Lecture Notes in Artificial Intelligence 9524

Subseries of Lecture Notes in Computer Science

More information about this series at http://www.springer.com/series/1244

Elizabeth Black · Sanjay Modgil · Nir Oren (Eds.)

Theory and Applications of Formal Argumentation

Third International Workshop, TAFA 2015
Buenos Aires, Argentina, July 25–26, 2015
Revised Selected Papers

Springer

Editors
Elizabeth Black
King's College London
London
UK

Sanjay Modgil
King's College London
London
UK

Nir Oren
University of Aberdeen
Aberdeen
UK

ISSN 0302-9743   ISSN 1611-3349   (electronic)
Lecture Notes in Artificial Intelligence
ISBN 978-3-319-28459-0   ISBN 978-3-319-28460-6   (eBook)
DOI 10.1007/978-3-319-28460-6

Library of Congress Control Number: 2015958911

LNCS Sublibrary: SL7 – Artificial Intelligence

Printed on acid-free paper

This Springer imprint is published by SpringerNature
The registered company is Springer International Publishing AG Switzerland

Preface

Recent years have witnessed a rapid growth of interest in formal models of argumentation and their application in diverse sub-fields and domains of the application of artificial intelligence. Specifically, formal models of argumentation have been developed for logic-based reasoning in the presence of uncertain, incomplete and inconsistent information, non-monotonic reasoning, decision making, and inter-agent communication and dialogue. Models of argumentation have also been developed for and applied in a multitude of fields including belief revision, the Semantic Web, grid applications, ontologies, recommender systems, machine learning, neural networks, trust computing, normative systems, social choice theory, judgment aggregation, game theory, law and medicine.

The Third International Workshop on the Theory and Applications of Formal Argumentation (TAFA 2015) aimed to promote further investigations into the use of formal argumentation and links with other fields of artificial intelligence. Co-located with the International Joint Conference on Artificial Intelligence (IJCAI 2015) in Buenos Aires, Argentina, TAFA 2015 built on the success of TAFA 2011 and TAFA 2013 with a range of strong papers submitted by authors from Europe, China, and Argentina. The workshop received 25 submissions, of which 16 were accepted for presentation after a rigorous review process. The workshop was attended by over 30 participants, and involved many lively and thought-provoking discussions. It also included a presentation of the results of the first International Competition on Computational Models of Argumentation[1].

We would like to thank the authors of this volume's papers for their high-quality contributions, and acknowledge the reviewers' efforts for their in-depth feedback to authors. The included papers point not only to the exciting work taking place in the field today, but also to challenges and exciting opportunities for future research in the area, which will no doubt lead to future volumes in this series of proceedings.

November 2015

Elizabeth Black
Sanjay Modgil
Nir Oren

---

[1] http://argumentationcompetition.org/2015/

Organization

TAFA 2015 took place at the Universidad de Buenos Aires, Facultad de Ciencias Económicas, Buenos Aires, Argentina, during July 25–26, 2015, as a workshop at IJCAI 2015, the 24th International Joint Conference on Artificial Intelligence.

Workshop Chairs

Elizabeth Black	King's College London, UK
Sanjay Modgil	King's College London, UK
Nir Oren	University of Aberdeen, UK

Program Committee

Leila Amgoud	IRIT - CNRS, France
Katie Atkinson	University of Liverpool, UK
Pietro Baroni	University of Brescia, Italy
Floris Bex	Utrecht University, The Netherlands
Elizabeth Black	King's College London, UK
Elise Bonzon	LIPADE - Université Paris Descartes, France
Richard Booth	University of Luxembourg, Luxembourg
Gerhard Brewka	Leipzig University, Germany
Katarzyna Budzynska	Polish Academy of Sciences, Poland, and University of Dundee, UK
Martin Caminada	University of Aberdeen, UK
Federico Cerutti	University of Aberdeen, UK
Carlos Chesñevar	UNS (Universidad Nacional del Sur), Argentina
Madalina Croitoru	LIRMM, University of Montpellier II, France
Sylvie Doutre	IRIT - University of Toulouse 1, France
Massimiliano Giacomin	University of Brescia, Italy
Tom Gordon	Fraunhofer FOKUS, Germany
Anthony Hunter	University College London, UK
Souhila Kaci	LIRMM, France
Joao Leite	Universidade Nova de Lisboa, Portugal
Beishui Liao	Zhejiang University, China
Nicolas Maudet	Université Paris 6, France
Sanjay Modgil	King's College London, UK
Pavlos Moraitis	Paris Descartes University, France
Nir Oren	University of Aberdeen, UK
Simon Parsons	University of Liverpool, UK
Henry Prakken	University of Utrecht and University of Groningen, The Netherlands
Odinaldo Rodrigues	King's College London, UK

Chiaki Sakama	Wakayama University, Japan
Guillermo R. Simari	Universidad Nacional del Sur in Bahia Blanca, Argentina
Hannes Strass	Leipzig University, Germany
Yuqing Tang	Carnegie Mellon University, USA
Matthias Thimm	Universität Koblenz-Landau, Germany
Francesca Toni	Imperial College London, UK
Alice Toniolo	University of Aberdeen, UK
Paolo Torroni	University of Bologna, Italy
Leon van der Torre	University of Luxembourg, Luxembourg
Srdjan Vesic	CRIL - CRNS, France
Serena Villata	Inria Sophia Antipolis, France
Toshiko Wakaki	Shibaura Institute of Technology, Japan
Simon Wells	Edinburgh Napier University, UK
Stefan Woltran	Vienna University of Technology, Austria
Adam Wyner	University of Aberdeen, UK

Additional Reviewers

Cyras, Kristijonas
Kontarinis, Dionysios
Linsbichler, Thomas

Contents

Comparing and Integrating Argumentation-Based with Matrix-Based Decision Support in *Arg&Dec*

Marco Aurisicchio[2], Pietro Baroni[1], Dario Pellegrini[1], and Francesca Toni[2]([⊠])

[1] Università degli Studi di Brescia, Brescia, Italy
pietro.baroni@unibs.it, pellegrini.dario.1303@gmail.com
http://www.unibs.it
[2] Imperial College London, London, UK
{m.aurisicchio,f.toni}@imperial.ac.uk
http://www.imperial.ac.uk

Abstract. The need of making decisions pervades every field of human activity. Several decision support methods and software tools are available in the literature, relying upon different modelling assumptions and often producing different results. In this paper we investigate the relationships between two such approaches: the recently introduced *QuAD frameworks*, based on the IBIS model and quantitative argumentation, and the *decision matrix* method, widely adopted in engineering. In addition, we describe *Arg&Dec* (standing for *Argue & Decide*), a prototype web application for collaborative decision-making, encompassing the two methodologies and assisting their comparison through automated transformation.

Keywords: Argumentation · Decision support · IBIS · Decision matrix

1 Introduction

The need of making decisions pervades every field of human activity and so does the opportunity of using a decision support methodology (typically supported by software tools) among the large variety available in the literature. This leads to the so-called *decision-making paradox* [25], which can be roughly summarized by the question: "What decision-making method should be used to choose the best decision-making method?". The problem is exacerbated by the fact that different available decision support methods may produce different results given the same input [24] and that many of them are subject to undesired behaviors, like *rank reversal* [23], in some cases.

In this light, the quest for a "universally best" decision support method appears to be ill-posed and should be replaced by context-sensitive analyses and comparisons of methods, with the crucial contribution of the domain experts involved in the decision processes. In particular, alternative methods should not only be compared in terms of their outputs but also on the initial modelling

© Springer International Publishing Switzerland 2015
E. Black et al. (Eds.): TAFA 2015, LNAI 9524, pp. 1–20, 2015.
DOI: 10.1007/978-3-319-28460-6_1

assumptions they adopt and, consequently, on their cognitive plausibility with respect to the (possibly implicit) mental models of the experts and/or to the way actual decision processes occur "into the wild".

This work contributes to this research line by investigating the relationships between the recently introduced *QuAD* (Quantitative Argumentation Debate) frameworks [3,4], based on the IBIS (Issue Based Information System) model [17] and quantitative argumentation, and the *decision matrix* method [20] commonly adopted in engineering for design decision-making.

More specifically, we pursue two complementary goals. First, we aim to draw a conceptual and formal comparison between argumentative QuAD frameworks and decision matrices, in order to point out their differences and commonalities, provide elements for an analysis of their appropriateness in different contexts, and investigate the possibility of a combined use thereof. Second, we aim to provide a software system assisting the above mentioned comparison. Given that most decision processes, especially in engineering, are multiparty, as they involve the cooperation of multiple experts or stakeholders, we aim to deliver a web-based application supporting cooperative work.

Accordingly, we provide a general analysis and discussion of QuAD frameworks and decision matrices, including their mutual translatability, and describe *Arg&Dec*[1], a prototype web application for collaborative decision-making, encompassing the two methodologies and assisting their empirical comparison through automated translation.

The paper is organised as follows. The necessary background being provided in Sects. 2 and 3 addresses the issues of comparison and transformation between QuAD frameworks and decision matrices, while Sect. 4 deals with the ranking methods in the two approaches. Section 5 then presents *Arg&Dec*. Finally, Sect. 6 concludes.

2   Background

IBIS and QuAD frameworks. QuAD frameworks [3,4] arise from a combination of the IBIS model [7,14,17] and a novel quantitative argumentation approach. We recall here the main underlying ideas and refer the reader to [4] for a detailed description and comparison with related formalisms, including abstract [12] and bipolar [9] argumentation.

IBIS [17] is a method to propose answers to issues and assess them through arguments. At the simplest level, an IBIS structure is a directed acyclic graph with four types of node: an *issue* node represents a problem being discussed, i.e. a question in need of an answer; an *answer* node gives a candidate solution to an issue; a *pro-argument* node represents an approval and a *con-argument* node represents an objection to an answer or to another argument. Figure 1 shows an example of IBIS graph (all figures in the paper are screenshots from *Arg&Dec*) in the design domain of Internal Combustion Engines (ICE) (nodes are labelled A1, A2, etc. for ease of reference).

---

[1] Available at www.arganddec.com.

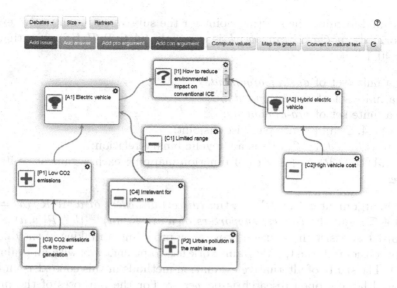

Fig. 1. A simple IBIS graph, as visualised in *Arg&Dec*.

An IBIS graph is typically constructed as follows: (1) an issue is captured; (2) answers are laid out and linked to the issue; (3) arguments are laid out and linked to either the answers or other arguments; (4) further issues may emerge during the process and be linked to either the answers or the arguments. In engineering design, answers and arguments may correspond to viewpoints of differents experts or stakeholders so that each move may also be regarded as a step in a dialectical process.

Several software tools implementing the IBIS model have been developed (e.g. Cohere and Compendium [5,6] or designVUE [2]). Most of them, however, only provide IBIS graph construction and visualization features, completely leaving to the user(s) the final evaluation of decision alternatives. QuAD frameworks overcome this limitation.

A QuAD framework provides a formal counterpart to an IBIS graph with some restrictions and one addition. Restrictions concern the graph structure: QuAD frameworks only represent graphs with a single specific issue. Thus, whereas IBIS graphs allow new issues to point to arguments, in QuAD frameworks arguments can only be pointed to by other arguments. This is not uncommon in focused design debates: while the design of any non-trivial system involves of course many issues, each issue is typically the subject of a focused debate concerning the various (technical, economical, and so on) aspects relevant to that issue. Extending the formalism in order to encompass a multiplicity of related debates, each represented by a QuAD framework, is a significant direction of future work.

The addition amounts to a numerical *base score* associated to each argument and answer, expressing a measure of importance according to the domain experts[2] and forming the starting point for the subsequent quantitative evaluation. Formally: a *QuAD framework* is a 5-tuple $\langle \mathcal{A}, \mathcal{C}, \mathcal{P}, \mathcal{R}, \mathcal{BS} \rangle$ such that (for scale $\mathbb{I}=[0,1]$):

- $\mathcal{A}$ is a finite set of *answer arguments*;
- $\mathcal{C}$ is a finite set of *con-arguments*;
- $\mathcal{P}$ is a finite set of *pro-arguments*;
- the sets $\mathcal{A}$, $\mathcal{C}$, and $\mathcal{P}$ are pairwise disjoint;
- $\mathcal{R} \subseteq (\mathcal{C} \cup \mathcal{P}) \times (\mathcal{A} \cup \mathcal{C} \cup \mathcal{P})$ is an acyclic binary relation;
- $\mathcal{BS} : (\mathcal{A} \cup \mathcal{C} \cup \mathcal{P}) \to \mathbb{I}$ is a total function mapping each argument to its *base score*.

Given argument $a \in \mathcal{A} \cup \mathcal{C} \cup \mathcal{P}$, the *(direct) attackers of a* are $\mathcal{R}^-(a) = \{b \in \mathcal{C} \mid (b,a) \in \mathcal{R}\}$ and the *(direct) supporters of a* are $\mathcal{R}^+(a) = \{b \in \mathcal{P} \mid (b,a) \in \mathcal{R}\}$.

In order to assist the decision process by providing a ranking of the different answers considered, the QuAD framework has to be endowed with an evaluation method. The study of alternative evaluation methods in this context is an interesting and largely open research issue *per se*. For the purposes of the present paper, it is sufficient to recall here the method to assign a *final score* to arguments as defined in [4]. The basic idea is that the final score of an argument is defined by a *score function $\mathcal{SF}$*, depending on the argument base score and on the final scores of its attackers and supporters. In this respect, note that we have defined direct attackers and supporters as *sets* taken from a (static) QuAD framework. However, in a dynamic design context these may actually be given in sequence: the final score of an argument is thus defined in terms of *sequences* of direct attackers and supporters. As in [4], we assume that these sequences are arbitrary permutations of the attackers and supporters (however, in a dynamic setting they may actually be given from the onset). For a generic argument a, let $(a_1, \ldots, a_n)$ be an arbitrary permutation of the $(n \geq 0)$ attackers in $\mathcal{R}^-(a)$. We denote as $SEQ_{\mathcal{SF}}(\mathcal{R}^-(a)) = (\mathcal{SF}(a_1), \ldots, \mathcal{SF}(a_n))$ the corresponding sequence of final scores. Similarly, letting $(b_1, \ldots, b_m)$ be an arbitrary permutation of the $(m \geq 0)$ supporters in $\mathcal{R}^+(a)$, we denote as $SEQ_{\mathcal{SF}}(\mathcal{R}^+(a)) = (\mathcal{SF}(b_1), \ldots, \mathcal{SF}(b_m))$ the corresponding sequence of final scores. Finally, with an abuse of notation, $\mathcal{R}^-(a)$ and $\mathcal{R}^+(a)$ will stand also for their arbitrary permutations $(a_1, \ldots, a_n)$ and $(b_1, \ldots, b_m)$ respectively. Using the hypothesis (implicitly adopted in [8] and [13]) of separability of the evaluations of attackers and supporters,[3] for an argument a, $\mathcal{SF}$ is defined recursively as

$$\mathcal{SF}(a) = g(\mathcal{BS}(a), \mathcal{F}_{att}(\mathcal{BS}(a), SEQ_{\mathcal{SF}}(\mathcal{R}^-(a))), \mathcal{F}_{supp}(\mathcal{BS}(a), SEQ_{\mathcal{SF}}(\mathcal{R}^+(a)))) \quad (1)$$

where g is an aggregation operator.

The functions $\mathcal{F}_{att}$ and $\mathcal{F}_{supp}$ provide a numerical value synthesising the contribution to the final score of the attackers and supporters, respectively. In [4]

---

[2] Suitable interpretation and elicitation of base scores are a crucial and non trivial issue: see some discussion in [4].

[3] Here, separability amounts to absence of interaction between attackers and supporters.

$\mathcal{F}_{att}$ (and dually $\mathcal{F}_{supp}$) is defined so that the contribution of an attacker (supporter) to the score of an argument decreases (increases) the argument score by an amount proportional both to (i) the score of the attacker (supporter), i.e. a strong attacker (supporter) has more effect than a weaker one, and to (ii) the previous score of the argument itself, i.e. an already strong argument benefits quantitatively less from a support than a weak one and an already weak argument suffers quantitatively less from an attack than a stronger one. Focusing on the case of a single attacker (supporter) with score $v \neq 0$, this leads to the following base expressions:[4]

$$f_{att}(v_0, v) = v_0 - v_0 \cdot v = v_0 \cdot (1 - v) \tag{2}$$
$$f_{supp}(v_0, v) = v_0 + (1 - v_0) \cdot v = v_0 + v - v_0 \cdot v \tag{3}$$

The definitions of $\mathcal{F}_{att}$ and $\mathcal{F}_{supp}$ have then the same recursive form. Let $*$ stand for either *att* or *supp*. Then:

$$\text{if } S = (v): \; \mathcal{F}_*(v_0, S) = f_*(v_0, v) \tag{4}$$
$$\text{if } S = (v_1, \ldots, v_n): \; \mathcal{F}_*(v_0, (v_1, \ldots, v_n)) = f_*(\mathcal{F}_*(v_0, (v_1, \ldots, v_{n-1})), v_n) \tag{5}$$

As shown in [4], these definitions have a simpler equivalent characterization:

$$\mathcal{F}_{att}(\mathcal{BS}(a), SEQ_{\mathcal{SF}}(\mathcal{R}^-(a))) = \mathcal{BS}(a) \cdot \prod_{b \subset \mathcal{R}^-(a)} (1 - \mathcal{SF}(b))$$

$$\mathcal{F}_{supp}(\mathcal{BS}(a), SEQ_{\mathcal{SF}}(\mathcal{R}^+(a))) = 1 - (1 - \mathcal{BS}(a)) \cdot \prod_{b \in \mathcal{R}^+(a)} (1 - \mathcal{SF}(b)).$$

Further, both $\mathcal{F}_{att}$ and $\mathcal{F}_{supp}$ return the special value *nil* when their second argument is an ineffective (namely empty or consisting of all zeros) sequence.

Finally, the operator $g : \mathbb{I} \times \mathbb{I} \cup \{nil\} \times \mathbb{I} \cup \{nil\} \to \mathbb{I}$ is defined on the basis of the idea that when the effect of attackers is null (i.e. the value returned by $\mathcal{F}_{att}$ is *nil*) the final score must coincide with the one established on the basis of supporters, and dually when the effect of supporters is null, while, when both are null, the base score is returned unchanged. When both attackers and supporters have an effect, the final score is obtained averaging the two contributions. As discussed in more detail in [4], this amounts to treating the aggregated effect of attackers and supporters equally in determining the final score of the argument. Formally the operator g is defined as follows:

$$g(v_0, v_a, v_s) = v_a \text{ if } v_s = nil \text{ and } v_a \neq nil$$
$$g(v_0, v_a, v_s) = v_s \text{ if } v_a = nil \text{ and } v_s \neq nil$$
$$g(v_0, v_a, v_s) = v_0 \text{ if } v_a = v_s = nil$$
$$g(v_0, v_a, v_s) = \frac{(v_a + v_s)}{2} \text{ otherwise}$$

This quantitative evaluation method has been integrated in and preliminarily experimented with the designVUE software tool [3,4]. This paper is a follow-up

---

[4] The expression of f_{supp} corresponds to the T-conorm operator also referred to as *probabilistic sum* in the literature [16].

of this experimentation, and, in particular, of a use-case in [4] on a design decision problem originally developed using the decision matrix approach, reviewed next.

Decision Matrices. A decision matrix provides a simple, yet clear and effective, scheme to compare a set of alternative solutions or options $\mathcal{CO}$ against a set of evaluation criteria $\mathcal{RO}$. Each option is evaluated qualitatively according to each criterion: the evaluation is expressed through one of the three symbols $+$, $-$, or 0, meaning respectively that it is positive, negative, or indifferent. Further each criterion $R \in \mathcal{RO}$ is assigned a numerical weight $w(R) \in [0,1]$, representing its importance. Formally, following [20]:

– a decision matrix is a 4-tuple $\langle \mathcal{CO}, \mathcal{RO}, \mathcal{QE}, w \rangle$, where $\mathcal{CO}$ is a set of *options*, $\mathcal{RO}$ is a set of *criteria*, $\mathcal{QE}$ is a total function $\mathcal{QE} : \mathcal{CO} \times \mathcal{RO} \rightarrow \{+, -, 0\}$ (called *qualitative evaluation*), and w is a total function $w : \mathcal{RO} \rightarrow [0,1]$ (called *weight*).

Letting $C_1, \ldots, C_m$ be an arbitrary but fixed ordering of $\mathcal{CO}$, and $R_1, \ldots, R_n$ an arbitrary but fixed ordering of $\mathcal{RO}$, the matrix is built by associating each option C_i with the i-th column, and each criterion R_j with the j-th row. For the sake of conciseness, we identify each option (criterion) with the corresponding

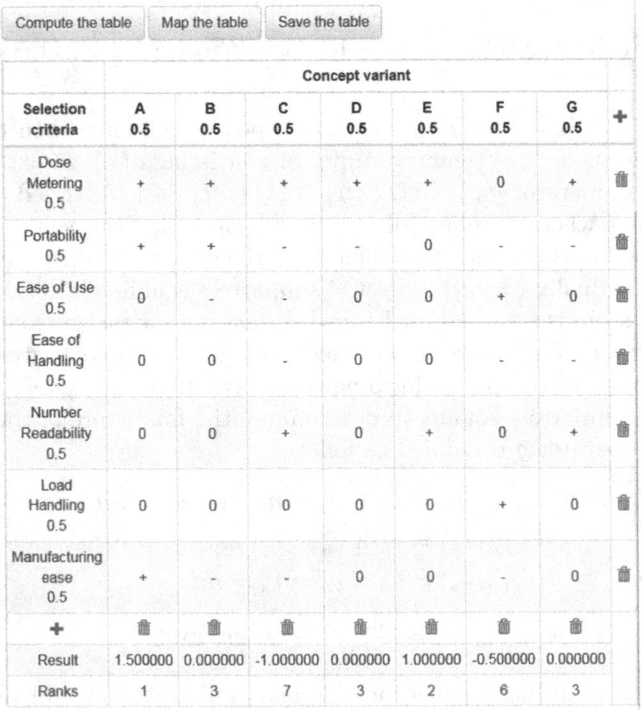

| Compute the table | Map the table | Save the table | | | | | |

	Concept variant							
Selection criteria	**A** 0.5	**B** 0.5	**C** 0.5	**D** 0.5	**E** 0.5	**F** 0.5	**G** 0.5	**+**
Dose Metering 0.5	+	+	+	+	+	0	+	🗑
Portability 0.5	+	+	-	-	0	-	-	🗑
Ease of Use 0.5	0	-	-	0	0	+	0	🗑
Ease of Handling 0.5	0	0	-	0	0	-	-	🗑
Number Readability 0.5	0	0	+	0	+	0	+	🗑
Load Handling 0.5	0	0	0	0	0	+	0	🗑
Manufacturing ease 0.5	+	-	-	0	0	-	0	🗑
+	🗑	🗑	🗑	🗑	🗑	🗑	🗑	
Result	1.500000	0.000000	-1.000000	0.000000	1.000000	-0.500000	0.000000	
Ranks	1	3	7	3	2	6	3	

Fig. 2. A decision matrix, as visualised in *Arg&Dec*.

column (row). Each cell contains the qualitative evaluation of the option C_i with respect to the criterion R_j.

Figure 2 provides an example matrix, adapted from [26], concerning the development of a syringe, with seven options (labelled A-G), namely master cylinder, rubber brake, ratchet, plunge stop, swash ring, lever set and dial screw, and seven criteria. The weight of each criterion is given below it in the matrix. Figure 2 also gives an evaluation result for each option, and a ranking computed from the results. The results are scores obtained combining the numerical weights, with each weight providing a positive, negative, or null contribution to the score of $C \in \mathcal{CO}$ depending on $\mathcal{QE}(C, R)$. Formally, letting $val(+) = 1$, $val(-) = -1$, $val(0) = 0$, the *matrix score* $\mathcal{MF}(C)$ of C is

$$\mathcal{MF}(C) = \sum_{R \in \mathcal{RO}} w(R) \cdot val(\mathcal{QE}(C, R))$$

3   QuAD Frameworks and Decision Matrices: Comparison and Transformation

While QuAD Frameworks (QFs) and Decision Matrices (DMs) are formally rather different, they share some common conceptual roots, in that they can be regarded, roughly, as involving the assessment and weighing of pros and cons, a common decision-making pattern whose formalization was first considered by Benjamin Franklin in a famous letter, generally regarded as the first attempt to define a decision support method [15]. In QFs pros and cons are represented explicitly through pro- and con-arguments, as in the IBIS model, while in DMs the pros and cons can be identified according to the + and − values , for instance in Fig. 2 *Ease of handling* is a con for concepts C, F and G (and a pro for no other), while *Load handling* is a pro for concept F (and a con for no other).

This similarity being acknowledged, several important differences can be pointed out. We focus here on structural aspects[5] first, deferring the comparison of their different ranking methods to Sect. 4. We analyse the differences in Subsect. 3.1, and identify opportunities of combination and transformation in Subsect. 3.2.

3.1   Different Methods for Different Problems?

As a first immediate observation, while QFs are bipolar, encompassing positive and negative influences, DMs are ternary, as they include indifferent evaluations too. This can be related to another important difference: in DMs each option is evaluated against every element of a fixed list of evaluation criteria, while in QFs the choice of pros and cons directly attached to each answer is free and, in general, they are not required to have any commonality, let alone belonging to a fixed list.

---

[5] The structural considerations we draw apply equally to QFs and to the underlying IBIS model.

Furthermore, QFs are open to dialectical developments, since pro- and con-arguments can in turn be supported/attacked by other pro/con-arguments, while DMs limit the analysis to exactly one level of pros and cons.

According to this basic analysis, we can describe DMs as more *rigid, systematic* and *flat* with respect to QFs: let us briefly justify these attributes. The DM method is more *rigid* as it requires an a-priori fixed, rather than open, list of evaluation criteria which can play the role of pros and cons. DM is more *systematic* because each of the criteria is evaluated for each of the options, while in QFs, if a pro or con is identified for an answer, it is not mandatory to consider its effect also on other answers. Finally DM is more *flat* as it hides any further debate underlying the pros and cons.

These properties may turn out to be an advantage or a limit depending on the features of the decision context. We will focus our discussion only on two features: *size* and *wickedness*. In our setting size simply concerns the number of elements to be taken into account, roughly speaking, the number of pros and cons. Wickedness [10,21] instead refers to a problem's inherent *structural complexity*. Wicked problems are "ill-formulated, where the information is confusing, where there are many clients and decision makers with conflicting values, and where the ramifications in the whole system are thoroughly confusing". They are opposed to "tame" or "benign" problems which are clearly "definable and separable and may have solutions that are findable" and where it is easy to check whether or not the problem has been solved. IBIS was in fact conceived as a way to tackle the mischievous nature of wicked problems since "through this counterplay of questioning and arguing, the participants form and exert their judgments incessantly, developing more structured pictures of the problem and its solutions" [17].

Size and wickedness affect important goals of decision problems: accuracy, feasibility, understandability and accountability, typically of concern to stakeholders with different roles in the decision process. For instance, the RAPID®model [22] identifies five roles: *recommenders* (R) are in charge of "providing the right data and analysis to make a sensible decision" (in our case of building a suitable QF or DM), acquiring *input* from any participants (I) able to make a useful contribution to the analysis; then the recommendation (in our case the QF or DM with the relevant ranking) is presented to some stakeholders (A) who have to *agree*, since they have a veto power, and to an authority (D) in charge of finally *deciding*; final decisions are then carried out by some *performers* (P). Different roles often correspond to different professional profiles and competences too: roles R and I need expertise in the application domain, while roles A and D may have managerial skills. As a consequence they also have different, possibly conflicting, priorities. On the one hand, R and I aim to *accuracy* of the analysis and recommendation, subject to several *feasibility* constraints, related not only to resources but also to knowledge requirements. On the other hand, A and D are interested in the *understandability* of the analysis in relation to their competences, given that they may lack technical expertise, and in the *accountability* of the final recommendation, given that they bear the final responsibility and may be asked to justify their choices.

Wickedness poses a challenge altogether to the notions of accuracy, feasibility, understandability and accountability, and calls for models able to reflect at least partially the structural complexity causing wickedness. Accuracy can generally be seen as a reason to increase the problem size, by including in the evaluation as many elements as possible. Apart from possibly hindering feasibility, this conflicts however with understandability and accountability, as a large number of detailed elements can hardly be mastered by non-experts and may obfuscate the key factors leading to decisions.

Let us now discuss the properties of DMs and QFs with respect to this analysis. DMs appear to meet well the requirements of *accuracy* and *understandability*. In fact, the DM model imposes to systematically identify all relevant criteria and to apply them uniformly, moreover its rigid and flat structure is quite easily understood and explained. *Feasibility* depends mainly on the actual possibility of assessing every alternative against every criterion, which may be a heavy requirement in some cases, as it corresponds to a possibly unachievable state of complete information. Information may be lacking in some cases: for instance experimental data concerning the side effects of a new therapy may not be available. Further, some criteria may simply be irrelevant or not applicable to some options. Consider the case of selecting among several candidate sites for oil exploration. The presence of suitable road infrastructures may be relevant for sites in the mainland, but is simply irrelevant for sea locations. Finally, DMs show a limited level of *accountability* due to their flat structure: while it is clear how the final ranking is derived from the matrix, no hint is given on how the matrix was filled in.

Increasing the *size* and *wickedness* of the problem, the appropriateness of DMs decreases. As to the size, a matrix with tens of rows loses understandability and the feasibility problems may only worsen. As to wickedness, the rigid and flat matrix structure does not fit the needs of a dialectical analysis. This raises accuracy issues: forcing a fluid evolving matter within the constraints of a square rigid box can only lead to modeling distortions and omissions. The role and meaning of the 0 value is particularly critical in this respect, since 0 may be used as a wildcard to cover, not just the intended indifferent/average evaluation, but also irrelevance, lack of information, judgment suspension.

Turning to QFs, *accuracy* appears to be a big concern. To put it simply, while it is easy to recognize an incomplete matrix, since it is only partially filled, it is impossible to discern an incomplete QF, due to its open ended nature. In this sense the accuracy burden entirely rests on modelers' shoulders since the model does not provide any, even implicit, guide, due to its flexibility. One may observe however that this is partly balanced by the fact that, for the same reasons, modeling distortions induced by the structure are less likely. *Feasibility* instead does not appear to raise specific criticalities: as far as the notions of pro- and con-argument are clear, a QF can easily be built reflecting the debate among the actors involved. As far as *understandability*, assuming that the basic notions of attack and support are clear, the structure of a QFs is easily understood, but the evaluation mechanism adopted in QFs is not straightforward (see also Sect. 4). Finally, *accountability* can be regarded as a strength of QFs given that the model allows and tracks the development of a dialectical analysis of arbitrary depth.

Concerning the effect of *size* and *wickedness*, QFs appear to be more robust. As to the latter, comments have been already given above. As to the size, the hierarchical rather than flat organization of QFs is able to accommodate a multilevel analysis where detailed evaluation criteria, lying on the lower levels of the graph, contribute as pros and cons to the evaluation of more synthetic evaluation criteria directly connected to the answers at the upper level. For instance, in the selection of a given technology with significant environmental impact, one may have a single con-argument *Pollution* directly connected to the answer, and then break down the relevant assessment at a lower level, adding arguments corresponding to more detailed items like *Air pollution, Water pollution, Soil pollution*, and so on. In this way, one can have a synthetic and easily understandable view just focusing on the upper part of the graph, while access to details can be achieved exploring the graph more deeply.

3.2 Combining Strengths: An Integrated View Through Transformation

The earlier discussion indicates that the two methods have complementary features:

- DMs feature accuracy, feasibility and understandability in problems of limited size and wickedness, and may suffer from limited accountability in every case;
- QFs are characterized by higher accountability in every case and are more robust in preserving feasibility and understandability with respect to increased problem size and/or wickedness, but they may suffer from limited accuracy in every case.

While a straightforward recipe could then be *"use a DM if your problem is small and tame, use a QF otherwise"*, their complementarity suggests that the two methods could also be exploited in combination, especially in the not uncommon case that the decision problem is mid-sized and mildly wicked. Indeed, converting a DM into an "equivalent" QF format might prompt the analysts to add additional levels of pros/cons thus getting a more accountable and possibly even more accurate representation without affecting, indeed exploiting, the advantages of the initial DM representation in terms of completeness of the assessment and of understandability. Conversely, converting the "top" part of a QF (e.g. in Fig. 1 the nodes A1, A2, P1, C1, and C2) into an "equivalent" DM format may help the analysts to identify some incompleteness, requiring a more systematic assessment, and to fill the relevant gaps, thus improving accuracy. Again, the advantages of having developed the initial analysis using a less rigid model are preserved. Indeed it seems desirable that an open dialectical process, meant to harness a recalcitrant problem, finally results in enabling the application of more plain techniques.

These considerations all point towards the usefulness of a tool supporting the construction of and transformation between DMs and QFs: its implementation will be described in Sect. 5. As prerequisites for the tool, we give here formal definitions of the transformation and, in Sect. 4, discuss issues concerning the rankings they impose.

As to the transformation from a DM to a QF, clearly each column C of the DM corresponds to a QF answer, while each criterion R plays the role of either a pro- or con-argument for C according to the positive or negative value of $\mathcal{QE}(C,R)$ (0 values are ignored). Weights of the criteria are assumed to play the role of base scores for the corresponding pro/con-arguments while answer arguments are assigned the default base score[6] 0.5 (see the top of the DM in Fig. 2). This leads to the following definition.

Definition 1. *Given* $\mathcal{DM} = \langle \mathcal{CO}, \mathcal{RO}, \mathcal{QE}, w \rangle$ *the corresponding* QF $T\mathcal{QF}(\mathcal{DM}) = \langle \mathcal{A}, \mathcal{C}, \mathcal{P}, \mathcal{R}, \mathcal{BS} \rangle$ *is defined as:*

- $\mathcal{A} = \mathcal{CO}$;
- $\mathcal{C} = \{ R \in \mathcal{RO} \mid \exists C \in \mathcal{CO} : \mathcal{QE}(C,R) = - \}$;
- $\mathcal{P} = \{ R \in \mathcal{RO} \mid \exists C \in \mathcal{CO} : \mathcal{QE}(C,R) = + \}$;
- $\mathcal{R} = \{(R,C) | \mathcal{QE}(C,R) = -\} \cup \{(R,C) | \mathcal{QE}(C,R) = +\}$;
- $\mathcal{BS} = \{(a, 0.5) \mid a \in \mathcal{A}\} \cup \{(b, w(b)) \mid b \in \mathcal{C} \cup \mathcal{P}\}$.

Note that, for each criterion R, both a pro- and a con-argument may be created.

As to the transformation from a QF to a DM, as already mentioned, only the pro/con-arguments directly linked to answers can be represented as criteria in the DM. Each matrix cell is filled with $+$ or $-$ according to the support or attack nature of the corresponding relation (if present) in the QF, and with 0 in case of no relation. The final score of the pro/con-arguments gives the weights. This leads to the following definition.

Definition 2. *Given* $\mathcal{QF} = \langle \mathcal{A}, \mathcal{C}, \mathcal{P}, \mathcal{R}, \mathcal{BS} \rangle$ *the corresponding* DM $T\mathcal{DM}(\mathcal{QF}) = \langle \mathcal{CO}, \mathcal{RO}, \mathcal{QE}, w \rangle$ *is defined as:*

- $\mathcal{CO} = \mathcal{A}$;
- $\mathcal{RO} = \{ a \in \mathcal{C} \cup \mathcal{P} \mid \exists b \in \mathcal{A} : (a,b) \in \mathcal{R} \}$;
- $\forall (C,R) \in \mathcal{CO} \times \mathcal{RO} : \mathcal{QE}(C,R) = +$ *if* $R \in \mathcal{P} \wedge (R,C) \in \mathcal{R}$; $\mathcal{QE}(C,R) = -$ *if* $R \in \mathcal{C} \wedge (R,C) \in \mathcal{R}$; $\mathcal{QE}(C,R) = 0$ *otherwise.*
- $\forall a \in \mathcal{RO} : w(a) = \mathcal{SF}(a)$.

4 Rankings in QuAD Frameworks and Decision Matrices

The transformations described in the previous section open the way to a comparison of the rankings produced by the two methods, resulting from their quantitative evaluations (see Sect. 2). First, note that these methods are not an intrinsic

---

[6] As explained in more detail in [4], this default assignment is not simply motivated by the fact that 0.5 is the middle point of the $[0, 1]$ interval: it represents the fact that there is no a-priori attitude towards the acceptance or rejection of an argument and ensures that, in the presence of symmetric attackers and supporters, $\mathcal{SF}(a)$ coincides with $\mathcal{BS}(a)$.

feature of the formalisms: other methods using the same input can be devised in either case. Indeed we can define a score function $\mathcal{SF}'$ for QFs inspired by the weighted sum used in DMs as follows, for any argument a:

- $\mathcal{SF}'(a) = \mathcal{BS}(a)$ if $\mathcal{R}^-(a) = \mathcal{R}^+(a) = \emptyset$;
- $\mathcal{SF}'(a) = \sum_{b \in \mathcal{R}^+(a)} \mathcal{SF}(b) - \sum_{c \in \mathcal{R}^-(a)} \mathcal{SF}'(c)$ otherwise.

Note that this definition ignores the base score except for leaf arguments.

Vice versa we can define a score method $\mathcal{MF}'$ for DMs replicating the features of the score function for QFs, by simply applying equation (1) to each option C as follows:

$$\mathcal{MF}'(C) = g(0.5, \mathcal{F}_{att}(0.5, SEQ_{\mathcal{W}}(\mathcal{M}^-(C))), \mathcal{F}_{supp}(0.5, SEQ_{\mathcal{W}}(\mathcal{M}^+(C))))$$

where $\mathcal{M}^-(C) = \{R \in \mathcal{RO} \mid \mathcal{QE}(C, R) = -\}$, $\mathcal{M}^+(C) = \{R \in \mathcal{RO} \mid \mathcal{QE}(C, R) = +\}$, and $SEQ_{\mathcal{W}}(\mathcal{M}^-(C))$ (resp. $SEQ_{\mathcal{W}}(\mathcal{M}^+(C))$) is an arbitrary permutation of the weights of the elements of $\mathcal{M}^-(C)$ (resp. $\mathcal{M}^+(C)$). Note that this method uses a base score of 0.5 for each option.

Leaving aside the possibility to reconcile the quantitative aspects of the two models by applying suitable (re)definitions, we focus on the differences between the quantitative evaluations in DMs and QFs as originally defined, by discussing their conceptual roots. Of course we will not include in the comparison the fact that QFs are more expressive, thus focusing on cases of QFs obtained (or obtainable) from a DM through the $\mathcal{TQF}$ transformation. Thus, letting $\mathcal{DM}$ be a DM and $\mathcal{TQF}(\mathcal{DM})$ the corresponding QF, we analyse, for each option C, the difference between the evaluations $\mathcal{MF}(C)$ in $\mathcal{DM}$ and $\mathcal{SF}(C)$ in $\mathcal{TQF}(\mathcal{DM})$. Moreover, we analyse the differences in the rankings induced by $\mathcal{MF}$ and $\mathcal{SF}$ over the set of all options $\mathcal{CO}$.

As a first elementary observation, we note that letting $T = \sum_{R \in \mathcal{RO}} w(R)$, the range of $\mathcal{MF}$ is the $[-T, T]$ interval, while the range of $\mathcal{SF}$ is $[0, 1]$. This means that for a given evaluation $\mathcal{SF}(C) \in [0, 1]$ one should consider in $[-T, T]$ the *corresponding value* $\mathcal{MF}_{corr}(\mathcal{SF}(C)) = 2T \cdot (\mathcal{SF}(C) - 0.5)$, and, conversely, for a given $\mathcal{MF}(C) \in [-T, T]$ the *corresponding value* $\mathcal{SF}_{corr}(\mathcal{MF}(C)) = 0.5 + \mathcal{MF}(C)/2T$. Thus a DM score $\mathcal{MF}(C)$ is *congruent with* a QF final score $\mathcal{SF}(C)$ if $\mathcal{MF}(C) = \mathcal{MF}_{corr}(\mathcal{SF}(C))$, or, equivalently, if $\mathcal{SF}(C) = \mathcal{SF}_{corr}(\mathcal{MF}(C))$.

Congruence is obviously attained for an option C in case $\mathcal{QE}(C, R) = 0$ for every $R \in \mathcal{RO}$, since in this case $\mathcal{MF}(C) = 0$ and the corresponding answer in $\mathcal{TQF}(\mathcal{DM})$ gets $\mathcal{SF}(C) = 0.5$, having neither attackers nor supporters. Congruence is also attained in the very simple situations where an option C has exactly one $+$ and all zeros, or exactly one $-$ and all zeros, under the mild additional condition that the weights in the decision matrix are normalized, i.e. that $T = 1$. Letting R be the only criterion such that $\mathcal{QE}(C, R) = +$, we have $\mathcal{MF}(C) = w(R)$, which, for $T = 1$ is congruent with

$\mathcal{SF}(C) = 1 - 0.5 \cdot (1 - w(R)) = 0.5 + w(R)/2$,

obtained for the case of a single supporter in $\mathcal{TQF}(\mathcal{DM})$. Similarly, if R is the only criterion such that $\mathcal{QE}(C, R) = -$, we have $\mathcal{MF}(C) = -w(R)$, which, for $T = 1$, is congruent with $\mathcal{SF}(C) = 0.5 \cdot (1 - w(R)) = 0.5 - w(R)/2$.

Apart from these and some other quite specific situations, congruence is in general not achieved . Indeed, in the computation of $\mathcal{MF}$, (signed) weights are simply summed up, while to obtain $\mathcal{SF}$ the weights of pros and cons are first combined separately with $\mathcal{F}_{supp}$ and $\mathcal{F}_{att}$, which are based on products (and take into account the base score) and then the results of these combinations are aggregated using the g operator, which behaves differently in the case where only attackers or only supporters are present with respect to the case where both are.

These differences not only obviously prevent congruence but may also affect the ranking, giving rise to different recommendations, as discussed next.

First, as also observed in [4], the g operator introduces a severe penalty for arguments with no supporters and a significant advantage for arguments with no attackers, with no counterpart in $\mathcal{MF}$. Dialectically this feature makes sense, as the inability to identify any, even weak, supporter (attacker) evidences a heavy asymmetry in the analysis, pointing out the undebated weakness (strength) of a given option. To give a simple example of its effects consider the QF shown in Fig. 3. Here, answer A1 having a single supporter P1 with $\mathcal{SF}(P1) = 0.6$ gets $\mathcal{SF}(A1) = 0.8$, while answer A2, with a supporter P2 with $\mathcal{SF}(P2) = 0.9$ and an attacker C1 with $\mathcal{SF}(C1) = 0.2$ gets $\mathcal{SF}(A2) = 0.675$. In the corresponding DM instead, A2 is ranked first with $\mathcal{MF}(A2) = 0.7$, while $\mathcal{MF}(A1) = 0.6$.

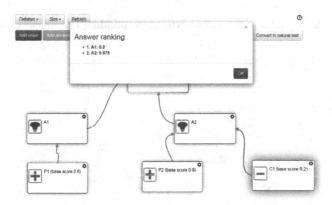

Fig. 3. A QF whose ranking differs from the corresponding DM since A1 has no attackers.

Further, in $\mathcal{MF}$ the final evaluation of each option basically depends only on the sum of the weights of the positive criteria and on the sum of the weights of the negative criteria. If weights are rearranged while keeping these two sums unchanged the final evaluation does not change. This does not happen with the use of $\mathcal{F}_{supp}$ and $\mathcal{F}_{att}$ in QFs. To exemplify consider Fig. 4 where answer A1 has two supporters P1 and P2 with $\mathcal{SF}(P1) = 0.9$, $\mathcal{SF}(P2) = 0.1$ and an attacker C1 with $\mathcal{SF}(C1) = 0.5$, while answer A2 has two supporters P3 and P4 with $\mathcal{SF}(P3) = 0.5$, $\mathcal{SF}(P4) = 0.5$ and the same attacker. In the corresponding DM A1 and A2 are ranked equally since $\mathcal{MF}(A1) = \mathcal{MF}(A2) = 0.5$, while the QF evaluation gives $\mathcal{SF}(A1) = 0.6025, \mathcal{SF}(A2) = 0.5625$.

Conversely, in Fig. 5 A1 has two attackers C1 and C2 with $\mathcal{SF}(C1) = 0.9$, $\mathcal{SF}(C2) = 0.1$ and a supporter P1 with $\mathcal{SF}(P1) = 0.5$, while A2 has two attackers C3 and C4 with $\mathcal{SF}(C3) = 0.5$, $\mathcal{SF}(C4) = 0.5$ and the same supporter. Again, in the corresponding DM A1 and A2 are ranked equally since $\mathcal{MF}(A1) = \mathcal{MF}(A2) = -0.5$, while the QF evaluation gives $\mathcal{SF}(A1) = 0.3975$, and $\mathcal{SF}(A2) = 0.4375$.

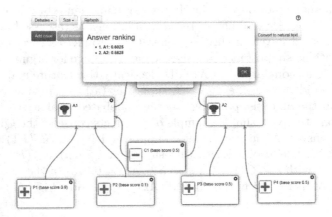

Fig. 4. A QF whose ranking differs from the corresponding DM since A1 has a strong supporter.

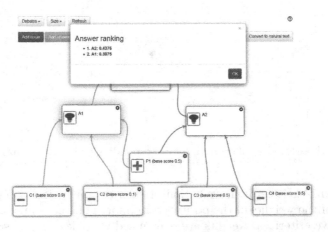

Fig. 5. A QF whose ranking differs from the corresponding DM since A1 has a strong attacker.

Intuitively, in QFs, having a strong supporter accompanied by a weak one is better than having two "average" supporters (an analogous observation applies to attackers). This behavior recalls the principles underlying bipolar qualitative decision models, like "decision makers are likely to consider degrees of strength at the ordinal rather than at the cardinal level" and "individuals appear to consider very few arguments (i.e. the most salient ones) when making their choice" [11]. In these models, pros and cons are ranked in levels of importance, and, for instance, a con at the highest level can only be countered by a pro at the same level, while compensation by many pros at lower levels is simply ruled out. Whereas these models encompass only a rather limited, purely ordinal, compensation between pros and cons, at the other extreme, the $\mathcal{MF}$ in DMs score allows a full linear compensation: many weak pros can effectively counter a strong con and similarly inverting the roles of pros and cons. The evaluation adopted in QFs can be regarded as an intermediate approach between these extremes: it is not so drastic to completely ignore weaker arguments with respect to stronger ones, but at the same time ascribes to stronger arguments a higher, more than linear, effect. The choice of the most suitable compensation method for a given decision problem depends of course on the domain and possibly on the attitude of decision makers. Getting different results with different methods may be puzzling for an unexperienced user: indeed, as already mentioned, the availability of multiple decision support methods leads to the so called *decision making paradox* [25]. However, it has the advantage of increasing user awareness that in some cases the evaluations supporting a decision are not rock solid and heavily depend on the modelling choices. If instead a user takes a single decision support model for granted without considering other possible choices, s/he may miss the opportunity to adopt an alternative available method which is more suited to her/his needs. This is related in turn to the largely open problem of defining correspondences between the features of a given application domain and the technical choices concerning the decision support method. While this issue is beyond the scope of this paper, we believe that it is important that these choices and their impact on decisions are explicit. *Arg&Dec*, described next, allows a direct comparison between QFs and DMs methods on the same problem and is a step in this direction.

5   The *Arg&Dec* Web Application

Arg&Dec is a web application supporting the definition of QFs and DMs and their mutual transformation. After signing in, the user can choose between two main sections: *Debates*, which is the default and concerns QFs, and *Tables*, concerning DMs. The user can create and edit QFs using buttons (one for each type of node that can be added to the graph, see top part of Fig. 1) and drag-and-drop facilities (to move nodes and to draw links between them). The properties of each node can be consulted/edited and the node can be deleted by clicking on the cogwheel symbol in the upper right corner of the box representing the node and then selecting the desired functions. DMs are created by adding rows and columns with two + buttons (respectively below the last row and at the right of the last column, see Fig. 2), the system then asks the basic information (name and weight for rows) required. Each matrix cell can be edited by simply clicking on it and each row/column can be deleted clicking on the trashbin symbol shown at its right/bottom. After creating a QF/DM the user can ask the system to compute the option ranking (using the methods described in Sect. 2) or to create the corresponding DM/QF using the mapping methods described in Sect. 3.2. As explained therein, when transforming a QF into a DM, pros and cons not directly linked to answers (e.g. in Fig. 1 nodes C3, C4, P2) are "lost". To partially compensate for this limitation and in the view of supporting the comparison between the two approaches *Arg&Dec* keeps track of the additional nodes "lost in transformation": when a DM is generated from a QF an option *Descendants* is shown when clicking on a DM cell corresponding to a node having further descendants in the QF. Selecting this option the user can then visualize a structured list of the "lost" descendants in the QF with their QF final score. To ease the comparison, when a DM has been generated starting from a QF, an additional button allows direct access to the generating DM, and similarly for a QF generated starting from a DM.

Concerning cooperative work, each QF/DM in *Arg&Dec* has an owner, who, through a simple checklist, can select which other users can have *Full* or *Read only* access to the QF/DM. Further, to enable multi-user visualization and editing, *Arg&Dec* implements a push notification mechanism: when more users open the same QF in their browsers at the same time, if a user makes a change to the QF the modification is notified immediately to the browsers of all the other users.

In order to improve the user interface, taking into account in particular the needs of non-expert users who may not be acquainted with QFs, *Arg&Dec* includes an experimental functionality of natural language presentation. In a similar spirit to the work of [18], this aims at synthesizing the motivations underlying the selection of the first ranked option. To exemplify, if the selected option has no cons, the fact that it has only pros is provided directly as a simple explanation. Otherwise, if the number of pros is much higher than the one of cons, an explanation focused on the cardinalities of pros and cons is given, while the notion of strength is mentioned and more emphasis is given to the average scores of pros and cons in case their cardinalities are closer or the number of cons is higher than the number of pros. The explanation is then extended recursively to the subtree of pros and cons rooted in the first ranked answer. The generated explanation can also be listened to thanks to a speech synthesis functionality.

As for technologies, *Arg&Dec* features a typical web application architecture with HTML, CSS, and AJAX on the client-side and PHP code executing queries on a MySQL DB on the server side, where all data are stored. On the client side, user interaction is managed by JavaScript code and several JavaScript libraries are used, including in particular jQuery, Bootstrap and Bootbox (for user interface features), and jsPlumb (for graph visualization). Further, Google Translator is used for speech synthesis.

The system has undergone a preliminary test phase with the aid of experts in engineering design at Imperial College London, several case studies (also taken from the experience described in [4]) were modeled and the transformation features in either direction were experimented with. The experts expressed an initial appreciation for the system functionalities and for the opportunity to compare different decision methods: a full validation of the system on a large number of realistic cases is planned for future work, as is the extension to support collaborative definitions of DMs.

6   Discussion and Conclusions

The paper develops a comparison between an argumentation-based, namely QuAD frameworks, and a matrix-based, namely Decision Matrices, decision support models from a conceptual and a technical perspective, introduces novel transformations between the two models, and presents the *Arg&Dec* web application which supports cooperative work for the definition, evaluation, and transformation of decision problems.

To the best of our knowledge, no systematic comparisons of argumentation-based versus matrix-based approaches, let alone software tools supporting this activity, are available in the literature. In this sense, there are no directly related works. It can be mentioned however that other proposals connecting argumentation formalisms with formal decision methods are available in the literature.

The work presented in [1] concerns a context where arguments can be distinguished into *practical* and *epistemic*. Practical arguments can be in favor or against some candidate options in a decision problem, while epistemic arguments may attack practical arguments and also attack each other. On the basis of these attacks, an abstract argumentation framework is built [12] and, accordingly, the acceptable arguments are identified. Then, for each candidate option, several evaluation principles can be considered: the most general evaluation principle is based on an aggregation function of the arguments in favor and against the option. In this general context, a specific typology of formal practical arguments is introduced. Basically, a practical argument uses a candidate option to derive either a desirable or undesirable consequence (called goal or rejection, respectively) and accordingly is in favor or against the candidate option used within the argument. Some relationships between this approach and some instances of Multi-Criteria Decision Making (MCDM) are then investigated. Differently from the proposal in [1], we do not assume the availability of a formal knowledge base for the construction of arguments and their attack relation, nor a crisp distinction between practical and epistemic arguments, since QuAD frameworks are meant to support debates occurring in application contexts where such formal basis is typically not available. Moreover while Decision Matrices belong to the MCDM family, the instances of MCDM considered in [1] do not cover the case of Decision Matrices as defined in the present paper.

In [19] a rule-based argumentation formalism is used to build arguments concerning decisions and their attack relations. Also in this case, only those arguments that are deemed acceptable according to an evaluation based on abstract argumentation semantics are used to determine the final decision, and for each candidate option, the goals which are supported by the acceptable arguments associated with this option are considered. The option(s) satisfying the highest numer of goals become recommended decisions. It is shown that the proposed formalism can be put in relationship with MCDM and, in particular, given a multi-criteria decision problem, it is shown that it is possible to generate an argument-based formalization producing the same results. It can be noted that some of the motivations presented in [19] are similar to ours, for instance it is remarked that using an argument-based decision method makes the decision process less opaque and aims at increasing accountability and reproducing the decision rationale. Similarly to the case of [1], the formalism adopted in [19] is more demanding than ours, since it encompasses the existence of a formal knowledge base. Differently from [1] and from our approach, the proposal of [19] encompasses only arguments in favor of a given option, which can be a significant limitation in a dialectical context. Concerning the relationship with MCDM, the mehod to generate an argument-based formalization proposed in [19] is applicable also to Decision Matrices. It can be observed however that it basically consists in "reproducing" the aggregation mechanism adopted (i.e. the matrix score) through a set of case-specific rules, some of which just map numbers into numbers to this purpose. Hence, this relationship basically corresponds to what we have observed at the beginning of Sect. 4 about the possibility of reproducing an approach within the other one by suitable ad hoc definitions, while one of the aims of the present paper was to analyze the motivations and different assumptions underlying the production of different outcomes by different formalisms. In this spirit, we regard a more systematic analysis of the relationships with MCDM as an important direction of future development.

While the two proposals discussed above are focused on decision support, for an extended discussion at a broader level of the relationships between QuAD frameworks and other argumentation-based models and software tools the reader is referred to [4]. Indeed, *Arg&Dec* has its basis in the experience of integrating the QuAD framework model within the designVUE [2] standalone software tool, described in [4]. We believe that comparison and integration of alternative, complementary decision models is a fruitful research direction to which this paper makes a first contribution. Future work includes a more extensive theoretical analysis of situations where the two models (dis)agree along with an analysis of general requirements of score functions (see some discussion in [4]), on-field experimentation with realistic case studies, in particular in the areas of engineering design and environmental planning, and further investigation on natural language presentation.

Acknowledgments. The authors thank the referees for their helpful comments and Antonio Rago for his help with *Arg&Dec* in the testing phase. F. Toni was partially supported by the EPSRC TRaDAr project, P. Baroni by the INDAM-GNCS project EMADS.

References

1. Amgoud, L., Prade, H.: Using arguments for making and explaining decisions. Artif. Intell. **173**(3–4), 413–436 (2009)
2. Aurisicchio, M., Bracewell, R.H.: Capturing an integrated design information space with a diagram based approach. J. Eng. Des. **24**, 397–428 (2013)
3. Baroni, P., Romano, M., Toni, F., Aurisicchio, M., Bertanza, G.: An argumentation-based approach for automatic evaluation of design debates. In: Leite, J., Son, T.C., Torroni, P., Torre, L., Woltran, S. (eds.) CLIMA XIV 2013. LNCS, vol. 8143, pp. 340–356. Springer, Heidelberg (2013)
4. Baroni, P., Romano, M., Toni, F., Aurisicchio, M., Bertanza, G.: Automatic evaluation of design alternatives with quantitative argumentation. Argument Comput. **6**(1), 24–49 (2015)
5. Shum, S.J.B., Selvin, A.M., Sierhuis, M., Conklin, J., Haley, C.B., Nuseibeh, B.: Hypermedia support for argumentation-based rationale: 15 years on from gIBIS and QOC. In: Dutoit, A.H., McCall, R., Mistrik, I., Paech, B. (eds.) Rationale Management in Software Engineering, pp. 111–132. Springer, Heidelberg (2006)
6. Shum, S.J.B.: Cohere: Towards web 2.0 argumentation. In: Besnard, P., Doutre, S., Hunter, A. (eds.) Proceedings of COMMA. Frontiers in Artificial Intelligence and Applications, vol. 172, pp. 97–108. IOS Press (2008)
7. Shum, S.J.B., Hammond, N.: Argumentation-based design rationale: What use at what cost? Int. J. Hum. Comput. Stud. **40**(4), 603–652 (1994)
8. Cayrol, C., Lagasquie-Schiex, M.C.: Gradual valuation for bipolar argumentation frameworks. In: Godo, L. (ed.) ECSQARU 2005. LNCS (LNAI), vol. 3571, pp. 366–377. Springer, Heidelberg (2005)
9. Cayrol, C., Lagasquie-Schiex, M.C.: On the acceptability of arguments in bipolar argumentation frameworks. In: Godo, L. (ed.) ECSQARU 2005. LNCS (LNAI), vol. 3571, pp. 378–389. Springer, Heidelberg (2005)
10. Churchman, C.W.: Wicked problems. Manage. Sci. **14**(4), B141–B142 (1967)
11. Dubois, D., Fargier, H., Bonnefon, J.F.: On the qualitative comparison of decisions having positive and negative features. J. Artif. Intell. Res. **32**, 385–417 (2008)
12. Dung, P.M.: On the acceptability of arguments and its fundamental role in non-monotonic reasoning, logic programming and n-person games. Artif. Intell. **77**(2), 321–357 (1995)
13. Evripidou, V., Toni, F.: Argumentation and voting for an intelligent user empowering business directory on the web. In: Krötzsch, M., Straccia, U. (eds.) RR 2012. LNCS, vol. 7497, pp. 209–212. Springer, Heidelberg (2012)
14. Fischer, G., Lemke, A.C., McCall, R., Morch, A.I.: Making argumentation serve design. Hum. Comput. Interact. **6**(3), 393–419 (1991)
15. Franklin, B.: Letter to Joseph Priestley. In: Labaree, L.W., Bell, W.J. (eds.) Mr. Franklin: A selection from his personal letters. Yale University Press, New Haven (1956)
16. Klement, E.P., Mesiar, R., Pap, E.: Triangular Norms. Kluwer, Dordrecht (2000)
17. Kunz, W., Rittel, H.: Issues as elements of information systems. Working Paper 131, Institute of Urban and Regional Development, University of California, Berkeley, California (1970)
18. Labreuche, C.: A general framework for explaining the results of a multi-attribute preference model. Artif. Intell. **175**(7–8), 1410–1448 (2011)

19. Müller, J., Hunter, A.: An argumentation-based approach for decision making. In: Proceedings of the IEEE 24th International Conference on Tools with Artificial Intelligence, (ICTAI 2012), pp. 564–571. IEEE Computer Society, 7–9 November 2012 (2012)
20. Pugh, S.: Total Design: Integrated Methods for Successful Product Engineering. Addison-Wesley, Wokingham (1991)
21. Rittel, H.W.J., Webber, M.M.: Dilemmas in a general theory of planning. Policy Sci. 4(4), 155–169 (1973)
22. Rogers, P., Blenko, M.W.: Who has the D? how clear decision roles enhance organizational performance. Harvard Bus. Rev. 84(1), 52–61 (2006)
23. Triantaphyllou, E.: Multi-Criteria Decision Making: A Comparative Study. Kluwer, London (2000)
24. Triantaphyllou, E., Baig, K.: The impact of aggregating benefit and cost criteria in four MCDA methods. IEEE Trans. Eng. Manage. 52(2), 213–226 (2005)
25. Triantaphyllou, E., Mann, S.H.: An examination of the effectiveness of multidimensional decision-making methods: a decision-making paradox. Decis. Support Syst. 5(3), 303–312 (1989)
26. Ulrich, K.T., Eppinger, S.D.: Product Design and Development, 3rd edn. Irwin McGraw-Hill, New York (2004)

Reasons and Options for Updating an Opponent Model in Persuasion Dialogues

Elizabeth Black[1]([⊠]) and Anthony Hunter[2]

[1] Department of Informatics, King's College London, London, UK
`elizabeth.black@kcl.ac.uk`
[2] Department of Computer Science, University College London, London, UK
`anthony.hunter@cs.ucl.ac.uk`

Abstract. Dialogical argumentation allows agents to interact by constructing and evaluating arguments through a dialogue. Numerous proposals have been made for protocols for dialogical argumentation, and recently there is interest in developing better strategies for agents to improve their own outcomes from the interaction by using an opponent model to guide their strategic choices. However, there is a lack of clear formal reasons for why or how such a model might be useful, or how it can be maintained. In this paper, we consider a simple type of persuasion dialogue, investigate options for using and updating an opponent model, and identify conditions under which such use of a model is beneficial.

1 Introduction

Argument dialogues are an established agreement technology; they provide a principled way of structuring rational interactions between participants (machine or human) who argue about the validity of certain claims in order to resolve their conflicting information, competing goals, incompatible intentions or opposing views of the world [1]. Such dialogues are typically defined by the *moves* that can be made and rules to determine which moves are permissible at any point in the dialogue. Much existing work in the field focusses on defining argument dialogues that allow achievement of a particular goal; for example, to persuade the other participant to accept some belief [2] or to agree on some action to achieve a shared goal [3]. However, successful achievement of a participant's dialogue goal normally depends on the *strategy* it employs to determine which of the permissible moves to make during the dialogue; the development of effective argument dialogue strategies is thus an important area of active research [4].

Recent work on argument dialogue strategy assumes the strategiser has some uncertain model of what its interlocutor knows, derived somehow from the strategiser's past interactions, which it uses to guide its choice of moves [5,6]. However, there is a lack of formal investigation into how such a model can be maintained and under what circumstances it can be useful. Rienstra *et al.* propose a mechanism for updating an opponent model with the addition of arguments proposed or received by the opponent [6], Black *et al.*'s approach involves also removing

© Springer International Publishing Switzerland 2015
E. Black et al. (Eds.): TAFA 2015, LNAI 9524, pp. 21–39, 2015.
DOI: 10.1007/978-3-319-28460-6_2

from the opponent model anything that is inconsistent with the observed opponent behaviour [5], while Hadjinikolis *et al.* consider how an agent can develop a model of the likelihood that an opponent will know a particular argument if it asserts some other argument [7,8]; however, none of these works formally investigate the impact of the model update mechanism on the dialogue outcome.

We are interested in understanding the different options for updating an opponent model and investigating the circumstances under which such a model can be useful. We consider a simple type of persuasion dialogue with two participants, the *persuader* and the *responder*. The persuader (who has an uncertain *model* of the responder) aims to convince the responder to accept the topic of the dialogue by asserting beliefs, while the responder replies honestly to indicate whether it is currently convinced of the acceptability of the topic.

We investigate the performance of two model update mechanisms, based on those used by Rienstra *et al.* [6] and Black *et al.* [5]. In the first (which we refer to as *basic*), beliefs asserted by the persuader are added to its model of the responder, while the second mechanism (which we refer to as *smart*) also removes from the persuader's model of the responder anything that is inconsistent with the moves the responder makes (under the assumption that the responder is honest). We do not focus here on how the persuader determines which beliefs to assert and which order to assert them in; we assume the persuader has a mechanism for determining some total ordering over its beliefs (which we refer to as its *strategy* and corresponds to the order in which it will assert its beliefs) and instead focus on whether it uses its model of the responder to decide when to give up trying to persuade the responder. We consider the case where the persuader will not give up until it has exhausted all its beliefs (called an *exhaustive* persuader) and the case where the persuader will give up as soon as, given its model of the responder, it believes it is not possible to successfully persuade the responder no matter which beliefs it asserts (called an *economical* persuader).

We formally investigate the performance of our model update mechanisms by identifying the situations in which it is possible that, *when following the same strategy*, a persuader of one type will successfully persuade the responder, while a persuader of another type will unsuccessfully terminate the dialogue before it has achieved its goal. This paper thus contributes to our understanding of when it can be advantageous to use a particular model update mechanism.

2   Simple Persuasion Dialogues

In our simple persuasion dialogues (adapted from the simple persuasion dialogues of Black *et al.* [5]) the persuader aims to convince the responder to accept the topic of the dialogue by asserting beliefs. We make no prescription as to which semantics the participants use to reason about the acceptability of beliefs. We assume only a finite logical language $\mathcal{L}$ and some function for determining the set of *acceptable* claims given some knowledge base of $\mathcal{L}$.

Definition 1. *For a knowledge base $\Phi \subseteq \mathcal{L}$, the function* Acceptable : $\wp(\mathcal{L}) \rightarrow$ $\wp(\mathcal{L})$ *returns the set of* **acceptable claims** *of Φ such that:* Acceptable$(\Phi) =$ $\{\alpha \in \mathcal{L} \mid \alpha$ *is acceptable given Φ under the chosen acceptability semantics}.*

There are many formalisms and associated acceptability semantics that may be used to instantiate Definition 1. For example: we could consider a standard propositional language $\mathcal{L}$ and specify that a claim α is acceptable given $\Phi \subseteq \mathcal{L}$ if and only if α can be classically entailed from Φ; it could be that $\mathcal{L}$ consists of atoms that represent abstract arguments and a claim α is acceptable given $\Phi \subseteq \mathcal{L}$ if and only if α is in the grounded extension of the argument framework constructed from Φ according to a particular defeat relation defined over $\mathcal{L}$ [9]; or $\Phi \subseteq \mathcal{L}$ may represent an ASPIC+ knowledge base and we may specify that α is acceptable given $\Phi \subseteq \mathcal{L}$ if and only if α is the claim of an admissible argument from the Dung-style argument framework constructed from Φ and a particular ASPIC+ argumentation system [10].

A simple persuasion dialogue has a *topic* (a wff of $\mathcal{L}$) and involves two *participants*, the *persuader* and the *responder*. Each participant has a *position* (a subset of $\mathcal{L}$) and the persuader has an uncertain *model* of the responder, which is a set consisting of those subsets of $\mathcal{L}$ that the persuader believes may be the responder's position. (Note that, unlike in [5], here we do not consider probabilities associated with the persuader's model.) We define a *dialogue scenario* by the participants, the participants' positions, the persuader's model of the responder and the topic. A dialogue scenario is *accurate* if the responder's position is a member of the persuader's model of the responder.

Definition 2. *A* **dialogue scenario** *is a tuple $(Ag, \mathsf{P}_0, \Upsilon_0, \tau)$ where:*

- *$Ag = \{ag_P, ag_R\}$ is the set of* **participants**, *ag_P is the* **persuader** *and ag_R is the* **responder***;*
- *$\mathsf{P}_0 : Ag \rightarrow \wp(\mathcal{L})$ is a function that returns each participant's* **position***;*
- *$\Upsilon_0 \subseteq \wp(\mathcal{L})$ is the persuader's* **model** *of the responder;*
- *$\tau \in \mathcal{L}$ is the* **topic** *of the dialogue.*

$(Ag, \mathsf{P}_0, \Upsilon_0, \tau)$ is **accurate** *iff $\mathsf{P}_0(ag_R) \in \Upsilon_0$. The set of all dialogue scenarios is denoted $\mathcal{S}$. The set of all accurate dialogue scenarios is denoted $\mathcal{S}_{acc}$.*

Example 1. Let $ds = (Ag, \mathsf{P}_0, \Upsilon_0, f)$ be a dialogue scenario. If $\mathsf{P}_0(ag_P) = \{a, b, c, d, e\}$, $\mathsf{P}_0(ag_R) = \{b\}$ and $\Upsilon_0 = \{\{a, b\}, \{a, c\}\}$, then ds is not accurate. If $\mathsf{P}_0(ag_P) = \{a, b, c, d, e\}$, $\mathsf{P}_0(ag_R) = \{b\}$ and $\Upsilon_0 = \{\{a, b\}, \{a, c\}, \{b\}\}$, then ds is accurate.

The set of *moves* used in simple persuasion dialogues is $\mathcal{M} = \{(\mathtt{open}, \tau), (\mathtt{assert}, \phi), (\mathtt{pass}), (\mathtt{close})\}$ where $\tau \in \mathcal{L}$ is the topic of the dialogue, $\phi \in \mathcal{L}$, and the function Sender : $\mathcal{M} \rightarrow Ag$ returns the *sender* of a move. A *simple persuasion dialogue* is a sequence of *dialogue states*, where each state consists of a *move* being made, a function that returns each participant's *position* after that move has been made, and a set that represents the persuader's *model* of the responder after that move has been made. The participants take it in turn to make moves. The persuader always starts by *opening* with the dialogue topic, following which it can *assert* a wff of $\mathcal{L}$ or make a *close* move. The responder can make a *close* or a *pass* move. The persuader cannot repeat assertions. The last move of the dialogue, and only the last move, is always a close move (and so either participant can chose to terminate the dialogue by making a close move); if this move is made by the responder, the dialogue is successful, otherwise it is unsuccessful. The *length* of a dialogue is equal to the number of dialogue states.

Definition 3. *A* **Simple Persuasion Dialogue** *of dialogue scenario* $(Ag, \mathsf{P}_0, \Upsilon_0, \tau)$ *is a sequence of* **dialogue states** $[(m_1, \mathsf{P}_1, \Upsilon_1), \ldots, (m_t, \mathsf{P}_t, \Upsilon_t)]$ *where* $\forall s$ *such that* $1 \leq s \leq t$:

1. $\mathsf{P}_s : Ag \rightarrow \wp(\mathcal{L})$;
2. $\Upsilon_s \subseteq \wp(\mathcal{L})$;
3. $m_s \in \{(\texttt{open}, \tau), (\texttt{assert}, \phi), (\texttt{pass}), (\texttt{close})\}$ *where* $\phi \in \mathcal{L}$;
4. $m_s = (\texttt{open}, \tau)$ *iff* $s = 1$;
5. *if* s *is odd, then* $\mathsf{Sender}(m_s) = ag_P$ *and* $m_s \in \{(\texttt{open}, \tau), (\texttt{assert}, \phi), (\texttt{close})\}$;
6. *if* s *is even, then* $\mathsf{Sender}(m_s) = ag_R$ *and* $m_s \in \{(\texttt{pass}), (\texttt{close})\}$;
7. $m_s = (\texttt{close})$ *iff* $s = t$;
8. *if* $m_s = (\texttt{assert}, \phi)$, *then* $\forall i$ *such that* $1 \leq i < s$, $m_i \neq (\texttt{assert}, \phi)$.

Let $d = [(m_1, \mathsf{P}_1, \Upsilon_1), \ldots, (m_t, \mathsf{P}_t, \Upsilon_t)]$ *be a simple persuasion dialogue: the* **length** *of* d, *denoted* $\mathsf{Length}(d)$, *is* t; d *is* **successful** *iff* $\mathsf{Sender}(m_t) = ag_R$.

The previous definition defines the protocol that participants of a simple persuasion dialogue must abide by. We also make some assumptions about the behaviour of the dialogue participants, namely: the persuader's position does not change during the dialogue (so it is not engaged with any processes external to the dialogue); the persuader only asserts things that are part of its own position (so it is honest); the responder's position is updated only to include things asserted by the persuader (so the responder trusts the persuader and is not engaged with any processes external to the dialogue); and the responder's moves accurately reflect whether it has been successfully convinced of the topic (so it is honest). If these assumptions hold we say the dialogue is *regular*.

Definition 4. *A simple persuasion dialogue* $[(m_1, \mathsf{P}_1, \Upsilon_1), \ldots, (m_t, \mathsf{P}_t, \Upsilon_t)]$ *of dialogue scenario* $(Ag, \mathsf{P}_0, \Upsilon_0, \tau)$ *is a* **regular simple persuasion dialogue** *iff* $\forall s$ *such that* $1 \leq s \leq t$:

1. $\mathsf{P}_s(ag_P) = \mathsf{P}_0(ag_P)$;
2. *if* $m_s = (\texttt{assert}, \phi)$, *then* $\phi \in \mathsf{P}_0(ag_P)$, *and* $\mathsf{P}_s(ag_R) = \mathsf{P}_{s-1}(ag_R) \cup \{\phi\}$;
3. $\tau \in \mathsf{Acceptable}(\mathsf{P}_{s-1}(ag_R))$ *iff* $s = t$ *and* $\mathsf{Sender}(m_s) = ag_R$.

The set of all regular simple persuasion dialogues of a dialogue scenario ds is denoted $\mathsf{Dialogues}_{\text{reg}}(ds)$.

The responder of a regular simple persuasion dialogue has no choice over the moves it can make; since we assume it to be honest, it terminates the dialogue with a close move if and only if it finds the topic to be acceptable, otherwise it makes a pass move. The persuader, however, can chose which beliefs to assert and whether to (unsuccessfully) terminate the dialogue; we consider conditions under which different types of persuader will terminate the dialogue in Sect. 3.

Example 2. Let $ds = (Ag, \mathsf{P}_0, \Upsilon_0, f)$ be a dialogue scenario with topic f such that $\mathsf{P}_0(ag_P) = \{a, b, c, d, e\}$, $\mathsf{P}_0(ag_R) = \{b\}$, $\Upsilon_0 = \{\{a, b\}, \{a, c\}\}$. The only sets of beliefs that determine the topic f to be acceptable (i.e., the only sets Φ such that $f \in \mathsf{Acceptable}(\Phi)$) are $\{b, c, d\}$ and $\{a, b, c\}$.

The following are each simple persuasion dialogues of ds. (In dialogues $d1$ and $d3$ the persuader's model of the responder is not updated, while in dialogues $d2$ and $d4$ the persuader's model is updated to include beliefs asserted by the persuader. We formally define model update methods in Sect. 3.)
$d1 = [((\text{open}, f), \mathsf{P}_1, \Upsilon_1), ((\text{pass}), \mathsf{P}_2, \Upsilon_2), ((\text{close}), \mathsf{P}_3, \Upsilon_3)]$ where

- $\forall i$ such that $1 \leq i \leq 3$, $\mathsf{P}_i(ag_P) = \{a, b, c, d, e\}$,
- $\forall i$ such that $1 \leq i \leq 3$, $\mathsf{P}_i(ag_R) = \{b\}$,
- $\forall i$ such that $1 \leq i \leq 3$, $\Upsilon_i = \{\{a, b\}, \{a, c\}\}$.

$d1$ is a regular unsuccessful dialogue.

$d2 = [((\text{open}, f), \mathsf{P}_1, \Upsilon_1), ((\text{pass}), \mathsf{P}_2, \Upsilon_2), ((\text{assert}, b), \mathsf{P}_3, \Upsilon_3), ((\text{pass}), \mathsf{P}_4, \Upsilon_4),$
$((\text{assert}, c), \mathsf{P}_5, \Upsilon_5), ((\text{pass}), \mathsf{P}_6, \Upsilon_6), ((\text{close}), \mathsf{P}_7, \Upsilon_7)]$ where

- $\forall i$ such that $1 \leq i \leq 7$, $\mathsf{P}_i(ag_P) = \{a, b, c, d, e\}$,
- $\forall i$ such that $1 \leq i \leq 4$, $\mathsf{P}_i(ag_R) = \{b\}$,
- $\forall i$ such that $5 \leq i \leq 7$, $\mathsf{P}_i(ag_R) = \{b, c\}$,
- $\Upsilon_1 = \Upsilon_2 = \{\{a, b\}, \{a, c\}\}$,
- $\Upsilon_3 = \Upsilon_4 = \{\{a, b\}, \{a, b, c\}\}$,
- $\forall i$ such that $5 \leq i \leq 7$, $\Upsilon_i = \{\{a, b, c\}\}$.

$d2$ is a regular unsuccessful dialogue.

$d3 = [((\text{open}, f), \mathsf{P}_1, \Upsilon_1), ((\text{pass}), \mathsf{P}_2, \Upsilon_2), ((\text{assert}, b), \mathsf{P}_3, \Upsilon_3), ((\text{pass}), \mathsf{P}_4, \Upsilon_4),$
$((\text{assert}, c), \mathsf{P}_5, \Upsilon_5), ((\text{pass}), \mathsf{P}_6, \Upsilon_6), ((\text{assert}, a), \mathsf{P}_7, \Upsilon_7), ((\text{close}), \mathsf{P}_8, \Upsilon_8)]$
where

- $\forall i$ such that $1 \leq i \leq 7$, $\mathsf{P}_i(ag_P) = \{a, b, c, d, e\}$,
- $\forall i$ such that $1 \leq i \leq 4$, $\mathsf{P}_i(ag_R) = \{b\}$,
- $\mathsf{P}_5(ag_R) = \mathsf{P}_6(ag_R) = \{b, c\}$,
- $\mathsf{P}_7(ag_R) = \mathsf{P}_8(ag_R) = \{a, b, c\}$,
- $\forall i$ such that $1 \leq i \leq 8$, $\Upsilon_i = \Upsilon_{i-1}$.

$d3$ is a regular successful dialogue.

$d4 = [((\text{open}, f), \mathsf{P}_1, \Upsilon_1), ((\text{pass}), \mathsf{P}_2, \Upsilon_2), ((\text{assert}, b), \mathsf{P}_3, \Upsilon_3), ((\text{close}), \mathsf{P}_4, \Upsilon_4)]$
where

- $\forall i$ such that $1 \leq i \leq 4$, $\mathsf{P}_i(ag_P) = \{a, b, c, d, e\}$,
- $\forall i$ such that $1 \leq i \leq 4$, $\mathsf{P}_i(ag_R) = \{b\}$,

- $\Upsilon_1 = \Upsilon_2 = \{\{a,b\}, \{a,c\}\}$,
- $\Upsilon_3 = \Upsilon_4 = \{\{a,b\}, \{a,b,c\}\}$.

$d4$ is not a regular dialogue, since at the point the responder successfully terminates the dialogue it does not find the topic to be acceptable.

We have now defined some assumptions about the behaviour of participants in a regular simple persuasion dialogue, however, we are yet to consider how the persuader updates or uses its model of the responder. In the following section we define different types of persuader according to the mechanism it uses to update its model of the responder and according to whether it will choose to unsuccessfully terminate the dialogue once, according to its (possibly incorrect) model, it believes it is impossible to convince the responder.

3   Updating and Using an Opponent Model

We first consider how a persuader may use its model of the responder to determine when to give up trying to persuade the responder. An *economical* persuader only makes a close move (and will always make a close move) when, according to its model of the responder, it believes there is no sequence of assertions it can make that will lead to a successful dialogue; that is, for every set Ψ that it believes could possibly be the responder's position, there is no subset of its own position that it can assert (i.e., contains no beliefs already asserted) and that, when combined with Ψ, would determine the topic to be acceptable.

Definition 5. *Let* $d = [(m_1, \mathsf{P}_1, \Upsilon_1), \ldots, (m_t, \mathsf{P}_t, \Upsilon_t)] \in \mathsf{Dialogues}_{\mathsf{reg}}((Ag, \mathsf{P}_0, \Upsilon_0, \tau))$. *We say* d *has an* **economical persuader** *iff:*

1. *if* $\mathsf{Sender}(m_t) = ag_P$, *then* $\forall \Psi \in \Upsilon_{t-1}$, $\nexists \Phi \subseteq \mathsf{P}_{t-1}(ag_P)$ *such that:*
   (a) $\Phi \neq \emptyset$,
   (b) $\Phi \cap \{\phi \mid \exists s$ *such that* $1 \leq s < t$ *and* $m_s = (\mathsf{assert}, \phi)\} = \emptyset$,
   (c) $\tau \in \mathsf{Acceptable}(\Psi \cup \Phi)$;
2. $\forall s$ *such that* $1 \leq s < t$ *and* s *is odd,* $\exists \Psi \in \Upsilon_{s-1}$ *such that* $\exists \Phi \subseteq \mathsf{P}_{s-1}(ag_P)$ *such that:*
   (a) $\Phi \neq \emptyset$,
   (b) $\Phi \cap \{\phi \mid \exists i$ *such that* $1 \leq i < s$ *and* $m_i = (\mathsf{assert}, \phi)\} = \emptyset$,
   (c) $\tau \in \mathsf{Acceptable}(\Psi \cup \Phi)$;

Example 3. Of the three regular dialogues given in Example 2 ($d1$, $d2$ and $d3$) only $d2$ and $d3$ have an economical persuader.

We now define three types of persuader whose performance we will later explore. An *exhaustive persuader* does not maintain its model of the responder and will only terminate the dialogue once it has exhausted all beliefs it can assert (i.e., does not consider its model when deciding whether to terminate the dialogue). A *basic persuader* is an economical persuader that only updates its opponent model to reflect that the responder is aware of things the persuader has asserted.

A persuader is *smart* if it is an economical persuader that updates its opponent model to reflect that the responder is aware of things the persuader has asserted and also removes from its model sets that are inconsistent with the responder's behaviour (assuming a regular dialogue). Thus, if the responder makes a pass move, a smart persuader removes from its model any sets that determine the topic to be acceptable (since it assumes the responder is honest).

Definition 6. *Let* $d = [(m_1, \mathsf{P}_1, \Upsilon_1), \ldots, (m_t, \mathsf{P}_t, \Upsilon_t)] \in \mathsf{Dialogues}_{\mathsf{reg}}((Ag, \mathsf{P}_0, \Upsilon_0, \tau))$.

d *has an* **exhaustive persuader** *iff: if* $\mathsf{Sender}(m_t) = ag_P$, *then* $\forall \phi \in \mathsf{P}_{t-1}(ag_P)$, $\exists s$ *such that* $1 \leq s < t$ *and* $m_s = (\mathsf{assert}, \phi)$ *and* $\forall s$ *such that* $1 \leq s \leq t$: $\Upsilon_s = \Upsilon_{s-1}$.

d *has a* **basic persuader** *iff* d *has an economical persuader and* $\forall s$ *such that* $1 \leq s \leq t$: *if* $m_s = (\mathsf{assert}, \phi)$, *then* $\Upsilon_s = \{\Psi \cup \{\phi\} \mid \Psi \in \Upsilon_{s-1}\}$; *otherwise* $\Upsilon_s = \Upsilon_{s-1}$.

d *has a* **smart persuader** *iff* d *has an economical persuader and* $\forall s$ *such that* $1 \leq s \leq t$: *if* $m_s = (\mathsf{assert}, \phi)$, *then* $\Upsilon_s = \{\Psi \cup \{\phi\} \mid \Psi \in \Upsilon_{s-1}\}$; *if* $m_s = (\mathsf{pass})$, *then* $\Upsilon_s = \{\Psi \in \Upsilon_{s-1} \mid \tau \notin \mathsf{Acceptable}(\Psi)\}$; *otherwise* $\Upsilon_s = \Upsilon_{s-1}$.

Example 4. Let $ds = (Ag, \mathsf{P}_0, \Upsilon_0, f)$ be the dialogue scenario given in Example 2 where $\mathsf{P}_0(ag_P) = \{a, b, c, d, e\}$, $\mathsf{P}_0(ag_R) = \{b\}$, $\Upsilon_0 = \{\{a, b\}, \{a, c\}\}$ and the only sets of beliefs that determine the topic of the dialogue to be acceptable (i.e., the only sets Φ such that $f \in \mathsf{Acceptable}(\Phi)$) are $\{b, c, d\}$ and $\{a, b, c\}$.

The persuader of the dialogue $d1$ given in Example 2 is neither exhaustive, basic nor smart. The persuader of the dialogue $d2$ given in Example 2 is basic. The persuader of the dialogue $d3$ given in Example 2 is exhaustive.

$d5 = [((\mathsf{open}, f), \mathsf{P}_1, \Upsilon_1), ((\mathsf{pass}), \mathsf{P}_2, \Upsilon_2), ((\mathsf{assert}, b), \mathsf{P}_3, \Upsilon_3), ((\mathsf{pass}), \mathsf{P}_4, \Upsilon_4),$
$((\mathsf{assert}, c), \mathsf{P}_5, \Upsilon_5), ((\mathsf{pass}), \mathsf{P}_6, \Upsilon_6), ((\mathsf{close}), \mathsf{P}_7, \Upsilon_7)]$ where

- $\forall i$ such that $1 \leq i \leq 7$, $\mathsf{P}_i(ag_P) = \{a, b, c, d, e\}$,
- $\forall i$ such that $1 \leq i \leq 4$, $\mathsf{P}_i(ag_R) = \{b\}$,
- $\forall i$ such that $5 \leq i \leq 7$, $\mathsf{P}_i(ag_R) = \{b, c\}$,
- $\Upsilon_1 = \Upsilon_2 = \{\{a, b\}, \{a, c\}\}$,
- $\Upsilon_3 = \{\{a, b\}, \{a, b, c\}\}$,
- $\Upsilon_4 = \{\{a, b\}\}$,
- $\Upsilon_5 = \{\{a, b, c\}\}$,
- $\Upsilon_6 = \Upsilon_7 = \emptyset$.

$d5$ is a regular unsuccessful dialogue with a smart persuader.

$d6 = [((\mathsf{open}, f), \mathsf{P}_1, \Upsilon_1), ((\mathsf{pass}), \mathsf{P}_2, \Upsilon_2), ((\mathsf{assert}, a), \mathsf{P}_3, \Upsilon_3), ((\mathsf{pass}), \mathsf{P}_4, \Upsilon_4),$
$((\mathsf{assert}, d), \mathsf{P}_5, \Upsilon_5), ((\mathsf{pass}), \mathsf{P}_6, \Upsilon_6), ((\mathsf{assert}, c), \mathsf{P}_7, \Upsilon_7), ((\mathsf{pass}), \mathsf{P}_8, \Upsilon_8),$
$((\mathsf{assert}, e), \mathsf{P}_9, \Upsilon_9), ((\mathsf{pass}), \mathsf{P}_{10}, \Upsilon_{10}), ((\mathsf{assert}, b), \mathsf{P}_{11}, \Upsilon_{11}), ((\mathsf{pass}), \mathsf{P}_{12}, \Upsilon_{12}),$
$((\mathsf{close}), \mathsf{P}_{13}, \Upsilon_{13})]$ where

- $\forall i$ such that $1 \leq i \leq 7$, $\mathsf{P}_i(ag_P) = \{a, b, c, d, e\}$,
- $\mathsf{P}_1(ag_R) = \mathsf{P}_2(ag_R) = \{b\}$,
- $\mathsf{P}_3(ag_R) = \mathsf{P}_4(ag_R) = \{a, b\}$,

- $P_5(ag_R) = P_6(ag_R) = \{a, b, d\}$,
- $P_7(ag_R) = P_8(ag_R) = \{a, b, c, d\}$,
- $\forall i$ such that $9 \leq i \leq 13$, $P_i(ag_R) = \{a, b, c, d, e\}$,
- $\forall i$ such that $1 \leq i \leq 13$, $\Upsilon_i = \Upsilon i - 1$.

$d6$ is a regular unsuccessful dialogue with an exhaustive persuader.

It follows from our definitions that if a regular dialogue of an *accurate* scenario has a basic or smart persuader, the persuader's model will remain accurate throughout the dialogue (i.e., the responder's actual beliefs will always be a member of the persuader's model).

Lemma 1. *If $ds \in \mathcal{S}_{acc}$ and $[(m_1, P_1, \Upsilon_1), \dots, (m_t, P_t, \Upsilon_t)] \in \mathsf{Dialogues}_{reg}(ds)$ has a basic or smart persuader, then for all i such that $1 \leq i \leq t$, $P_i(ag_R) \in \Upsilon_i$.*

In the following section, we define how a dialogue is generated from a particular dialogue scenario by a particular type of persuader.

4   Generating Dialogues

We are interested in exploring the usefulness of our model update mechanisms when the persuader uses its model of the responder to decide when to unsuccessfully terminate the dialogue. We are not concerned here with the strategical choices the persuader makes to determine which beliefs to assert and which order to assert them in, but rather assume that the persuader has some mechanism for determining this. We define a *strategy* for a dialogue scenario as a sequence of beliefs that is some permutation of the persuader's position, corresponding to the order in which it will assert beliefs. Different dialogues may be generated from the same dialogue scenario by persuaders of different types following the same strategy, since an economical persuader will choose to terminate the dialogue once it thinks it is in a hopeless position according to its model of the responder, and a basic and a smart persuader's models may diverge.

Definition 7. *A **strategy** of a dialogue scenario $(Ag, P_0, \Upsilon_0, \tau) \in \mathcal{S}$ is a sequence $[\alpha_1, \dots, \alpha_n]$ such that $\{\alpha_1, \dots, \alpha_n\} = P_0(ag_P)$ and $\forall i, i'$ such that $1 \leq i, i' \leq n$, $\alpha_i = \alpha_{i'}$ iff $i = i'$.*

Example 5. Let $ds = (Ag, P_0, \Upsilon_0, f)$ be the dialogue scenario given in Example 2 where $P_0(ag_P) = \{a, b, c, d, e\}$, $P_0(ag_R) = \{b\}$ and $\Upsilon_0 = \{\{a, b\}, \{a, c\}\}$. Examples of strategies of ds are $[b, c, a, d, e]$ and $[b, c, a, e, d]$. However, $[b, c, e]$ is not a strategy of ds and $[b, c, a, c, d, e]$ is not a strategy of ds.

Whether the persuader makes a close move is determined by its initial position, the assertions it has already made and (in the case of an economical persuader) its model of the responder; whether the responder makes a close move is determined by its initial position and the assertions made by the persuader. Thus each possible strategy maps to exactly one dialogue for each type of persuader and a given dialogue scenario, where the assertions made during the dialogue correspond to a prefix of the strategy; we say this is the *dialogue of the persuader type generated by the strategy from the dialogue scenario*.

Definition 8. *Let* $ds \in \mathcal{S}$, $\mathrm{T} \in \{\text{exh}, \text{bas}, \text{sm}\}$ *and* $st = [\alpha_1, \ldots, \alpha_n]$ *be a strategy of* ds. *The* **dialogue of type** T **generated by** st **from** ds, *denoted* $\text{Dialogue}(ds, \mathrm{T}, st)$, *is* $d = [(m_1, \mathsf{P}_1, \Upsilon_1), \ldots, (m_t, \mathsf{P}_t, \Upsilon_t)]$ $(t \leq 2n + 2)$ *such that*

1. $d \in \text{Dialogues}_{\text{reg}}(ds)$,
2. $\forall i$ *such that* $1 < i < t$ *and* i *is odd,* $m_i = (\text{assert}, \alpha_x)$ *where* $x = \frac{i-1}{2}$,
3. *if* $\mathrm{T} = \text{exh}$, *then* d *has an exhaustive persuader,*
4. *if* $\mathrm{T} = \text{bas}$, *then* d *has a basic persuader,*
5. *if* $\mathrm{T} = \text{sm}$, *then* d *has a smart persuader.*

Example 6. Let $ds = (Ag, \mathsf{P}_0, \Upsilon_0, f)$ be the dialogue scenario given in Example 2 where $\mathsf{P}_0(ag_P) = \{a, b, c, d, e\}$, $\mathsf{P}_0(ag_R) = \{b\}$, $\Upsilon_0 = \{\{a, b\}, \{a, c\}\}$ and the only sets of beliefs that determine the topic f to be acceptable (i.e., the only sets Φ such that $f \in \text{Acceptable}(\Phi)$) are $\{b, c, d\}$ and $\{a, b, c\}$.
Let $st1 = [b, c, a, d, e]$, $st2 = [b, c, a, e, d]$, $st3 = [a, d, c, e, b]$ be strategies of ds.
$\text{Dialogue}(ds, \text{bas}, st1) = \text{Dialogue}(ds, \text{bas}, st2) = d2$ (as given in Example 2).
$\text{Dialogue}(ds, \text{sm}, st1) = \text{Dialogue}(ds, \text{sm}, st2) = d5$ (as given in Example 4).
$\text{Dialogue}(ds, \text{exh}, st3) = d6$ (as given in Example 4).

It follows from Definition 6 that if a basic and a smart persuader each follow the same strategy, the smart persuader's model will be a subset of the basic persuader's model at corresponding points in the two dialogues produced.

Lemma 2. *If* $ds \in \mathcal{S}$ *and* st *is a strategy of* ds *such that* $\text{Dialogue}(ds, \text{bas}, st) = [(m_{b_1}, \mathsf{P}_{b_1}, \Upsilon_{b_1}), \ldots, (m_{b_n}, \mathsf{P}_{b_n}, \Upsilon_{b_n})]$ *and* $\text{Dialogue}(ds, \text{sm}, st) = [(m_{s_1}, \mathsf{P}_{s_1}, \Upsilon_{s_1}), \ldots, (m_{s_m}, \mathsf{P}_{s_m}, \Upsilon_{s_m})]$, *then* $\forall i$ *such that* $1 \leq i \leq m$, *if* $i \leq n$, *then* $\Upsilon_{s_i} \subseteq \Upsilon_{b_i}$.

It follows from our definitions and the previous lemma, that the smart dialogue generated by a particular strategy from a dialogue scenario is never longer than the basic dialogue generated with the same strategy, which is never longer than the exhaustive dialogue generated.

Proposition 1. *If* $ds \in \mathcal{S}$ *and* st *is a strategy of* ds, *then*

$$\text{Length}(\text{Dialogue}(ds, \text{exh}, st)) \geq \text{Length}(\text{Dialogue}(ds, \text{bas}, st))$$
$$\geq \text{Length}(\text{Dialogue}(ds, \text{sm}, st)).$$

In the following section, we compare the performance of the different types of persuader we have defined (exhaustive, basic, smart). In particular, we identify the situations in which a persuader of one type can be successful while a persuader of another type may be unsuccessful.

5   Performance of Model Update Mechanisms

We are interested in identifying the situations when a persuader of one type can have an advantage over a persuader of another type; i.e., when, following a particular strategy, a persuader of one type will successfully convince the responder, while a persuader of another type will not. We show that, for accurate scenarios, there is no difference in success of the different persuader types (Table 1). For accurate scenarios, the only difference in the dialogues produced by the different types of persuader with a particular strategy is that, if the dialogues produced are unsuccessful, a smart persuader may terminate the dialogue before a basic persuader, who may terminate before an exhaustive persuader.

We show that, for scenarios that are not accurate, it is possible for an exhaustive persuader to generate a successful dialogue, while a basic and a smart persuader each generate an unsuccessful dialogue with the same strategy. We also show that it is possible for an exhaustive and a basic persuader to each generate a successful dialogue, while a smart persuader generates an unsuccessful dialogue with the same strategy. (These results are summarised in Table 2.)

5.1   Performance of Mechanisms for Accurate Scenarios

If we consider only accurate scenarios, if a persuader of a particular type generates a successful dialogue with a given strategy, then a persuader of either of the other types will generate the same dialogue with the same strategy. This follows from Lemma 1, the definitions of basic, smart and exhaustive persuaders (Definition 6) and the assumptions we have made about regular dialogues (Definition 4).

Lemma 3. *If $ds \in \mathcal{S}_{acc}$ and st is a strategy of ds such that* Dialogue(ds, T, st) *is successful (where* $\text{T} \in \{\text{exh}, \text{bas}, \text{sm}\}$*) then* $\forall \text{T}' \in \{\text{exh}, \text{bas}, \text{sm}\}$, Dialogue$(ds, \text{T}, st) = $ Dialogue(ds, T', st).

If we again consider only accurate scenarios, but with a strategy that generates an unsuccessful dialogue for one persuader type, then the same strategy will also generate an unsuccessful dialogue for each of the other persuader types (in this case the dialogue generated by a smart persuader may be shorter than the dialogue generated by a basic persuader, which may be shorter than the dialogue generated by an exhaustive persuader, which must be of length $2n + 3$ where n is the size of the persuader's position). Again, this follows from Lemma 1, the definitions of basic, smart and exhaustive persuaders (Definition 6) and the assumptions we have made about regular dialogues (Definition 4).

Lemma 4. *If $ds \in \mathcal{S}_{acc}$ and st is a strategy of ds such that* Dialogue(ds, T, st) *is unsuccessful (where* $\text{T} \in \{\text{exh}, \text{bas}, \text{sm}\}$*) then* $\forall \text{T}' \in \{\text{exh}, \text{bas}, \text{sm}\}$, Dialogue$(ds, \text{T}', st)$ *is also unsuccessful.*

It is clear from the above results that there are no accurate dialogue scenarios for which there is any difference in success of the different agent types.

Proposition 2. $\nexists ds \in \mathcal{S}_{acc}$ *such that st is a strategy of ds,* Dialogue(ds, T, st) *is successful,* Dialogue(ds, T', st) *is unsuccessful,* $\text{T}, \text{T}' \in \{\text{exh}, \text{bas}, \text{sm}\}$ *and* $\text{T}' \neq \text{T}$.

It is straightforward to construct examples to show that there are accurate dialogue scenarios in which, when following the same strategy, all agent types will be successful (similarly unsuccessful). This gives us the following propositions.

Proposition 3. $\exists ds \in S_{acc}$ *such that st is a strategy of ds and* $\forall T \in$ {exh, bas, sm}, Dialogue(ds, T, st) *is successful.*

Proposition 4. $\exists ds \in S_{acc}$ *such that st is a strategy of ds and* $\forall T \in$ {exh, bas, sm}, Dialogue(ds, T, st) *is unsuccessful.*

These results are summarised in Table 1.

Table 1. For an accurate dialogue scenario and a particular strategy, identifies possible combinations of outcomes by persuader type.

Outcome by persuader type			Outcome combination possible for accurate dialogue scenarios?
Exhaustive	Basic	Smart	
Successful	Successful	Successful	Yes (Proposition 3)
Unsuccessful	Unsuccessful	Unsuccessful	Yes (Proposition 4)
Successful	Unsuccessful	Unsuccessful	No (Proposition 2)
Unsuccessful	Successful	Unsuccessful	No (Proposition 2)
Unsuccessful	Unsuccessful	Successful	No (Proposition 2)
Unsuccessful	Successful	Successful	No (Proposition 2)
Successful	Unsuccessful	Successful	No (Proposition 2)
Successful	Successful	Unsuccessful	No (Proposition 2)

5.2 Performance of Mechanisms for Scenarios that are Not Accurate

For any dialogue scenario (accurate or not), if the dialogue generated by an exhaustive persuader with a particular strategy is unsuccessful, then the dialogue generated by a basic persuader with the same strategy is unsuccessful; similarly, if the dialogue generated by a basic persuader with a particular strategy is unsuccessful, then the dialogue generated by a smart persuader with the same strategy is unsuccessful. This follows from Lemma 2, the definition of an exhaustive persuader (Definition 6) and the assumptions we have made about regular dialogues (Definition 4).

Lemma 5. *Let* $ds \in S$ *and st be a strategy of ds.*
If Dialogue(ds, exh, st) *is unsuccessful, then* Dialogue(ds, bas, st) *is unsuccessful.*
If Dialogue(ds, bas, st) *is unsuccessful, then* Dialogue(ds, sm, st) *is unsuccessful.*

It follows straightforwardly from the above lemma that there are no dialogue scenarios for which (when following the same strategy) a smart persuader will be successful while either an exhaustive or a basic persuader will be unsuccessful, nor are there any dialogue scenario for which a basic persuader will be successful but an exhaustive persuader (with the same strategy) will be unsuccessful.

Proposition 5. $\nexists ds \in S \setminus S_{acc}$ such that st is a strategy of ds, Dialogue(ds, sm, st) is successful, Dialogue(ds, T, st) is unsuccessful, and $\text{T} \in \{\text{exh}, \text{bas}\}$.

Proposition 6. $\nexists ds \in S \setminus S_{acc}$ such that st is a strategy of ds, Dialogue(ds, bas, st) is successful and Dialogue(ds, exh, st) is unsuccessful.

We now show by example that all other combinations of difference in outcome from the different persuader types are possible. First, we show that there exists a dialogue scenario that is not accurate in which all persuader types are successful.

Proposition 7. $\exists ds \in S \setminus S_{acc}$ such that st is a strategy of ds, and $\forall \text{T} \in \{\text{exh}, \text{bas}, \text{sm}\}$, Dialogue$(ds, \text{T}, st)$ is successful.

Proof. Let $ds = (Ag, \mathsf{P}_0, \Upsilon_0, f)$ be a dialogue scenario with topic f such that $\mathsf{P}_0(ag_P) = \{a, b, c, d, e\}$, $\mathsf{P}_0(ag_R) = \{b\}$, $\Upsilon_0 = \{\{d\}\}$. The only sets of beliefs that determine the topic f to be acceptable (i.e., the only sets Φ such that $f \in \mathsf{Acceptable}(\Phi)$) are $\{a, b, c\}$ and $\{a, c, d, e\}$.
Following the strategy $[a, c, e, d, b]$, each of the persuader types produces a successful dialogue where after it has asserted a and then c the responder will close the dialogue, indicating it has been persuaded.

We now show that there exists a dialogue scenario that is not accurate in which all persuader types are unsuccessful.

Proposition 8. $\exists ds \in S \setminus S_{acc}$ such that st is a strategy of ds, and $\forall \text{T} \in \{\text{exh}, \text{bas}, \text{sm}\}$, Dialogue$(ds, \text{T}, st)$ is unsuccessful.

Proof. Let $ds = (Ag, \mathsf{P}_0, \Upsilon_0, f)$ be a dialogue scenario with topic f such that $\mathsf{P}_0(ag_P) = \{a, b, c, d, e\}$, $\mathsf{P}_0(ag_R) = \{b, d\}$, $\Upsilon_0 = \{\{a\}, \{d, e\}\}$. The only sets of beliefs that determine the topic f to be acceptable (i.e., the only sets Φ such that $f \in \mathsf{Acceptable}(\Phi)$) are $\{a, b, c\}$ and $\{a, c, d, e\}$.
For all possible strategies of this dialogue scenario, each of the different persuader types will produce an unsuccessful dialogue (since there is no superset of the responder's initial position that determines the topic to be acceptable).

We now show the existence of a dialogue scenario that is not accurate in which, when following a particular strategy, an exhaustive persuader will be successful but both a basic and a smart persuader will be unsuccessful.

Proposition 9. $\exists ds \in S \setminus S_{acc}$ such that st is a strategy of ds, Dialogue(ds, exh, st) is successful, and $\forall \text{T} \in \{\text{bas}, \text{sm}\}$, Dialogue$(ds, \text{T}, st)$ is unsuccessful.

Proof. Let $ds = (Ag, \mathsf{P}_0, \Upsilon_0, f)$ be a dialogue scenario with topic f such that $\mathsf{P}_0(ag_P) = \{a, b, c, d\}$, $\mathsf{P}_0(ag_R) = \{b, e\}$, $\Upsilon_0 = \{\{a, b\}, \{b, c\}\}$. The only sets of beliefs that determine the topic f to be acceptable (i.e., the only sets Φ such that $f \in \mathsf{Acceptable}(\Phi)$) are $\{a, c, d\}$ and $\{b, d, e\}$.
    No matter what strategy they are following, both a smart and a basic persuader will choose to terminate the dialogue unsuccessfully without asserting

any beliefs, since according to their model of the responder they believe there is no way the responder can successfully be persuaded (as there is no superset of any element of its model that determines the topic to be acceptable). However, an exhaustive persuader with a strategy that chooses to assert d first will be successful.

Finally, we show the existence of a dialogue scenario that is not accurate in which, when following a particular strategy, both an exhaustive and a basic persuader will be successful but a smart persuader will be unsuccessful.

Proposition 10. $\exists ds \in S \setminus S_{acc}$ *such that st is a strategy of ds,* $\forall \text{T} \in \{\text{exh}, \text{bas}\}$ Dialogue(ds, T, st) *is successful, and* Dialogue(ds, sm, st) *is unsuccessful.*

Proof. *Let* $ds = (Ag, \text{P}_0, \Upsilon_0, f)$ *be a dialogue scenario with topic* f *such that* $\text{P}_0(ag_P) = \{a, b, c, d, e\}$, $\text{P}_0(ag_R) = \{a, b\}$, $\Upsilon_0 = \{\{b, e\}, \{b, d\}, \{c\}\}$. *The only sets of beliefs that determine the topic* f *to be acceptable (i.e., the only sets* Φ *such that* $f \in \text{Acceptable}(\Phi)$*) are* $\{a, b, d\}$, $\{a, b, e\}$, $\{b, c\}$ *and* $\{a, b, d, e\}$. *Consider the strategy* $st = [a, e, b, d, c]$.

Dialogue$(ds, \text{exh}, st) = [((\text{open}, f), \text{P}_1, \Upsilon_0), ((\text{pass}), \text{P}_2, \Upsilon_0), ((\text{assert}, a), \text{P}_3, \Upsilon_0),$ $((\text{pass}), \text{P}_4, \Upsilon_0), ((\text{assert}, e), \text{P}_5, \Upsilon_0), ((\text{close}), \text{P}_6, \Upsilon_0)]$ *where*

- $\forall i$ *such that* $1 \leq i \leq 6$, $\text{P}_i(ag_P) = \{a, b, c, d, e\}$,
- $\forall i$ *such that* $1 \leq i \leq 4$, $\text{P}_i(ag_R) = \{a, b\}$,
- $\text{P}_5(ag_R) = \text{P}_6(ag_R) = \{a, b, e\}$.

Dialogue$(ds, \text{bas}, st) = [((\text{open}, f), \text{P}_1, \Upsilon_1), ((\text{pass}), \text{P}_2, \Upsilon_2), ((\text{assert}, a), \text{P}_3, \Upsilon_3),$ $((\text{pass}), \text{P}_4, \Upsilon_4), ((\text{assert}, e), \text{P}_5, \Upsilon_5), ((\text{close}), \text{P}_6, \Upsilon_6)]$ *where*

- $\forall i$ *such that* $1 \leq i \leq 6$, $\text{P}_i(ag_P) = \{a, b, c, d, e\}$,
- $\forall i$ *such that* $1 \leq i \leq 4$, $\text{P}_i(ag_R) = \{a, b\}$,
- $\text{P}_5(ag_R) = \text{P}_6(ag_R) = \{a, b, e\}$,
- $\Upsilon_1 = \Upsilon_2 = \{\{b, e\}, \{b, d\}, \{c\}\}$,
- $\Upsilon_3 = \Upsilon_4 = \{\{a, b, e\}, \{a, b, d\}, \{a, c\}\}$,
- $\Upsilon_3 = \Upsilon_4 = \{\{a, b, e\}, \{a, b, d\}, \{a, c\}\}$,
- $\Upsilon_5 = \Upsilon_6 = \{\{a, b, e\}, \{a, b, d, e\}, \{a, c, e\}\}$.

Dialogue$(ds, \text{sm}, st) = [((\text{open}, f), \text{P}_1, \Upsilon_1), ((\text{pass}), \text{P}_2, \Upsilon_2), ((\text{assert}, a), \text{P}_3, \Upsilon_3),$ $((\text{pass}), \text{P}_4, \Upsilon_4), ((\text{close}), \text{P}_5, \Upsilon_5)]$ *where*

- $\forall i$ *such that* $1 \leq i \leq 6$, $\text{P}_i(ag_P) = \{a, b, c, d, e\}$,
- $\forall i$ *such that* $1 \leq i \leq 5$, $\text{P}_i(ag_R) = \{a, b\}$,
- $\Upsilon_1 = \Upsilon_2 = \{\{b, e\}, \{b, d\}, \{c\}\}$,
- $\Upsilon_3 = \{\{a, b, e\}, \{a, b, d\}, \{a, c\}\}$,
- $\Upsilon_4 = \Upsilon_5 = \{\{a, c\}\}$.

Thus we see that while the exhaustive and basic persuader types are each successful, the smart persuader incorrectly perceives there to be no chance of convincing the responder and terminates the dialogue unsuccessfully.

These results are summarised in Table 2. They demonstrate the potential disadvantage of behaving economically (that is, choosing to give up trying to persuade the responder as soon as, according to one's image of the responder, success seems impossible) in the case where the persuader's image of the responder may not be accurate. Furthermore, they show that a smart persuader may incorrectly perceive its position to be hopeless while a basic persuader may not. We now consider the conditions under which an exhaustive persuader is successful but an economical persuader (basic or smart) is not, following which we consider the conditions under which an exhaustive and a basic persuader are successful but a smart persuader is not.

For a dialogue scenario that is not accurate, it follows from our definitions that the dialogue produced by an exhaustive persuader with a particular strategy is successful but the dialogue produced by a basic persuader with the same strategy is unsuccessful if and only if: the arguments asserted by the basic persuader are a strict prefix of those asserted by the exhaustive persuader (condition 1 in Proposition 11); the topic of the dialogue is determined to be acceptable by the union of the responder's initial position with the arguments asserted by the exhaustive persuader (condition 2); there is no strict prefix of the arguments asserted by the exhaustive persuader that, when combined with the responder's initial position, determines the topic to be acceptable (condition 3); for every element of the persuader's initial model of the responder, there is no subset of the persuader's initial position that contains the arguments asserted by the basic persuader and that, when combined with the responder's initial position, determines the topic to be acceptable (condition 4); for every strict prefix of the arguments asserted by the basic persuader, there is some subset of the persuader's initial position that contains that prefix and some element of the persuader's initial model such that the union of the two determines the topic to be acceptable (condition 5). Furthermore, it follows from these results that for every element Ψ of the persuader's initial model of the responder: if Ψ is

Table 2. For a not-accurate dialogue scenario that is not accurate and a particular dialogue strategy, identifies possible combinations of outcomes by persuader type.

Outcome by persuader type			Outcome combination possible for dialogue scenarios that are not accurate?
Exhaustive	Basic	Smart	
Successful	Successful	Successful	Yes (Proposition 7)
Unsuccessful	Unsuccessful	Unsuccessful	Yes (Proposition 8)
Successful	Unsuccessful	Unsuccessful	Yes (Proposition 9)
Unsuccessful	Successful	Unsuccessful	No (Proposition 6)
Unsuccessful	Unsuccessful	Successful	No (Proposition 5)
Unsuccessful	Successful	Successful	No (Proposition 5/6)
Successful	Unsuccessful	Successful	No (Proposition 5)
Successful	Successful	Unsuccessful	Yes (Proposition 10)

a proper subset of the responder's initial position, then there is a belief that the responder is aware of and of which the persuader has no knowledge; if the responder's initial position is a proper subset of Ψ, then there is some belief in Ψ that is not in the responder's initial position and not asserted by the exhaustive persuader; otherwise there is something in the responder's initial position that is not in Ψ and there is something in Ψ that is not in the responder's initial position, and either there is a belief in the responder's initial position that is not present in the persuader's initial position, or there is a belief in Ψ that is not in the responder's initial position and is not asserted by the exhaustive persuader (condition 6).

Proposition 11. *Let* $ds = (Ag, \mathsf{P}_0, \Upsilon_0, \tau) \in \mathcal{S} \setminus \mathcal{S}_{acc}$ *and* $st = [\alpha_1, \ldots, \alpha_n]$ *be a strategy of* ds.
$\mathsf{Dialogue}(ds, \mathsf{bas}, st)$ *is unsuccessful and* $\mathsf{Dialogue}(ds, \mathsf{exh}, st)$ *is successful where* $\mathsf{Dialogue}(ds, \mathsf{bas}, st) = [(\mathsf{open}, \tau), (\mathsf{pass}), (\mathsf{assert}, \alpha_1), (\mathsf{pass}), \ldots, (\mathsf{assert}, \alpha_j), (\mathsf{pass}), (\mathsf{close})]$ *and* $\mathsf{Dialogue}(ds, \mathsf{exh}, st) = [(\mathsf{open}, \tau), (\mathsf{pass}), (\mathsf{assert}, \alpha_1), (\mathsf{pass}), \ldots, (\mathsf{assert}, \alpha_k), (\mathsf{close})]$ *iff*

1. $j < k$,
2. $\tau \in \mathsf{Acceptable}(\{\alpha_1, \ldots, \alpha_k\} \cup \mathsf{P}_0(ag_R))$,
3. $\nexists i$ *such that* $1 \leq i < k$ *and* $\tau \in \mathsf{Acceptable}(\{\alpha_1, \ldots, \alpha_i\} \cup \mathsf{P}_0(ag_R))$,
4. $\forall \Psi \in \Upsilon_0, \nexists \Phi \subseteq \mathsf{P}_0(ag_P)$ *such that* $\{\alpha_1, \ldots, \alpha_j\} \subset \Phi$ *and* $\tau \in \mathsf{Acceptable}(\Psi \cup \Phi)$,
5. $\forall i$ *such that* $1 \leq i < j$, $\exists \Psi \in \Upsilon_0$ *such that* $\exists \Phi \subseteq \mathsf{P}_0(ag_P)$ *such that* $\{\alpha_1, \ldots, \alpha_i\} \subset \Phi$ *and* $\tau \in \mathsf{Acceptable}(\Psi \cup \Phi)$, *and*
6. $\forall \Psi \in \Upsilon_0$, *either*
   - $\Psi \subset \mathsf{P}_0(ag_R)$ *and* $\exists \phi \in \mathsf{P}_0(ag_R) \setminus \Psi$ *such that* $\phi \notin \mathsf{P}_0(ag_P)$,
   - $\mathsf{P}_0(ag_R) \subset \Psi$ *and* $\exists \phi$ *such that* $\phi \in \Psi \setminus \mathsf{P}_0(ag_R)$ *and* $\phi \notin \{\alpha_1, \ldots, \alpha_k\}$,
   otherwise
   - $\exists \phi \in \mathsf{P}_0(ag_R) \setminus \Psi$, $\exists \psi \in \Psi \setminus \mathsf{P}_0(ag_R)$, *and either*
     - $\mathsf{P}_0(ag_R) \setminus \mathsf{P}_0(ag_P) \neq \emptyset$, *or*
     - $\exists \phi$ *such that* $\phi \in \Psi \setminus \mathsf{P}_0(ag_R)$ *and* $\phi \notin \{\alpha_1, \ldots, \alpha_k\}$.

Proof. Left to right. Condition 1 follows directly from the definition of successful dialogues (Definition 3) and Proposition 1. Conditions 2-5 follow directly from the definitions of a basic persuader, an exhaustive persuader, an economical persuader and a regular dialogue (Definitions 4, 5 and 6).
Since $ds \notin \mathcal{S}_{acc}$, it cannot be the case that $\mathsf{P}_0(ag_R) \in \Upsilon_0$ (Definition 2), thus $\forall \Psi \in \Upsilon_0$, either $\Psi \subset \mathsf{P}_0(ag_R)$, $\mathsf{P}_0(ag_R) \subset \Psi$, or $\exists \phi \in \mathsf{P}_0(ag_R) \setminus \Psi$ and $\exists \psi \in \Psi \setminus \mathsf{P}_0(ag_R)$. We now consider these three cases in turn.

Let $\Psi \in \Upsilon_0$ such that $\Psi \subset \mathsf{P}_0(ag_R)$. Since $\tau \in \mathsf{Acceptable}(\{\alpha_1, \ldots, \alpha_k\} \cup \mathsf{P}_0(ag_R))$ and $\Psi \subset \mathsf{P}_0(ag_R)$, $\tau \in \mathsf{Acceptable}(\Lambda \cup \Psi \cup \{\alpha_1, \ldots, \alpha_k\})$ where $\Lambda = \mathsf{P}_0(ag_R) \setminus \Psi$. From 4, $\nexists \Phi \subseteq \mathsf{P}_0(ag_P)$ such that $\{\alpha_1, \ldots, \alpha_j\} \subset \Phi$ and $\tau \in \mathsf{Acceptable}(\Psi \cup \Phi)$. Therefore, $\exists \phi \in \Lambda$ such that $\phi \notin \mathsf{P}_0(ag_P)$ and thus $\exists \phi \in \mathsf{P}_0(ag_R) \setminus \Psi$ such that $\phi \notin \mathsf{P}_0(ag_P)$.

Let $\Psi \in \Upsilon_0$ such that $\mathsf{P}_0(ag_R) \subset \Psi$. It follows from 4 that $\tau \notin \mathsf{Acceptable}(\Psi \cup \{\alpha_1, \ldots, \alpha_k\})$. Since $\tau \in \mathsf{Acceptable}(\{\alpha_1, \ldots, \alpha_k\} \cup \mathsf{P}_0(ag_R))$ and $\mathsf{P}_0(ag_R) \subset \Psi$, it must be the case that $\exists \phi$ such that $\phi \in \Psi \setminus \mathsf{P}_0(ag_R)$ and $\phi \notin \{\alpha_1, \ldots, \alpha_k\}$.

Let $\Psi \in \Upsilon_0$ such that $\exists \phi \in \mathsf{P}_0(ag_R) \setminus \Psi$ and $\exists \psi \in \Psi \setminus \mathsf{P}_0(ag_R)$. Assume $\mathsf{P}_0(ag_R) \setminus \mathsf{P}_0(ag_P) = \emptyset$ (i.e., $\mathsf{P}_0(ag_R) \subseteq \mathsf{P}_0(ag_P)$). Since $\mathsf{P}_0(ag_R) \subseteq \mathsf{P}_0(ag_P)$, it follows from 4 that $\tau \notin \mathsf{Acceptable}(\Psi \cup \{\alpha_1, \ldots, \alpha_k\} \cup \mathsf{P}_0(ag_R))$. Since $\tau \in \mathsf{Acceptable}(\{\alpha_1, \ldots, \alpha_k\} \cup \mathsf{P}_0(ag_R))$, it follows that $\exists \phi \in \Psi$ such that $\phi \notin (\{\alpha_1, \ldots, \alpha_n\} \cup \mathsf{P}_0(ag_R))$. Therefore either $\mathsf{P}_0(ag_R) \setminus \mathsf{P}_0(ag_P) \neq \emptyset$, or $\exists \phi$ such that $\phi \in \Psi \setminus \mathsf{P}_0(ag_R)$ and $\phi \notin \{\alpha_1, \ldots, \alpha_k\}$.

Right to left. Follows from conditions 2-5 and from the definitions of a basic persuader, an exhaustive persuader, an economical persuader and a regular dialogue (Definitions 4, 5 and 6).

Also considering only non-accurate dialogue scenarios, it similarly follows from our definitions that the dialogue produced by a basic persuader with a particular strategy is successful but the dialogue produced by a smart persuader with the same strategy is unsuccessful if and only if: the arguments asserted by the smart persuader are a strict prefix of those asserted by the basic persuader (condition 1, Proposition 12); the topic of the dialogue is determined to be acceptable by the union of responder's initial position with the arguments asserted by the basic persuader (condition 2); there is no strict prefix of the arguments asserted by the basic persuader that, when combined with the responder's initial position, determines the topic to be acceptable (condition 3); for every element Ψ of the persuader's initial model of the responder, either Ψ determines the topic to be acceptable, or there is some strict prefix of the arguments asserted by the smart persuader that when combined with Ψ determines the topic to be acceptable, or there is no subset of the persuader's initial position that contains the arguments asserted by the smart persuader and when combined with Ψ determines the topic to be acceptable (condition 4); for every strict prefix $p1$ of the arguments asserted by the smart persuader, there is some element Ψ of the persuader's initial model such that there is no strict prefix $p2$ of $p1$ (including the empty prefix) that when combined with Ψ determines the topic to be acceptable and such that there exists some subset of the persuader's initial position that contains $p1$ and when combined with Ψ determines the topic to be acceptable.

Proposition 12. *Let $ds = (Ag, \mathsf{P}_0, \Upsilon_0, \tau) \in \mathcal{S} \setminus \mathcal{S}_{acc}$ and $st = [\alpha_1, \ldots, \alpha_n]$ be a strategy of ds.*

Dialogue(ds, sm, st) is unsuccessful and Dialogue(ds, bas, st) is successful where Dialogue$(ds, \mathsf{sm}, st) = [(\mathsf{open}, \tau), (\mathsf{pass}), (\mathsf{assert}, \alpha_1), (\mathsf{pass}), \ldots, (\mathsf{assert}, \alpha_j), (\mathsf{pass}), (\mathsf{close})]$ and Dialogue$(ds, \mathsf{bas}, st) = [(\mathsf{open}, \tau), (\mathsf{pass}), (\mathsf{assert}, \alpha_1), (\mathsf{pass}), \ldots, (\mathsf{assert}, \alpha_k), (\mathsf{close})]$ iff

1. $j < k$,
2. $\tau \in \mathsf{Acceptable}(\{\alpha_1, \ldots, \alpha_k\} \cup \mathsf{P}_0(ag_R))$,
3. $\forall i$ such that $1 \leq i < k$, $\exists \Psi \in \Upsilon_0$ such that $\exists \Phi \subseteq \mathsf{P}_0(ag_P)$ such that $\{\alpha_1, \ldots, \alpha_i\} \subset \Phi$ and $\tau \in \mathsf{Acceptable}(\Psi \cup \Phi)$.
4. $\forall \Psi \in \Upsilon_0$ such that $\tau \notin \mathsf{Acceptable}(\Psi)$ and $\nexists i$ such that $1 \leq i < j$ and $\tau \in \mathsf{Acceptable}(\Psi \cup \{\alpha_1, \ldots, \alpha_i\})$, $\nexists \Phi \subseteq \mathsf{P}_0(ag_P)$ such that $\{\alpha_1, \ldots, \alpha_j\} \subset \Phi$ and $\tau \in \mathsf{Acceptable}(\Psi \cup \Phi)$,

5. $\forall i$ such that $1 \leq i < j$, $\exists \Psi \in \Upsilon_0$ such that $\tau \notin$ Acceptable(Ψ), $\nexists h$ such that $1 \leq h < i$ and $\tau \in$ Acceptable$(\Psi \cup \{\alpha_1, \ldots, \alpha_h\})$, and $\exists \Phi \subseteq P_0(ag_P)$ such that $\{\alpha_1, \ldots, \alpha_i\} \subset \Phi$ and $\tau \in$ Acceptable$(\Psi \cup \Phi)$.

Proof. Follows from the definitions of successful dialogues, a basic persuader, a smart persuader, an economical persuader and a regular dialogue (Definitions 3, 4, 5 and 6) and Proposition 1.

Propositions 11 and 12 identify the necessary and sufficient conditions under which, while following the same strategy, a persuader of one type will successfully convince the responder, while a persuader of another type will not. These results help us to understand the situations in which the use of the different update mechanisms considered here can be disadvantageous.

6   Discussion

In this paper we have formally investigated the use of two approaches (basic and smart) for updating an uncertain opponent model in simple persuasion dialogues, where the persuader uses such a model to determine whether there is any chance of the dialogue leading to success, giving up and unsuccessfully terminating the dialogue as soon as it believes this not to be the case. We have shown that, if the persuader's initial model of the responder is accurate (i.e., represents the responder's actual position as being possible) there is no difference in the outcomes produced by the different persuader types with a particular strategy (where a strategy here predetermines the sequence of assertions to make), but a smart persuader may produce a shorter dialogue than a basic persuader, and a basic persuader may produce a shorter dialogue than an exhaustive persuader. In the case where the persuader's initial model of the responder does not represent the responder's actual initial position as a possibility, we have shown that it is possible for an exhaustive persuader to succeed in persuading the responder, while both a basic and a smart persuader following the same strategy will fail, and that it is possible for an exhaustive and basic persuader to be successful while a smart persuader following the same strategy will fail, and identified the conditions under which these cases occur.

These results help us to understand the situations under which it can be useful to apply the basic or the smart model update mechanism. If shorter dialogues are desirable and it is certain that the responder's actual initial position is captured as a possibility in the persuader's model, then a smart persuader will produce the best outcome, only producing an unsuccessful dialogue if neither a basic nor exhaustive persuader would succeed with the same strategy, but potentially terminating the dialogue at an earlier stage than the other types of persuader. If the persuader's model might not contain the responder's actual initial position as a possibility, then both a smart and a basic persuader risks incorrectly perceiving its position to be hopeless and unsuccessfully terminating the dialogue when in fact continuing with its strategy would lead to success.

Other works have investigated the use of a model of what is known to the opponent in order to generate a proponent's dialogue strategy. Rienstra *et al.* [6] apply a variation of the maxmin algorithm to an uncertain opponent model in order to determine the moves that produce the best expected outcome, while Black *et al.* [5] use automated planning techniques to generate a strategy with the highest chance of success given an uncertain opponent model. In contrast, here we do not consider here the generation of a dialogue strategy (we assume a sequence of assertions to make); however, our results can be beneficial in such settings, particularly in understanding the situations in which a possible strategy might be incorrectly classified as hopeless (using the results from Propositions 11 and 12). In their work, Rienstra *et al.* [6] apply the basic model update mechanism and Black *et al.* [5] use the smart approach, however neither explicitly considers the effect the update mechanism has on the outcome of the dialogue. Hadjinikolis *et al.* [7,8] propose a method an agent can use to augment an opponent model with extra information, based on previous dialogue experience, however they do not consider how this relates to dialogue outcome.

Hunter [11] also considers different mechanisms for updating an opponent model during a dialogue, where this opponent model represents the strength of belief the persuader believes its opponent has in different arguments (in the sense that it finds them convincing). In contrast, our opponent model represents the beliefs the persuader believes the responder is aware of and the responder's belief in the claims of arguments can be captured with the Acceptable function. Hunter considers how the accuracy of a user model can be improved through the use of moves that query the opponent's beliefs; it will be interesting to consider how an opponent model in our setting can be improved with such moves.

While the persuasion dialogue we consider here is simple, in that it is unidirectional and the responder's choice of moves is determined by its position and what has been asserted by the persuader, we believe that the results we present here provide useful foundations for exploring the behaviour of such model update functions in more complex persuasion situations, where each participant is asserting beliefs with the aim of persuading the other. The intuition underlying each of the basic and the smart update functions (to add to one's model beliefs that are asserted and to remove from one's model anything that is inconsistent with the opponent's behaviour) are also applicable in the symmetric persuasion setting, and we plan to adapt the results presented here to the symmetric persuasion setting in future work.

We also plan in future work to allow the assignment of probabilities to our uncertain opponent model and adapt our model update mechanisms to manage these, as is considered by Rienstra *et al.* [6] and Hunter [11]. The combination of probability with argumentation is a growing area of interest; e.g., recent work has proposed a framework for analysing the expected utility of probabilistic strategies for argument dialogues [12], while Oren *et al.* consider the use of a probabilistic audience model to determine convincing arguments to move in a monologue [13]. It will be interesting to investigate how the choice of update mechanism for a probabilistic opponent model impacts on dialogue outcome.

Acknowledgements. This work was partially supported by the the UK Engineering and Physical Sciences Research Council, grant ref. EP/M01892X/1.

References

1. Modgil, S., et al.: The added value of argumentation. In: Ossowski, S. (ed.) Agreement Technologies. Law, Governance and Technology Series, vol. 8, pp. 357–403. Springer, Heidelberg (2013)
2. Prakken, H.: Formal systems for persuasion dialogue. Knowl. Eng. Rev. **21**(02), 163–188 (2006)
3. Black, E., Atkinson, K.: Choosing persuasive arguments for action. In: 10th International Conference on Autonomous Agents and Multiagent Systems, pp. 905–912 (2011)
4. Thimm, M.: Strategic argumentation in multi-agent systems. Künstliche Intelligenz, Spec. Issue Multi-Agent Decis. Making **28**(3), 159–168 (2014)
5. Black, E., Coles, A., Bernardini, S.: Automated planning of simple persuasion dialogues. In: Bulling, N., van der Torre, L., Villata, S., Jamroga, W., Vasconcelos, W. (eds.) CLIMA 2014. LNCS, vol. 8624, pp. 87–104. Springer, Heidelberg (2014)
6. Rienstra, T., Thimm, M., Oren, N.: Opponent models with uncertainty for strategic argumentation. In: 23rd International Joint Conference on Artificial Intelligence, pp. 332–338 (2013)
7. Hadjinikolis, C., Siantos, Y., Modgil, S., Black, E., McBurney, P.: Opponent modelling in persuasion dialogues. In: 23rd International Joint Conference on Artificial Intelligence, pp. 164–170 (2013)
8. Hadjinikolis, C., Modgil, S., Black, E.: Building support-based opponent models in persuasion dialogues. In: Theory and Applications of Formal Argumentation: Third International Workshop, TAFA 2015, Buenos Aires, Argentina, 25–26 July 2015, Revised Selected papers. Springer LNAI 9524 (2016)
9. Dung, P.M.: On the acceptability of arguments and its fundamental role in non-monotonic reasoning, logic programming and n-person games. Artif. Intell. **77**(2), 321–357 (1995)
10. Modgil, S., Prakken, H.: A general account of argumentation with preferences. Artif. Intell. **195**, 361–397 (2013)
11. Hunter, A.: Modelling the persuadee in asymmetric argumentation dialogues for persuasion. In: 24th International Joint Conference on Artificial Intelligence, pp. 3055–3061 (2015)
12. Hunter, A.: Probabilistic strategies in dialogical argumentation. In: Straccia, U., Calì, A. (eds.) SUM 2014. LNCS, vol. 8720, pp. 190–202. Springer, Heidelberg (2014)
13. Oren, N., Atkinson, K., Li, H.: Group persuasion through uncertain audience modelling. In: 4th International Conference on Computational Models of Argument, pp. 350–357 (2012)

Abstract Solvers for Dung's Argumentation Frameworks

Remi Brochenin[1], Thomas Linsbichler[2], Marco Maratea[1(✉)],
Johannes Peter Wallner[3], and Stefan Woltran[2]

[1] University of Genoa, Genoa, Italy
marco@dibris.unige.it
[2] TU Wien, Vienna, Austria
[3] HIIT, Department of Computer Science, University of Helsinki, Helsinki, Finland

Abstract. Abstract solvers are a quite recent method to uniformly describe algorithms in a rigorous formal way and have proven successful in declarative paradigms such as Propositional Satisfiability and Answer Set Programming. In this paper, we apply this machinery for the first time to a dedicated AI formalism, namely Dung's abstract argumentation frameworks. We provide descriptions of several advanced algorithms for the preferred semantics in terms of abstract solvers and, moreover, show how slight adaptions thereof directly lead to new algorithms.

1 Introduction

Dung's concept of abstract argumentation [12] is nowadays a core formalism in AI [2,21]. The problem of solving certain reasoning tasks on such frameworks is the centerpiece of many advanced higher-level argumentation systems. The problems to be solved are however intractable and might even be hard for the second level of the polynomial hierarchy [13,15]. Thus, efficient and advanced algorithms have to be developed in order to deal with real-world size data with reasonable performance. The argumentation community is currently facing this challenge [7] and a first solver competition[1] has been organized in 2015. Thus, a number of new algorithms and systems are currently under development. Being able to precisely analyze and compare already developed and new algorithms is a fundamental step in order to understand the ideas behind such high-performance systems, and to build a new generation of more efficient algorithms and solvers.

Usually, algorithms are presented by means of pseudo-code descriptions, but other communities have experienced that analyzing algorithms on this basis may not be fruitful. More formal descriptions, which allow, e.g. for a uniform representation, have thus been developed: a recent and successful approach in this direction is the concept of *abstract solvers* [19]. Hereby, one characterizes the states of computation as nodes of a graph, the techniques as arcs between nodes, and the whole solving process as a path in the graph. This concept not

---

[1] http://argumentationcompetition.org.

© Springer International Publishing Switzerland 2015
E. Black et al. (Eds.): TAFA 2015, LNAI 9524, pp. 40–58, 2016.
DOI: 10.1007/978-3-319-28460-6_3

only proved successful for SAT [19], but also has been applied for several variants
of Answer-Set Programming [4,16,17].

In this paper, we make a first step to investigate the appropriateness of
abstract solvers for dedicated AI formalisms and focus on certain problems in
Dung's argumentation frameworks. In order to understand whether abstract
solvers are powerful enough, we consider quite advanced algorithms – ranging
from dedicated [20] to reduction-based [5,14] approaches (see [8] for a recent
survey) – for solving problems that are hard for the second level of the polynomial hierarchy. We show that abstract solvers allow for convenient algorithm
design resulting in a clear and mathematically precise description, and how formal properties of the algorithms are easily specified by means of related graph
properties. We also illustrate how abstract solvers simplify the *combination* of
techniques implemented in different solvers in order to define new solving procedures. Consequently, our findings not only prove that abstract solvers are a
valuable tool for specifying and analysing argumentation algorithms, but also
indicate the broad range the novel concept of abstract solvers can be applied to.

To sum up, our main contributions are as follows:

- We provide a full formal description of recent algorithms [5,14,20] for reasoning tasks under the preferred semantics in terms of abstract solvers, thus
  enabling a comparison of these approaches at a formal level.
- We give proofs illustrating how formal correctness of the considered algorithms
  can be shown with the help of descriptions in terms of abstract solvers.
- We outline how our reformulations can be used to gain more insight into the
  algorithms and how novel combinations of "levels" of abstract solvers might
  pave the way for new solutions.

The paper is structured as follows. Section 2 introduces the required preliminaries about abstract argumentation frameworks and abstract solvers. Then,
Sect. 3 shows how our target algorithms are reformulated in terms of abstract
solvers and introduces a new solving algorithm obtained from combining the target algorithms. The paper ends in Sect. 4 with final remarks and possible topics
for future research.

2   Preliminaries

In this section we first review (abstract) argumentation frameworks [12] and
their semantics (see [1] for an overview), and then introduce abstract transition
systems [19] on the concrete instance describing the DPLL-procedure [9].

Abstract Argumentation Frameworks. An *argumentation framework (AF)* is a pair
$F = (A, R)$ where A is a finite set of arguments and $R \subseteq A \times A$ is the *attack
relation*. Semantics for argumentation frameworks assign to each AF $F = (A, R)$
a set $\sigma(F) \subseteq 2^A$ of *extensions*. We consider here for σ the functions *adm*, *com*, and
prf, which stand for admissible, complete, and preferred semantics. Towards the
definitions of the semantics we need some formal concepts. For an AF $F = (A, R)$,

an argument $a \in A$ is defended (in F) by a set $S \subseteq A$ if for each $b \in A$ such that $(b, a) \in R$, there is a $c \in S$, such that $(c, b) \in R$ holds.

Definition 1. *Let $F = (A, R)$ be an AF. A set $S \subseteq A$ is* conflict-free *(in F), denoted $S \in cf(F)$, if there are no $a, b \in S$ such that $(a, b) \in R$. For $S \in cf(F)$, it holds that*

- *$S \in adm(F)$ if each $a \in S$ is defended by S;*
- *$S \in com(F)$ if $S \in adm(F)$ and for each $a \in A$ defended by S, $a \in S$ holds;*
- *$S \in prf(F)$ if $S \in adm(F)$ (resp. $S \in com(F)$) and there is no $T \in adm(F)$ (resp. $T \in com(F)$) with $T \supset S$.*

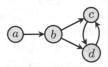

Fig. 1. AF F with $prf(F) = \{\{a, c\}, \{a, d\}\}$.

Example 1. Consider the AF $F = (\{a, b, c, d\}, \{(a, b), (b, c), (b, d), (c, d), (d, c)\})$ depicted in Fig. 1 where nodes of the graph represent arguments and edges represent attacks. The extensions of F under admissible, complete, and preferred semantics are as follows: $adm(F) = \{\emptyset, \{a\}, \{a, c\}, \{a, d\}\}$, $com(F) = \{\{a\}, \{a, c\}, \{a, d\}\}$, and $prf(F) = \{\{a, c\}, \{a, d\}\}$.

Given an AF $F = (A, R)$, an argument $a \in A$, and a semantics σ, the problem of skeptical acceptance asks whether it is the case that a is contained in all σ-extensions of F. While skeptical acceptance is trivial for *adm* and decidable in polynomial time for *com*, it is Π_2^P-complete for *prf*, see [10, 12, 13]. The class $\Pi_2^P = \text{coNP}^{\text{NP}}$ denotes the class of problems P, such that the complementary problem $\overline{P}$ can be decided by a nondeterministic polynomial time algorithm that has (unrestricted) access to an NP-oracle.

Abstract Solvers. Most SAT solvers are based on the Davis-Putnam-Logemann-Loveland (DPLL) procedure [9]. We give an abstract transition system for DPLL following the work of Nieuwenhuis et al. in [19], and start with basic notation.

For a Conjunctive Normal Form (CNF) formula φ (resp. a set of literals M), we denote the set of atoms occurring in φ (resp. in M) by $atoms(\varphi)$ (resp. $atoms(M)$). We identify a consistent set E of literals (i.e. a set that does not contain complementary literals such as a and $\neg a$) with an assignment to $atoms(E)$ as follows: if $a \in E$ then a maps to *true*, while if $\neg a \in E$ then a maps to *false*. For sets X and Y of atoms such that $X \subseteq Y$, we identify X with an assignment over Y as follows: if $a \in X$ then a maps to *true*, while if $a \in Y \setminus X$ then a maps to *false*. By $\text{Sat}(\varphi)$ we refer to the set of satisfying assignments of φ.

We now introduce the abstract procedure for deciding whether a CNF formula is satisfiable. A *decision* literal is a literal annotated by d, as in l^d. An *annotated literal* is a literal, a decision literal or the false constant $\perp$. For a set X of atoms, a *record* relative to X is a string E composed of annotated literals over X without repetitions. For instance, $\emptyset$, $\neg a^d$ and $a \, \neg a^d$ are records relative to the set $\{a\}$. We say that a record E is *inconsistent* if it contains $\perp$ or both a literal l and its complement $\bar{l}$, and consistent otherwise. We sometimes identify a record with the set containing all its elements without annotations. For example, we identify the consistent record $b^d \, \neg a$ with the consistent set $\{\neg a, b\}$ of literals, and so with the assignment which maps a to *false* and b to *true*.

Each CNF formula φ determines its DPLL *graph* DP_φ. The set of nodes of DP_φ consists of the records relative to $atoms(\varphi)$ and the distinguished states *Accept* and *Reject*. A node in the graph is *terminal* if no edge originates from it; in practice, the terminal nodes are *Accept* and *Reject*. The edges of the graph DP_φ are specified by the transition rules presented in Fig. 2. In solvers, generally the oracle rules are chosen with the preference order following the order in which they are stated in Fig. 2, but the failing rule which has a higher priority than all the oracle rules.

Oracle rules

Backtrack $El^d E'' \Rightarrow E\bar{l}$ if $\begin{cases} El^d E'' \text{ is inconsistent and} \\ E'' \text{ contains no decision literal} \end{cases}$

UnitPropagate E $\Rightarrow El$ if $\begin{cases} l \text{ does not occur in } E \text{ and} \\ \text{all the literals of } \overline{C} \text{ occur in } E \text{ and} \\ C \vee l \text{ is a clause in } \varphi \end{cases}$

Decide E $\Rightarrow El^d$ if $\begin{cases} E \text{ is consistent and} \\ \text{neither } l \text{ nor } \bar{l} \text{ occur in } E \end{cases}$

Failing rule
Fail E $\Rightarrow$ *Reject* if $\{ E \text{ is inconsistent and decision-free}$

Succeeding rule
Succeed E $\Rightarrow$ *Accept* if $\{$ no other rule applies

Fig. 2. The transition rules of DP_φ.

Intuitively, every state of the DPLL graph represents some hypothetical state of the DPLL computation whereas a path in the graph is a description of a process of search for a satisfying assignment of a given CNF formula. The rule *Decide* asserts that we make an arbitrary decision to add a literal or, in other words, to assign a value to an atom. Since this decision is arbitrary, we are allowed to backtrack at a later point. The rule *UnitPropagate* asserts that we can add a literal that is a logical consequence of our previous decisions and the given formula. The rule *Backtrack* asserts that the present state of computation is failing but can be fixed: at some point in the past we added a decision literal whose value we can now reverse. The rule *Fail* asserts that the current state of computation has failed and cannot be fixed. The rule *Succeed* asserts that the current state of computation corresponds to a successful outcome.

To decide the satisfiability of a CNF formula it is enough to find a path in DP_φ leading from node $\emptyset$ to a terminal node. If it is *Accept*, then the formula is satisfiable, and if it is *Reject*, then the formula is unsatisfiable. Since there is no infinite path, a terminal node is always reached.

3   Algorithms for Preferred Semantics

In this section we abstract two SAT-based algorithms for preferred semantics, namely PrefSat [5] (implemented in the tool ARGSEMSAT [6]) for extension enumeration, and an algorithm for deciding skeptical acceptance of CEGARTIX [14]. Moreover, we abstract the dedicated approach for enumeration of [20]. In Sect. 3.4 we show how our graph representations can be used to develop novel algorithms, by combining parts of PrefSat and parts of the dedicated algorithm.

We will present these algorithms in a uniform way, abstracting from some minor tool-specific details. Moreover, even if abstract solvers are mainly conceived as a modeling formalism, in our solutions a certain level of systematicity can be outlined, that helps in the design of such abstract solvers. In fact, common to all algorithms is a conceptual two-level architecture of computation, similar to Answer Set Programming solvers for disjunctive logic programs [4]. The lower level corresponds to a DPLL-like search subprocedure, while the higher level part takes care of the control flow and drives the overall algorithm. For PrefSat and CEGARTIX, the subprocedures actually are delegated to a SAT solver, while the dedicated approach carries out a tailored search procedure.

Each algorithm uses its own data structures, and, by slight abuse of notation, for a given AF $F = (A, R)$ we denote their used variables in our graph representation by $atoms(F)$. For this set it holds that $A \subseteq atoms(F)$, i.e. the status of the arguments can be identified from this set of atoms. The states of our graph representations of all algorithms are either

1. an annotated triple $(\epsilon, E', E)_i$ where $i \in \{out, base, max\}$, $\epsilon \subseteq 2^A$ is a set of sets of arguments, and both E' and E are records over $atoms(F)$; or
2. $Ok(\epsilon)$ for $\epsilon \subseteq 2^A$; or
3. a distinguished state *Accept* or *Reject*.

The intended meaning of a state $(\epsilon, E', E)_i$ is that ϵ is the set of already found preferred extensions of F (visited part of the search space), E' is a record representing the current candidate extension (which is admissible or complete in F), and E is a record that may be currently modified by a subprocedure. Note that both E and E' are records, since they will be modified by subprocedures, while found preferred extensions will be translated to a set of arguments before being stored in ϵ. The annotation i denotes the current (sub)procedure we are in. Both *base* and *max* correspond to different lower level computations, typically

SAT calls, while *out* is used solely for (simple) checks outside such subprocedures. Transition rules reflecting the higher level of computation shift these annotations, e.g. from a terminated subprocedure *base* to subprocedure *max*, and transition rules mirroring rules "inside" a SAT solver do not modify i.

The remaining states denote terminated computation: $Ok(\epsilon)$ contains all solutions, while *Accept* or *Reject* denote an answer to a decision problem.

In order to show acyclicity of graphs later in this section, we define a strict partial order on states.

Definition 2. *Let E be a record. E can be written as $L^0 l_1^d L^1 \ldots l_p^d L^p$ where $l_1^d, \ldots, l_p^d$ are all the decision literals of E. We define $s(E) = |L^0|, |L^1|, \ldots, |L^p|$.*

Definition 3. *Let ϵ_1, ϵ_2 be sets of arguments, E_1', E_2', E_1, E_2 be records, and $i_1, i_2 \in \{base, max, out\}$. We define the following strict partial orders (i.e. irreflexive and transitive binary relations):*

$<_\epsilon$: $\epsilon_1 <_\epsilon \epsilon_2$ *iff* $\epsilon_1 \subset \epsilon_2$.
$<_{E'}$: $E_1' <_{E'} E_2'$ *iff* $e(E_1') \subset e(E_2')$.
$<_E$: $E_1 <_E E_2$ *iff* $s(E_1) <_{lex} s(E_2)$, *where $<_{lex}$ is the lexicographic order.*
$<_i$: *base $<_i$ max $<_i$ out.*

The strict partial order $<$ on states is defined such that for any two states $S_1 = (\epsilon_1, E_1', E_1)_{i_1}$ and $S_2 = (\epsilon_2, E_2', E_2)_{i_2}$, $S_1 < S_2$ iff

(i) $\epsilon_1 <_\epsilon \epsilon_2$, *or*
(ii) $\epsilon_1 = \epsilon_2$ *and* $i_1 <_i i_2$, *or*
(iii) $\epsilon_1 = \epsilon_2$ *and* $i_1 = i_2$ *and* $E_1' <_{E'} E_2'$, *or*
(iv) $\epsilon_1 = \epsilon_2$ *and* $i_1 = i_2$ *and* $E_1' = E_2'$ *and* $E_1 <_E E_2$.

One can check that all orders on elements are transitive and irreflexive. Therefore the construction of $<$ also ensures these properties for the order of states.

The SAT-based algorithms construct formulas by an oracle function f s.t. $A \subseteq atoms(f(\epsilon, E, F, \alpha)) \subseteq atoms(F)$ for all possible arguments of f, in particular for $\alpha \in A$. The formulas $f(\epsilon, E, F, \alpha)$ are adapted from [3]. The argument α is relevant only for CEGARTIX to decide skeptical acceptance of α. Finally, we use $e(E) = E \cap A$ to project the arguments from a record E.

3.1   SAT-Based Algorithm for Enumeration

PrefSat (Algorithm 1 of [5]) is a SAT-based algorithm for finding all preferred extensions of a given AF F. The algorithm maintains a list of visited preferred extensions. It first searches for a complete extension not contained in previously found preferred extensions. If such an extension is found, it is iteratively extended until we reach a subset-maximal complete extension, i.e. a preferred extension. This preferred extension is stored, and we repeat the process.

In PrefSat we have two subprocedures that are delegated to a SAT solver. The first has to generate a complete extension not contained in one of the enumerated

i-oracle rules ($i \in \{base, max\}$)

$Backtrack_i$ $(\epsilon, E', El^d E'')_i \Rightarrow (\epsilon, E', E\bar{l})_i$ if $\begin{cases} El^d E'' \text{ is inconsistent and} \\ E'' \text{ contains no decision literal} \end{cases}$

$UnitPropagate_i$ $(\epsilon, E', E)_i \Rightarrow (\epsilon, E', El)_i$ if $\begin{cases} l \text{ does not occur in } E \text{ and} \\ \text{all the literals of } \overline{C} \text{ occur in } E \text{ and} \\ C \vee l \text{ is a clause in } f_i^{com}(\epsilon, E', F, \alpha) \end{cases}$

$Decide_i$ $(\epsilon, E', E)_i$ $\Rightarrow (\epsilon, E', El^d)_i$ if $\begin{cases} E \text{ is consistent and} \\ \text{neither } l \text{ nor } \bar{l} \text{ occur in } E \end{cases}$

Succeeding rules

$Succeed_{base}$ $(\epsilon, E', E)_{base}$ $\Rightarrow (\epsilon, E, \emptyset)_{max}$ if $\{$ no other rule applies

$Succeed_{max}$ $(\epsilon, E', E)_{max}$ $\Rightarrow (\epsilon, E, \emptyset)_{max}$ if $\{$ no other rule applies

Failing rules

$Fail_{base}$ $(\epsilon, E', E)_{base}$ $\Rightarrow Ok(\epsilon)$ if $\{$ E is inconsistent and decision-free

$Fail_{max}$ $(\epsilon, E', E)_{max} \Rightarrow (\epsilon \cup \{e(E')\}, \emptyset, \emptyset)_{base}$ if $\{$ E is inconsistent and decision-free

Fig. 3. The rules of $\text{ENUM}_{\overline{f}}^F$.

preferred extensions, and the second searches for a complete extension that is a strict superset of a given one.

We now represent PrefSat via abstract solver. The graph $\text{ENUM}_{\overline{f}}^F$ for an AF $F = (A, R)$ and a vector of oracle functions $\overline{f}$ is defined by the states over $atoms(F)$ and the transition rules presented in Fig. 3. Its initial state is $(\emptyset, \emptyset, \emptyset)_{base}$. We assume the functions f_{base}^{com} and f_{max}^{com} that generate CNF formulas for $\epsilon \subseteq 2^A$, a record E, and an argument $\alpha \in A$ such that:

1. $\{e(M) \mid M \in \text{Sat}(f_{base}^{com}(\epsilon, E, F, \alpha))\} = \{E'' \in com(F) \mid \neg\exists E' \in \epsilon : E'' \subseteq E'\}$;
2. $\{e(M) \mid M \in \text{Sat}(f_{max}^{com}(\epsilon, E, F, \alpha))\} = \{E'' \in com(F) \mid e(E) \subset E''\}$.

We remark that α is not relevant for enumeration of extensions and only used for acceptance later on. In a state $(\epsilon, E', E)_i$, the set ϵ represents preferred extensions found as of now, E' is a record for the complete extension found in the previous subprocedure, and E is a record for the complete extension that the current oracle is trying to build. The annotation $i \in \{base, max\}$ corresponds to different kinds of SAT calls.

If the conditions of a rule with annotation i check for consistency, we implicitly refer to the formula generated by f_i^{com}. That is, if a $Fail_i$ rule is applied to the state $(\epsilon, E', E)_i$ for $i \in \{base, max\}$, the formula $f_i^{com}(\epsilon, E', F, \alpha)$ is unsatisfiable. Conversely, when a $Succeed_i$ rule is applied, the formula $f_i^{com}(\epsilon, E', F, \alpha)$ is satisfied by E. Notice that $Fail_i$ and $Succeed_i$ might shift i to reflect a change of type of SAT calls. When $i = base$, the oracle searches for a complete extension that has not been found before. In case of failure all the preferred extensions have been found. In case of success, it is necessary to search whether there are strictly larger complete extensions than the one found. This is handled by subprocedure max. In case of success, $Succeed_{max}$ is applied and the procedure is repeated, since the current complete extension might still not be maximal. Failure by $Fail_{max}$ means we have found a preferred extension.

Example 2. Again consider the AF F depicted in Fig. 1. We have seen in Example 1 that F has two preferred extensions, namely $\{a, c\}$ and $\{a, d\}$. Figure 4 shows a possible path in the graph ENUM_{f}^{F}. As expected, the computation terminates in the state $Ok(\{\{a, d\}, \{a, c\}\})$. Note that we abbreviate the parts of the path where we are "inside" the SAT-solver. Also, we only show literals over A, and do not state the extra literals that may have been assigned during the call to the SAT-solver. By *unsat* we represent an inconsistent and decision-free record.

$$
\begin{aligned}
&\text{Initial state}: && (\emptyset, \emptyset, \emptyset)_{base} \\
&\text{base-oracle}: && (\emptyset, \emptyset, E_1 \supseteq \{a, \neg b, \neg c, \neg d\})_{base} \\
&Succeed_{base}: && (\emptyset, E_1, \emptyset)_{max} \\
&\text{max-oracle}: && (\emptyset, E_1, E_2 \supseteq \{a, \neg b, \neg c, d\})_{max} \\
&Succeed_{max}: && (\emptyset, E_2, \emptyset)_{max} \\
&\text{max-oracle}: && (\emptyset, E_2, unsat)_{max} \\
&Fail_{max}: && (\{\{a, d\}\}, \emptyset, \emptyset)_{base} \\
&\text{base-oracle}: && (\{\{a, d\}\}, \emptyset, E_3 \supseteq \{a, \neg b, c, \neg d\})_{base} \\
&Succeed_{base}: && (\{\{a, d\}\}, E_3, \emptyset)_{max} \\
&\text{max-oracle}: && (\{\{a, d\}\}, E_3, unsat)_{max} \\
&Fail_{max}: && (\{\{a, d\}, \{a, c\}\}, \emptyset, \emptyset)_{base} \\
&\text{base-oracle}: && (\{\{a, d\}, \{a, c\}\}, \emptyset, unsat)_{base} \\
&Fail_{base}: && Ok(\{\{a, d\}, \{a, c\}\})
\end{aligned}
$$

Fig. 4. Path in ENUM_{f}^{F} where F is the AF from Fig. 1.

It remains to show that ENUM_{f}^{F} correctly describes PrefSat by showing that we reach a terminal state containing all preferred extensions of F. We begin with a lemma stating that we only add preferred extensions to ϵ which have not been found at this point.

Lemma 1. *For any AF F if the rule $Fail_{max}$ is applied from state $(\epsilon, E', E)_{max}$ in the graph $\text{ENUM}_{(f_{base}^{com}, f_{max}^{com})}^{F}$ then $e(E') \in prf(F)$ and $e(E') \notin \epsilon$.*

Proof. Let $S_1 = (\epsilon_1, E_1', E_1)_{max}$ be the state from which $Fail_{max}$ is applied. This means that f_{max}^{com} is unsatisfiable, hence, by the definition of formula f_{max}^{com}, there is no $C \in com(F)$ with $C \supset e(E_1')$. To get $e(E_1') \in prf(F)$ it remains to show that $e(E_1') \in com(F)$. Observe that $Succeed_{base}$ is applied at least once, since every AF has a complete extension. Moreover, the value of E_1' is only updated by an application of $Succeed_{base}$ or $Succeed_{max}$. In both cases $e(E_1')$ corresponds to a complete extension of F, since E_1' is a satisfying assignment of the formula f_{base}^{com} or f_{max}^{com}, respectively. Therefore E_1' is a complete extension of F.

Since the initial state is $(\emptyset, \emptyset, \emptyset)_{base}$, an application of $Succeed_{base}$ must precede $Fail_{max}$. From this application of $Succeed_{base}$ it follows that there is a record E' such that $\neg \exists C \in \epsilon : e(E') \subseteq C$. Moreover every application of $Succeed_{max}$ updates E' by a proper superset of itself. Therefore $e(E'_1) \supseteq e(E')$ and also $\neg \exists C \in \epsilon : e(E'_1) \subseteq C$, in particular $e(E'_1) \notin \epsilon$. ☐

Now we are ready to show correctness of ENUM_{f}^{F}.

Theorem 1. *For any AF F, the graph $\mathrm{ENUM}_{(f_{base}^{com}, f_{max}^{com})}^{F}$ is finite, acyclic and the only terminal state reachable from the initial state is $Ok(\epsilon)$ where $\epsilon = prf(F)$.*

Proof. In order to show that ENUM_{f}^{F} is finite, consider some state $(\epsilon, E', E)_i$ of ENUM_{f}^{F}. Since both E and E' are records over $atoms(F)$, and F is finite by definition, the number of possible records E and E' is finite. Similarly, there is only a finite number of sets of sets of arguments ϵ. Finally, ENUM_{f}^{F} only contains states with $i \in \{base, max\}$. Thus the number of states is finite in the graph ENUM_{f}^{F}.

In order to show that it is acyclic recall the strict partial order $<$ on states from Definition 3. We show that each transition rule is increasing w.r.t. $<$. To this end consider two states $S_1 = (\epsilon_1, E'_1, E_1)_{i_1}$ and $S_2 = (\epsilon_2, E'_2, E_2)_{i_2}$. First of all, the i-oracle rules (i.e. $Backtrack_i$, $UnitPropagate_i$, and $Decide_i$) fulfill $S_1 < S_2$ because of (iv). For all of these rules $\epsilon_1 = \epsilon_2$, $E'_1 = E'_2$ and $i_1 = i_2$, but $s(E_1)$ is lexicographically smaller than $s(E_2)$, therefore $E_1 <_l E_2$. Moreover, $Fail_{max}$ fulfills $S_1 < S_2$ due to (i) since $e(E'_1) \notin \epsilon_1$ by Lemma 1. $Succeed_{base}$ guarantees $S_1 < S_2$ because of (ii). Finally, $Succeed_{max}$ fulfills $S_1 < S_2$ due to (iii), since the max-oracle rules work on the formula f_{max}^{com} and the extension associated with a satisfying assignment $E_1 = E'_2$ thereof must be a proper superset of $e(E'_1)$. Therefore, for any two states S_1 and S_n such that S_n is reachable from S_1 in ENUM_{f}^{F} it holds that $S_1 < S_n$, showing that the graph is acyclic.

The only terminal state reachable from the initial state is $Ok(\epsilon)$ (via rule $Fail_{base}$) since all states $S = (\epsilon, E, E')_i$ of ENUM_{f}^{F} have $i \in \{base, max\}$ and for each $i \in \{base, max\}$ there is a rule $Succeed_i$ with the condition "no other rule applies". It remains to show that, when state $Ok(\epsilon)$ is reached, ϵ coincides with $prf(F)$. Since elements are only added to ϵ by application of the rule $Fail_{max}$ we know from Lemma 1 that for each $P \in \epsilon$ it holds that $P \in prf(F)$. To reach $Ok(\epsilon)$, the rule $Fail_{base}$ must have been applied from state $(\epsilon, E', E)_{base}$. This means, by the definition of f_{base}^{com}, that for each complete extension C of F there is some $P \in \epsilon$ such that $C \subseteq P$. Hence $\epsilon = prf(F)$. ☐

3.2   SAT-Based Algorithm for Acceptance

CEGARTIX [14] is a SAT-based tool for deciding several acceptance questions for AFs. Here we focus on Algorithm 1 of [14] for deciding skeptical acceptance under preferred semantics of an argument α. Similarly as PrefSat, CEGARTIX traverses the search space of a certain semantics, generates candidate extensions not contained in already visited preferred extensions, and maximizes the candidate until a preferred extension is found. The main differences to PrefSat are (1) the parametrized use of base semantics σ (the search space), which can be either admissible or complete semantics, and (2) the incorporation of the queried argument α. To prune the search space, α must not to be contained in the candidate σ-extension before maximization. Again, we have two kinds of SAT-calls.

The graph $\text{SKEPT-PRF}_{\overline{f}}^{F,\alpha}$ for an AF F, an argument α and a vector of oracle functions $\overline{f}$ is defined by the states over $atoms(F)$ and the rules in Fig. 3 replacing the $Fail_i$ rules and adding the out rules as depicted in Fig. 5. The initial state is $(\emptyset, \emptyset, \emptyset)_{base}$. For $\sigma \in \{adm, com\}$ we assume the functions f_{base}^{σ} and f_{max}^{σ} such that:

1. $\{e(M) \mid M \in \text{Sat}(f_{base}^{\sigma}(\epsilon, E, F, \alpha))\} = \{E'' \in \sigma(F) \mid \alpha \notin E'' \wedge \neg \exists E' \in \epsilon : E'' \subseteq E'\}$;
2. $\{e(M) \mid M \in \text{Sat}(f_{max}^{\sigma}(\epsilon, E, F, \alpha))\} = \{E'' \in \sigma(F) \mid e(E) \subset E''\}$.

Failing rules

$Fail_{base}$ $(\epsilon, E', E)_{base} \rightarrowtail Accept$ if $\{$ E is inconsistent and decision-free

$Fail_{max}$ $(\epsilon, E', E)_{max} \Rightarrow (\epsilon, E', \emptyset)_{out}$ if $\{$ E is inconsistent and decision-free

$Fail_{out}$ $(\epsilon, E', E)_{out} \Rightarrow (\epsilon \cup \{e(E')\}, \emptyset, \emptyset)_{base}$ if $\{$ $\alpha \in e(E')$

Succeeding rules

$Succeed_{out}$ $(\epsilon, E', E)_{out} \Rightarrow Reject$ if $\{$ $\alpha \notin e(E')$

Fig. 5. Changed transition rules for $\text{SKEPT-PRF}_{\overline{f}}^{F,\alpha}$.

The graph $\text{SKEPT-PRF}_{\overline{f}}^{F,\alpha}$ is nearly identical to $\text{ENUM}_{\overline{f}}^{F}$. It differs only in case of failure in subprocedure $base$ or max. When all the preferred extensions have been enumerated in subprocedure $base$, we can report a positive outcome with $Accept$, since we have ensured that α belongs to all of them. In subprocedure max, when a preferred extension has been found, it is here necessary to check whether α belongs to it. The out rules correspond to an if-then-else construct: if the condition $\alpha \notin E'$ holds then we follow the $Succeed_{out}$ rule else follow the $Fail_{out}$ rule. In other words, if α is not in the extension then the procedure can terminate with a negative answer; else proceed as in the previous graph: add the preferred extension to ϵ and search for a new one by going back to $base$.

Example 3. Again consider the AF F from Fig. 1 and note that skeptical acceptance of argument c does not hold as c is not contained in the preferred extension $\{a, d\}$ of F. Accordingly, the possible path of the graph $\text{SKEPT-PRF}_{\overline{f}}^{F,c}$ which is depicted in Fig. 6a (with base semantics adm) terminates in the $Reject$-state.

On the other hand, argument a is skeptically accepted under preferred semantics in F as it belongs to all preferred extensions enumerated in $\{\{a, d\}, \{a, c\}\}$.

For checking whether a is skeptically accepted in F, a possible path in the graph $\text{SKEPT-PRF}_{f}^{F,a}$ (again with base semantics adm) is shown in Fig. 6b. As expected, the path terminates in the state $Accept$.

$Inital\ state$: $(\emptyset, \emptyset, \emptyset)_{base}$
$base\text{-}oracle$: $(\emptyset, \emptyset, E_1 \supseteq \{a, \neg b, \neg c, \neg d\})_{base}$
$Succeed_{base}$: $(\emptyset, E_1, \emptyset)_{max}$
$max\text{-}oracle$: $(\emptyset, E_1, E_2 \supseteq \{a, \neg b, c, \neg d\})_{max}$
$Succeed_{max}$: $(\emptyset, E_2, \emptyset)_{max}$
$max\text{-}oracle$: $(\emptyset, E_2, unsat)_{max}$
$Fail_{max}$: $(\emptyset, E_2, \emptyset)_{out}$
$Fail_{out}$: $(\{\{a, c\}\}, \emptyset, \emptyset)_{base}$
$base\text{-}oracle$: $(\{\{a, c\}\}, \emptyset, E_3 \supseteq \{a, \neg b, \neg c, d\})_{base}$
$Succeed_{base}$: $(\{\{a, c\}\}, E_3, \emptyset)_{max}$
$max\text{-}oracle$: $(\{\{a, c\}\}, E_3, unsat)_{max}$
$Fail_{max}$: $(\{\{a, c\}\}, E_3, \emptyset)_{out}$
$Succeed_{out}$: $Reject$

(a) Reject-path for argument c in $\text{SKEPT-PRF}_{f}^{F,c}$.

$Initial\ state$: $(\emptyset, \emptyset, \emptyset)_{base}$
$base\text{-}oracle$: $(\emptyset, \emptyset, E_1 \supseteq \{\neg a, \neg b, \neg c, \neg d\})_{base}$
$Succeed_{base}$: $(\emptyset, E_1, \emptyset)_{max}$
$max\text{-}oracle$: $(\emptyset, E_1, E_2 \supseteq \{a, \neg b, \neg c, \neg d\})_{max}$
$Succeed_{max}$: $(\emptyset, E_2, \emptyset)_{max}$
$max\text{-}oracle$: $(\emptyset, E_2, E_3 \supseteq \{a, \neg b, \neg c, d\})_{max}$
$Succeed_{max}$: $(\emptyset, E_3, \emptyset)_{max}$
$max\text{-}oracle$: $(\emptyset, E_3, unsat)_{max}$
$Fail_{max}$: $(\emptyset, E_3, \emptyset)_{out}$
$Fail_{out}$: $(\{\{a, d\}\}, \emptyset, \emptyset)_{base}$
$base\text{-}oracle$: $(\{\{a, d\}\}, \emptyset, unsat)_{base}$
$Fail_{base}$: $Accept$

(b) Accept-path for argument a in $\text{SKEPT-PRF}_{f}^{F,a}$.

Fig. 6. Possible paths in $\text{SKEPT-PRF}_{f}^{F,\alpha}$.

We will use the following lemma to show correctness of $\text{SKEPT-PRF}_{f}^{F,\alpha}$. Its proof is almost identical to the one of Lemma 1 and therefore omitted.

Lemma 2. *For any AF F, if the rule $Fail_{out}$ is applied from state $(\epsilon, E', E)_{out}$ in the graph $\text{SKEPT-PRF}_{(f_{base}^{\sigma}, f_{max}^{\sigma})}^{F,\alpha}$ with $\sigma \in \{adm, com\}$ then $e(E') \in prf(F)$ and $e(E') \notin \epsilon$.*

Theorem 2. *For any AF $F = (A, R)$, argument $\alpha \in A$, and $\sigma \in \{adm, com\}$, the graph $\text{SKEPT-PRF}_{(f_{base}^{\sigma}, f_{max}^{\sigma})}^{F,\alpha}$ is finite, acyclic and any terminal state reachable from the initial state is either Accept or Reject; Accept is reachable iff α is skeptically accepted in F w.r.t. prf.*

Proof. (1) SKEPT-PRF$_{\overline{f}}^{F,\alpha}$ is finite and acyclic: In order to show finiteness note that the states $(\epsilon, E', E)_i$ of SKEPT-PRF$_{\overline{f}}^{F,\alpha}$ coincide with the states of ENUM$_{\overline{f}}^F$, there is just an additional option *out* for i. Hence finiteness follows from Theorem 1. In order to show that SKEPT-PRF$_{\overline{f}}^{F,\alpha}$ is acyclic we have to show that the rules that differ in SKEPT-PRF$_{\overline{f}}^{F,\alpha}$ from ENUM$_{\overline{f}}^F$ (i.e. the ones listed in Fig. 5) are increasing with respect to the ordering $<$ from Definition 3: $Fail_{out}$ fulfills $S_1 < S_2$ due to (i) by Lemma 2, $Fail_{max}$ guarantees $S_1 < S_2$ because of (ii), and $Fail_{base}$ and $Succeed_{out}$ end in terminal states.

(2) Any terminal state of SKEPT-PRF$_{\overline{f}}^{F,\alpha}$ reachable from the initial state is either *Reject* or *Accept*: Consider the state $S = (\epsilon, E, E')_i$. If $i \in \{base, max\}$ then there is a rule $Succeed_i$ with the condition "no other rule applies", hence S cannot be a terminal state. If $i = out$, the rules $Fail_{out}$ and $Succeed_{out}$ are complete in the sense that if one rule does not apply the other rule applies and vice versa. Therefore only *Reject* and *Accept* can be terminal states.

(3) *Reject* is reachable from the initial state iff α is not skeptically accepted by F w.r.t. *prf*: $\Rightarrow$: Assume *Reject* is reachable. Hence also $(\epsilon, E', E)_{out}$ with $\alpha \notin e(E')$ is reachable. Moreover $Fail_{max}$ was applied at a state $(\epsilon, E', E'')_{max}$, meaning that $f_{max}^\sigma(\epsilon, E', F, \alpha)$ is unsatisfiable, i.e. there is no σ-extension C with $C \supset e(E')$. It remains to show that $e(E') \in \sigma(F)$. That is by the fact that there must be a preceding application of the rule $Succeed_{base}$ from some state $(\epsilon, E''', E')_{base}$ with $e(E')$ being a σ-extension of F by the definition of f_{base}^σ. Now as $e(E') \in \sigma(F)$, $\neg\exists C \supset e(E') : C \in \sigma(F)$, and $\alpha \notin e(E')$, we have that α is not skeptically accepted by F w.r.t. *prf*. $\Leftarrow$: Assume α is skeptically rejected by F w.r.t. *prf*. Hence there is some $P \in prf(F)$ with $\alpha \notin P$. Now assume, towards a contradiction, that *Reject* is not reachable. This means by (1) and (2), that *Accept* is reachable. Hence $Fail_{base}$ is applicable from a state $(\epsilon, E', E)_{base}$. By the definition of f_{base}^σ, this means that there is no σ-extension C of F with $\alpha \notin C$ and $\neg\exists E'' \in \epsilon : C \subseteq E''$. Now note that $Fail_{out}$ is the only rule where elements are added to ϵ. Moreover, by Lemma 2, we know that elements added are preferred extensions of F. But therefore for each $C \in \sigma(F)$ with $\alpha \notin C$ it holds that $\exists E'' \in prf(F) : C \subseteq E'' \wedge \alpha \in E''$, a contradiction. $\square$

Finally note that from Theorem 1 it follows that *Accept* is reachable from the initial state if and only if α is skeptically accepted by F, which completes the correctness statement for SKEPT-PRF$_{\overline{f}}^{F,\alpha}$.

3.3   Dedicated Approach for Enumeration

Algorithm 1 of [20] presents a direct approach for enumerating preferred extensions. One function is important for this algorithm, which is called IN-TRANS. It marks an argument $x \in A$ as belonging to the extension which is currently constructed, and marks all attackers $\{y \mid (y, x) \in R\}$ and all attacked arguments $\{y \mid (x, y) \in R\}$ as outside of this extension. Intuitively, IN-TRANS *decides* to accept x, and then *propagates* the immediate consequences to the neighboring nodes. It actually does an additional task. It labels the attacked arguments as "attacked", and the attackers that are not yet labelled as attacked as "to be attacked": this allows later to easily check the admissibility of the extension by just looking whether there is any argument "to be attacked".

The algorithm is recursive, and stores the admissible extensions in a global variable. First, it checks whether all the arguments are marked as either belonging to or being outside the extension, and if so it returns after adding the extension to the global variable if the extension is actually admissible. Second, it applies the function IN-TRANS to some unmarked argument and calls itself recursively. Third, it reverts the effects of IN-TRANS, marks the argument it chose as outside of this extension, and calls itself recursively. This can be seen as a *backtrack*.

We have defined an equivalent representation of this algorithm that follows the framework of abstract solvers with binary logics as previously used in this article. Binary truth values are sufficient to represent the arguments marked, but we see the labels "attacked" and "to be attacked" as an optimization as they can be easily recovered at the end of the algorithm. Indeed, they correspond to the condition "there is an argument a such that E does not attack a and a attacks E" of the rule $Fail_{out}$.

Oracle rules

$Backtrack'_{max}$ $(\epsilon, \emptyset, Ea^d E'')_{max} \Rightarrow (\epsilon, \emptyset, E \neg a)_{max}$ if $\begin{cases} Ea^d E'' \text{ is inconsistent and} \\ E'' \text{ contains no decision literal} \end{cases}$

$Propagate'_{max}$ $(\epsilon, \emptyset, E)_{max} \Rightarrow (\epsilon, \emptyset, E \neg a)_{max}$ if $\{ E \text{ attacks } a \text{ or } a \text{ attacks } E$

$Decide'_{max}$ $(\epsilon, \emptyset, E)_{max} \Rightarrow (\epsilon, \emptyset, Ea^d)_{max}$ if $\begin{cases} E \text{ is consistent and} \\ \text{neither } a \text{ nor } \neg a \text{ occur in } E \text{ and} \\ Propagate'_{max} \text{ does not apply} \end{cases}$

Succeeding and failing rules

$Fail_{max}$ $(\epsilon, \emptyset, E)_{max} \Rightarrow Ok(\epsilon)$ if $\{ E \text{ is incons. and decision-free}$

$Succeed_{max}$ $(\epsilon, \emptyset, E)_{max} \Rightarrow (\epsilon, \emptyset, E)_{out}$ if $\{ \text{no other rule applies}$

$Fail_{out}$ $(\epsilon, \emptyset, E)_{out} \Rightarrow (\epsilon, \emptyset, E\perp)_{max}$ if $\begin{cases} \exists E' \in \epsilon : E \subseteq E' \text{ or} \\ \text{there is an argument } a \text{ s.t.} \\ E \text{ does not attack } a \text{ and} \\ a \text{ attacks } E \end{cases}$

$Succeed_{out}$ $(\epsilon, \emptyset, E)_{out} \Rightarrow (\epsilon \cup \{e(E)\}, \emptyset, E\perp)_{max}$ if $\{ \text{no other rule applies}$

Fig. 7. The rules of the graph DIRECT^F.

The graph DIRECT^F for an AF F is defined by the states over $atoms(F)$ and the transition rules presented in Fig. 7. Its initial state is $(\emptyset, \emptyset, \emptyset)_{max}$. The structure of the graph is similar to that of $\mathrm{ENUM}_{\overline{f}}^F$. It differs from this graph in two ways. First, it has only one subprocedure. Second, the rules of the oracle differ from the previous oracle rules since they are not a call to a SAT solver; we primed them to emphasize the difference.

More precisely, among the oracle rules, propagation now only occurs so as to negatively add an atom if it attacks or is attacked by an atom of the extension being built. The $Decide'_{max}$ rule only adds atoms positively, which is useful in Algorithm 2 of [20], but does not seem to be crucial here. When a record assigning all arguments is found, the rule $Succeed_{max}$ is applied so as to allow the test of the outer rules to be carried on. If the record corresponds to a preferred extension, then it is stored by $Succeed_{out}$ and the process of trying all possible records continues. In both $Succeed_{out}$ and $Fail_{out}$, the use of one of the rules $Backtrack'_{max}$ or $Fail_{max}$ is forced by making the record inconsistent. This way the process of browsing records is forced to continue.

Example 4. A possible path in the graph DIRECT^F for the AF F in Fig. 1 is shown in Fig. 8. One difference can be seen by the fact that the result of the modified oracle rules may be contained in an already found preferred extension. Then $\bot$ is added to the current record by $Fail_{out}$, followed by backtracking to the last decision literal.

Initial state :	$(\emptyset, \emptyset, \emptyset)_{max}$
$Decide'_{max}$:	$(\emptyset, \emptyset, c^d)_{max}$
$Propagate'_{max}$:	$(\emptyset, \emptyset, c^d \neg b \neg d)_{max}$
$Decide'_{max}$:	$(\emptyset, \emptyset, c^d \neg b \neg da^d)_{max}$
$Succeed_{max}$:	$(\emptyset, \emptyset, c^d \neg b \neg da^d)_{out}$
$Succeed_{out}$:	$(\{\{a,c\}\}, \emptyset, c^d \neg b \neg da^d \bot)_{max}$
$Backtrack'_{max}$:	$(\{\{a,c\}\}, \emptyset, c^d \neg b \neg d \neg a)_{max}$
$Succeed_{max}$:	$(\{\{a,c\}\}, \emptyset, c^d \neg b \neg d \neg a)_{out}$
$Fail_{out}$:	$(\{\{a,c\}\}, \emptyset, c^d \neg b \neg d \neg a \bot)_{max}$
$Backtrack'_{max}$:	$(\{\{a,c\}\}, \emptyset, \neg c)_{max}$
	$\ldots$
$Succeed_{max}$:	$(\{\{a,c\}\}, \emptyset, \neg ca^d \neg bd^d)_{out}$
$Succeed_{out}$:	$(\{\{a,c\}, \{a,d\}\}, \emptyset, \neg ca^d \neg bd^d \bot)_{max}$
$Backtrack'_{max}$:	$(\{\{a,c\}, \{a,d\}\}, \emptyset, \neg ca^d \neg b \neg d)_{max}$
$Succeed_{max}$:	$(\{\{a,c\}, \{a,d\}\}, \emptyset, \neg ca^d \neg b \neg d)_{out}$
$Fail_{out}$:	$(\{\{a,c\}, \{a,d\}\}, \emptyset, \neg ca^d \neg b \neg d \bot)_{max}$
$Backtrack'_{max}$:	$(\{\{a,c\}, \{a,d\}\}, \emptyset, \neg c \neg a)_{max}$
	$\ldots$
$Succeed_{max}$:	$(\{\{a,c\}, \{a,d\}\}, \emptyset, \neg c \neg a \neg b \neg d)_{out}$
$Fail_{out}$:	$(\{\{a,c\}, \{a,d\}\}, \emptyset, \neg c \neg a \neg b \neg d \bot)_{max}$
$Fail_{max}$:	$Ok(\{\{a,d\}, \{a,c\}\})$

Fig. 8. Path in DIRECT^F where F is the AF from Fig. 1.

Lemma 3. *For any AF F, if the rule $Succeed_{out}$ is applied from state $(\epsilon, \emptyset, E)_{out}$ in the graph DIRECT^F then $e(E) \in prf(F)$ and $e(E) \notin \epsilon$.*

Proof. The application of $Succeed_{out}$ from state $S_{out} = (\epsilon, \emptyset, E)_{out}$ must have been preceded by $Succeed_{max}$ from the state $S_{max} = (\epsilon, \emptyset, E)_{max}$ which only differs from S_{out} in i. We now analyze the record E as it is constructed by the rules $Decide'_{max}$, $Propagate'_{max}$ and $Backtrack'_{max}$. The application of $Decide'_{max}$ adds literal a, literal $\neg b$ is added by $Propagate'_{max}$ for all b being in conflict with a in F. Therefore $e(E)$ is conflict-free in F. Moreover $e(E)$ is admissible since if "there is an argument a such that E does not attack a and a attacks E", then $Fail_{out}$ is applied instead of $Succeed_{out}$. To get $e(E) \in prf(F)$ it remains to show that there is no $D \in adm(F)$ with $D \supset e(E)$. Assume there is such a $D \in adm(F)$. Then there must be some $a \in D$ with $a \notin e(E)$. Now observe that the graph first adds a to the record and afterwards $\neg a$. Therefore D must have been discovered in advance. But then $\exists D \in \epsilon : e(E) \subseteq D$, hence $Fail_{out}$ is applied instead of $Succeed_{out}$. This condition is also the reason why $e(E) \notin \epsilon$ is guaranteed when $Succeed_{out}$ is applied from state S_{out}.   □

Theorem 3. *For any AF F, the graph DIRECT^F is finite, acyclic and the only terminal state reachable from its initial state is $Ok(\epsilon)$ where $\epsilon = prf(F)$.*

Proof. Since states of DIRECT^F consist of the same elements as states of $\mathrm{ENUM}^F_{\bar{f}}$, finiteness of DIRECT^F follows in the same way as in Theorem 1.

To show that DIRECT^F is acyclic we will, again as in the proof of Theorem 1, show that each transition rule of DIRECT^F is increasing w.r.t. a strict partial order on states. To this end we define the strict partial order $<_D$ such that for any two states $S_1 = (\epsilon_1, \emptyset, E_1)_{i_1}$ and $S_2 = (\epsilon_2, \emptyset, E_2)_{i_2}$, $S_1 <_D S_2$ iff

(i) $\epsilon_1 <_\epsilon \epsilon_2$, or
(ii) $\epsilon_1 = \epsilon_2$ and $E_1 <_E E_2$, or
(iii) $\epsilon_1 = \epsilon_2$ and $E_1 = E_2$ and $i_1 <_i i_2$,

where $<_\epsilon$, $<_E$ and $<_i$ are the orders from Definition 3. First of all, the oracle rules (i.e. $Backtrack'_{max}$, $UnitPropagate'_{max}$, and $Decide'_{max}$) and $Fail_{out}$ fulfill $S_1 <_D S_2$ because of (ii). For all of these rules $\epsilon_1 = \epsilon_2$, but $s(E_1)$ is lexicographically smaller than $s(E_2)$, therefore $E_1 <_E E_2$. Moreover, $Succeed_{out}$ fulfills $S_1 <_D S_2$ due to (i) since $e(E_1) \notin \epsilon_1$ by Lemma 3. $Succeed_{max}$ guarantees $S_1 <_D S_2$ because of (iii).

The only terminal state reachable from the initial state is $Ok(\epsilon)$ since all states $(\epsilon, \emptyset, E')_i$ of DIRECT^F have $i \in \{max, out\}$ and for each $i \in \{max, out\}$ there is a rule $Succeed_i$ with the condition "no other rule applies". It remains to show that, when state $Ok(\epsilon)$ is reached, ϵ is the set of preferred extensions of F. Since elements are only added to ϵ by rule $Succeed_{out}$ we know from Lemma 3 that for each $P \in \epsilon$ it holds that $P \in prf(F)$. On the other hand, the oracle rules guarantee that each conflict-free set C of F a set $(\epsilon, \emptyset, E)_{out}$ with $e(E) = C$ is reached. If C is then admissible and maximal w.r.t. ϵ (which contains only preferred extensions of F as observed before), C is added to ϵ. Therefore each $P \in prf(F)$ is contained in ϵ.   □

3.4 Combining Algorithms

We can now define a new algorithm which is a combination of the PrefSat approach and the dedicated approach. In fact, it replaces the loop of SAT-calls for maximizing a complete extension of PrefSat by a part of the dedicated algorithm of [20]. In particular, instead of having subsequent oracle calls for maximization, we utilize the dedicated algorithm with a different initialization and stop already when the first preferred extension has been found. The graph MIX-PRF$_{\overline{f}}^{F}$ representing this algorithm consists of the oracle rules and the rules $Succeed_{max}$ and $Fail_{out}$ of DIRECT^{F}, the $base$-oracle rules and the rule $Fail_{base}$ of ENUM$_{\overline{f}}^{F}$ and the rules in Fig. 9. The initial state is $(\emptyset, \emptyset, \emptyset)_{base}$.

As in ENUM$_{\overline{f}}^{F}$, whenever a $Succeed_{base}$ rule is applied, a complete extension has been generated and it has to be validated or extended by the subprocedure identified with max. When $Succeed_{max}$ is applied, a preferred extension has been found and the search for another complete extension can be started. Whenever an extension has been found by procedure $base$, there is a preferred extension that is a superset of the found extension. Hence, there is no need for a rule $Fail_{max}$, since subprocedure max will always succeed.

Succeeding and failing rules
$Succeed_{base}$ $(\epsilon, \emptyset, E)_{base} \Rightarrow (\epsilon, \emptyset, e(E))_{max}$ if $\{$ no other rule applies
$Succeed_{out}$ $(\epsilon, \emptyset, E)_{out} \Rightarrow (\epsilon \cup \{e(E)\}, \emptyset, \emptyset)_{base}$ if $\{$ no other rule applies

Fig. 9. The rules of the graph MIX-PRF$_{\overline{f}}^{F}$.

Lemma 4. *For any AF $F = (A, R)$, if the rule $Succeed_{out}$ is applied from state $(\epsilon, \emptyset, E)_{out}$ in the graph MIX-PRF$_{\overline{f}}^{F}$ then $e(E) \in prf(F)$ and $e(E) \notin \epsilon$.*

Proof. By the definition of f_{base}^{com} we know that when the rule $Succeed_{base}$ is applied at state $(\epsilon, \emptyset, E)_{base}$ it holds that $e(E)$ is a complete extension of F. By the same reasoning as in the proof of Lemma 3, $e(E) \in prf(F)$ and $e(E) \notin \epsilon$. □

Theorem 4. *For any AF F, the graph MIX-PRF$_{\overline{f}}^{F}$ is finite, acyclic and the only terminal state reachable from its initial state is $Ok(\epsilon)$ where $\epsilon = prf(F)$.*

Proof. Since states of MIX-PRF$_{\overline{f}}^{F}$ coincide with the ones of ENUM$_{\overline{f}}^{F}$, finiteness of MIX-PRF$_{\overline{f}}^{F}$ follows in the same way as in Theorem 1.

For acyclicity of MIX-PRF$_{\overline{f}}^{F}$ we begin with the following observation. Consider a state $S = (\epsilon, \emptyset, E)_{max}$ and assume none of the max-oracle-rules apply. Then $Succeed_{max}$ with the condition "no other rule applies" applies and we only change the index of the state to then have just an if-else-decision between $Fail_{out}$ and

$Succeed_{out}$. We get the same behavior when removing the rule $Succeed_{max}$ and changing $Fail_{out}$ and $Succeed_{out}$ in the following way:

$$Fail'_{out} \quad (\epsilon, \emptyset, E)_{max} \Rightarrow (\epsilon, \emptyset, E\bot)_{max} \quad \text{if} \begin{cases} \text{no other rule applies and} \\ (\exists E' \in \epsilon : E \subseteq E' \text{ or} \\ \text{there is an argument } a \text{ such that} \\ E \text{ does not attack } a \text{ and } a \text{ attacks } E) \end{cases}$$

$$Succeed'_{out} \quad (\epsilon, \emptyset, E)_{max} \Rightarrow (\epsilon \cup \{e(E)\}, \emptyset, \emptyset)_{base} \text{ if} \{ \text{no other rule applies}$$

We show that the modified version MIX-PRF$_{\overline{f}}^{F}$ is acyclic and therefore get, by the considerations above, that MIX-PRF$_{\overline{f}}^{F}$ is acyclic. We do so by showing that all rules in the modified version of MIX-PRF$_{\overline{f}}^{F}$ are increasing w.r.t. the strict partial order $<$ from Definition 3. The $base$-oracle-rules and $Fail_{base}$ were shown to be increasing in the proof of Theorem 1. Moreover, $Succeed_{base}$ is increasing because of (ii). The max-oracle-rules and $Fail'_{out}$ are increasing due to (iv). Finally, $Succeed'_{out}$ is increasing by (i) (cf. Lemma 4).

The only terminal state reachable from the initial state is $Ok(\epsilon)$ since for each $i \in \{base, max, out\}$ there is a rule $Succeed_i$ with the condition "no other rule applies". It remains to show that ϵ coincides with the preferred extensions of F. Since extensions are exclusively added by the application of $Succeed_{out}$ it follows from Lemma 4 that $\epsilon \subseteq prf(F)$. The state $Ok(\epsilon)$ must have been reached by the application of $Fail_{base}$. Hence, by definition of f_{base}^{com}, we know that there is no complete extension C of F such that $\forall E' \in \epsilon : C \not\subseteq E'$. Therefore also for each $P \in prf(F)$, $\exists E' \in \epsilon : P \subseteq E'$. Since ϵ only contains preferred extensions of F we get $P \in \epsilon$, and finally $prf(F) \subseteq \epsilon$. □

4   Discussion and Conclusions

In this paper we have shown the applicability and the advantages of using a rigorous formal way for describing certain algorithms for solving decision problems for AFs through graph-based abstract solvers instead of pseudo-code-based descriptions. Both SAT-based and dedicated approaches have been analyzed and compared. Moreover, by a combination of these approaches we have obtained a novel algorithm for enumeration of preferred extensions.

Our work shows the potential of abstract transition systems to describe, compare and combine algorithms also in the research field of abstract argumentation, as already happened in, e.g. SAT, SMT and ASP. In particular, the last feature, which allows the design of new solving procedures by combining reasoning modules from different algorithms, seems to be particularly appealing. However, we do not claim about the efficiency of a new tool built on this basis, given that it usually requires many iterations of theoretical analysis, practical engineering, and domain-specific optimizations to develop efficient systems.

We have focused on the well-studied preferred semantics and presented core algorithms. However, the machinery can be easily employed to describing algorithms for other reasoning tasks, such as credulous acceptance, or different semantics, e.g. semi-stable and stage semantics, as employed in CEGARTIX [14].

Moreover, specific optimization techniques can be taken into account by means of modular addition of transition rules to the graph describing the core parts of the algorithms. As future work we plan to make these points more concrete.

Moreover, we envisage to formally describe further algorithms for reasoning tasks within abstract argumentation (see e.g. [8,11,18]). In particular, the results of the competition suggest promising candidates for the application of the newly gained technique of algorithm combination via abstract solvers.

Acknowledgements. This work has been funded by the Austrian Science Fund (FWF) through project I1102, and by Academy of Finland through grants 251170 COIN and 284591.

References

1. Baroni, P., Caminada, M.W.A., Giacomin, M.: An introduction to argumentation semantics. Knowl. Eng. Rev. **26**(4), 365–410 (2011)
2. Bench-Capon, T.J.M., Dunne, P.E.: Argumentation in artificial intelligence. Artif. Intell. **171**(10–15), 619–641 (2007)
3. Besnard, P., Doutre, S.: Checking the acceptability of a set of arguments. In: Delgrande, J.P., Schaub, T. (eds.) Proceedings of the 10th International Workshop on Non-Monotonic Reasoning, NMR 2004, pp. 59–64 (2004)
4. Brochenin, R., Lierler, Y., Maratea, M.: Abstract disjunctive answer set solvers. In: Schaub, T., Friedrich, G., O'Sullivan, B. (eds.) Proceedings of the 21st European Conference on Artificial Intelligence, ECAI 2014. FAIA, vol. 263, pp. 165–170. IOS Press (2014)
5. Cerutti, F., Dunne, P.E., Giacomin, M., Vallati, M.: Computing preferred extensions in abstract argumentation: a SAT-based approach. In: Black, E., Modgil, S., Oren, N. (eds.) TAFA 2013. LNCS, vol. 8306, pp. 176–193. Springer, Heidelberg (2014)
6. Cerutti, F., Giacomin, M., Vallati, M.: ArgSemSAT: Solving argumentation problems using SAT. In: Parsons, S., Oren, N., Reed, C., Cerutti, F. (eds.) Proceedings of the 5th International Conference on Computational Models of Argument, COMMA 2014. FAIA, vol. 266, pp. 455–456. IOS Press (2014)
7. Cerutti, F., Oren, N., Strass, H., Thimm, M., Vallati, M.: A benchmark framework for a computational argumentation competition. In: Parsons, S., Oren, N., Reed, C., Cerutti, F. (eds.) Proceedings of the 5th International Conference on Computational Models of Argument, COMMA 2014. FAIA, vol. 266, pp. 459–460. IOS Press (2014)
8. Charwat, G., Dvořák, W., Gaggl, S.A., Wallner, J.P., Woltran, S.: Methods for solving reasoning problems in abstract argumentation - a survey. Artif. Intell. **220**, 28–63 (2015)
9. Davis, M., Logemann, G., Loveland, D.: A machine program for theorem proving. Commun. ACM **5**(7), 394–397 (1962)
10. Dimopoulos, Y., Torres, A.: Graph theoretical structures in logic programs and default theories. Theoret. Comput. Sci. **170**(1–2), 209–244 (1996)
11. Doutre, S., Mengin, J.: Preferred extensions of argumentation frameworks: query answering and computation. In: Goré, R.P., Leitsch, A., Nipkow, T. (eds.) IJCAR 2001. LNCS (LNAI), vol. 2083, pp. 272–288. Springer, Heidelberg (2001)

12. Dung, P.M.: On the acceptability of arguments and its fundamental role in nonmonotonic reasoning, logic programming and n-person games. Artif. Intell. **77**(2), 321–358 (1995)
13. Dunne, P.E., Bench-Capon, T.J.M.: Coherence in finite argument systems. Artif. Intell. **141**(1/2), 187–203 (2002)
14. Dvořák, W., Järvisalo, M., Wallner, J.P., Woltran, S.: Complexity-sensitive decision procedures for abstract argumentation. Artif. Intell. **206**, 53–78 (2014)
15. Dvořák, W., Woltran, S.: Complexity of semi-stable and stage semantics in argumentation frameworks. Inf. Process. Lett. **110**(11), 425–430 (2010)
16. Lierler, Y.: Abstract answer set solvers with backjumping and learning. Theory Pract. Log. Program. **11**(2–3), 135–169 (2011)
17. Lierler, Y.: Relating constraint answer set programming languages and algorithms. Artif. Intell. **207**, 1–22 (2014)
18. Modgil, S., Caminada, M.W.A.: Proof theories and algorithms for abstract argumentation frameworks. In: Rahwan, I., Simari, G.R. (eds.) Argumentation in Artificial Intelligence, pp. 105–129. Springer, Heidelberg (2009)
19. Nieuwenhuis, R., Oliveras, A., Tinelli, C.: Solving SAT and SAT modulo theories: From an abstract Davis-Putnam-Logemann-Loveland procedure to DPLL(T). J. ACM **53**(6), 937–977 (2006)
20. Nofal, S., Atkinson, K., Dunne, P.E.: Algorithms for decision problems in argument systems under preferred semantics. Artif. Intell. **207**, 23–51 (2014)
21. Rahwan, I., Simari, G.R. (eds.): Argumentation in Artificial Intelligence. Springer, Heidelberg (2009)

A Discussion Game for Grounded Semantics

Martin Caminada[1,2](✉)

[1] University of Aberdeen, Aberdeen, Scotland, UK
[2] Cardiff University, Cardiff, Wales, UK
caminadam@cardiff.ac.uk

Abstract. We introduce an argument-based discussion game where the ability to win the game for a particular argument coincides with the argument being in the grounded extension. Our game differs from previous work in that (i) the number of moves is *linear* (instead of exponential) w.r.t. the strongly admissible set that the game is constructing, (ii) winning the game does not rely on cooperation from the other player (that is, the game is winning strategy based), (iii) a *single* game won by the proponent is sufficient to show grounded membership, and (iv) the game has a number of properties that make it more in line with natural discussion.

1 Introduction

In informal argumentation, discussions play a prominent role. Yet the aspect of discussion has received relatively little attention in formal argumentation theory, especially within the research line of Dung-style argumentation [12]. Whereas other aspects of informal argumentation, like argument schemes [21], claims and conclusions [15,21], assumptions [2,13,30] and preferences [18,20] have successfully been modelled in the context of (instantiated) Dung-style argumentation, dialectical aspects are often regarded as being part of a research field seperate from inference-based argumentation [22,24,25]. The scarce work that does consider dialectical aspects in the context of argument-based entailment tends to do so for the purpose of defining proof procedures [11,27] that, although useful for software implementation [23], are not meant to actually resemble informal discussion.

One exception to this is the Grounded Persuasion Game of Caminada and Podlaszewski [9], which provides a labelling-based discussion game for grounded semantics. The game is defined such that an argument is in the grounded extension iff there exists at least one game for it that is won by the proponent. However, the Grounded Persuasion Game has a number of shortcomings. For instance, it can be that an argument is in the grounded extension but the proponent does not have a winning strategy for it. That is, although it is possible to win the game, this depends partly on the cooperation of the opponent. Furthermore, in the Grounded Persuasion Game it is the proponent who first introduces the arguments that he later needs to defend against, a phenomenon that rarely occurs in natural discussions other than by mistake.

In the current paper, we present a modified and slightly simplified discussion game for grounded semantics, called the Grounded Discussion Game, that

© Springer International Publishing Switzerland 2015
E. Black et al. (Eds.): TAFA 2015, LNAI 9524, pp. 59–73, 2015.
DOI: 10.1007/978-3-319-28460-6_4

addresses above mentioned shortcomings. Overall, our aim is to provide a discussion game that can be used in the context of human-computer interaction, for the purpose of explaining argument-based inference. This can be helpful to allow users to understand why a particular advice was given by a knowledge-based system, and to examine whether particular objections the user might have can properly be addressed. In this way, we see interactive discussion as an alternative for argument visualisation [28,29]. Our current work, which is focussed on grounded semantics, fits in a line of research where similar discussion games have been stated also for preferred [7] and stable [10]. With respect to the previously stated games for grounded semantics [3,9,19,27] our aim is to satisfy the following properties:

1. Correctness and completeness for grounded semantics w.r.t. the presence of a winning strategy. It should be the case that an argument is in the grounded extension iff the proponent has a winning strategy for it (unlike for instance [9]).
2. Similarity to natural discussion. No party should be required to introduce arguments that he subsequently has to argue against (unlike for instance [9]). Also, there should be moves in which a player can indicate agreement ("fair enough") at specific points of the discussion (unlike for instance the Standard Grounded Game [3,19,27], where such moves are absent).
3. Efficiency. The number of moves should be *linear* in relation to the size of the strongly admissible labelling [5] the game is constructing. This is for instance violated by the Standard Grounded Game [3,19,27], where the number of moves can be *exponential* in relation to the size of the strongly admissible labelling the game is constructing (see [5, Section 5.3] for details). A similar observation can be made for other tree-based proof procedures [11,14].

The remaining part of this paper is structured as follows. First, in Sect. 2 we provide some preliminaries of argumentation theory. Then, in Sect. 3 we present our new Grounded Discussion Game, and show that it satisfies the above mentioned properties. We round off in Sect. 4 with a discussion of the obtained results and how these relate to previous research. Due to space constraints, some of the proofs have been moved to a seperate technical report [6].

2   Formal Preliminaries

Abstract argumentation theory [12] in essence is about how to select nodes from a graph called an *argumentation framework*.

Definition 1 ([12]). *An* argumentation framework *is a pair* (Ar, att) *where* Ar *is a finite set of entities called arguments, and* att *is a binary relation on* Ar. *We say that* A *attacks* B *iff* $(A, B) \in att$.

For current purposes, we apply the labelling-based version of argumentation semantics [8] instead of the original extension-based version of [12]. It should be noticed, however, that an extension is essentially the **in** labelled part of a labelling [8].

Definition 2 ([8]). *Let* (Ar, att) *be an argumentation framework. An* argument labelling *is a total function* $\mathcal{L}ab : Ar \to \{\text{in}, \text{out}, \text{undec}\}$. *An argument labelling is called an* admissible *labelling iff for each* $A \in Ar$ *it holds that:*

- *if* $\mathcal{L}ab(A) = \text{in}$ *then for each* B *that attacks* A *it holds that* $\mathcal{L}ab(B) = \text{out}$
- *if* $\mathcal{L}ab(A) = \text{out}$ *then there exists a* B *that attacks* A *such that* $\mathcal{L}ab(B) = \text{in}$

$\mathcal{L}ab$ *is called a* complete *labelling iff it is an admissible labelling and for each* $A \in Ar$ *it also holds that:*

- *if* $\mathcal{L}ab(A) = \text{undec}$ *then there exists a* B *that attacks* A *such that* $\mathcal{L}ab(B) \neq$ *out, and there exists no* B *that attacks* A *such that* $\mathcal{L}ab(B) = \text{in}$

As a labelling is essentially a function, we sometimes write it as a set of pairs. Also, if $\mathcal{L}ab$ is a labelling, we write $\text{in}(\mathcal{L}ab)$ for $\{A \in Ar \mid \mathcal{L}ab(A) = \text{in}\}$, $\text{out}(\mathcal{L}ab)$ for $\{A \in Ar \mid \mathcal{L}ab(A) = \text{out}\}$ and $\text{undec}(\mathcal{L}ab)$ for $\{A \in Ar \mid \mathcal{L}ab(A) = \text{undec}\}$. As a labelling is also a partition of the arguments into sets of in-labelled arguments, out-labelled arguments and undec-labelled arguments, we sometimes write it as a triplet $(\text{in}(\mathcal{L}ab), \text{out}(\mathcal{L}ab), \text{undec}(\mathcal{L}ab))$.

Definition 3 ([8]). *Let* $\mathcal{L}ab$ *be a complete labelling of argumentation framework* $AF = (Ar, att)$. $\mathcal{L}ab$ *is said to be the* grounded *labelling iff* $\text{in}(\mathcal{L}ab)$ *is minimal (w.r.t. set inclusion) among all complete labellings of* AF.

The discussion game to be presented in Sect. 3 of this paper is based on the concept of strong admissibility [1,5]. Hence, we briefly recall its basic definitions.

Definition 4 ([5]). *Let* $\mathcal{L}ab$ *be an admissible labelling of argumentation framework* (Ar, att). *A* min-max numbering *is a total function* $\mathcal{MM}_{\mathcal{L}ab} : \text{in}(\mathcal{L}ab) \cup \text{out}(\mathcal{L}ab) \to \mathbb{N} \cup \{\infty\}$ *such that for each* $A \in \text{in}(\mathcal{L}ab) \cup \text{out}(\mathcal{L}ab)$ *it holds that:*

- *if* $\mathcal{L}ab(A) = \text{in}$ *then* $\mathcal{MM}_{\mathcal{L}ab}(A) = max\left(\{\mathcal{MM}_{\mathcal{L}ab}(B) \mid B \text{ attacks } A \text{ and } \mathcal{L}ab(B) = \text{out}\}\right) + 1$ *(with* $max(\emptyset)$ *defined as* 0*)*
- *if* $\mathcal{L}ab(A) = \text{out}$ *then* $\mathcal{MM}_{\mathcal{L}ab}(A) = min\left(\{\mathcal{MM}_{\mathcal{L}ab}(B) \mid B \text{ attacks } A \text{ and } \mathcal{L}ab(B) = \text{in}\}\right) + 1$ *(with* $min(\emptyset)$ *defined as* ∞*)*

Theorem 1 ([5]). *Every admissible labelling has a unique min-max numbering.*

Definition 5 ([5]). *A* strongly admissible *labelling is an admissible labelling whose min-max numbering yields natural numbers only (so no argument is numbered* ∞*).*

Theorem 2 ([5]). *An argument is labelled* in *(resp.* out*) by at least one strongly admissible labelling iff it is labelled* in *(resp.* out*) by the grounded labelling.*

As an example, consider the argumentation framework shown below, which we refer to as AF_{ex}. Here $\mathcal{L}ab_1 = (\{A, C, E, G\}, \{B, D, H\}, \{F\})$ is an admissible (though not complete) labelling with associated min-max numbering $\mathcal{MM}_{\mathcal{L}ab_1} = \{(A\!:\!1), (B\!:\!2), (C\!:\!3), (D\!:\!4), (E\!:\!5), (G\!:\!\infty), (H\!:\!\infty)\}$, which implies that $\mathcal{L}ab_1$

is not strongly admissible. Furthermore, $\mathcal{L}ab_2 = (\{A, C, E\}, \{B, D, F\}, \{G, H\})$ is an admissible (and complete) labelling with associated min-max numbering $\mathcal{MM}_{\mathcal{L}ab_2} = \{(A\!:\!1), (B\!:\!2), (C\!:\!3), (D\!:\!4), (E\!:\!5), (F\!:\!2)\}$, which implies that $\mathcal{L}ab_2$ is indeed a strongly admissible labelling.

From Theorem 2, together with the fact that the grounded extension consists of the in-labelled arguments of the grounded labelling [8], it follows that to show that an argument is in the grounded extension, it is sufficient to construct a strongly admissible labelling that labels the argument in.

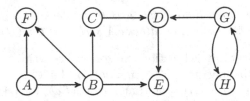

3   The Grounded Discussion Game

The Grounded Discussion Game that we will define in the current section has two players (proponent and opponent) and is based on four different moves, each of which has an argument as a parameter.

$HTB(A)$ ("A has to be the case"). With this move, the proponent claims that A has to be labelled in by every complete labelling, and hence also has to be labelled in by the grounded labelling.

$CB(B)$ ("B can be the case, or at least cannot be ruled out"). With this move, the opponent claims that B does not have to be labelled out by every complete labelling. That is, the opponent claims there exists a complete labelling where B is labelled in or undec, and that B is therefore not labelled out by the grounded labelling.

$CONCEDE(A)$ ("I agree that A has to be the case"). With this move, the opponent indicates that he now agrees with the proponent (who previously did a $HTB(A)$ move) that A has to be the case (labelled in by every complete labelling, including the grounded).

$RETRACT(B)$ ("I give up that B can be the case"). With this move, the opponent indicates that he no longer believes that B can be in or undec. That is, the opponent acknowledges that B has to be labelled out by every complete labelling, including the grounded.

One of the key ideas of the discussion game is that the proponent has burden of proof. He has to establish the acceptance of the main argument and make sure the discussion does not go around in circles. The opponent merely has to cast sufficient doubts.

The game starts with the proponent uttering a HTB statement. After each HTB statement (either the first one or a subsequent one) the opponent utters a sequence of one or more *CB*, *CONCEDE* and *RETRACT* statements, after which the proponent again utters an *HTB* statement, etc. In AF_{ex} the discussion could go as follows.

(1) P :*HTB(C)*   (4) O :*CONCEDE(A)*
(2) O :*CB(B)*   (5) O :*RETRACT(B)*
(3) P :*HTB(A)*   (6) O :*CONCEDE(C)*

In the above discussion, *C* is called *the main argument* (the argument the discussion starts with). The discussion above ends with the main argument being conceded by the opponent, so we say that the proponent wins the discussion.

As an example of a discussion that is lost by the proponent, it can be illustrative to examine what happens if, still in AF_{ex}, the proponent claims that *B* has to be the case.

(1) P :*HTB(B)*   (2) O :*CB(A)*

After the second move, the discussion is terminated, as the proponent cannot make any further move, since *A* does not have any attackers. This brings us to the precise preconditions of the discussion moves.

HTB(A) Either this is the first move, or the previous move was *CB(B)*, where *A* attacks *B*, and no *CONCEDE* or *RETRACT* move is applicable.

CB(A) *A* is an attacker of the last *HTB(B)* statement that is not yet conceded, the directly preceeding move was not a *CB* statement, argument *A* has not yet been retracted, and no *CONCEDE* or *RETRACT* move is applicable.

CONCEDE(A) There has been a *HTB(A)* statement in the past, of which every attacker has been retracted, and *CONCEDE(A)* has not yet been moved.

RETRACT(A) There has been a *CB(A)* statement in the past, of which there exists an attacker that has been conceded, and *RETRACT(A)* has not yet been moved.

Apart from the preconditions mentioned above, all four statements also have the additional precondition that no *HTB-CB* repeats have occurred. That is, there should be no argument for which *HTB* has been uttered more than once, *CB* has been uttered more than once, or both *HTB* and *CB* have been uttered. In the first and second case, the discussion is going around in circles, which the proponent has to prevent as he has burden of proof. In the third case, the proponent has been contradicting himself, as his statements are not conflict-free. In each of these three cases, the discussion comes to an end with no move being applicable anymore. The above conditions are made formal as follows.

Definition 6. *Let AF = (Ar, att) be an argumentation framework. A grounded discussion is a sequence of discussion moves constructed by applying the following principles.*

BASIS *(HTB). If $A \in Ar$ then $[HTB(A)]$ is a grounded discussion.*

STEP *(HTB). If $[M_1, \ldots, M_n]$ $(n \geq 1)$ is a grounded discussion without HTB-CB repeats,[1] and no CONCEDE or RETRACT move is applicable,[2] and $M_n = CB(A)$ and B is an attacker of A then $[M_1, \ldots, M_n, HTB(B)]$ is also a grounded discussion.*

STEP *(CB). If $[M_1, \ldots, M_n]$ $(n \geq 1)$ is a grounded discussion without HTB-CB repeats, and no CONCEDE or RETRACT move is applicable, and M_n is not a CB move, and there is a move $M_i = HTB(A)$ $(i \in \{1 \ldots n\})$ such that the discussion does not contain CONCEDE(A), and for each move $M_j = HTB(A')$ $(j > i)$ the discussion contains a move CONCEDE(A'), and B is an attacker of A such that the discussion does not contain a move RETRACT(B), then $[M_1, \ldots, M_n, CB(B)]$ is a grounded discussion.*

STEP *(CONCEDE). If $[M_1, \ldots, M_n]$ $(n \geq 1)$ is a grounded discussion without HTB-CB repeats, and CONCEDE(B) is applicable then $[M_1, \ldots, M_n, CONCEDE(B)]$ is a grounded discussion.*

STEP *(RETRACT). If $[M_1, \ldots, M_n]$ $(n \geq 1)$ is a grounded discussion without HTB-CB repeats, and RETRACT(B) is applicable then $[M_1, \ldots, M_n, RETRACT(B)]$ is a grounded discussion.*

It can be observed that the preconditions of the moves are such that a proponent move (*HTB*) can never be applicable at the same moment as an opponent move (*CB, CONCEDE* or *RETRACT*). That is, proponent and opponent essentially take turns in which each proponent turn consists of a single *HTB* statement, and every opponent turn consists of a sequence of *CONCEDE, RETRACT* and *CB* moves.

Definition 7. *A grounded discussion $[M_1, \ldots, M_n]$ is called terminated iff there exists no move M_{n+1} such that $[M_1, \ldots, M_n, M_{n+1}]$ is a grounded discussion. A terminated grounded discussion (with A being the main argument) is won by the proponent iff the discussion contains CONCEDE(A), otherwise it is won by the opponent.*

To illustrate why the discussion has to be terminated after the occurrence of a *HTB-CB* repeat, consider the following discussion in AF_{ex}.

(1) P :$HTB(G)$ (3) P :$HTB(G)$
(2) O :$CB(H)$

After the third move, an *HTB-CB* repeat occurs and the discussion is terminated (opponent wins). Hence, termination after a *HTB-CB* repeat is necessary to prevent the discussion from going on perpetually.

---

[1] We say that there is a *HTB-CB* repeat iff $\exists i, j \in \{1 \ldots n\} \exists A \in Ar : (M_i = HTB(A) \vee M_i = CB(A)) \wedge (M_j = HTB(A) \vee M_j = CB(A)) \wedge i \neq j$.

[2] A move CONCEDE(B) is applicable iff the discussion contains a move $HTB(A)$ and for every attacker A of B the discussion contains a move RETRACT(B), and the discussion does not already contain a move CONCEDE(B). A move RETRACT(B) is applicable iff the discussion contains a move $CB(B)$ and there is an attacker A of B such that the discussion contains a move CONCEDE(A), and the discussion does not already contain a move RETRACT(B).

Theorem 3. *Every discussion will terminate after a finite number of steps.*

From the fact that a discussion terminates after an *HTB-CB* repeat, the following result follows.

Lemma 1. *No discussion can contain a CONCEDE and RETRACT move for the same argument.*

3.1 Soundness

Now that the workings of the game have been outlined, the next step will be to formally prove its soundness and completeness w.r.t. grounded semantics. We start with soundness: if a discussion is won by the proponent, then the main argument is in the grounded extension. In order to prove this, we first have to introduce the notions of the proponent labelling and the opponent labelling.

Definition 8. *Let $[M_1, \ldots, M_n]$ be a grounded discussion (in argumentation framework (Ar, att)) without any HTB-CB repeats.*
The proponent labelling $\mathcal{L}ab_P$ is defined as
$\mathrm{in}(\mathcal{L}ab_P) = \{A \mid \exists i \in \{1 \ldots n\}: M_i = HTB(A)\}$
$\mathrm{out}(\mathcal{L}ab_P) = \{A \mid \exists i \in \{1 \ldots n\}: M_i = CB(A)\}$
$\mathrm{undec}(\mathcal{L}ab_P) = Ar \setminus (\mathrm{in}(\mathcal{L}ab_P) \cup \mathrm{out}(\mathcal{L}ab_P))$
The opponent labelling $\mathcal{L}ab_O$ is defined as
$\mathrm{in}(\mathcal{L}ab_O) = \{A \mid \exists i \in \{1 \ldots n\}: M_i = CONCEDE(A)\}$
$\mathrm{out}(\mathcal{L}ab_O) = \{A \mid \exists i \in \{1 \ldots n\}: M_i = RETRACT(A)\}$
$\mathrm{undec}(\mathcal{L}ab_O) = Ar \setminus (\mathrm{in}(\mathcal{L}ab_O) \cup \mathrm{out}(\mathcal{L}ab_O)).$

Notice that the well-definedness of $\mathcal{L}ab_O$ in Definition 8 does not depend on the absence of *HTB-CB* repeats (this is due to Lemma 1) whereas the well-definedness of $\mathcal{L}ab_P$ does. When applying $\mathcal{L}ab_O$, we will therefore often do so without having ruled out any *HTB-CB* repeats, as for instance in the following theorem.

Theorem 4. *Let $\mathcal{L}ab_O$ be the opponent's labelling w.r.t. discussion $[M1, \ldots, M_n]$. $\mathcal{L}ab_O$ is strongly admissible.*

Theorem 4 states that at any stage of the discussion, $\mathcal{L}ab_O$ is strongly admissible (this can be proved by induction over the number of *CONCEDE* and *RETRACT* moves [6]). Hence, when the game is terminated and won by the proponent, we have a strongly admissible labelling where (by definition of winning) the main argument is labelled **in**. It then follows (Theorem 2) that the main argument is labelled **in** by the grounded labelling and is therefore an element of the grounded extension [8], leading to the following theorem.

Theorem 5. *Let $[M_1, \ldots, M_n]$ be a terminated grounded discussion, won by the proponent, with main argument A. It holds that A is in the grounded extension.*

As an aside, although it is possible to infer that an argument is in the grounded extension when the proponent wins a discussion (Theorem 5) we cannot infer that an argument is *not* in the grounded extension when the proponent loses a discussion. This is because loss of a game could be due to the proponent following a flawed strategy. For instance, in AF_{ex} one could have the following discussion:

(1) P : $HTB(E)$	(4) O : $CB(H)$
(2) O : $CB(D)$	(5) P : $HTB(G)$
(3) P : $HTB(G)$	

The discussion is terminated at step (5) due to a HTB-CB repeat ($HTB(G)$). The main argument is not conceded, so the proponent loses. Still the proponent could have won by moving $HTB(C)$ instead of $HTB(G)$ at step (3).

3.2 Completeness

Now that the soundness of the game has been shown, we shift our attention to completeness. The obvious thing to prove regarding completeness would be the converse of Theorem 5: if A is in the grounded extension, then there exists a discussion won by the proponent with A as the main argument. However, our aim is to prove a slightly stronger property. Instead of there being just a single discussion won by the proponent, which might be due to the opponent actually providing cooperation during the game, we require the proponent to have a winning strategy. That is, when an argument is in the grounded extension, the proponent will be able to win the game, irrespective of how the opponent choses to play it.

The idea is that a strongly admissible labelling (for instance the grounded labelling) with its associated min-max numbering can serve as a roadmap for winning the discussion. The proponent will be able to win if, whenever he has to do a HTB move, he prefers to use an **in** argument with the lowest min-max number that attacks the directly preceding CB move. We refer to this as a *lowest number strategy*.[3]

We first observe that when applying such a strategy, the game stays within the boundaries of the strongly admissible labelling (that is, within its **in** and **out** labelled part). As long as each HTB move of the proponent is related to an **in**-labelled argument, it follows that all the attackers are labelled **out** (Definition 2, first bullet) so each CB move the opponent utters in response will be related to an **out**-labelled argument. This **out**-labelled argument will then have at least one **in**-labelled attacker (Definition 2, second bullet) as a candidate for the proponent's subsequent HTB move.

The next thing to be observed is that when the proponent applies a lowest number strategy, the game will not terminate due to any HTB-CB repeats. This

---

[3] We write "*a* lowest number strategy" instead of "*the* lowest number strategy" as a lowest number strategy might not be unique due to different lowest numbered **in**-labelled arguments being applicable at a specific point. In that case it suffices to pick an arbitrary one.

is due to the facts that (1) after a move $HTB(A)$ is played (for some argument A) all subsequent CB and HTB moves will be related to arguments with lower min-max numbers than A until a move $CONCEDE(A)$ is played, and (2) after a move $CB(A)$ is played (for some argument A), all subsequent HTB and CB moves will be related to arguments with lower min-max numbers than A, until a move $RETRACT(A)$ is played. We refer to [6] for details.

Lemma 2. *If the proponent uses a lowest number strategy, then no HTB-CB repeats occur.*

We are now ready to present the main result regarding completeness of the discussion game.

Theorem 6. *Let A be an argument in the grounded extension of argumentation framework (Ar, att). If the proponent uses a lowest number strategy, he will win the discussion for main argument A.*

Theorem 6 partly follows from the facts that each discussion will terminate in a finite number of moves (Theorem 3) and, as the proponent uses a lowest number strategy, termination cannot be due to any HTB-CB repeat (Lemma 2). We refer to [6] for details. As the presence of a winning strategy trivially implies the presence of at least one discussion that is won by the proponent, we immediately obtain the following result.

Corollary 1. *Let A be an argument in the grounded extension of argumentation framework (Ar, att). There exists at least one terminated grounded discussion, won by the proponent, for main argument A.*

3.3   Efficiency

Now that soundness and completeness of the game have been shown, we proceed to examine its efficiency. Theorem 3 states that every discussion will terminate, and we are interested in how many steps are required for this. For this, we need the following lemma (proof in [6]).

Lemma 3. *Let A be an argument in the grounded extension of argumentation framework (Ar, att). When the proponent uses a lowest number strategy for the discussion of A, then once the game is terminated it holds that $\mathcal{L}ab_O = \mathcal{L}ab_P$.*

In a terminated discussion yielded by a lowest number strategy, there exists a one-to-one relation between HTB moves and arguments in $\text{in}(\mathcal{L}ab_P)$ (as no HTB move is repeated, as there are no HTB-CB repeats), a one-to-one relationship between CB moves and arguments in $\text{out}(\mathcal{L}ab_P)$ (as no CB move is repeated, as there are non HTB-CB repeats), a one-to-one relation between $CONCEDE$ moves and arguments in $\text{in}(\mathcal{L}ab_O)$ (as no $CONCEDE$ move can be repeated) and a one-to-one relation between $RETRACT$ moves and arguments in $\text{out}(\mathcal{L}ab_O)$ (as no $RETRACT$ move can be repeated). Hence, the total number of moves is $|\text{in}(\mathcal{L}ab_P)| + |\text{out}(\mathcal{L}ab_P)| + |\text{in}(\mathcal{L}ab_O)| + |\text{out}(\mathcal{L}ab_O)|$. Due to the facts that

$in(\mathcal{L}ab_P) \cap out(\mathcal{L}ab_P) = \emptyset$, $in(\mathcal{L}ab_O) \cap out(\mathcal{L}ab_O) = \emptyset$, and $\mathcal{L}ab_P = \mathcal{L}ab_O$ (Lemma 3), this is equivalent to $2 \cdot |in(\mathcal{L}ab_P) \cup out(\mathcal{L}ab_P)|$ and to $2 \cdot |in(\mathcal{L}ab_O) \cup out(\mathcal{L}ab_O)|$, so to two times the *size* [5] of either $\mathcal{L}ab_P$ or $\mathcal{L}ab_O$.

Theorem 7. *Let A be an argument in the grounded extension of argumentation framework $AF = (Ar, att)$. When the proponent uses a lowest number strategy for A, the resulting terminated discussion will have a number of moves that is linear w.r.t. the size of the strongly admissible labelling that is has been constructed.*

4   Discussion and Related Work

As was shown in Sect. 3, the Grounded Discussion Game is based on the concept of strong admissibility. In essence, it constructs a strongly admissible labelling where the main argument is labelled **in** (Theorem 4). Moreover, the presence of a strongly admissible labelling provides the proponent with a winning strategy for the game (Theorem 6). These observations make it possible to compare the Grounded Discussion Game with two previously defined games that are also based on strong admissibility: the Standard Grounded Game [3,19,27] and the Grounded Persuasion Game [9].

4.1   The Standard Grounded Game

The Standard Grounded Game (SGG) [3,19,27] is one of the earliest dialectical proof procedures for grounded semantics. Each game[4] consists of a sequence $[A_1, \ldots, A_n]$ $(n \geq 1)$ of arguments, moved by the proponent and opponent taking turns, with the proponent starting. That is, a move A_i $(i \in \{1 \ldots n\})$ is a proponent move iff i is odd, and an opponent move iff i is even. Each move, except the first one, is an attacker of the previous move. In order to ensure termination even in the presence of cycles, the proponent is not allowed to repeat any of his moves. A game is terminated iff no next move is possible; the player making the last move wins.

As an example, in AF_{ex} $[C, B, A]$ is terminated and won by the proponent (as A has no attackers, the opponent cannot move anymore) whereas $[G, H]$ is terminated and won by the opponent (as the only attacker of H is G, which the proponent is not allowed to repeat). It is sometimes possible for the proponent to win a game even if the main argument is not in the grounded extension. An example would be $[F, B, A]$. This illustrates that in order to show that an argument is in the grounded extension, a single game won by the proponent is not sufficient. Instead, what is needed is a *winning strategy*. This is essentially a tree in which each node is associated with an argument such that (1) each path from the root to a leaf constitutes a terminated discussion won by the proponent, (2) the children of each proponent node (a node corresponding with a proponent move) coincide with all attackers of the associated argument,

---

[4] What we call an SGG game is called a "line of dispute" in [19].

and (3) each opponent node (a node corresponding with an opponent move) has precisely one child, whose argument attacks the argument of the opponent node.

It has been proved that an argument is in the grounded extension iff the proponent has a winning strategy for it in the SGG [3,27]. Moreover, it has also been shown that an SGG winning strategy defines a strongly admissible labelling, when labelling each argument of a proponent node in, each argument of an opponent node out and all remaining arguments undec [5].

As an example, in AF_{ex} the winning strategy for argument E would be the tree consisting of the two branches $E-B-A$ and $E-D-C-B-A$, thus proving its membership of the grounded extension by yielding the strongly admissible labelling $(\{A,C,E\},\{B,D\},\{F,G,H\})$. As can be observed from this example, a winning strategy of the SGG can contain some redundancy when it comes to multiple occurrences of the same arguments in different branches. In the current example, the redundancy is relatively mild (consisting of just the two arguments A and B) but other cases have been found where the SGG requires a number of moves in the winning strategy that is *exponential* w.r.t. the size of the strongly admissible labelling the winning strategy is defining [5, Figure 2].[5] Hence, one of the advantages of our newly defined GDG compared to the SGG is that we go from an exponential [5, Figure 2] to a linear (Theorem 7) number of moves.[6]

4.2   The Grounded Persuasion Game

One of the main aims of the Grounded Persuasion Game (GPG) [9] was to bring the proof procedures of grounded semantics more in line with Mackenzie-style dialogue theory [16,17] The game has two participants (P and O) and four types of moves: claim (the first move in the discussion, with which P utters the main claim that a particular argument has to be labelled in), why (with which O asks why a particular argument has to be labelled in a particular way), because (with which P explains why a particular argument has to be labelled a particular way) and concede (with which O indicates agreement with a particular statement of P). During the game, both P and O keep *commitment stores*, partial labellings (which we will refer to as $\mathcal{P}$ and $\mathcal{O}$) which keep track of which arguments they think are in and out during the course of the discussion. For P, a commitment is added every time he utters a claim or because statement. For O, a commitment is added every time he utters a concede statement. An *open issue* is an argument where only one player has a commitment. Some of the key rules of the Grounded Persuasion Game are as follows (full details in [9]).

---

[5] A similar observation can be made for other tree-based proof procedures [11,14].

[6] As each move contains a single argument, this means the "communication complexity" (the total number of arguments that needs to be communicated) is also linear. This contrasts with the computational complexity of playing the game, which is polynomial ($O(n^3)$, where n is the number of arguments) due to the fact that selecting the next move can have $O(n^2)$ complexity (see [6] for details). This is still less than when applying Standard Grounded Game, whose overall complexity would be exponential (even if each move could be selected in just one step) due to the requirement of a winning strategy, which as we have seen can be exponential in size.

- If O utters a why in(A) statement (resp. a why out(A) statement) then P has to reply with because out($B_1, \ldots, B_n$) where $B_1, \ldots, B_n$ are all attackers of A (resp. with because in(B) where B is an attacker of A).
- Any why statement of O has to be related to the most recently created open issue in the discussion.
- A because statement is not allowed to use an argument that is already an open issue.
- Once O has enough evidence to agree with P that a particular argument has to be labelled in (because for each of its attackers, O is already committed that the attacker is labelled out) or has to be labelled out (because it has an attacker of which O is already committed that it is labelled in), O has to utter the relevant concede statement immediately.

Unlike the SGG, in the GPG it is not necessary to construct a winning strategy to show grounded membership. Instead, an argument A is in the grounded extension iff there exists *at least one game* that starts with P uttering "claim in(A)" and is won by P [9].[7]

As a general property of the Grounded Persuasion Game, it can be observed that at every stage of the discussion, O's commitment store $\mathcal{O}$ is an admissible labelling [9].[8]

As an example, for argument E in AF_{ex} the discussion could go as follows.

	in($\mathcal{P}$)	out($\mathcal{P}$)	in($\mathcal{O}$)	out($\mathcal{O}$)
(1) P: claim in(E)	E			
(2) O: why in(E)	E			
(3) P: because out(B, D)	E	B,D		
(4) O: why out(B)	E	B,D		
(5) P: because in(A)	E,A	B,D		
(6) O: concede in(A)	E,A	B,D	A	
(7) O: concede out(B)	E,A	B,D	A	B
(8) O: why out(D)	E,A	B,D	A	B
(9) P: because in(C)	E,A,C	B,D	A	B
(10) O: concede in(C)	E,A,C	B,D	A,C	B
(11) O: concede out(D)	E,A,C	B,D	A,C	B,D
(12) O: concede in(E)	E,A,C	B,D	A,C,E	B,D

In the above game, the main claim in(E) is conceded so the proponent wins. As was mentioned above, a "because" statement is not allowed to use an argument that is already an open issue. This is to ensure termination even in the presence of cycles. However, this condition has an undesirable side effect. Consider what happens when, at move (4) of the above discussion, the opponent would have decided to utter "why out(D)" instead of "why out(B)".

---

[7] A discussion is won by P iff at the end of the game O is committed that the argument the discussion started with is labelled in.

[8] That is, if one regards all arguments where O does not have any commitments to be labelled undec.

$$(4')O : \text{why out}(D) \qquad E \qquad B, D$$
$$(5')P : \text{because in}(C) \qquad E, C \qquad B, D$$
$$(6')O : \text{why in}(C) \qquad E, C \qquad B, D$$

After move $(6')$ the proponent cannot reply with "because $\text{out}(B)$" as $\text{out}(B)$ is an open issue, so the game is terminated (according to the rules of [9]) without the main claim being conceded, meaning the proponent loses. Moreover, there is nothing the proponent could have done differently in order to win the game, in spite of E being in the grounded extension. One of the advantages of our currently defined Grounded Discussion Game is that such anomalies cannot occur (Theorem 6). Once the proponent utters $HTB(E)$ he can win the game, regardless of whether the opponent responds with $CB(B)$ or with $CB(D)$.

Another difference between the GPG and our currently defined GDG is related to the player who introduces the counterarguments in the discussion. In the GPG this is always the proponent, who for instance explicitly has to list all the attackers against an argument he is actually trying to defend (like "P: because $\text{out}(B, A)$" in the above discussion). However, in natural discussion it would be rare for any participant to provide counterarguments against his own position, other than by mistake. The GDG, however, is such that in a game won by the proponent, each of the counterarguments uttered against proponent's position is uttered by the opponent.

4.3   Summary and Analysis

Overall, the differences between our approach and the other games are summarised in the following table.

	SGG	GPG	GDG
number of moves needed to show strong admissibility	exp [5]	linear [5]	linear (Th. 7)
supports RETRACT and/or CONCEDE moves	no	yes	yes
both proponent and opponent introduce arguments	yes	no	yes
single successful game implies grounded membership	no	yes	yes
grounded membership implies ∃ winning strategy	yes	no	yes

Apart from the technical considerations mentioned above, the research agenda of developing argument-based discussion games is also relevant because it touches some of the foundations of argumentation theory. Whereas for instance classical logic entailment is based on the notion of *truth*, this notion simply does not exist in abstract argumentation and would be problematic even in instantiated argumentation.[9] But if not truth, then what actually is it that is actually yielded by formal argumentation theory? Our view is that argumentation theory yields what can be defended in rational discussion. As our Grounded Discussion Game is essentially a form of persuasion dialogue [31] we have shown that grounded semantics can be seen as a form of persuasion dialogue. Furthermore, Caminada et al. have for instance shown that (credulous) preferred semantics can be seen as a particular form of Socratic dialogue [4,7]. Hence, different argumentation semantics correspond to different types of discussion [7], an observation that is not just relevant for philosophical reasons, but also opens up opportunities for argument-based human computer interaction. In further research we hope to report on whether engaging in the Grounded Discussion Game increases people's trust in particular forms of argument-based inference. An implementation, that can serve as the basis for this, is currently under development.

Acknowledgements. This work has been supported by the Engineering and Physical Sciences Research Council (EPSRC, UK), grant ref. EP/J012084/1 (SAsSy project).

References

1. Baroni, P., Giacomin, M.: On principle-based evaluation of extension-based argumentation semantics. Artif. Intell. **171**(10–15), 675–700 (2007)
2. Bondarenko, A., Dung, P.M., Kowalski, R.A., Toni, F.: An abstract, argumentation-theoretic approach to default reasoning. Artif. Intell. **93**, 63–101 (1997)
3. Caminada, M.W.A.: For the sake of the Argument. Explorations into argument-based reasoning. Doctoral dissertation Free University Amsterdam (2004)
4. Caminada, M.W.A.: A formal account of socratic-style argumentation. J. Appl. Log. **6**(1), 109–132 (2008)
5. Caminada, M.W.A.: Strong admissibility revisited. In: Parsons, S., Oren, N., Reed, C., Cerutti, F. (eds.) Computational Models of Argument; Proceedings of COMMA 2014, pp. 197–208. IOS Press (2014)
6. Caminada, M.W.A.: A discussion protocol for grounded semantics (proofs). Technical report, University of Aberdeen (2015)
7. Caminada, M.W.A., Dvořák, W., Vesic, S.: Preferred semantics as socratic discussion. J. Log. Comput. (2014). (in print)
8. Caminada, M.W.A., Gabbay, D.M.: A logical account of formal argumentation. Stud. Logica **93**(2–3), 109–145 (2009). Special issue: new ideas in argumentation theory
9. Caminada, M.W.A., Podlaszewski, M.: Grounded semantics as persuasion dialogue. In: Verheij, B., Szeider, S., Woltran, S. (eds.) Computational Models of Argument - Proceedings of COMMA 2012, pp. 478–485 (2012)
10. Caminada, M.W.A., Wu, Y.: An argument game of stable semantics. Log. J. IGPL **17**(1), 77–90 (2009)
11. Dung, P.M., Mancarella, P., Toni, F.: Computing ideal sceptical argumentation. Artif. Intell. **171**(10–15), 642–674 (2007)

---

[9] For instance, if a conclusion is considered justified in ASPIC+ [21,26], does this imply the conclusion is also *true*?.

12. Dung, P.M.: On the acceptability of arguments and its fundamental role in non-monotonic reasoning, logic programming and n-person games. Artif. Intell. **77**, 321–357 (1995)
13. Dung, P.M., Kowalski, R.A., Toni, F.: Assumption-based argumentation. In: Simari, G., Rahwan, I. (eds.) Argumentation in Artificial Intelligence, pp. 199–218. Springer, Heidelberg (2009)
14. Fan, X., Toni, F.: A general framework for sound assumption-based argumentation dialogues. Artif. Intell. **216**, 20–54 (2014)
15. Gorogiannis, N., Hunter, A.: Instantiating abstract argumentation with classical logic arguments: Postulates and properties. Artif. Intell. **175**(9–10), 1479–1497 (2011)
16. Mackenzie, J.D.: Question-begging in non-cumulative systems. J. Philos. Log. **8**, 117–133 (1979)
17. Mackenzie, J.D.: Four dialogue systems. Stud. Logica **51**, 567–583 (1990)
18. Modgil, S.: Reasoning about preferences in argumentation frameworks. Artif. Intell. **173**, 901–1040 (2009)
19. Modgil, S., Caminada, M.W.A.: Proof theories and algorithms for abstract argumentation frameworks. In: Rahwan, I., Simari, G.R. (eds.) Argumentation in Artificial Intelligence, pp. 105–129. Springer, Heidelberg (2009)
20. Modgil, S., Prakken, H.: A general account of argumentation with preferences. Artif. Intell. **195**, 361–397 (2013)
21. Modgil, S., Prakken, H.: The ASPIC+ framework for structured argumentation: a tutorial. Argum. Comput. **5**, 31–62 (2014). Special Issue: Tutorials on Structured Argumentation
22. Parsons, S., Wooldridge, M., Amgoud, L.: Properties and complexity of formal inter-agent dialogues. J. Log. Comput. **13**(3), 347–376 (2003)
23. Podlaszewski, M., Wu, Y., Caminada, M.: An implementation of basic argumentation components. In: The 10th International Conference on Autonomous Agents and Multiagent Systems, vol. 3, pp. 1307–1308 (2011)
24. Prakken, H.: Coherence and flexibility in dialogue games for argumentation. J. Log. Comput. **15**(6), 1009–1040 (2005)
25. Prakken, H.: Formal systems for persuasion dialogue. Knowl. Eng. Rev. **21**, 163–188 (2006)
26. Prakken, H.: An abstract framework for argumentation with structured arguments. Argum. Comput. **1**(2), 93–124 (2010)
27. Prakken, H., Sartor, G.: Argument-based extended logic programming with defeasible priorities. J. Appl. Non-Classical Log. **7**, 25–75 (1997)
28. Schulz, C.: Graphical representation of assumption-based argumentation. In: Proceedings of the 29th AAAI Conference on Artificial Intelligence, pp. 4204–4205 (2015)
29. Schulz, C., Toni, F.: Logic programming in assumption-based argumentation revisited - semantics and graphical representation. In: Proceedings of the 29th AAAI Conference on Artificial Intelligence, pp. 1569–1575 (2015)
30. Toni, F.: A tutorial on assumption-based argumentation. Argum. Comput. **5**, 89–117 (2014). Special Issue: Tutorials on Structured Argumentation
31. Walton, D.N., Krabbe, E.C.W.: Commitment in Dialogue: Basic Concepts of Interpersonal Reasoning. SUNY Series in Logic and Language. State University of New York Press, Albany (1995)

An Axiomatic Approach to Support
in Argumentation

Claudette Cayrol and Marie-Christine Lagasquie-Schiex[✉]

IRIT-UPS, Toulouse, France
{ccayrol,lagasq}@irit.fr

Abstract. In the context of bipolar argumentation (argumentation with
two kinds of interaction, attacks and supports), we present an axiomatic
approach for taking into account a special interpretation of the support
relation, the necessary support. We propose constraints that should be
imposed to a bipolar argumentation system using this interpretation.
Some of these constraints concern the new attack relations, others concern acceptability. We extend basic Dung's framework in different ways
in order to propose frameworks suitable for encoding these constraints.
By the way, we propose a formal study of properties of necessary support.

Keywords: Abstract argumentation · Bipolar argumentation · Axiom-
atization of necessary support

1 Introduction

The main feature of argumentation framework is the ability to deal with
incomplete and/or contradictory information, especially for reasoning [2,15].
Moreover, argumentation can be used to formalize dialogues between several
agents by modeling the exchange of arguments in, *e.g.*, negotiation between
agents [4]. An argumentation system (AS) consists of a collection of arguments
interacting with each other through a relation reflecting conflicts between them,
called *attack*. The issue of argumentation is then to determine "acceptable" sets
of arguments (*i.e.*, sets able to defend themselves collectively while avoiding
internal attacks), called *"extensions"*, and thus to reach a coherent conclusion.
Formal frameworks have greatly eased the modeling and study of AS. In particular, the framework of [15] allows for abstracting the "concrete" meaning of the
arguments and relies only on binary interactions that may exist between them.

In this paper, we are interested in bipolar AS (BAS), which handle a second kind of interaction, the support relation. This relation represents a positive
interaction between arguments and has been first introduced by [18,27]. In [8],
the support relation is left general so that the bipolar framework keeps a high
level of abstraction. However there is no single interpretation of the support,
and a number of researchers proposed specialized variants of the support relation: deductive support [5], necessary support [21,22], evidential support [23,24],

© Springer International Publishing Switzerland 2015
E. Black et al. (Eds.): TAFA 2015, LNAI 9524, pp. 74–91, 2015.
DOI: 10.1007/978-3-319-28460-6_5

backing support [13]. Each specialization can be associated with an appropriate modelling using an appropriate complex attack. These proposals have been developed quite independently, based on different intuitions and with different formalizations. [10] presents a comparative study in order to restate these proposals in a common setting, the bipolar argumentation framework (see also [13] for another survey). The idea is to keep the original arguments, to add complex attacks defined by the combination of the original attack and the support, and to modify the classical notions of acceptability. An important result of [10] is the highlight of a kind of duality between the deductive and the necessary specialization of support, which results in a duality in the modelling by complex attacks. In this context, new different papers have recently been written: some of them give a translation between necessary supports and evidential supports [25]; others propose a justification of the necessary support using the notion of sub-arguments [26]; an extension of the necessary support is presented in [20]. From all these works it seems interesting to focus on the necessary support. However, different interpretations remain possible, leading to different ways of introducing new attacks and different ways to define acceptability of sets of arguments.

Our purpose is to propose a kind of "axiomatic approach" for studying how necessary support should be taken into account. Indeed we propose requirements (or constraints) that should be imposed to a bipolar argumentation system as "axioms" describing a desired behaviour of this system. Some of these constraints concern the new attack relations, others concern acceptability. We extend basic Dung's framework in different ways in order to propose frameworks suitable for encoding these contraints. By the way, we propose a formal study of properties of necessary support.

Some background is given in Sect. 2 for AS and BAS, in particular the duality identified in [10]. Section 3 presents constraints that should be imposed for taking into account necessary support. Then different frameworks for handling these constraints are described in Sect. 4. Section 5 concludes and suggests perspectives of our work. The proofs are given in [11].

2   Background on Abstract Bipolar Argumentation Systems

Bipolar abstract argumentation systems extend Dung's argumentation systems. So first we recall Dung's framework for abstract argumentation systems.

2.1   Dung's Framework

Dung's abstract framework consists of a set of arguments and only one type of interaction between them, namely attack. The important point is the way arguments are in conflict.

Definition 1 (Dung AS). *A Dung's argumentation system (AS, for short) is a pair* $\langle \mathbf{A}, \mathbf{R} \rangle$ *where*

- $\mathbf{A}$ *is a finite and non-empty set of arguments and*
- $\mathbf{R}$ *is a binary relation over* $\mathbf{A}$ *(a subset of* $\mathbf{A} \times \mathbf{A}$*), called the* attack *relation.*

An argumentation system can be represented by a directed graph, called the *interaction graph*, in which nodes represent arguments and edges are defined by the attack relation: $\forall a, b \in \mathbf{A}$, $a\mathbf{R}b$ is represented by $a \nrightarrow b$.

Definition 2 (Admissibility in AS). *Given* $\langle \mathbf{A}, \mathbf{R} \rangle$ *and* $S \subseteq \mathbf{A}$.

- S *is* conflict-free *in* $\langle \mathbf{A}, \mathbf{R} \rangle$ *iff[1] there are no arguments* $a, b \in S$, *s.t.[2]* $a\mathbf{R}b$.
- $a \in \mathbf{A}$ *is* acceptable *in* $\langle \mathbf{A}, \mathbf{R} \rangle$ *wrt[3]* S *iff* $\forall b \in \mathbf{A}$ *s.t.* $b\mathbf{R}a$, $\exists c \in S$ *s.t.* $c\mathbf{R}b$.
- S *is* admissible *in* $\langle \mathbf{A}, \mathbf{R} \rangle$ *iff* S *is conflict-free and each argument in* S *is acceptable wrt* S.

Standard semantics introduced by Dung (preferred, stable, grounded) enable to characterize admissible sets of arguments that satisfy some form of optimality.

Definition 3 (Extensions). *Given* $\langle \mathbf{A}, \mathbf{R} \rangle$ *and* $S \subseteq \mathbf{A}$.

- S *is a* preferred extension *of* $\langle \mathbf{A}, \mathbf{R} \rangle$ *iff it is a maximal (wrt* $\subseteq$*) admissible set.*
- S *is a* stable extension *of* $\langle \mathbf{A}, \mathbf{R} \rangle$ *iff it is conflict-free and for each* $a \notin S$, *there is* $b \in S$ *s.t.* $b\mathbf{R}a$.
- S *is* the grounded extension *of* $\langle \mathbf{A}, \mathbf{R} \rangle$ *iff it is the least (wrt* $\subseteq$*) admissible set* X *s.t. each argument acceptable wrt* X *belongs to* X.

Example 1. *Let* AS *be defined by* $\mathbf{A} = \{a, b, c, d, e\}$ *and* $\mathbf{R} = \{(a, b), (b, a), (b, c), (c, d), (d, e), (e, c)\}$. *There are two preferred extensions (*$\{a\}$ *and* $\{b, d\}$*), one stable extension (*$\{b, d\}$*) and the grounded extension is the empty set.*

2.2   Abstract Bipolar Argumentation Systems

The abstract bipolar argumentation framework presented in [8,9] extends Dung's framework in order to take into account both negative interactions expressed by the attack relation and positive interactions expressed by a support relation (see [3] for a more general survey about bipolarity in argumentation).

Definition 4 (BAS). *A bipolar argumentation system (BAS, for short) is a tuple* $\langle \mathbf{A}, \mathbf{R}_{att}, \mathbf{R}_{sup} \rangle$ *where*

- $\mathbf{A}$ *is a finite and non-empty set of arguments,*
- $\mathbf{R}_{att}$ *is a binary relation over* $\mathbf{A}$ *called the* attack *relation and*
- $\mathbf{R}_{sup}$ *is a binary relation over* $\mathbf{A}$ *called the* support *relation.*

---

[1] if and only if.
[2] such that.
[3] with respect to.

A BAS can still be represented by a directed graph[4], called the *bipolar interaction graph*, with two kinds of edges. Let a_i and $a_j \in \mathbf{A}$, $a_i\mathbf{R}_{att}a_j$ (resp. $a_i\mathbf{R}_{sup}a_j$) means that a_i attacks a_j (resp. a_i supports a_j) and it is represented by $a \nrightarrow b$ (resp. $a \rightarrow b$).

Handling support and attack at an abstract level has the advantage to keep genericity. An abstract bipolar framework is useful as an analytic tool for studying different notions of complex attacks, complex conflicts, and new semantics taking into account both kinds of interactions between arguments. However, the drawback is the lack of guidelines for choosing the appropriate definitions and semantics depending on the application. For solving this problem, some specializations of the support relation have been proposed and discussed recently. The distinction between deductive and necessary support has appeared first. Then, several interpretations have been given to the necessary support (sub-argument relation [26], evidential support [23–25], backing support [13]).

Deductive Support. The deductive support has first appeared in [5]. This variant is intended to enforce the following constraint: If $b\mathbf{R}_{sup}c$ then "the acceptance of b implies the acceptance of c", and as a consequence "the non-acceptance of c implies the non-acceptance of b".

In relevant literature, this interpretation is usually taken into account by adding two kinds of complex attack. The idea is to produce a new AS, containing original and new attacks, and then to use standard semantics.

The first new attack, called mediated attack in [5], occurs when $b\mathbf{R}_{sup}c$ and $a\mathbf{R}_{att}c$: "the acceptance of a implies the non-acceptance of c" and so "the acceptance of a implies the non-acceptance of b".

Definition 5 ([5] Mediated Attack). *Let* BAS $= \langle \mathbf{A}, \mathbf{R}_{att}, \mathbf{R}_{sup}\rangle$. *There is a mediated attack from a to b iff there is a sequence* $a_1\mathbf{R}_{sup}\ldots\mathbf{R}_{sup}a_{n-1}$, *and* $a_n\mathbf{R}_{att}a_{n-1}, n \geq 3$, *with* $a_1 = b$, $a_n = a$.

Another complex attack, called supported attack in [9] occurs when $a\mathbf{R}_{sup}c$ and $c\mathbf{R}_{att}b$: "the acceptance of a implies the acceptance of c" and "the acceptance of c implies the non-acceptance of b"; so, "the acceptance of a implies the non-acceptance of b".

Definition 6 ([9] Supported Attack). *Let* BAS $= \langle \mathbf{A}, \mathbf{R}_{att}, \mathbf{R}_{sup}\rangle$. *There is a supported attack from a to b iff there is a sequence* $a_1\mathbf{R}_{sup}\ldots\mathbf{R}_{sup}a_{n-1}$ *and* $a_{n-1}\mathbf{R}_{att}a_n, n \geq 3$, *with* $a_1 = a, a_n = b$.

So, with the deductive interpretation of the support, new kinds of attack, from a to b, can be considered in the following cases:

Supported attacks: Mediated attacks:

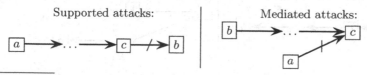

---

[4] This is an abuse of language since, strictly speaking, this is an edge-labeled graph (with two labels) rather than a directed graph.

Necessary Support. The necessary support has been first proposed by [21,22] with the following interpretation (issued from logic programming): If $c\mathbf{R}_{sup}b$ then "the acceptance of c is necessary to get the acceptance of b", or equivalently "the acceptance of b implies the acceptance of c". A example of this kind of support could be:

Example 2. *A dialog between three customers about the qualities of services of their hotel:*

- *"This hotel is very well managed." (Argument a)*
- *"Yes. In particular, the hotel staff is very competent." (Argument b)*
- *"They are not competent! The rooms are dirty." (Argument c)*

Here b necessarily supports a and c attacks b ($c \nrightarrow b \rightarrow a$). The link between b and a is similar to the notion of subargument used in [26]; this is another justification for necessary support.

As for deductive support, the idea is to add complex attacks in order to use standard semantics on a new AS. The first added complex attack, called extended attack in [21] and secondary attack in [9] has been proposed in the following case: Suppose that $a\mathbf{R}_{att}c$ and $c\mathbf{R}_{sup}b$. "The acceptance of a implies the non-acceptance of c" and so "the acceptance of a implies the non-acceptance of b". Another kind of complex attack may be considered when $c\mathbf{R}_{sup}a$ and $c\mathbf{R}_{att}b$: "the acceptance of a implies the acceptance of c" and "the acceptance of c implies the non-acceptance of b". So, "the acceptance of a implies the non-acceptance of b". This new attack from a to b has been proposed in [22].
    The formal definition of these two attacks is:

Definition 7 ([22] **Extended Attack**). *Let* BAS $= \langle \mathbf{A}, \mathbf{R}_{att}, \mathbf{R}_{sup} \rangle$. *There is an* extended attack *from a to b iff*

- *either $a\mathbf{R}_{att}b$ (direct attack),*
- *or there is a sequence $a_1\mathbf{R}_{att}a_2\mathbf{R}_{sup}\ldots\mathbf{R}_{sup}a_n, n \geq 3$, with $a_1 = a, a_n = b$ (Case 1),*
- *or there is a sequence $a_1\mathbf{R}_{sup}\ldots\mathbf{R}_{sup}a_n$, and $a_1\mathbf{R}_{att}a_p, n \geq 2$, with $a_n = a, a_p = b$ (Case 2).*

So, with the necessary interpretation of the support, new kinds of attack, from a to b, can be considered in the following cases:

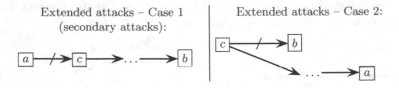

Extended attacks – Case 1
(secondary attacks):

Extended attacks – Case 2:

Duality Between Deductive and Necessary Support. Deductive support and necessary support have been introduced independently. Nevertheless, they correspond to dual interpretations of the notion of support. Let us denote $a \xrightarrow{D} b$ (resp. $a \xrightarrow{N} b$) when there exists a deductive (resp. necessary) support from a to b. As $a \xrightarrow{D} b$ means that "the acceptance of a implies the acceptance of b", and $a \xrightarrow{N} b$ means that "the acceptance of a is necessary to get the acceptance of b", it follows that $a \xrightarrow{N} b$ is equivalent to $b \xrightarrow{D} a$.

Following this duality, it is easy to see that the mediated attack obtained by combining the attack relation $\mathbf{R}_{\mathrm{att}}$ and the support relation $\mathbf{R}_{\mathrm{sup}}$ exactly corresponds to the secondary attack obtained by combining the attack relation $\mathbf{R}_{\mathrm{att}}$ and the support relation $\mathbf{R}_{\mathrm{sup}}^{-1}$ which is the symmetric relation of $\mathbf{R}_{\mathrm{sup}}$ ($\mathbf{R}_{\mathrm{sup}}^{-1} = \{(b,a)|(a,b) \in \mathbf{R}_{\mathrm{sup}}\}$). Similarly, the supported attack obtained by combining the attack relation $\mathbf{R}_{\mathrm{att}}$ and the support relation $\mathbf{R}_{\mathrm{sup}}$ exactly corresponds to the second case of extended attack obtained by combining the attack relation $\mathbf{R}_{\mathrm{att}}$ and the support relation $\mathbf{R}_{\mathrm{sup}}^{-1}$.

So in the following, we only focus on the necessary support since, taking advantage of the duality, all the results we obtain can be easily translated into results for deductive supports.

3 Axiomatic Approach for Handling Necessary Support

In relevant literature, as described in the previous section, taking into account support generally leads to add new attacks. It is the case for instance with the necessary support that leads to extended attacks. This approach has the main advantage to produce a Dung AF, and so it is useless to redefine basic notions such as conflict-freeness nor the semantics. However, a deeper analysis of the original interpretation of necessary support suggests other ways to handle this support. These other ways propose a richer reading of the notion of support; as a counterpart, new types of argumentation system must be defined. In this section, we discuss several constraints induced by the intended meaning of necessary support, and we show that new frameworks must be proposed for encoding these constraints.

Let us come back to the original interpretation of necessary support: If $c\mathbf{R}_{\mathrm{sup}}b$, "the acceptance of c is necessary to get the acceptance of b". Analysing this interpretation leads to at least four kinds of constraints.

Transitivity (TRA). This first requirement concerns the relation $\mathbf{R}_{\mathrm{sup}}$ alone. It expresses transitivity[5] of the necessary support. This is justified by the fact that "a supports b that supports c" is interpreted as "the acceptance of c implies the acceptance of b that implies the acceptance of a", and so "the acceptance of c implies the acceptance of a". For instance, this interpretation obviously holds when the support models the notion of subargument as in [26]. It induces that a sequence of supports can be considered as a support:

---

[5] Irreflexivity has also been considered for instance in [21,22].

Definition 8 (Constraint TRA). $\forall a, b \in \mathbf{A}$, *if* $\exists n > 1$ *such that* $a = a_1 \mathbf{R}_{\mathrm{sup}} \ldots \mathbf{R}_{\mathrm{sup}} a_n = b$, *then* a supports b.

Closure (CLO). A second constraint also concerns the relation $\mathbf{R}_{\mathrm{sup}}$ alone and expresses the fact that if $c\mathbf{R}_{\mathrm{sup}}b$, then "the acceptance of b implies the acceptance of c". So, if $c\mathbf{R}_{\mathrm{sup}}b$, and there exists an extension S containing b, then S also contains c. This constraint can be expressed by the property of closure of an extension under $\mathbf{R}_{\mathrm{sup}}^{-1}$.[6]

Definition 9 (Constraint CLO). *Let s be a semantics and E be an extension under s.* $\forall a, b \in \mathbf{A}$, *if* $a\mathbf{R}_{\mathrm{sup}}b$ *and* $b \in E$, *then* $a \in E$.

Moreover, an interesting variant of this constraint could be induced by a slightly different reading of the original interpretation: "the acceptance of c is necessary to get the acceptance of b" because c *is the only attacker of a particular attacker of b*. This reading implies that there implicitly exists a special attack to b which can be only defeated by c. This interpretation will lead us to propose a framework with meta-arguments (see Sect. 4.2).

Conflicting Sets (CFS). Now, we consider constraints induced by the presence of both attacks and supports in a BAS. Starting from the original interpretation, if $a\mathbf{R}_{\mathrm{att}}c$ and $c\mathbf{R}_{\mathrm{sup}}b$, "the acceptance of a implies the non-acceptance of c" and "the acceptance of b implies the acceptance of c". So, using contrapositives, "the acceptance of a implies the non-acceptance of b", and then "the acceptance of b implies the non-acceptance of a". Thus, we obtain a symmetric constraint involving a and b. However, the fact that "the acceptance of a implies the non-acceptance of b" is not equivalent to the fact that there is an attack from a to b. We have only the sufficient condition. So, the creation of a complex attack (here a secondary attack) from a to b can be viewed in some sense too strong. Hence, faced with the case when $a\mathbf{R}_{\mathrm{att}}c$ and $c\mathbf{R}_{\mathrm{sup}}b$, we propose to assert a conflict between a and b, or in other words that the set $\{a, b\}$ is a conflicting set. Similarly, if $c\mathbf{R}_{\mathrm{att}}b$ and $c\mathbf{R}_{\mathrm{sup}}a$, "the acceptance of a implies the acceptance of c" and so "the acceptance of a implies the non-acceptance of b".

Definition 10 (Constraint CFS). $\forall a, b, c \in \mathbf{A}$. *If ($a\mathbf{R}_{\mathrm{att}}c$ and c supports b) or ($c\mathbf{R}_{\mathrm{att}}b$ and c supports a) then $\{a, b\}$ is a conflicting set.*

Note that the Dung's abstract framework is not suitable for expressing such a constraint. So we will present in Sect. 4.1 a new framework for handling conflicting sets of arguments.

Addition of New Attacks (nATT, n+ATT). According to the applications and the previous works presented in literature, we may impose stronger constraints corresponding to the addition of new attacks. Two cases may be considered:

---

[6] Note that if $c\mathbf{R}_{\mathrm{sup}}b$ and $c\mathbf{R}_{\mathrm{att}}b$, as an extension must be conflict-free, there is no extension containing both c and b, so the constraint trivially holds. Some works, as for instance [10], exclude the case when $c\mathbf{R}_{\mathrm{sup}}b$ and $c\mathbf{R}_{\mathrm{att}}b$.

Definition 11 (Constraint nATT). *If $a\mathbf{R}_{att}c$ and $c\mathbf{R}_{sup}b$, then there is a new attack from a to b.*

Definition 12 (Constraint n+ATT). *If $(a\mathbf{R}_{att}c$ and $c\mathbf{R}_{sup}b)$ or $(c\mathbf{R}_{att}b$ and $c\mathbf{R}_{sup}a)$, then there is a new attack from a to b.*

nATT (resp. **n+ATT**) corresponds to the addition of secondary (resp. extended) attacks. In Sect. 4.3 we present two frameworks for handling these constraints.

Continuing the discussion one step further, if the fact that "the acceptance of a implies the non-acceptance of b" is represented by an attack from a to b, due to contrapositive, this new attack must be symmetric. However, in that case, each attack should be turned into a symmetric one. Thus, we move towards symmetric argumentation frameworks which have been studied in [14]. We will not consider this case in the current paper. Some of the above constraints can be handled in a Dung's abstract framework (**CLO**, **TRA**, **nATT** and **n+ATT**) with the advantage of reusing all known Dung's results. However, as we noticed above, constraint **CFS** cannot be encoded in a Dung's framework. So in the next section we propose different variants of Dung's framework and of the bipolar framework in order to take into account these constraints.

4 New Frameworks for Handling Necessary Supports

Starting from the constraints discussed in Sect. 3, we propose several frameworks for handling necessary support. The first two are driven by Constraint **CLO** whereas the last two are driven by the constraints **nATT** and **n+ATT**. The section will end by a comparison of these frameworks.

4.1 Handling Conflicting Sets of Arguments

We propose a generalized bipolar abstract argumentation framework consisting of a set of arguments, a binary relation representing an attack between arguments, a binary relation representing a support between arguments and a set of conflicting sets of arguments. Intuitively, knowing that a attacks b is stronger than knowing that $\{a, b\}$ is a conflicting set of arguments. Knowing that a set of arguments S is conflicting will only prevent any extension from containing S. Moreover, a conflicting set may contain more than two arguments.

Definition 13 (Generalized BAS, GBAS). *A generalized bipolar argumentation system is a tuple $\langle \mathbf{A}, \mathbf{R}_{att}, \mathbf{R}_{sup}, \mathbf{C} \rangle$ where*

- $\mathbf{A}$ *is a finite and non-empty set of arguments,*
- $\mathbf{R}_{att}$ *is a binary relation over $\mathbf{A}$ called the attack relation,*
- $\mathbf{R}_{sup}$ *is a binary relation over $\mathbf{A}$ called the support relation and*
- $\mathbf{C}$ *is a finite set of subsets of $\mathbf{A}$ such that $\forall (a, b) \in \mathbf{R}_{att}, \{a, b\} \in \mathbf{C}$.*

Conflict-freeness in a generalized bipolar argumentation system is defined as follows:

Definition 14 (Conflict-freeness in a GBAS). *Let* $\langle \mathbf{A}, \mathbf{R}_{\mathrm{att}}, \mathbf{R}_{\mathrm{sup}}, \mathbf{C} \rangle$ *be a GBAS and* $S \subseteq \mathbf{A}$. *S is conflict-free in the GBAS iff there does not exist* $C \in \mathbf{C}$ *such that* $C \subseteq S$.

However, the definition of semantics depends on the interpretation of the support and also on the constraints that have to be enforced. The generalized bipolar framework can be instantiated for encoding necessary support, due to the following definition:

Definition 15 (The GBAS Associated with a BAS). *Let* BAS $=$ $\langle \mathbf{A}, \mathbf{R}_{\mathrm{att}}, \mathbf{R}_{\mathrm{sup}} \rangle$ *with* $\mathbf{R}_{\mathrm{sup}}$ *being a set of necessary supports. The tuple* GBAS $=$ $\langle \mathbf{A}, \mathbf{R}_{\mathrm{att}}, \mathbf{R}_{\mathrm{sup}}, \mathbf{C} \rangle$ *with*

$$
\begin{aligned}
\mathbf{C} = \ & \{\{a,b\} | (a,b) \in \mathbf{R}_{\mathrm{att}}\} \\
& \cup \{\{a,b\} | a\mathbf{R}_{\mathrm{att}}c \text{ and } c \text{ supports } b\} \\
& \cup \{\{a,b\} | c\mathbf{R}_{\mathrm{att}}b \text{ and } c \text{ supports } a\}
\end{aligned}
$$

is the generalized argumentation system associated with BAS.

It is easy to see that the generalized argumentation system associated with BAS enables to enforce the constraints **TRA** and **CFS**, whereas it satisfies neither Constraint **nATT**, nor Constraint **n+ATT**.

The next step is the study of acceptability in a GBAS in order to check whether Contraint **CLO** is taken into account. For that purpose, the first proposal is to use conflict-freeness as defined in Definition 14 and admissible, preferred and stable extensions as defined in Dung's systems. In this case, it can be proved that every stable extension is closed under $\mathbf{R}_{\mathrm{sup}}^{-1}$.

Proposition 1. *Let* BAS $=$ $\langle \mathbf{A}, \mathbf{R}_{\mathrm{att}}, \mathbf{R}_{\mathrm{sup}} \rangle$ *and its associated* GBAS. *Let* $S \subseteq \mathbf{A}$. *If S is conflict-free in* GBAS, *and for each* $a \notin S$, *there is* $b \in S$ *s.t.* $b\mathbf{R}_{\mathrm{att}}a$, *then S is closed under* $\mathbf{R}_{\mathrm{sup}}^{-1}$.

However, this approach produces many conflicts, without adding any attacks. So in many cases, there will be no stable extension. Moreover, Constraint **CLO** is generally not satisfied with the preferred semantics. The following example illustrates these two drawbacks.

Example 3. *Consider* BAS *represented by the following graph.*

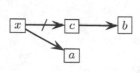

$\mathbf{C} = \{\{x,c\}, \{x,b\}, \{a,c\}\}$. *Using the classical definition of semantics with conflict-freeness as defined in Definition 14, the preferred extensions of the associated* GBAS *are* $\{a,x\}$ *and* $\{a,b\}$, *and there is no stable extension. Moreover, the preferred extension* $\{a,b\}$ *is not closed under* $\mathbf{R}_{\mathrm{sup}}^{-1}$.

The preferred semantics has to be redefined in order to enforce Constraint **CLO**. So, our second proposal is to enforce a notion of coherence by combining conflict-freeness and closure under $\mathbf{R}_{\mathrm{sup}}^{-1}$. Moreover it can be proven that:

Proposition 2. *Let $\langle \mathbf{A}, \mathbf{R}_{\mathrm{att}}, \mathbf{R}_{\mathrm{sup}} \rangle$ and its associated GBAS. Let $S \subseteq \mathbf{A}$. If S is closed under $\mathbf{R}_{\mathrm{sup}}^{-1}$ then (S is conflict-free in GBAS iff S is conflict-free in $\langle \mathbf{A}, \mathbf{R}_{\mathrm{att}} \rangle$).*

Definition 16 (Coherence in a GBAS). *Let $\langle \mathbf{A}, \mathbf{R}_{\mathrm{att}}, \mathbf{R}_{\mathrm{sup}}, \mathbf{C} \rangle$ be a GBAS and $S \subseteq \mathbf{A}$. S is coherent in the GBAS iff S is conflict-free in $\langle \mathbf{A}, \mathbf{R}_{\mathrm{att}} \rangle$ and S is closed under $\mathbf{R}_{\mathrm{sup}}^{-1}$.*

Using coherence in place of conflict-freeness leads to new definitions:

Definition 17 (Admissibility in a GBAS). *Let $\langle \mathbf{A}, \mathbf{R}_{\mathrm{att}}, \mathbf{R}_{\mathrm{sup}}, \mathbf{C} \rangle$ be a GBAS and $S \subseteq \mathbf{A}$.*

- *S is admissible in the GBAS iff S is coherent in the GBAS and $\forall a \in S$, $\forall b \in \mathbf{A}$ s.t. $b\mathbf{R}_{\mathrm{att}}a$, $\exists c \in S$ s.t. $c\mathbf{R}_{\mathrm{att}}b$.*
- *S is a preferred extension of the GBAS iff it is a maximal (wrt $\subseteq$) admissible set.*
- *S is a stable extension of the GBAS iff S is coherent[7] in the GBAS and for each $a \not\subseteq S$, there is $b \in S$ s.t. $b\mathbf{R}_{\mathrm{att}}a$.*

Example 3 (cont'd). *Taking into account coherence, as in Definition 17, $\{a, x\}$ is the unique preferred extension of the associated GBAS, and it is closed under $\mathbf{R}_{\mathrm{sup}}^{-1}$.*

So, using Definitions 17 and 16, the associated GBAS enables to enforce Constraint **CLO**.[8] Moreover, as in Dung's framework, stable extensions are also preferred.

Proposition 3. *Let $\langle \mathbf{A}, \mathbf{R}_{\mathrm{att}}, \mathbf{R}_{\mathrm{sup}}, \mathbf{C} \rangle$ be a GBAS and $S \subseteq \mathbf{A}$. If S is a stable extension of the GBAS then S is also a preferred extension of the GBAS.*

A thorough study of the generalized bipolar abstract argumentation framework would demand to define other semantics such as grounded one. However, this is not our purpose in this paper. We focus on the way to enforce different kinds of constraints related to necessary support.

4.2 A Meta-Framework Encoding Necessary Support

The fact that "the acceptance of c is necessary to get the acceptance of b" can be encoded in another way. As explained in Sect. 3, the idea is to assume the existence of a special argument attacking b for which c is the *only* attacker. More precisely, if $c\mathbf{R}_{\mathrm{sup}}b$, we create a new argument N_{cb} and two attacks $c\mathbf{R}_{\mathrm{att}}N_{cb}$ and

---

[7] Due to Proposition 1, coherent may be replaced by conflict-free.

[8] Note that enforcing coherence makes the set C useless due to Proposition 2.

$N_{cb}\mathbf{R}_{att}b$. As c is the unique attacker of N_{cb}, "the acceptance of b implies the acceptance of c". The meaning of N_{cb} could be that the support from c to b is not active. A similar idea can be found in [12,28] for the more general purpose of representing recursive and defeasible attacks and supports.

Definition 18 (The MAS Associated with a BAS). *Let* BAS $= \langle \mathbf{A}, \mathbf{R}_{att},$ $\mathbf{R}_{sup} \rangle$ *with* $\mathbf{R}_{sup}$ *being a set of necessary supports. Let* $\mathbf{A}_n = \{ N_{cb} | (c, b) \in \mathbf{R}_{sup} \}$ *and* $\mathbf{R}_n = \{ (c, N_{cb}) | (c, b) \in \mathbf{R}_{sup} \} \cup \{ (N_{cb}, b) | (c, b) \in \mathbf{R}_{sup} \}$. *The tuple* MAS $=$ $\langle \mathbf{A} \cup \mathbf{A}_n, \mathbf{R}_{att} \cup \mathbf{R}_n \rangle$ *is the meta-argumentation system* [9] *associated with* BAS.

Let us check whether the minimal requirements are satisfied. Let us first consider constraint **TRA**. From $a\mathbf{R}_{sup}b$ and $b\mathbf{R}_{sup}c$, we obtain the sequence of attacks $a\mathbf{R}_{att}N_{ab}\mathbf{R}_{att}b\mathbf{R}_{att}N_{bc}\mathbf{R}_{att}c$. So, the acceptance of c implies the acceptance of b, which in turn implies the acceptance of a, as if we had directly encoded $a\mathbf{R}_{sup}c$. So, **TRA** is taken into account. The same result holds for **CLO**:

Proposition 4. *Let* BAS $= \langle \mathbf{A}, \mathbf{R}_{att}, \mathbf{R}_{sup} \rangle$ *and its associated* MAS. *Let* $S \subseteq$ $\mathbf{A} \cup \mathbf{A}_n$. *If* S *is admissible in* MAS, *then* $S \cap \mathbf{A}$ *is closed under* $\mathbf{R}_{sup}^{-1}$ *in* BAS.

Constraint **CFS** is not enforced. We only have the following property:

Proposition 5. *Let* BAS $= \langle \mathbf{A}, \mathbf{R}_{att}, \mathbf{R}_{sup} \rangle$ *and its associated* MAS. *Let* a, b, c *be arguments of* $\mathbf{A}$. *If* $(a\mathbf{R}_{att}c$ *and* c supports $b)$ *or* $(c\mathbf{R}_{att}b$ *and* c supports $a)$ *then no admissible set in* MAS *contains* $\{a, b\}$.

Note that this result is weaker than **CFS** since it does not imply that $\{a, b\}$ is a conflicting set.

Obviously, stronger constraints such as **nATT** or **n+ATT** are not directly enforced. If $a\mathbf{R}_{att}c$ and $c\mathbf{R}_{sup}b$, we obtain the sequence $a\mathbf{R}_{att}c\mathbf{R}_{att}N_{cb}\mathbf{R}_{att}b$. No attack from a to b is added. However, we will see in Sect. 4.4 that the meta-argumentation framework associated with BAS enables to recover the extensions obtained when enforcing Constraint **nATT**.

4.3   A Framework with Complex Attacks

In this subsection we discuss two frameworks enabling to handle necessary support through the addition of complex attacks. According to the various interpretations of the necessary support, all the complex attacks are not justified. For instance, if the necessary support models a subargument relation as in [26], only the secondary attack makes sense. Other works [22] have considered both cases of extended attack. However, to the best of our knowledge, there has been no formal study of the properties of these extended attacks, and of the consequences of these attacks on the acceptable sets of arguments.

From Definition 7, new attacks called n+-attacks can be generated inductively as follows:

---

[9] Note that it is an argumentation system in dung's sense.

Definition 19 (n+-attacks). *Let* BAS $= \langle \mathbf{A}, \mathbf{R}_{att}, \mathbf{R}_{sup} \rangle$ *with* $\mathbf{R}_{sup}$ *being a set of necessary supports. There exists a* **n+-attack** *from a to b iff*

- *either* $a\mathbf{R}_{att}b$, *or there is a (case 1 or case 2) extended attack from a to b,*
- *or there exists an argument c s.t. a* **n+-attacks** *c and c* supports *b,*
- *or there exists an argument c s.t. c* supports *a and c* **n+-attacks** *b.*

$\mathbf{N}+_{\mathbf{R}_{att}}^{\mathbf{R}_{sup}}$ *denoted the set of* **n+-attacks** *generated by* $\mathbf{R}_{sup}$ *on* $\mathbf{R}_{att}$. *The AS defined by* $\langle \mathbf{A}, \mathbf{N}+_{\mathbf{R}_{att}}^{\mathbf{R}_{sup}} \rangle$ *is denoted by* AS^{N^+}.

Obviously Constraints **TRA**, **nATT** and **n+ATT** are enforced in AS^{N^+}.

Let us now consider the case when the extended attacks are restricted to secondary attacks (Case 1 of extended attacks). Following the above definition, our purpose is to define a **n-attack** from a to b when either $a\mathbf{R}_{att}b$, or there exists a secondary attack from a to b, or there exists an argument c s.t. a **n-attacks** c and c supports b. Indeed, it is easy to prove that the formal definition of this **n-attack** can be simplified as follows:

**Definition 20
(n-attacks).** *Let* BAS $= \langle \mathbf{A}, \mathbf{R}_{att}, \mathbf{R}_{sup} \rangle$. *There is a* **n-attack** *from a to b iff*

- *either* $a\mathbf{R}_{att}b$,
- *or there is a secondary attack from a to b.*

$\mathbf{N}_{\mathbf{R}_{att}}^{\mathbf{R}_{sup}}$ *denoted the set of* **n-attacks** *generated by* $\mathbf{R}_{sup}$ *on* $\mathbf{R}_{att}$. *The AS defined by* $\langle \mathbf{A}, \mathbf{N}_{\mathbf{R}_{att}}^{\mathbf{R}_{sup}} \rangle$ *is denoted by* AS^N.

Note that both AS^N and AS^{N^+} are Dung's argumentation systems; so the classical notions given in Definitions 2 and 3 can be applied without restriction, nor redefinition.

Obviously Constraints **TRA** and **nATT** are enforced in AS^N, whereas Constraint **n+ATT** is not.

Definition 19 looks complex. However the following proposition enables to rewrite **n+-attacks** and **n-attacks** in a form which will be much easier to handle for studying their properties.

Proposition 6. *Let* BAS $= \langle \mathbf{A}, \mathbf{R}_{att}, \mathbf{R}_{sup} \rangle$. *There is an* **n+-attack** *from a to b iff there is a sequence* $a_1\mathbf{R}_{att}b_1\mathbf{R}_{sup}\ldots\mathbf{R}_{sup}b_m$, *with* $b_m = b$ *and* $m \geq 1$, *and a sequence* $a_1\mathbf{R}_{sup}\ldots\mathbf{R}_{sup}a_n$ *with* $a_n = a$ *and* $n \geq 1$.

n+-attacks as defined by Proposition 6 can be illustrated by the following figure:

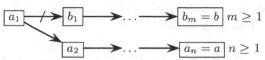

Moreover, Proposition 6 can be used for identifying the following particular cases:

- The case when $m = n = 1$ corresponds to a direct attack from a to b.
- The case when $n = 1$ and $m \geq 1$ corresponds to a n-attack from a to b (direct or secondary attacks, see Definition 20).
- The case when $n = 1$ and $m > 1$ corresponds to an extended attack - Case 1 (secondary attack) from a to b (see Definition 7).
- The case when $n > 1$ and $m = 1$ corresponds to an extended attack - Case 2 from a to b (see Definition 7).

An obvious consequence of this proposition is:

Corollary 1. *Let* $\mathsf{BAS} = \langle \mathbf{A}, \mathbf{R}_{\mathrm{att}}, \mathbf{R}_{\mathrm{sup}} \rangle$ *and its associated* AS^N *and* AS^{N^+}. *Let* $S \subseteq \mathbf{A}$. *If* S *is conflict-free in* AS^{N^+}, *then* S *is conflict-free in* AS^N.

As said above, in some works necessary support can be handled by only considering n-attacks, that is by adding secondary attacks. However, although both cases of extended attacks are independent, we show that taking into account only n-attacks is already enough for inducing constraints on AS^{N^+}.

Proposition 7. *Let* $\mathsf{BAS} = \langle \mathbf{A}, \mathbf{R}_{\mathrm{att}}, \mathbf{R}_{\mathrm{sup}} \rangle$ *and its associated* AS^N. *If a* n+-attack *from* a *to* b *can be built from* BAS, *there exists no admissible set in* AS^N *containing* $\{a, b\}$.

As an immediate consequence (contrapositive of Proposition 7), we have:

Corollary 2. *Let* $\mathsf{BAS} = \langle \mathbf{A}, \mathbf{R}_{\mathrm{att}}, \mathbf{R}_{\mathrm{sup}} \rangle$ *and the associated* AS^N *and* AS^{N^+}. *Let* $S \subseteq \mathbf{A}$. *If* S *is admissible in* AS^N, *then* S *is conflict-free in* AS^{N^+}.

Example 4. *Consider* BAS *represented by the following graph:*

The associated AS^N *only contains the original attack from* c *to* b *(there is no secondary attack). If we consider only* n-attacks, *there is no conflict between* a *and* b. *However, it can be proved that no admissible set in* AS^N *contains* $\{a, b\}$.

The following results establish links between extensions in AS^N and AS^{N^+}.

Proposition 8. *Let* $\mathsf{BAS} = \langle \mathbf{A}, \mathbf{R}_{\mathrm{att}}, \mathbf{R}_{\mathrm{sup}} \rangle$ *and the associated* AS^N *and* AS^{N^+}. *Let* $S \subseteq \mathbf{A}$. *If* S *is admissible in* AS^N, *then* S *is also admissible in* AS^{N^+}.

The converse of Proposition 8 generally does not hold as shown by the following example.

Example 5. *Consider* BAS *and its associated* AS^N *and* AS^{N^+} *represented by the following graphs:*

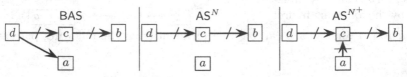

The set $\{a, b\}$ is admissible in AS^{N^+} but is not admissible in AS^N (since a does not attack c in AS^N).

However, the converse of Proposition 8 holds for maximal admissible sets:

Proposition 9. Let $\mathsf{BAS} = \langle \mathbf{A}, \mathbf{R}_{\mathrm{att}}, \mathbf{R}_{\mathrm{sup}} \rangle$ and its associated AS^N and AS^{N^+}. Let $S \subseteq \mathbf{A}$. S is maximal admissible in AS^{N^+} iff S is maximal admissible in AS^N.

The same holds for stable semantics:

Proposition 10. Let $\mathsf{BAS} = \langle \mathbf{A}, \mathbf{R}_{\mathrm{att}}, \mathbf{R}_{\mathrm{sup}} \rangle$ and its associated AS^N and AS^{N^+}. Let $S \subseteq \mathbf{A}$. S is stable in AS^{N^+} iff S is stable in AS^N.

We conclude this section by providing results about the property of closure under the relation $\mathbf{R}_{\mathrm{sup}}^{-1}$.

Proposition 11. Let $\mathsf{BAS} = \langle \mathbf{A}, \mathbf{R}_{\mathrm{att}}, \mathbf{R}_{\mathrm{sup}} \rangle$ and its associated AS^{N^+}. Let $S \subseteq \mathbf{A}$ and $a, b \in \mathbf{A}$.

- If S is conflict-free in AS^{N^+}, $a \in S$ and $b\mathbf{R}_{\mathrm{sup}}a$, then $S \cup \{b\}$ is conflict-free in AS^{N^+}.
- If S is maximal (wrt $\subseteq$) conflict-free in AS^{N^+}, then S is closed for the relation $\mathbf{R}_{\mathrm{sup}}^{-1}$.

Proposition 11 does not hold when considering AS^N instead of AS^{N^+}, as shown by the following example.

Example 4 (cont'd). $S = \{a, b\}$ is maximal conflict-free in AS^N but it is not closed under $\mathbf{R}_{\mathrm{sup}}^{-1}$. We have $c\mathbf{R}_{\mathrm{sup}}a$ but $S \cup \{c\}$ is not conflict-free in AS^N.

However, the property of closure under $\mathbf{R}_{\mathrm{sup}}^{-1}$ is recovered in AS^N, if preferred (resp. stable) extensions are considered.

Proposition 12. Let $\mathsf{BAS} = \langle \mathbf{A}, \mathbf{R}_{\mathrm{att}}, \mathbf{R}_{\mathrm{sup}} \rangle$ and the associated AS^N and AS^{N^+}. Let $S \subseteq \mathbf{A}$.

- If S is a preferred extension in AS^N (resp. AS^{N^+}), then S is closed for the relation $\mathbf{R}_{\mathrm{sup}}^{-1}$.
- If S is stable in AS^N (resp. AS^{N^+}), then S is closed for the relation $\mathbf{R}_{\mathrm{sup}}^{-1}$.

Due to Proposition 12, each stable (resp. preferred) extension of AS^N (resp. AS^{N^+}) is closed under $\mathbf{R}_{\mathrm{sup}}^{-1}$. In that sense, Constraint **CLO** is enforced in AS^N (resp. AS^{N^+}).

It remains to consider Constraint **CFS**. This constraint is obviously satisfied by AS^{N^+} since a new attack is built for each conflict in the sense of **CFS**, whereas the Dung's argumentation system AS^N does not capture all the conflicts induced by **CFS**, as illustrated by the following example.

Example 3 (cont'd). *In the associated* AS^N, *there is one* **n-attacks** *from* x *to* c *and one from* x *to* b. $\{a, x\}$ *is the unique preferred extension of* AS^N. *It is also stable. Note that* $\{a, c\}$ *is conflict-free in* AS^N. *Nevertheless* $\{a, c\}$ *is a conflicting set in the sense of* **CFS**.

4.4   Comparison Between the Different Frameworks

In the previous sections, starting from a set of constraints, several frameworks (GBAS, MAS, AS^N and AS^{N^+}) have been proposed for handling necessary support. In this section, we compare these frameworks wrt two different points of view: the satisfaction of the constraints and the extensions that are produced.

First, the following table synthesizes the previous results:

	GBAS	MAS	AS^N	AS^{N^+}
TRA	X	X	X	X
CLO	X	X	X	X
CFS	X	–	–	X
nATT	–	–	X	X
n+ATT	–	–	–	X

X (resp. $-$) means that the corresponding property is (resp. not) satisfied in the corresponding framework.

Now, let us consider AS^N and GBAS. We know that AS^N does not satisfy **CFS** whereas GBAS does. However, due to Proposition 7, if S is a conflicting set of GBAS, it is conflicting in AS^{N^+} and then there is no admissible set of AS^N containing S. Moreover, it can be proved that each preferred extension of GBAS is (generally strictly) included in a preferred extension of AS^N. This is illustrated by the following example.

Example 6. *Consider* BAS *represented by:*

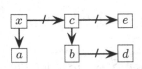

In the associated GBAS, *we have* $\mathbf{C} = \{\{x, c\}, \{x, b\}, \{c, e\}, \{b, d\}, \{a, c\}, \{b, e\}\}$. *The unique preferred extension of* GBAS *is* $\{a, x, e\}$. *In the associated* AS^N, *the* **n-attacks** *from* x *to* b *is used for ensuring the acceptability of* d *wrt* $\{a, x, e\}$. *So, the unique preferred extension is* $\{a, d, x, e\}$.

Proposition 13. *Let* BAS $= \langle \mathbf{A}, \mathbf{R}_{\text{att}}, \mathbf{R}_{\text{sup}} \rangle$ *and its associated* GBAS *and* AS^N. *Let* $S \subseteq \mathbf{A}$.

– *If* S *is admissible in* GBAS, *then* S *is also admissible in* AS^N.
– *If* S *is a preferred extension in* GBAS, *then* S *is included in a preferred extension of* AS^N.
– *If* S *is a stable extension in* GBAS, *then* S *is also a stable extension of* AS^N.

Note that Proposition 13 holds when considering AS^{N^+} instead of AS^N, due to Propositions 8, 9 and 10.

The next issue concerns the comparison between AS^N and the associated MAS of BAS. It seems that encoding a necessary support $c\mathbf{R}_{\mathrm{sup}}b$ by a meta-argument N_{cb} and the sequence $a\mathbf{R}_{\mathrm{att}}c\mathbf{R}_{\mathrm{att}}N_{cb}\mathbf{R}_{\mathrm{att}}b$ is less strong than encoding n-attacks. However, there is a correspondence between the extensions which are obtained in each framework.

Proposition 14. *Let* $\mathsf{BAS} = \langle \mathbf{A}, \mathbf{R}_{\mathrm{att}}, \mathbf{R}_{\mathrm{sup}} \rangle$ *and its associated* MAS *and* AS^N.

- *Let* $S \subseteq \mathbf{A} \cup \mathbf{A}_n$. *If* S *is admissible in* MAS, *then* $S \cap \mathbf{A}$ *is also admissible in* AS^N.
- *Let* $S \subseteq \mathbf{A} \cup \mathbf{A}_n$. *If* S *is stable in* MAS, *then* $S \cap \mathbf{A}$ *is also stable in* AS^N.
- *Let* $S \subseteq \mathbf{A}$. *If* S *is a preferred extension in* AS^N, *there exists* S' *admissible in* MAS *such that* $S = S' \cap \mathbf{A}$.
- *Let* $S \subseteq \mathbf{A}$. *If* S *is a stable extension in* AS^N, *then there exists* S' *stable in* MAS *such that* $S = S' \cap \mathbf{A}$.

From Propositions 13 and 14, the following comparison between GBAS and MAS can be easily established.

Proposition 15. *Let* $\mathsf{BAS} = \langle \mathbf{A}, \mathbf{R}_{\mathrm{att}}, \mathbf{R}_{\mathrm{sup}} \rangle$ *and its associated* MAS *and* GBAS. *Let* $S \subseteq \mathbf{A}$.

- *If* S *is a preferred extension of* GBAS, *then there exists* S' *preferred in* MAS *such that* $S \subseteq S' \cap \mathbf{A}$.
- *If* S *is a stable extension of* GBAS, *then there exists* S' *stable in* MAS *such that* $S = S' \cap \mathbf{A}$.

The following example illustrates the above propositions.

Example 6 (cont'd). *Consider the associated* MAS *represented by:*

In GBAS, *the unique preferred extension is the set* $\{a, x, e\}$ *(no stable extension in* GBAS). *In* AS^N, *the unique preferred (and also stable) extension is the set* $\{a, x, e, d\}$. *In* MAS, *the unique preferred (and also stable) extension is the set* $\{a, x, e, N_{cb}, d\}$.

5   Conclusion and Future Works

Recent studies in argumentation have addressed the notion of support, with several interpretations (such as deductive, evidential, necessary, backing) and several approaches developed independently. In this paper we focus on necessary support and show that the intended meaning of necessary support can induce different ways to handle it. Our main contribution is to propose an axiomatic approach that is helpful for understanding and comparing the different existing proposals for handling support. First, we have proposed different kinds of constraints that should be imposed to a bipolar argumentation system using necessary supports. Then we have studied different frameworks suitable for encoding these contraints.

This paper reports a preliminary work that could be pursued along different lines. First, our study must be deepened in order to give a more high-level analysis and comparison of all these frameworks. Then the axiomatic approach could be enriched by considering other constraints, such as for instance the strong requirement leading to the addition of symmetric attacks in the case of a necessary support. Moreover, it would be interesting to define such an axiomatic for other interpretations of support, or to consider other frameworks which do not explicitely define a notion of support, such as Abstract Dialectical Frameworks [6]. Another direction for further research would be to study how to encode necessary (or other variants) support by the addition of attacks of various strengths (see for instance [7,16,17,19]). Moreover it would be interesting to see the link between our approaches and the ranking semantics proposed by [1].

References

1. Amgoud, L., Ben-Naim, J.: Ranking-based semantics for argumentation frameworks. In: Liu, W., Subrahmanian, V.S., Wijsen, J. (eds.) SUM 2013. LNCS, vol. 8078, pp. 134–147. Springer, Heidelberg (2013)
2. Amgoud, L., Cayrol, C.: A reasoning model based on the production of acceptable arguments. Ann. Math. Artif. Intell. **34**, 197–216 (2002)
3. Amgoud, L., Cayrol, C., Lagasquie-Schiex, M.C., Livet, P.: On bipolarity in argumentation frameworks. Int. J. Intell. Syst. **23**, 1062–1093 (2008)
4. Amgoud, L., Maudet, N., Parsons, S.: Modelling dialogues using argumentation. In: Fourth International Conference on MultiAgent Systems (ICMAS 2000), Boston, MA, USA, pp. 31–38, July 2000
5. Boella, G., Gabbay, D.M., van der Torre, L., Villata, S.: Support in abstract argumentation. In: Proceeding of the 2010 Conference on Computational Models of Argument: Proceedings of COMMA 2010, pp. 111–122. IOS Press, Amsterdam (2010)
6. Brewka, G., Woltran, S.: Abstract dialectical frameworks. In: Proceedings of the 20th International Conference on the Principles of Knowledge Representation and Reasoning, pp. 102–111, Toronto, Canada (2010)
7. Cayrol, C., Devred, C., Lagasquie-Schiex, M.C.: Acceptability semantics accounting for strength of attacks in argumentation. In: Proceedings of European Conference in Artificial Intelligence (ECAI), pp. 995–996. IOS Press (2010)
8. Cayrol, C., Lagasquie-Schiex, M.C.: On the acceptability of arguments in bipolar argumentation frameworks. In: Godo, L. (ed.) ECSQARU 2005. LNCS (LNAI), vol. 3571, pp. 378–389. Springer, Heidelberg (2005)
9. Cayrol, C., Lagasquie-Schiex, M.C.: Coalitions of arguments: a tool for handling bipolar argumentation frameworks. Int. J. Intell. Syst. **25**, 83–109 (2010)
10. Cayrol, C., Lagasquie-Schiex, M.C.: Bipolarity in argumentation graphs: towards a better understanding. Int. J. Approximate Reasoning **54**(7), 876–899 (2013). http://dx.doi.org/10.1016/j.ijar.2013.03.001
11. Cayrol, C., Lagasquie-Schiex, M.C.: An axiomatic approach to support in argumentation. Technical Report RR-2015-04-FR, IRIT (2015). http://www.irit.fr/publis/ADRIA/PapersMCL/Rapport-IRIT-2015-04.pdf

12. Cohen, A., Gottifredi, S., García, A.J., Simari, G.R.: An approach to abstract argumentation with recursive attack and support. J. Appl. Logic **13**, 509–533 (2014)
13. Cohen, A., Gottifredi, S., García, A.J., Simari, G.R.: A survey of different approaches to support in argumentation systems. Knowl. Eng. Rev. **29**, 513–550 (2014). http://journals.cambridge.org/article_S0269888913000325
14. Coste-Marquis, S., Devred, C., Marquis, P.: Symmetric argumentation frameworks. In: Godo, L. (ed.) ECSQARU 2005. LNCS (LNAI), vol. 3571, pp. 317–328. Springer, Heidelberg (2005)
15. Dung, P.M.: On the acceptability of arguments and its fundamental role in non-monotonic reasoning, logic programming and n-person games. Artif. Intell. **77**, 321–357 (1995)
16. Dunne, P.E., Hunter, A., McBurney, P., Parsons, S., Wooldridge, M.: Weighted argument systems: Basic definitions, algorithms, and complexity results. Artif. Intell. **175**(2), 457–486 (2011)
17. Kaci, S., Labreuche, C.: Arguing with valued preference relations. In: Liu, W. (ed.) ECSQARU 2011. LNCS, vol. 6717, pp. 62–73. Springer, Heidelberg (2011)
18. Karacapilidis, N., Papadias, D.: Computer supported argumentation and collaborative decision making: the hermes system. Inf. Syst. **26**(4), 259–277 (2001)
19. Martinez, D.C., Garcia, A.J., Simari, G.R.: An abstract argumentation framework with varied-strength attacks. In: Proceedings of International Conference on the Principles of Knowledge Representation and Reasoning (KR), pp. 135–143 (2008)
20. Nouioua, F.: AFs with necessities: further semantics and labelling characterization. In: Liu, W., Subrahmanian, V.S., Wijsen, J. (eds.) SUM 2013. LNCS, vol. 8078, pp. 120–133. Springer, Heidelberg (2013)
21. Nouioua, F., Risch, V.: Bipolar argumentation frameworks with specialized supports. In: Proceedings of the IEEE International Conference on Tools with Artificial Intelligence (ICTAI), pp. 215–218. IEEE Computer Society (2010)
22. Nouioua, F., Risch, V.: Argumentation frameworks with necessities. In: Benferhat, S., Grant, J. (eds.) SUM 2011. LNCS, vol. 6929, pp. 163–176. Springer, Heidelberg (2011)
23. Oren, N., Norman, T.J.: Semantics for evidence-based argumentation. In: Besnard, P., Doutre, S., Hunter, A. (eds.) Proceedings of the 2nd International Conference on Computational Models of Argument (COMMA), pp. 276–284. IOS Press (2008)
24. Oren, N., Reed, C., Luck, M.: Moving between argumentation frameworks. In: Proceeding of the Conference on Computational Models of Argument (COMMA), pp. 379–390. IOS Press, Amsterdam (2010)
25. Polberg, S., Oren, N.: Revisiting support in abstract argumentation systems. In: Parsons, S. (ed.) Proceedings of the Conference on Computational Models of Argument (COMMA), pp. 369–376. IOS Press (2014)
26. Prakken, H.: On support relations in abstract argumentation as abstraction of inferential relations. In: Schaub, T. (ed.) Proceedings of the European Conference on Artificial Intelligence (ECAI), pp. 735–740 (2014)
27. Verheij, B.: Deflog: on the logical interpretation of prima facie justified assumptions. J. Logic Comput. **13**, 319–346 (2003)
28. Villata, S., Boella, G., Gabbay, D.M., van der Torre, L.: Modelling defeasible and prioritized support in bipolar argumentation. Ann. Math. Artif. Intell. **66**(1–4), 163–197 (2012). http://dx.doi.org/10.1007/s10472-012-9317-7

Non-Monotonic Inference Properties
for Assumption-Based Argumentation

Kristijonas Čyras[(✉)] and Francesca Toni

Imperial College London, London, UK
{k.cyras13,ft}@imperial.ac.uk

Abstract. Cumulative Transitivity and Cautious Monotonicity are widely considered as important properties of non-monotonic inference and equally as regards to information change. We propose three novel formulations of each of these properties for Assumption-Based Argumentation (ABA)—an established structured argumentation formalism, and investigate these properties under a variety of ABA semantics.

Keywords: Assumption-Based Argumentation · Non-monotonic inference · Argumentation dynamics

1 Introduction

In the 1980s, several non-monotonic reasoning formalisms were proposed (see [2] for an overview). Systemic investigations into aspects of Cautious Monotonicity and Cumulative Transitivity of non-monotonic inference followed (e.g. [24,25]). Those works also contribute to the well-studied area of analysing non-monotonic reasoning with respect to information change (see e.g. [29]).

Since the early 1990s, argumentation (as overviewed in [28]) has emerged as a generic framework for non-monotonic reasoning, admitting existing non-monotonic reasoning formalisms as instances (see e.g. [7,16]). Recently, some forms of structured argumentation (see [5] for an overview) have been investigated in terms of non-monotonic inference (see Sect. 4). Contributing to this area of research, we here analyse a well-established structured argumentation formalism, Assumption-Based Argumentation (ABA) [7,30], against the non-monotonic inference properties of Cumulative Transitivity and Cautious Monotonicity in the spirit of [24,25]. Since ABA is an instance of a well-known structured argumentation framework ASPIC[+] (see [26] for a tutorial), this work is potentially applicable to a wider array of argumentation systems.

Originally, the non-monotonic inference properties in question were defined with respect to non-monotonic entailment. Yet, ABA (as well as a significant portion of other structured argumentation formalisms) is defined in terms of *extensions* (e.g. sets of arguments). We thus first reformulate the properties to be applicable to extension-based non-monotonic reasoning formalisms (but see e.g. [11,15] for different approaches). The essential idea is to characterize what happens to extensions when a certain change in knowledge occurs. The following

© Springer International Publishing Switzerland 2015
E. Black et al. (Eds.): TAFA 2015, LNAI 9524, pp. 92–111, 2015.
DOI: 10.1007/978-3-319-28460-6_6

will serve as an abstract pattern for producing the concrete instances of the properties (from now on, CUT and MON stand for Cumulative Transitivity and Cautious Monotonicity, respectively):

Let $\mathcal{K}$ be a knowledge base. Suppose that an 'entity' ψ 'belongs' to an extension E of $\mathcal{K}$, and let E' be an extension of the knowledge base $\mathcal{K}'$, which is obtained by 'adding' ψ to $\mathcal{K}$. Then

$$\text{CUT}: \quad E \text{ 'contains' } E'; \qquad\qquad \text{MON}: \quad E' \text{ 'contains' } E.$$

These properties concern what happens when a conclusion that is reached—which could have been already present as a hard fact, or inferred defeasibly—is added to the knowledge base and reasoned with anew. Arguably, there are many ways to interpret both properties, e.g. as checking that accepting a conclusion does not yield overwhelming changes in reasoning. One of our contributions is to provide three instantiations of both CUT and MON applicable to ABA. We will also discuss some possible interpretations of those instantiations.

The abstract formulation above, aiming to be universal, is informal: notions like 'entity' act as placeholders for alternative formal concepts (e.g. conclusion of an argument); 'containment' need not be understood in set-theoretic terms. For ABA, we will provide rigorously defined instances of the abstract formulation.

To ease the intuition behind the properties, consider the following illustration.

Example 1. Three prospective academic partners—*Al*, *Ben* and *Dan*—invite you to dine at a new restaurant. On the eve of the dinner it turns out that no one has booked a table in advance and, unfortunately, you will have to sit in pairs at two separate tables. You are the one invited, so you will have to choose whom to sit with. In a playful manner, your associates start competing for your company: both Ben and Dan claim that Al is *antisocial*, while Al retorts that Ben is *back-stabbing*. Somewhat puzzled, you casually inquire about the restaurant. Ben replies that it is a *gourmet* place. You then recall that Dan is a *disagreeable* person over fancy food. It is high time to decide, so what will be the verdict?

The reasoning may unfold as follows. Ben defends himself against Al by insisting that the latter is antisocial. Meanwhile, Al has nothing against his attacker Dan. The latter is not a good option, assuming that Ben is right about gourmet food. No more hesitating, and you decide to go for Ben.

Now, how would the information that you are really in a gourmet place change your reasoning, if at all? One can argue that, knowing as a matter of fact it is a gourmet restaurant immediately discards Dan as an option. So if Dan is out of consideration, then Al is attacked only by Ben, and in turn attacks him back. Thus, both Ben and Al defend themselves, and hence are acceptable choices. In terms of non-monotonic inference, CUT insists you should not draw any new conclusions, while MON demands not to lose previous inferences. Sticking to your first choice would satisfy both requirements, whereas choosing Al over Ben would violate both properties, indicating a revision of your previous decision.

In this work we investigate how ABA (background in Sect. 2) behaves when employed to formalize this sort of situations. In particular, in Sect. 3 we provide three instantiations of each of CUT and MON, and analyse their satisfaction under six extension-based ABA semantics. After discussing related work (Sect. 4), we conclude in Sect. 5.

2 Background

In this section, we provide background on ABA, following [30].

An **ABA framework** is a tuple $(\mathcal{L}, \mathcal{R}, \mathcal{A}, \bar{\ })$ consisting of the following elements. $(\mathcal{L}, \mathcal{R})$ is a deductive system with a language $\mathcal{L}$ and a set $\mathcal{R}$ of rules: rules in $\mathcal{R}$ are assumed to be of the form $\varphi_0 \leftarrow \varphi_1, \ldots, \varphi_m$ with $m \geq 0$ and $\varphi_i \in \mathcal{L}$ for $i \in \{0, \ldots, m\}$; φ_0 is referred to as the *head*, and $\varphi_1, \ldots, \varphi_m$ is referred to as the *body* of the rule; if $m = 0$, then the rule is said to have an empty body and we write it as $\varphi_0 \leftarrow \top$. The set $\mathcal{A} \subseteq \mathcal{L}$ is non-empty, referred to as **assumptions**. The so called *contrary mapping* $\bar{\ }: \mathcal{A} \to \mathcal{L}$ is a total function and for $\alpha \in \mathcal{A}$, the $\mathcal{L}$-formula $\bar{\alpha}$ is referred to as the **contrary** of α.

We restrict the discussion to the so called *flat* ABA frameworks, where no assumption $\alpha \in \mathcal{A}$ can be the head of any rule from $\mathcal{R}$.

A **deduction** *for* $\varphi \in \mathcal{L}$ *supported by* $S \subseteq \mathcal{L}$ *and* $R \subseteq \mathcal{R}$, denoted by $S \vdash^R \varphi$, is a finite tree with the root labeled by φ, leaves labeled by $\top$ or elements from S, the children of non-leaf nodes ψ labeled by the elements of the body of some rule from $\mathcal{R}$ with the head ψ, and R being the set of all such rules. An **argument** A with *conclusion* $\varphi \in \mathcal{L}$ and *support* $A \subseteq \mathcal{A}$, written as $\mathsf{A} : A \vdash \varphi$, is a deduction for φ supported by A and some $R \subseteq \mathcal{R}$. We say that $\mathsf{A}' : A' \vdash \varphi'$ **attacks** $\mathsf{A} : A \vdash \varphi$ (on some $\alpha \in A$) just in case φ' is the contrary $\bar{\alpha}$ of some $\alpha \in A$.

Given an ABA framework $(\mathcal{L}, \mathcal{R}, \mathcal{A}, \bar{\ })$, we denote the set of constructible arguments by *Args*, the attack relation by $\rightsquigarrow$, and the corresponding *argument framework* by $(Args, \rightsquigarrow)$. For a set $S \subseteq Args$, we say that: S attacks an argument A', written $S \rightsquigarrow \mathsf{A}'$, if some $\mathsf{A} \in S$ attacks A'; S attacks a set $S' \subseteq Args$ of arguments, written $S \rightsquigarrow S'$, if S attacks some $\mathsf{A}' \in S'$; S is *conflict-free* if $S \not\rightsquigarrow S$; and S *defends* $\mathsf{A} \in Args$ if for each $\mathsf{A}' \rightsquigarrow \mathsf{A}$ we have $S \rightsquigarrow \mathsf{A}'$. For an argument A, let $Cn(\mathsf{A})$ be the conclusion of A and $asm(\mathsf{A})$ the support of A. We extend this notation so that for a set $S \subseteq Args$ of arguments, $Cn(S) = \{Cn(\mathsf{A}) : \mathsf{A} \in S\}$ and $asm(S) = \{\alpha \in \mathcal{A} : \alpha \in asm(\mathsf{A}), \mathsf{A} \in S\}$.

ABA semantics are defined as follows. A set $E \subseteq Args$, also called an **extension** (of $(\mathcal{L}, \mathcal{R}, \mathcal{A}, \bar{\ })$ or $(Args, \rightsquigarrow)$), is: *admissible*, if E is conflict-free and defends all $\mathsf{A} \in E$; *preferred*, if E is $\subseteq$-maximally admissible; *sceptically preferred*, if E is the intersection of all the preferred extensions; *complete*, if E is admissible and contains all arguments it defends; *grounded*, if E is $\subseteq$-minimally complete; *stable*, if E is admissible and $E \rightsquigarrow \mathsf{A}$ for all $\mathsf{A} \in Args \setminus E$; and *ideal*, if E is $\subseteq$-maximal such that E is admissible and contained in all the preferred extensions.

Grounded, sceptically preferred and ideal semantics fall into the category of *sceptical* reasoning, whereby conclusions are drawn from a unique extension. Meanwhile stable, preferred and complete semantics represent *credulous* reasoning, in that multiple conflicting extensions can be present.

We also recall (see e.g. [16]) that the grounded extension G of any $(\mathcal{L}, \mathcal{R}, \mathcal{A}, \bar{\ })$ always exists and is unique, and can be constructed inductively as $G = \bigcup_{i \geq 0} G_i$, where G_0 is the set of arguments that are not attacked at all, and for every $i \geq 0$, G_{i+1} is the set of arguments that are defended by G_i.

To simplify proofs of our results, we restrict to finite argument frameworks, as is common in literature.

3   Inference Properties for ABA

In this section we formulate and analyse non-monotonic inference properties regarding ABA. There will be three different settings of instantiations of CUT and MON. Each property will also have a strong and a weak version. The strong properties will quantify over all extensions, indicating the necessity to preserve the previously accepted conclusions after a change in information. Meanwhile, the weak properties, by quantifying existentially over extensions, will insist on the possibility, rather than necessity, to preserve the previously accepted conclusions. When referring to a property, we will have in mind its strong version, unless specified otherwise.

Throughout this section we use the following notation, unless stated otherwise. We take as given a fixed, but otherwise arbitrary (flat) ABA framework $\mathcal{F} = (\mathcal{L}, \mathcal{R}, \mathcal{A}, {}^-)$, and its corresponding argument framework $(Args, \rightsquigarrow)$. To instantiate the abstract formulations of CUT and MON given in the Introduction, we replace a knowledge base $\mathcal{K}$ with $\mathcal{F}$, fix an argumentation semantics σ and let E be an extension of $\mathcal{F}$ under $\sigma \in$ {grounded, ideal, sceptically preferred, stable, preferred, complete}. An 'entity' ψ will come from the set $Cn(E)$ of conclusions of E. By default, the knowledge base $\mathcal{K}'$ will be represented by $\mathcal{F}'$, which will be the ABA framework obtained by 'adding' (to be formalized) ψ to $\mathcal{F}$. The corresponding argument framework of $\mathcal{F}'$ will be denoted by $(Args', \rightsquigarrow')$. Still further, E' will denote an extension of $\mathcal{F}'$ under the same fixed semantics σ. To avoid trivialities, we consider cases only where under a particular semantics σ, each of $\mathcal{F}$ and $\mathcal{F}'$ admits at least one extension, E and E', respectively.

3.1   Strict Cumulative Transitivity and Cautious Monotonicity

We now rigorously formulate the first type of properties for ABA. (Recall that E is an extension of $\mathcal{F}$ under a fixed semantics σ.) Initially, given some $\psi \in Cn(E) \setminus \mathcal{A}$, define $\mathcal{F}' = (\mathcal{L}, \mathcal{R} \cup \{\psi \leftarrow \top\}, \mathcal{A}, {}^-)$. The following then are the first concrete instances of non-monotonic inference properties that we consider.

STRONG STRICT CUT :	For all extensions E' of $\mathcal{F}'$ we have $Cn(E') \subseteq Cn(E)$;
WEAK STRICT CUT :	There is an extension E' of $\mathcal{F}'$ with $Cn(E') \subseteq Cn(E)$;
STRONG STRICT MON :	For all extensions E' of $\mathcal{F}'$ we have $Cn(E) \subseteq Cn(E')$;
WEAK STRICT MON :	There is an extension E' of $\mathcal{F}'$ with $Cn(E) \subseteq Cn(E')$.

STRICT CUT and STRICT MON concern what happens when a conclusion (not itself an assumption) is reached and then considered as a fact (i.e. a rule with empty body) to reason again. The conclusion may be learned as an objective truth, e.g. verifying that you are in a gourmet restaurant. In essence, STRICT properties regard *strengthening of information* and what effect it has on different ABA semantics in terms of extensions. A reasoner employing ABA semantics can utilize these properties to anticipate its behaviour regarding changes that strengthen knowledge.

The following remarks are in place. First, satisfaction of a strong property will always imply satisfaction of the corresponding weak property. Second, under sceptical semantics, weak and strong formulations actually coincide, because the extension is unique. Further, as grounded, ideal, stable and preferred extensions are complete [16,18], a strong property satisfied under complete semantics holds for the other four. Similarly, if a strong property is violated under stable semantics, then it fails under both preferred and complete semantics, because stable extensions are also preferred [7].

Our first result shows that grounded semantics fulfils (the strong versions of) both CUT and MON in the STRICT setting.

Proposition 2. *Grounded semantics satisfies both STRICT CUT and STRICT MON.*

Proof. Let G be the grounded extension of $\mathcal{F}$. If $G = \emptyset$, then $\mathcal{F}' = \mathcal{F}$, so the properties are trivially satisfied. Otherwise, pick a conclusion $\psi \in Cn(G) \setminus \mathcal{A}$ and suppose that $\mathsf{B}_1 : B_1 \vdash \psi, \ldots, \mathsf{B}_n : B_n \vdash \psi$ are all the arguments in G that have conclusion ψ. Let G' be the grounded extension of $\mathcal{F}' = (\mathcal{L}, \mathcal{R} \cup \{\psi \leftarrow \top\}, \mathcal{A}, \bar{})$.

We prove $G \subseteq G'$ by induction on the construction of G.

For the basis step, let $G_0 \subseteq G$ be the set of arguments not attacked in $\mathcal{F}$. Since $Cn(Args') = Cn(Args)$, arguments from G_0 are unattacked in $\mathcal{F}'$, so we get $G_0 \subseteq G'$.

For the inductive step, let $G_{i+1} \subseteq G$ be the set of arguments attacked in $\mathcal{F}$ but defended by $G_i \subseteq G$, assuming $G_i \subseteq G'$ as an induction hypothesis. Suppose that $\mathsf{A}' : A' \vdash \varphi$ attacks G_{i+1} in $\mathcal{F}'$. We split into cases.

- If $\mathsf{A}' \in Args$, then $\mathsf{A}' \rightsquigarrow G_{i+1}$, so that $G_i \rightsquigarrow \mathsf{A}'$, and so $G' \rightsquigarrow' \mathsf{A}'$ too.
- Else, if $\mathsf{A}' \notin Args$, then there is some $\mathsf{A} : A \vdash \varphi \in Args$ from which A' can be obtained by replacing occurrences of the deduction $B_j \vdash^{R_j} \psi$ (for some j) in A with the deduction $\emptyset \vdash^{\{\psi \leftarrow \top\}} \psi$. (Such A' and A are called **counterpart** arguments and satisfy $asm(\mathsf{A}) = asm(\mathsf{A}') \cup B_j$.) We then have $\mathsf{A} \rightsquigarrow G_{i+1}$, so that $G_i \rightsquigarrow \mathsf{A}$ on some $\alpha \in A \setminus B_j = A'$ (because $B_j \subseteq asm(G)$), which yields $G' \rightsquigarrow' \mathsf{A}'$.

In any event, G' defends G_{i+1}, so that $G_{i+1} \subseteq G'$.

By induction it holds that $G_i \subseteq G'$ for every $i \geq 0$, so that $G \subseteq G'$, and hence $Cn(G) \subseteq Cn(G')$, giving STRICT MON.

For STRICT CUT, given that we already have $G \subseteq G'$, it suffices to show that $Cn(G' \setminus G) \subseteq Cn(G)$. We prove this by induction on the construction of G'.

For the basis step, let $G'_0 \subseteq G' \setminus G$ be the set of arguments from $Args' \setminus Args$ unattacked in $\mathcal{F}'$. Pick $\mathsf{A}' \in G'_0$, if any. Consider a counterpart $\mathsf{A} \in Args$ with

$asm(A) = asm(A') \cup B_j$ (for some j) and $Cn(A) = Cn(A')$ (so every occurrence of the deduction $\emptyset \vdash^{\{\psi \leftarrow \top\}} \psi$ in A' is replaced with the deduction $B_j \vdash^{R_j} \psi$ in A). Such an A can be attacked in $\mathcal{F}$ only on some $\beta \in B_j$, whereby G defends A, because $B_j \subseteq asm(G)$. Consequently, $Cn(A') \in Cn(G)$, and therefore, $Cn(G'_0) \subseteq Cn(G)$.

For the inductive step, let $G'_{i+1} \subseteq G' \setminus G$ be the set of arguments attacked in $\mathcal{F}'$ but defended by $G \cup G'_i$, assuming $Cn(G'_i) \subseteq Cn(G)$ as an induction hypothesis. Pick $A' \in G'_{i+1}$, if any, and consider a counterpart $A \in Args$ with $asm(A) = asm(A') \cup B_j$ (for some j) and $Cn(A) = Cn(A')$. Then A can be attacked in $\mathcal{F}$ in two ways:

- either on some $\beta \in B_j$, whence G defends A in $\mathcal{F}$;
- or on some $\alpha \in asm(A) \setminus B_j$, whence A' is attacked in $\mathcal{F}'$ (on α), and so defended in $\mathcal{F}'$ by $G \cup G'_i$, so that G defends A in $\mathcal{F}$, because $Cn(G \cup G'_i) \subseteq Cn(G)$.

In any case, $A \in G$, and so $Cn(G'_{i+1}) \subseteq Cn(G)$.

By induction, $Cn(G') \subseteq Cn(G)$ holds as required to satisfy STRICT CUT. □

So we know that strong, and hence weak, STRICT CUT and STRICT MON hold for grounded semantics. What is more, weak versions of both properties are satisfied under complete semantics, as we see next.

Proposition 3. *Complete semantics satisfies both WEAK STRICT CUT and WEAK STRICT MON.*

Proof. We prove that for each complete extension E of $\mathcal{F}$, and for each conclusion $\psi \in Cn(E) \setminus \mathcal{A}$, there is a complete extension E' of $\mathcal{F}' = (\mathcal{L}, \mathcal{R} \cup \{\psi \leftarrow \top\}, \mathcal{A}, \overline{})$ such that $Cn(E') = Cn(E)$.

So let E be a complete extension of $\mathcal{F}$ and fix $\psi \in Cn(E) \setminus \mathcal{A}$. Suppose that $B_1 : B_1 \vdash \psi, \ldots, B_n : B_n \vdash \psi$ are all the arguments in E with conclusion ψ. Now, $Args' \setminus Args$ consists of arguments $A' : A' \vdash \varphi$ which are constructed from arguments $A : A \vdash \varphi$ in $Args$ that use some deduction(s) of the form $\Psi \vdash^R \psi$, by replacing (some) such deduction(s) with $\emptyset \vdash^{\{\psi \leftarrow \top\}} \psi$. (Such A and A' are said to be **corresponding** to each other.) Let E^+ be the collection of $A' \in Args' \setminus Args$ whose corresponding A is in E. We claim that $E' = E \cup E^+$ is the required complete extension of $\mathcal{F}'$.

- First, E' is conflict-free, as $Cn(E^+) \subseteq Cn(E)$.
- Second, E' defends every argument it contains: if $A' \in Args' \setminus Args$ attacks E' in $\mathcal{F}'$, but $E' \not\leadsto' A'$, then a counterpart (as in the proof of Proposition 2) argument A attacks E in $\mathcal{F}$, but $E \not\leadsto A$, contradicting admissibility of E.
- Finally, for completeness, assume E' defends $A' \in Args'$. Then there are two cases.
  - If $A' \in Args$, then, as $Cn(E^+) \subseteq Cn(E)$, we have that E defends A' in $\mathcal{F}'$.
  - Else, if $A' \notin Args$, then assume $A' \notin E^+$ for a contradiction. Then a counterpart $A \in Args$ is not in E, and so some C attacks A in $\mathcal{F}$, but $E \not\leadsto C$. As E defends all B_js, we have $C \leadsto' A'$, but $E' \not\leadsto' C$, which is a contradiction.

In any event, $A' \in E'$. Hence, E' is complete.

Since clearly $Cn(E') = Cn(E)$, E' is the required complete extension of $\mathcal{F}'$.   □

We can actually extend the proof above to be applicable to both preferred and stable semantics, as follows.

Proposition 4. *Preferred and stable semantics satisfy both WEAK STRICT CUT and WEAK STRICT MON.*

Proof. We first prove that for every preferred extension E of $\mathcal{F}$, there is a preferred extension E' of $\mathcal{F}'$ with $Cn(E') = Cn(E)$. Since preferred extensions are complete, it suffices to show that the corresponding complete extension $E' = E \cup E^+$ (as defined in the proof of Proposition 3) is preferred in $\mathcal{F}'$. And indeed, if E' were not $\subseteq$-maximally admissible, then some $A' \in Args' \setminus E'$ could be added to E' without sacrificing admissibility. But then a counterpart $A \in Args$ (possibly $A = A'$, if A' does not use ψ) could be added to E without losing its admissibility, whence E would not be preferred in $\mathcal{F}$.

Likewise, we show that if E is stable, then E' is also stable. Suppose $A' \notin E'$. If $A' \in Args$, then $A' \notin E$, so $E \rightsquigarrow A'$, and hence $E' \rightsquigarrow' A'$. Else, if $A' \notin Args$, then a counterpart A is not in E and $E \rightsquigarrow A$, so that $E' \rightsquigarrow' A'$ too. Consequently, E' is a stable extension of $\mathcal{F}'$.   □

Having the results above, we conclude with the following.

Corollary 5. *Sceptically preferred and ideal semantics satisfy STRICT CUT.*

Proof. Using notation from the proof of Proposition 3, let $S = \bigcap_i E_i$ be the intersection of all the preferred extensions E_i of $(\mathcal{L}, \mathcal{R}, \mathcal{A}, {}^-)$. Pick $\psi \in Cn(S) \setminus \mathcal{A}$ and consider $\mathcal{F}' = (\mathcal{L}, \mathcal{R} \cup \{\psi \leftarrow \top\}, \mathcal{A}, {}^-)$. Let $S' = \bigcap_j E'_j$ be the intersection of all the preferred extensions E'_j of $\mathcal{F}'$. We show $Cn(S') \subseteq Cn(S)$. According to Proposition 4, for every preferred extension E of $\mathcal{F}$, there is a preferred extension E' of $\mathcal{F}'$ such that $Cn(E') = Cn(E)$. Therefore, S' cannot contain arguments with conclusions not in $Cn(S)$. So STRICT CUT holds under sceptically preferred semantics.

Likewise, for the ideal extension I of $\mathcal{F}$ and $\psi \in Cn(I) \setminus \mathcal{A}$, if I' is the ideal extension of $\mathcal{F}' = (\mathcal{L}, \mathcal{R} \cup \{\psi \leftarrow \top\}, \mathcal{A}, {}^-)$, then, being contained in all preferred extensions of $\mathcal{F}'$, it has $Cn(I') \subseteq Cn(I)$. Thus, STRICT CUT holds under ideal semantics.   □

The following formalization of the example from the Introduction reveals that neither of the (strong) properties holds for credulous reasoning. This violation is intuitive, as credulous semantics allow for multiple extensions, with different conclusions.

Example 6 (STRICT CUT and STRICT MON violations). Let $\mathcal{L} = \{\alpha, \beta, \delta, a, b, d, \psi\}$, where: α, β, δ are the assumptions of choosing Al, Ben and Dan (resp.); a, b and d stand for 'antisocial', 'back-stabbing' and 'disagreeable' (resp.); and ψ expresses that we are in a gourmet place. So $\mathcal{A} = \{\alpha, \beta, \delta\}$, with contraries $\overline{\alpha} = a$, $\overline{\beta} =$

$b,\ \overline{\delta} = d$. Then $\mathcal{R} = \{b \leftarrow \alpha,\ a \leftarrow \delta,\ a \leftarrow \beta,\ \psi \leftarrow \beta,\ d \leftarrow \psi\}$ completes the formalization: e.g. the rule $b \leftarrow \alpha$ represents Al's claim about Ben; the rule $d \leftarrow \psi$ indicates that Dan is a disagreeable company in a gourmet place. (In further examples, both $\mathcal{L}$ and $\mathcal{A}$ will be omitted, as they are implicit from $\mathcal{R}$ and the contrary relation.) The corresponding argument framework $(Args, \rightsquigarrow)$ can be represented graphically as follows (nodes hold arguments and directed edges indicate attacks):

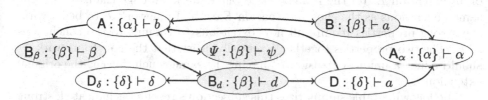

Here, $\mathcal{F} = (\mathcal{L}, \mathcal{R}, \mathcal{A}, {}^{-})$ has a unique preferred (also stable and ideal) extension $E = \{\mathsf{B}, \mathsf{B}_\beta, \mathsf{B}_d, \Psi\}$ (gray arguments) with $Cn(E) = \{a, \beta, d, \psi\}$. Now suppose that after deciding to sit with Ben, you check the menu and realize you are indeed in a gourmet restaurant. As knowledge changes—your belief that this is a gourmet place being strengthened—you wonder whether you would make the same decision now.

Consider thus $\mathcal{F}' = (\mathcal{L}, \mathcal{R} \cup \{\psi \leftarrow\ \}, \mathcal{A},\ )$. In $Args'$, we get two new arguments: $\Psi' : \{\} \vdash \psi$ and $\mathsf{B}' : \{\} \vdash d$. While Ψ' neither attacks, nor is attacked by anything, B' is unattacked but attacks both D_δ and D. So $(Args', \rightsquigarrow')$ has two preferred extensions (which are also stable): $E_1 = \{\mathsf{B}, \mathsf{B}_\beta, \mathsf{B}_d, \mathsf{B}', \Psi, \Psi'\}$ (with $Cn(E_1) = Cn(E)$) and $E_2 = \{\mathsf{A}_\alpha, \mathsf{A}, \mathsf{B}', \Psi'\}$. Taking E_2 with $Cn(E_2) \not\subseteq Cn(E) \not\subseteq Cn(E_2)$ yields violations of STRICT CUT and STRICT MON under credulous reasoning. We also have $Cn(E) \not\subseteq Cn(\{\mathsf{B}', \Psi'\}) = Cn(E_1 \cap E_2)$, so STRICT MON is violated under both ideal and sceptically preferred semantics.

We see that a reasoner using ABA could find itself in a situation where adding credulously inferred information leads to a multitude of extensions. Even if the extension to begin with is unique, as in Example 6, strengthening some of its conclusions can result in more than one acceptable extension. Whether or not this behaviour is desirable depends on the application, anticipated changes in information and intended flexibility of the reasoner. For instance, one may wish for the reasoner to be credulous and try many different scenarios in order not to fixate on one particular decision. In contrast, sceptical semantics (except grounded) provide insurance that no new conclusions are attained—fulfil STRICT CUT, while ensuring that some are dropped (e.g. β, d). However, a sceptical reasoner may completely lose some previously acceptable choices (such as β in Example 6).

Example 6 also reveals contrast between STRICT CUT and STRICT MON under sceptically preferred and ideal semantics: adding a previously attained conclusion as a fact leaves all the original preferred extensions intact, yet allows for new ones, thus possibly shrinking their intersection. Hence, the sceptically preferred extension E' (as well as the ideal extension) of the ABA framework $\mathcal{F}'$ after the change in information will satisfy STRICT CUT; indeed, we have $Cn(E_1 \cap E_2) = Cn(\{B', \Psi'\}) \subseteq Cn(E)$ in Example 6. For the same reason, STRICT MON is violated under both sceptically preferred and ideal semantics, as illustrated in Example 6.

We observe that under credulous semantics, the strong properties gain importance in settings where there is a unique credulous extension to begin with, such as in Example 6. Indeed, while the weak properties merely ask for the existence of an extension E' (of the framework $\mathcal{F}'$ after the knowledge change) with the same conclusions as the chosen extension E of the framework $\mathcal{F}$ to begin with, the strong properties require all new extensions to commit to the conclusions of E. The two properties together essentially insist that the new framework $\mathcal{F}'$ should admit a unique extension E' having the same conclusions as the original extension E.

The following table summarizes this subsection's results (as indicated, strong and weak versions coincide under sceptical reasoning, and for credulous semantics the status of the weak property is indicated in parentheses).

STRICT Cumulative Transitivity and Cautious Monotonicity

Property	Grounded	Ideal	Sceptically pref.	Stable	Preferred	Complete
STRICT CUT	✓	✓	✓	X (✓)	X (✓)	X (✓)
STRICT MON	✓	X	X	X (✓)	X (✓)	X (✓)

Only grounded semantics allows for safely strengthening information. However, as the grounded extension of a given ABA framework can be empty (e.g. Example 6), other semantics may be needed to make decisions. In that case, ideal and sceptically preferred semantics, for instance, guarantee that no new conclusions will be attained after strengthening information, yet some important ones may be lost: in Example 6, neither semantics allows to decide whom to dine with, because $\alpha, \beta, \delta \notin Cn(E_1 \cap E_2)$. Credulous semantics provide even less certainty (or more flexibility—depending on the way one intends to use it) unless one has a procedure allowing to pick the extension with the same conclusions as the extension to begin with (such an extension is guaranteed to exist due to satisfaction of the weak properties).

3.2   Defeasible Cumulative Transitivity and Cautious Monotonicity

We now formulate another type of variants of CUT and MON. Given $\psi \in Cn(E) \setminus \mathcal{A}$, define $\mathcal{F}' = (\mathcal{L} \cup \{y\}, \mathcal{R} \setminus \{r \in \mathcal{R} \; : \; \text{head of r is } \psi\}, \mathcal{A} \cup \{\psi\}, ^-).$[1] Then

STRONG DEF CUT :   For all extensions E' of $\mathcal{F}'$ we have $Cn(E') \subseteq Cn(E)$;

WEAK DEF CUT :   There is an extension E' of $\mathcal{F}'$ with $Cn(E') \subseteq Cn(E)$;

STRONG DEF MON :   For all extensions E' of $\mathcal{F}'$ we have $Cn(E) \subseteq Cn(E')$;

WEAK DEF MON :   There is an extension E' of $\mathcal{F}'$ with $Cn(E) \subseteq Cn(E')$.

---

[1] The modification of the rules in $\mathcal{F}'$ is required to preserve flatness. We also slightly abuse the notation by using $^-$ for both contrary mappings: the implicit presumption is that the original contrary mapping $^-$ is extended with the assignment $\overline{\psi} = y$, where y is new to $\mathcal{L}$.

Unlike the STRICT setting, DEF CUT and DEF MON regard situations where a previously accepted conclusion (inferred possibly *defeasibly* using assumptions) is converted into an assumption itself, and can afterwards be drawn only *defeasibly*. For instance, instead of relying on Ben's claim about gourmet food, you may initially guess that you are in a gourmet place.

The same results (as in Sect. 3.1) hold in the defeasible (DEF) setting, and proofs follow a similar pattern.

Proposition 7. *Grounded semantics satisfies both DEF CUT and DEF MON.*

Proof. Let G be the grounded extension of $\mathcal{F}$. If $G = \emptyset$, then $\mathcal{F}' = \mathcal{F}$, so the properties are trivially satisfied. Otherwise, pick $\psi \in Cn(G) \backslash \mathcal{A}$ and let $\mathsf{B}_1 : B_1 \vdash \psi, \ldots, \mathsf{B}_n : B_n \vdash \psi \in G$ be all the arguments in G that conclude ψ. Let G' be the grounded extension of $\mathcal{F}' = (\mathcal{L} \cup \{y\}, \mathcal{R} \backslash \{r \in \mathcal{R} : \text{head of } r \text{ is } \psi\}, \mathcal{A} \cup \{\psi\}, \overline{})$ (where $\overline{\psi} = y$).

We first prove $Cn(G) \subseteq Cn(G')$ by induction on the construction of G.

For the basis step, let $G_0 \subseteq G$ be the set of arguments that are not attacked in $\mathcal{F}$ and pick $\mathsf{A} \in G_0$. There are two cases, as follows.

- If $\mathsf{A} \in Args \cap Args'$, then it is not attacked in $\mathcal{F}'$, because $Cn(Args') = Cn(Args)$.
- If $\mathsf{A} \in Args \backslash Args'$, then it uses some deduction(s) of the form $\Psi \vdash^R \psi$. Hence, there is a **corresponding** argument $\mathsf{A}' \in Args' \backslash Args$ (having $Cn(\mathsf{A}') = Cn(\mathsf{A})$) with (all) the deduction(s) $\Psi \vdash^R \psi$ replaced by the deduction $\{\psi\} \vdash^\emptyset \psi$. Note that A' cannot be attacked in $\mathcal{F}'$ on ψ, since $\overline{\psi} = y$ is new to the language.

In any case, we get that $Cn(\mathsf{A}) \in Cn(G')$.

For the inductive step, let $G_{i+1} \subseteq G$ be the set of arguments that are attacked in $\mathcal{F}$ but defended by $G_i \subseteq G$, where $Cn(G_i) \subseteq Cn(G')$ is assumed as an induction hypothesis. Pick $\mathsf{A} \in G_{i+1}$, if any. We split into cases.

- If $\mathsf{A} \in Args \cap Args'$, then it is defended by G_i in $\mathcal{F}$. So, on the one hand, G' defends A in $\mathcal{F}$ too, as $Cn(G_i) \subseteq Cn(G')$. On the other hand, if $\mathsf{C}' \in Args' \backslash Args$ attacks A in $\mathcal{F}'$ and is not attacked by G', then a **counterpart** argument $\mathsf{C} \in Args \backslash Args'$ (which uses some fixed deduction $B_j \vdash^{R_j} \psi$ instead of $\{\psi\} \vdash^\emptyset \psi$) attacks A in $\mathcal{F}$ and is not attacked by G_i (because $Cn(G_i) \subseteq Cn(G')$ and $B_j \subseteq asm(G)$), which is a contradiction.
- Else, if $\mathsf{A} \in Args \backslash Args'$, then like in the basis case, a corresponding argument $\mathsf{A}' \in Args \backslash Args$ (with deduction(s) $\Psi \vdash^R \psi$ replaced by the deduction $\{\psi\} \vdash^\emptyset \psi$) satisfying $Cn(\mathsf{A}') = Cn(\mathsf{A})$ is defended in $\mathcal{F}'$ by G' (as $asm(\mathsf{A}') \backslash \{\psi\} \subseteq asm(\mathsf{A})$, G_i defends A in $\mathcal{F}$, $Cn(G_i) \subseteq Cn(G')$ and $\overline{\psi} = y$ is new).

In any event, $Cn(G_{i+1}) \subseteq Cn(G')$.

By induction, $Cn(G) \subseteq Cn(G')$, as required for DEF MON.

For the satisfaction of DEF CUT under grounded semantics, we next show that $Cn(G' \backslash G) \subseteq Cn(G)$ holds by induction on the construction of G'.

For the basis step, let $G'_0 \subseteq G'$ be the set of arguments from $Args'$ that are not attacked in $\mathcal{F}'$, and pick $\mathsf{A}' \in G'_0$, if any.

- If $A' \in Args' \cap Args$, then it is not attacked in $\mathcal{F}$ either, so $A \in G$.
- If $A' \in Args' \setminus Args$, then a counterpart argument $A \in Args \setminus Args'$ (having $Cn(A) = Cn(A')$ and every occurrence of the deduction $\{\psi\} \vdash^\emptyset \psi$ in A' replaced by some deduction $B_j \vdash^{R_j} \psi$ in A) is defended by G in $\mathcal{F}$, because $Cn(Args) = Cn(Args')$ (so that A cannot be attacked in $\mathcal{F}$ on $asm(A) \setminus B_j$) and $B_j \subseteq asm(G)$ (so that G defends A in $\mathcal{F}$ from attacks on B_j).

In any case, $Cn(A') \in Cn(G)$, and so $Cn(G'_0) \subseteq Cn(G)$.

For the inductive step, let $G'_{i+1} \subseteq G'$ be the set of arguments from $Args'$ that are attacked in $\mathcal{F}'$ but defended by G'_i, where $Cn(G'_i) \subseteq Cn(G)$. Pick $A' \in G'_{i+1}$, if any.

- If $A' \in Args' \cap Args$, then G defends it in $\mathcal{F}$.
- If $A' \in Args' \setminus Args$, then a counterpart argument $A \in Args \setminus Args'$ can be attacked in $\mathcal{F}$ in two ways:
  - either on some $\beta \in B_j$: such attacks G defends against;
  - or on some $\alpha \in asm(A) \setminus B_j$, in which case A' is attacked in $\mathcal{F}'$ (on α), and so defended by G'_i, so that G defends A in $\mathcal{F}$.

In any event, $Cn(A') \in Cn(G)$, and so $Cn(G'_{i+1}) \subseteq Cn(G)$.

By induction, $Cn(G') \subseteq Cn(G)$, as required for DEF CUT.   □

Proposition 8. *Complete semantics satisfies WEAK DEF CUT and WEAK DEF MON.*

Proof. We show for every complete extension E of $\mathcal{F}$, for each $\psi \in Cn(E) \setminus \mathcal{A}$, there is a complete extension E' of $\mathcal{F}' = (\mathcal{L} \cup \{y\}, \mathcal{R} \setminus \{r \in \mathcal{R} : \text{head of } r \text{ is } \psi\}, \mathcal{A} \cup \{\psi\}, \overline{})$ (where $\overline{\psi} = y$) such that $Cn(E') = Cn(E)$.

Let E be a complete extension of $\mathcal{F}$ and fix $\psi \in Cn(E) \setminus \mathcal{A}$ (assuming again that $B_1 : B_1 \vdash \psi$, ..., $B_n : B_n \vdash \psi \in E$ are all the arguments in E concluding ψ). Now, $Args' \setminus Args$ consists of arguments $A' : A' \vdash \varphi$ constructed from the corresponding arguments $A : A \vdash \varphi \in Args$ that use some deduction $\Psi \vdash^R \psi$. Let E^+ be the set of all such arguments A' for which $A \in E$, and put $E' = (E \cap Args') \cup E^+$ (note that the argument $\{\psi\} \vdash \psi$ is in E' too, because $B_j \in E$ for all j). Then $Cn(E) = Cn(E')$, so it suffices to prove that such E' is a complete extension of $\mathcal{F}'$.

- First, E' is conflict-free, because $Cn(E^+) \subseteq Cn(E)$ and $\overline{\psi} = y \notin \mathcal{L}$.
- Second, E' defends itself. Indeed, any $C \in Args \cap Args'$ that attacks E' in $\mathcal{F}$ on some $\alpha \in asm(E') \setminus \{\psi\} \subseteq asm(E)$ is attacked by E', because $Cn(E') = Cn(E)$ and E is complete. On the other hand, if $C' \in Args' \setminus Args$ attacks E' in $\mathcal{F}'$, but $E' \not\rightarrow' C'$, then a counterpart argument C with $Cn(C) = Cn(C')$ and some deduction $B_j \vdash^{R_j} \psi$ replacing (all) the deduction(s) $\{\psi\} \vdash^\emptyset \psi$ attacks E in $\mathcal{F}$, and we have $E \not\rightarrow C$ (because $B_j \subseteq asm(E)$), contradicting admissibility of E.
- Finally, E' is complete. For suppose towards a contradiction that E' defends some $A' \in Args' \setminus Args$, but $A' \notin E^+$ (as in the proof of Proposition 3, we do not consider $A' \in Args$, for it would be defended by E and hence would belong to E). Consider thus a corresponding argument $A \in Args$ of A'. Then there are two cases.

- Either A has some deduction(s) $B_j \vdash^{R_j} \psi$ replacing (all) the deduction(s) $\{\psi\} \vdash^{\emptyset} \psi$ (so A is also a counterpart of A') and A $\notin E$, in which case A is not defended by E against some attack C $\rightsquigarrow$ A. As E defends B_j (for all j), we have C' $\rightsquigarrow'$ A', for a counterpart C' of C. But as $E \not\rightsquigarrow$ C and $\psi \in asm(E')$, we get $E' \not\rightsquigarrow'$ C', which is a contradiction to A' being defended by E'.
- Or else, A uses deduction(s) of the form $\Psi \vdash^R \psi$, where $\Psi \neq B_j$ for any j. But then $E \rightsquigarrow$ A, and so E', being conflict-free, cannot defend A.

We obtain a contradiction in any case, so that A' $\in E^+$ after all.

Consequently, E', as defined above, is the required complete extension.   □

Like with Proposition 4 and Corollary 5 (resp.), we have the following results.

Proposition 9. *Preferred and stable semantics satisfy WEAK DEF CUT and WEAK DEF MON.*

Proof. The proof is *verbatim* to the proof of Proposition 4, with $E' = (E \cap Args') \cup E^+$ as in the proof of Proposition 8.   □

Corollary 10. *Sceptically preferred and ideal semantics satisfy DEF CUT.*

The following example exhibits a violation of both DEF CUT and DEF MON under the remaining semantics.

Example 11 (DEF CUT and DEF MON violations. Based on Example 6). Suppose that instead of relying on Ben about the restaurant (remove $\psi \leftarrow \beta$), you guess it to be a gourmet place to begin with (add ψ to assumptions). Reason then according to $(\mathcal{L} \cup \{y\}, \mathcal{R} \setminus \{\psi \leftarrow \beta\}, \mathcal{A} \cup \{\psi\}, \quad)$ (where $\psi = y$), with $(Args', \rightsquigarrow')$ as follows:

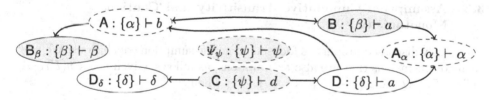

There are two preferred extensions (which are also stable): $E'_1 = \{B, B_\beta, C, \Psi_\psi\}$ (gray) and $E'_2 = \{A_\alpha, A, C, \Psi_\psi\}$ (dashed). The sceptically preferred (also ideal) extension is $E' = \{C, \Psi_\psi\}$ with $Cn(E') \not\supseteq \{a, \beta, \psi, d\} = Cn(E)$, where E is as in Example 6. So DEF MON fails under both sceptically preferred and ideal semantics. DEF CUT and DEF MON fail in credulous reasoning, as $Cn(E) \not\subseteq Cn(E'_2) \not\subseteq Cn(E)$.

We see that even when starting with a unique credulous extension, assuming a previously defeasibly inferred conclusion opens up space for multiple credulous extensions. This may be desirable in situations where revision of decisions based on defeasible assumptions (β in Example 11) is important. At the same time, such behaviour results into possibly losing conclusions in sceptical reasoning (except, as before, under grounded semantics). This nevertheless may be sensible, if, for instance, differentiating defeasible information is needed (e.g. ψ versus $\psi \leftarrow \beta$).

Below is a summary of results in this subsection (using the same notational conventions as at the end of Sect. 3.1).

DEFEASIBLE Cumulative Transitivity and Cautious Monotonicity

Property	Grounded	Ideal	Sceptically pref.	Stable	Preferred	Complete
DEF CUT	✓	✓	✓	X (✓)	X (✓)	X (✓)
DEF MON	✓	X	X	X (✓)	X (✓)	X (✓)

Conclusions drawn using grounded semantics can be safely turned into assumptions and inferred defeasibly instead. However, such a change would not allow for new conclusions under the other two sceptical semantics, yet could lead to a decision vacuum: neither of α, β, δ belongs to $Cn(E')$ in Example 11. Credulous semantics, meanwhile, allow for greater dynamicity, which could be desirable: if independently from what Ben says a reasoner believes to be in a gourmet place and thus does not care about Dan, then Al can be as likely a choice as Ben, and so the conclusions may need revision.

Naturally, somewhat different formulations of the properties in the defeasible setting could be investigated. For example, the contrary of the new assumption ψ could instead be one of the existing symbols in $\mathcal{L}$, based on the rules and contraries of the assumptions that allowed to derive ψ in the first place. However, such behaviour need not be desirable in general: if you assume to begin with that you are about to dine in a gourmet place, then, arguably, this assumption should not be contingent on the objections against Ben. We chose the formulation above, readily applicable to all ABA frameworks, as the first step in our analysis. Different and more complex settings are left for future work.

3.3 Assumption Cumulative Transitivity and Cautious Monotonicity

Previously discussed properties focused on non-assumption conclusions. We now turn to conclusions that are also assumptions, as follows. Given $\psi \in Cn(E) \cap \mathcal{A}$, define $\mathcal{F}' = (\mathcal{L}, \mathcal{R} \cup \{\psi \leftarrow \top\}, \mathcal{A} \setminus \{\psi\}, ^{-})$.[2] Then

STRONG ASM CUT :   For all extensions E' of $\mathcal{F}'$ we have $Cn(E') \subseteq Cn(E)$;

WEAK ASM CUT :   There is an extension E' of $\mathcal{F}'$ with $Cn(E') \subseteq Cn(E)$;

STRONG ASM MON :   For all extensions E' of $\mathcal{F}'$ we have $Cn(E) \subseteq Cn(E')$;

WEAK ASM MON :   There is an extension E' of $\mathcal{F}'$ with $Cn(E) \subseteq Cn(E')$.

ASM CUT and ASM MON focus on previously accepted assumptions *being confirmed* and made into facts to reason again. For instance, you might have guessed

---

[2] Again, for brevity reasons, the same symbol $^{-}$ is used for both contrary mappings: in $\mathcal{F}'$, the original contrary mapping $^{-}$ is implicitly restricted to a diminished set of assumptions.

that you are in a gourmet restaurant, and after deciding whom to sit with you may check the menu to confirm your guess and scrutinize your decision.

As for satisfaction of the properties, the same results (as in Sects. 3.1 and 3.2) hold with proofs following the same pattern.

Proposition 12. *Grounded semantics satisfies* ASM CUT *and* ASM MON.

Proof. Let G be the grounded extension of $\mathcal{F}$. If $G = \emptyset$, then $\mathcal{F}' = \mathcal{F}$, so the properties are trivially satisfied. Otherwise, pick $\psi \in Cn(G) \cap \mathcal{A}$ and let G' be the grounded extension of $\mathcal{F}' = (\mathcal{L}, \mathcal{R} \cup \{\psi \leftarrow \top\}, \mathcal{A} \setminus \{\psi\}, \overline{})$.

First show $Cn(G) \subseteq Cn(G')$ by induction on the construction of G.

For the basis step, let $G_0 \subseteq G$ be the set of arguments that are not attacked in $\mathcal{F}$. Pick $A \in G_0$, if any. We split into two cases.

- If $\psi \notin asm(A)$, then A remains unattacked in $\mathcal{F}'$. Hence $A \in G'$.
- Otherwise, if $\psi \in asm(A)$, then in $Args'$, A is replaced by its **counterpart** A' with $asm(A) = asm(A') \cup \{\psi\}$ and $Cn(A') = Cn(A)$ (the deduction $\emptyset \vdash^{\{\psi \leftarrow \top\}} \psi$ replaces (all) the deduction(s) $\{\psi\} \vdash^{\emptyset} \psi$). Since there were no attacks against A in $\mathcal{F}$, the counterpart A' is unattacked in $\mathcal{F}'$ either. Hence, $A' \in G'$.

In any case, we have $Cn(G_0) \subseteq Cn(G')$.

For the inductive step, let $G_{i+1} \subseteq G$ be the set of arguments that are attacked in $\mathcal{F}$ but defended by G_i, where $Cn(G_i) \subseteq Cn(G')$. Suppose that in $\mathcal{F}'$, an argument $A' \in Args'$ attacks the set $G'_{i+1} \subseteq Args'$ of arguments which are obtained from G_{i+1} by replacing the assumption ψ with the rule $\psi \leftarrow \top$.[3] We split into cases.

- If $A' \in Args$, then $G_i \rightsquigarrow A'$, so that $G' \rightsquigarrow' A'$ too.
- Otherwise, if $A' \notin Args$, then A' is constructed from the counterpart $A \in Args$ such that $A \rightsquigarrow G_{i+1}$. Now, if $G' \not\rightsquigarrow' A'$, it means that $G_i \rightsquigarrow A$ on ψ. This effectively yields $G \rightsquigarrow G$, contradicting conflict-freeness of G. Hence, $G' \rightsquigarrow' A'$.

Thus, $Cn(G_{i+1}) \subseteq Cn(G')$, and so $Cn(G) \subseteq Cn(G')$ by induction, as required.

To show ASM CUT holds under grounded semantics, prove $Cn(G') \subseteq Cn(G)$ by induction on the construction of G'.

For the basis step, let $G'_0 \subseteq G'$ be the set of arguments that are not attacked in $\mathcal{F}'$, and pick $A' \in G'_0$, if any. We split into cases.

- If $A' \in Args$, then A' can be attacked in $\mathcal{F}$ only on ψ. But since $\psi \in Cn(G)$, we would then have A' defended by G, so that $A' \in G$.
- Otherwise, if $A' \notin Args$, then the counterpart $A \in Args$ can be attacked in $\mathcal{F}$ only on $\psi \in Cn(G)$, and so is defended by G.

In any case, $Cn(A') \in Cn(G)$ holds true.

For the inductive step, let $G'_{i+1} \subseteq G'$ be the set of arguments attacked in $\mathcal{F}'$ but defended by G'_i, where $Cn(G'_i) \subseteq Cn(G)$. Pick $A' \in G'_{i+1}$, if any. We split into cases.

---

[3] Deduction(s) $\Phi \vdash^R \varphi$ with $\psi \in \Phi$ are replaced with the deduction(s) $\Phi \setminus \{\psi\} \vdash^{R' \cup \{\psi \leftarrow \top\}} \varphi$ such that $R' \subseteq R$ is the set of rules from R that do not contain ψ in their bodies.

- If $A' \in Args$, then A' can be attacked in $\mathcal{F}$ either on any $\alpha \in asm(A') \setminus \{\psi\}$, or on ψ itself. Consider each case separately.
  - Suppose first that $B \rightsquigarrow A'$ on some $\alpha \in asm(A') \setminus \{\psi\}$. Then either B or its counterpart $B' \in Args'$ (if such can possibly be obtained from B) attacks A' in $\mathcal{F}'$ on α. In any event, G'_i defends against this attack, and since it holds that $Cn(G'_i) \subseteq Cn(G)$ by induction hypothesis, we get either $G \rightsquigarrow B$, or $G \rightsquigarrow B'$.
  - In the latter case, if $B \rightsquigarrow A'$ on ψ, then since $\psi \in Cn(G)$, we have $G \rightsquigarrow B$. In any event $A' \in G$.
- Otherwise, suppose $A' \notin Args$. Then consider its counterpart $A \in Args$ and assume $B \rightsquigarrow A$ on some $\alpha \in asm(A)$. Then, like before:
  - either $\alpha = \psi$, in which case $G \rightsquigarrow B$, so that $A \in G$;
  - or $\alpha \neq \psi$, whence either B (or its counterpart $B' \in Args'$) attacks A' in $\mathcal{F}'$, but as G'_i defends against this attack, we get $G \rightsquigarrow B$ (or $G \rightsquigarrow B'$), and so $A \in G$.

Consequently, $Cn(A') \in Cn(G)$, and by induction, $Cn(G') \subseteq Cn(G)$, as required. $\qquad\square$

Proposition 13. *Complete semantics satisfies* WEAK ASM CUT *and* WEAK ASM MON.

Proof. Show for every complete extension E of $\mathcal{F}$, for each $\psi \in Cn(E) \setminus \mathcal{A}$, there is a complete extension E' of $\mathcal{F}' = (\mathcal{L}, \mathcal{R} \cup \{\psi \leftarrow \top\}, \mathcal{A} \setminus \{\psi\}, \overline{})$ with $Cn(E') = Cn(E)$.

Let E be a complete extension of $\mathcal{F}$. Now, $Args' \setminus Args$ consists of arguments A' that are counterpart to $A \in Args$ with $\psi \in asm(A)$. Let $E^- \subseteq E$ be the set of arguments from E that use the assumption ψ and let $E^+ \subseteq Args'$ be the set of all the counterparts of arguments in E^-. Put $E' = (E \setminus E^-) \cup E^+$. The following then hold.

- E' is conflict-free, because $Cn(E^+) \subseteq Cn(E)$.
- E' defends itself: if $A' \in Args' \setminus Args$ attacks E' in $\mathcal{F}'$, but $E' \not\rightsquigarrow' A'$, then the counterpart argument $A \in Args$ attacks E; yet, $E \not\rightsquigarrow A$ (because $\psi \in Cn(E)$), contradicting admissibility of E.
- E' is complete. Suppose for a contradiction that E' defends $A' \in Args' \setminus Args$, but $A' \notin E^+$ (as in the proof of Proposition 3, we do not consider $A' \in Args$). Then the counterpart argument $A \in Args$ of A' does not belong to E, and hence is not defended by E against some attack $C \rightsquigarrow A$. As $\psi \in Cn(E)$, we have $C' \rightsquigarrow' A'$, for the counterpart C' of C. But since $E \not\rightsquigarrow C$ and $\psi \in Cn(E')$, we get $E' \not\rightsquigarrow' C'$, which is a contradiction to E' defending A'.

Then $Cn(E') = Cn(E)$ yields that E' is the required complete extension of $\mathcal{F}'$. $\qquad\square$

The next two results follow from the ones above, as with the other properties.

Proposition 14. *Preferred and stable semantics satisfy* WEAK ASM CUT *and* WEAK MON.

Corollary 15. *Sceptically preferred and ideal semantics satisfy ASM CUT.*

To show that the properties are violated under the remaining semantics, we consider a situation where, in contrast to Examples 6 and 11, one argument depends on two assumptions, one of which is to be turned into a fact, as follows.

Example 16 (ASM CUT and ASM MON violations). Consider $\mathcal{R} = \{d \leftarrow \alpha,$ $a \leftarrow \beta,\ b \leftarrow \alpha, \delta\}$ with $\overline{\alpha} = a$, $\overline{\beta} = b$, $\overline{\delta} = d$. This yields the following $(Args, \leadsto)$:

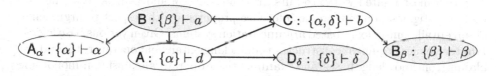

Here, $E = \{B, B_\beta, D_\delta\}$ (gray) is a unique preferred (also stable and ideal) extension of $(Args, \leadsto)$. Taking $\delta \in Cn(E) \cap \mathcal{A}$ results in $\mathcal{F}' = (\mathcal{L}, \mathcal{R} \cup \{\delta \leftarrow \top\}, \mathcal{A} \setminus \{\delta\}, \overline{\ })$ in which C and D_δ are replaced by their counterparts $C' : \{\alpha\} \vdash b$ and $D'_\delta : \{\} \vdash \delta$:

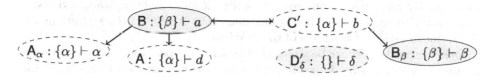

Therefore, $\mathcal{F}'$ admits two preferred extensions: $E'_1 = \{B, B_\beta, D'_\delta\}$ (gray) and $E'_2 = \{A_\alpha, C', D'_\delta, A\}$ (dashed) with $Cn(E) \not\subseteq Cn(E'_2) \not\subseteq Cn(E)$. The sceptically preferred and ideal extension is $E' = \{D'_\delta\}$ with $Cn(E) \not\subseteq Cn(E')$.

Compared to sceptical semantics, credulous ones are more dynamic. Here, confirming δ results in retracting β (as well as a) under both ideal and sceptically preferred semantics. Meanwhile, the same change effectively removes A's attack on C, still leaving C defeasible, yet rendering B to lose its position as the sole defender against A, hence enabling mutual acceptability of α and δ, under, say, complete semantics. This allows for a possibly desirable revision of conclusions.

The following is a summary of this subsection's results (notation as before).

ASSUMPTION Cumulative Transitivity and Cautious Monotonicity

Property	Grounded	Ideal	Sceptically pref.	Stable	Preferred	Complete
ASM CUT	✓	✓	✓	X (✓)	X (✓)	X (✓)
ASM MON	✓	X	X	X (✓)	X (✓)	X (✓)

Confirmation of some defeasible information can lead to an increased number of options in credulous reasoning. This could be desirable if, for instance, one of the choices (like C with conclusion b in Example 16) depends on an assumption (δ) and is not considered acceptable to begin with (C has no defense against A), but becomes viable (via C') as soon as the assumption is confirmed ($\delta \leftarrow \top$) and ceases to be questioned (D'_δ). Meanwhile, if confirming information widens the array of credulous choices, then a sceptical reasoner could opt for fewer—more certain—conclusions, as witnessed by the sceptical (bar grounded) semantics satisfying `ASM CUT` but failing `ASM MON`.

4   Related Work

The two most related works to ours are Hunter's [23] and Dung's [17]. The former investigates non-monotonic inference properties with respect to argument–claim entailment in logic-based argumentation systems. Given various base logics, Hunter defines argument construction-mimicking entailment operators to produce claims from knowledge bases, and examines those operators against non-monotonic inference properties (Cumulative Transitivity and Cautious Monotonicity among them). Meanwhile, Dung analyses, among other aspects of argumentation dynamics, Cumulativity (i.e. Cumulative Transitivity plus Cautious Monotonicity) of ASPIC$^+$ under stable extension semantics. The main concern there is that confirmation of some conclusions in an extension should strengthen other conclusions in that extension. To formalize this, Dung introduces two axioms—a variant of Cumulativity and another one regarding attack monotonicity. Stable extension semantics with respect to either of the main four ASPIC$^+$ attack relations are shown not to satisfy at least one of those axioms.

Other related works can be seen to fall under two broad research topics in argumentation: (i) analysing desirable properties of argumentation formalisms, and (ii) relating belief change and argumentation. Regarding (i), with the exceptions of [17,23], existing works on properties of argumentation disregard the issues of argumentation dynamics: for example, [12] propose rationality postulates for rule-based argumentation systems; [19] provide guidelines for argumentation-based practical reasoning; [22] postulate and examine properties of attack relations (and the corresponding extensions under alternative semantics) over classical logic-based argument graphs. As far as (ii) is concerned, argumentation dynamics has recently been studied with respect to Abstract Argumentation [16] and some other argumentation-based approaches to non-monotonic reasoning, such as DeLP [21] (see e.g. [3,8,13,14,20]). To the best of our knowledge, [17] is the only work in the direction of investigating structured, extension-based argumentation with regards to non-monotonic inference properties á la [24].

Our work differs from [17] in several aspects. First, we consider Cumulative Transitivity and Cautious Monotonicity as two separate properties, rather than one. Also, our reformulations of the properties are not restricted to one particular semantics (stable), but allow for any semantics. Still further, we consider three types of information change, including strengthening (`STRICT`) and confirmation (`ASM`), and analyse their influence to argumentation processes in ABA. Finally, we do not insist that properties have to be necessarily fulfilled, but maintain that their satisfaction is conditional on applications.

5 Conclusions

This paper researches extension-based structured argumentation dynamics in the spirit of non-monotonic inference properties of [24,25]. To this end, we offer reformulations of non-monotonic inference properties in terms of extensions. Particularly, we introduce (strong and weak versions of) six properties applicable to the well-known structured argumentation formalism Assumption-Based Argumentation (ABA) and investigate their satisfaction under six key ABA semantics. Three pairs of properties reflect different modifications of knowledge in ABA frameworks, and each item of a pair concerns either Cumulative Transitivity (CUT) or Cautious Monotonicity (MON) of extension-based non-monotonic inference. While conceptually the three types of information change are different, we show that technically they lead to the same outcomes in the sense of a property being satisfied in either all or none of the three settings, under a particular semantics. Consequently, irrespective of the knowledge representation in ABA and the nature of the anticipated changes in information, one can choose semantics best suited for the application, depending on the desirable properties of the reasoner.

Credulous semantics violate the strong properties. This is expected, due to presence of choice between extensions that share conclusions. Meanwhile, the weak properties are satisfied under credulous semantics. This essentially says that ABA frameworks do not lose the extension based on which a change in knowledge occurs. As for further results on credulous reasoning, we can also identify a certain provocative aspect of our findings: even when a stable/preferred extension to begin with is unique, changing (even strengthening) information in ABA can lead to more than one stable/preferred extension afterwards (Examples 6, 11 and 16). We believe this phenomenon deserves further study in terms of characterization of ABA frameworks and/or semantics for which it occurs.

In terms of sceptical reasoning, intuitively, the most sceptical (grounded) semantics satisfies all the properties. This is because grounded extensions commit to the most certain conclusions to begin with, and changing the way they are represented in ABA frameworks does not influence their (and other arguments') acceptance. Somewhat surprisingly, the other two sceptical semantics—sceptically preferred and ideal—fail MON, yet fulfill CUT. Such a behaviour is present because changes in information can increase the number of, particularly, preferred extensions, whence their intersection shrinks, resulting in violation of MON, at the same time satisfying CUT.

The results can serve as guidelines regarding argumentation dynamics for modeling common-sense reasoning using ABA. Due to the same property satisfaction outcomes, irrespective of knowledge representation in ABA, one has a range of differently behaving semantics to choose among, contingent on the intended behaviour of the reasoner. Depending on application, one may wish to rely on the static grounded semantics to prevent overwhelming changes in reasoning, or use a much more dynamic credulous semantics to be flexible about revising decisions.

This work serves as one of the first steps towards investigating extension-based structured argumentation dynamics. Current results cover ABA, and hence (by virtue of results in [27]) ASPIC$^+$ without preferences, with regards to CUT and MON. Future work directions include different formulations of the properties, as well as analysis of extension-based formalisms of argumentation with preferences against variants of the non-monotonic inference properties in question. As to the latter, ABA Equipped with Preferences (known as p_ABA [31]) is of particular interest, as well as other formalisms, such as ASPIC$^+$, Value-Based Argumentation [4] or PAFs [1]. It may also be possible to use the abstract formulations of the properties to analyse other non-monotonic reasoning formalisms, such as default logic and logic programming (see e.g. [9,10]), from a slightly different perspective than in the existing work (e.g. [6,11,15]).

References

1. Amgoud, L., Vesic, S.: Rich preference-based argumentation frameworks. Int. J. Approximate Reasoning **55**(2), 585–606 (2014)
2. Antoniou, G.: Nonmonotonic Reasoning. MIT Press, Cambridge (1997)
3. Baroni, P., Boella, G., Cerutti, F., Giacomin, M., van der Torre, L., Villata, S.: On the input/output behavior of argumentation frameworks. Artif. Intell. **217**, 144–197 (2014)
4. Bench-Capon, T.: Persuasion in practical argument using value based argumentation frameworks. J. Logic Comput. **13**(3), 429–448 (2003)
5. Besnard, P., García, A., Hunter, A., Modgil, S., Prakken, H., Simari, G., Toni, F.: Introduction to structured argumentation. Argum. Comput. **5**(1), 1–4 (2014)
6. Bochman, A.: A foundational theory of belief and belief change. Artif. Intell. **108**(1–2), 309–352 (1999)
7. Bondarenko, A., Dung, P.M., Kowalski, R., Toni, F.: An abstract, argumentation-theoretic approach to default reasoning. Artif. Intell. **93**(97), 63–101 (1997)
8. Booth, R., Kaci, S., Rienstra, T., van der Torre, L.: A logical theory about dynamics in abstract argumentation. In: Liu, W., Subrahmanian, V.S., Wijsen, J. (eds.) SUM 2013. LNCS, vol. 8078, pp. 148–161. Springer, Heidelberg (2013)
9. Brewka, G., Eiter, T.: Preferred answer sets for extended logic programs. Artif. Intell. **109**(1–2), 297–356 (1999)
10. Brewka, G., Eiter, T.: Prioritizing default logic. In: Intellectics and Computational Logic, pp. 27–45 (2000)
11. Brewka, G., Niemelä, I., Truszczynski, M.: Nonmonotonic reasoning. In: van Harmelen, F., Lifschitz, V., Bruce, P. (eds.) Handbook of Knowledge Representation, pp. 239–284. Elsevier (2007)
12. Caminada, M., Amgoud, L.: On the evaluation of argumentation formalisms. Artif. Intell. **171**(5–6), 286–310 (2007)
13. Cayrol, C., De Saint-Cyr, F., Lagasquie-Schiex, M.: Change in abstract argumentation frameworks: adding an argument. J. Artif. Intell. Res. **38**(1), 49–84 (2010)
14. Coste-Marquis, S., Konieczny, S., Mailly, J.G., Marquis, P.: On the revision of argumentation systems: minimal change of arguments status. In: KR (2014)
15. Dix, J.: A classification theory of semantics of normal logic programs: I. strong properties. Fundamenta Informaticae **22**(3), 227–255 (1995)

16. Dung, P.M.: On the acceptability of arguments and its fundamental role in non-monotonic reasoning, logic programming and n-person games. Artif. Intell. **77**, 321–357 (1995)
17. Dung, P.M.: An axiomatic analysis of structured argumentation for prioritized default reasoning. In: ECAI, pp. 267–272 (2014)
18. Dung, P.M., Mancarella, P., Toni, F.: Computing ideal sceptical argumentation. Artif. Intell. **171**(10–15), 642–674 (2007)
19. Dung, P.M., Mancarella, P., Toni, F.: Some design guidelines for practical argumentation systems. In: COMMA, pp. 183–194 (2010)
20. Falappa, M., García, A., Kern-Isberner, G., Simari, G.: On the evolving relation between belief revision and argumentation. Knowl. Eng. Rev. **26**(01), 35–43 (2011)
21. García, A., Simari, G.: Defeasible logic programming: DeLP-servers, contextual queries, and explanations for answers. Argum. Computat. **5**(1), 63–88 (2014)
22. Gorogiannis, N., Hunter, A.: Instantiating abstract argumentation with classical logic arguments: postulates and properties. Artif. Intell. **175**(9–10), 1479–1497 (2011)
23. Hunter, A.: Base logics in argumentation. In: COMMA, pp. 275–286 (2010)
24. Kraus, S., Lehmann, D., Magidor, M.: Nonmonotonic reasoning, preferential models and cumulative logics. Artif. Intell. **44**(1–2), 167–207 (1990)
25. Makinson, D.: General theory of cumulative inference. In: Reinfrank, M., de Kleer, J., Ginsberg, M.L., Sandewall, E. (eds.) Non-Monotonic Reasoning. Lecture Notes in Computer Science, vol. 346, pp. 1–18. Springer, Heidelberg (1989)
26. Modgil, S., Prakken, H.: The ASPIC+ framework for structured argumentation: a tutorial. Argum. Comput. **5**(1), 31–62 (2014)
27. Prakken, H.: An abstract framework for argumentation with structured arguments. Argum. Comput. **1**(2), 93–124 (2010)
28. Rahwan, I., Simari, G.: Argumentation in Artificial Intelligence. Springer, Heidelberg (2009)
29. Rott, H.: Change, Choice and Inference: A Study of Belief Revision and Non-monotonic Reasoning. Oxford University Press, Oxford (2001)
30. Toni, F.: A tutorial on assumption-based argumentation. Argum. Comput. **5**(1), 89–117 (2014)
31. Wakaki, T.: Assumption-based argumentation equipped with preferences. In: Dam, H.K., Pitt, J., Xu, Y., Governatori, G., Ito, T. (eds.) PRIMA 2014. LNCS, vol. 8861, pp. 116–132. Springer, Heidelberg (2014)

On Explanations for Non-Acceptable Arguments

Xiuyi Fan$^{(\boxtimes)}$ and Francesca Toni

Imperial College London, London, UK
{xf309,ft}@imperial.ac.uk

Abstract. Argumentation has the unique advantage of giving explanations to reasoning processes and results. Recent work studied how to give explanations for arguments that are acceptable, in terms of arguments defending it. This paper studies the counterpart of this problem by formalising explanations for arguments that are not acceptable. We give two different views (an argument-view and an attack-view) in explaining the non-acceptability of an argument and show the computation of explanations with debate trees.

1   Introduction

Argumentation (see e.g. [18,20] for an overview) can be viewed as a process of generating *explanations*. Indeed, an arguing process transparently explains the procedure and the results of reasoning. Given a topic, the process of arguing can be viewed as identifying *related* information and generating an *explanation* for the topic, usually through some fictitious *proponent* and *opponent* debate game. Hence, arguing for an argument can be deemed to explain it.

Recent work [14,15] has proposed explaining the acceptability of an argument a as a set of arguments defending a. However, this approach fails to address the case when a is not acceptable; as, intuitively, an argument is not acceptable because it lacks appropriate defences against some attackers.

We propose two alternative views for explaining why some argument a is not acceptable. In the *argument-view*, we view an explanation for a with a defending set S as a set of argument A attacking S such that if A is removed, then a becomes acceptable. In the *attack-view*, we see an explanation for a as a set of attacks such that, if removed, a becomes acceptable. We analyse the relations between these two views of explanations.

We develop our notions of explanations in the context of Abstract Argumentation (AA) [9] as AA is arguably the most widely used argumentation framework with great simplicity. Also, the main approach we use in this work relies on a proof theory developed for AA, namely, dispute trees [10,11]. Moreover, most other argumentation frameworks, e.g. Assumption-based Argumentation [11,25] and ASPIC+ [17], are instances of AA; hence results obtained in AA apply to those frameworks as well. We will focus our discussion on the admissibility semantics thus equate arguments' acceptability with admissibility.

We motivate our approach with the following example on argumentation-based decision making, adapted from [13]:

© Springer International Publishing Switzerland 2015
E. Black et al. (Eds.): TAFA 2015, LNAI 9524, pp. 112–127, 2015.
DOI: 10.1007/978-3-319-28460-6_7

Example 1. An agent needs to decide on accommodation in London, amongst three options: Imperial College Student Accommodation (ic), the John Howard Hotel (jh), and the Ritz Hotel (ritz). The main decision criterion is whether the accommodation is quiet. The agent believes that both ic and ritz are quiet, but jh is not. The decision to not choose ic can be represented by the following AA framework $\langle \mathcal{A}, \mathcal{R} \rangle$ (as conventional, represented as a directed graph with nodes being arguments in $\mathcal{A}$ and arcs being attacks in $\mathcal{R}$):

a: Choose ic.
b: Why not jh?
d: Because it is not quiet.
c: Why not ritz?

Here, the argument a is not acceptable as it cannot defend against argument c, even with the help of other arguments. Although b also attacks a, this attack is countered by d. Thus, one may conclude that either the *argument c* or the *attack* from c to a explains the non-acceptability of a, as *by removing either the argument or the attack a is acceptable*. Identifying the source of non-acceptability can then help repairing the AA framework to ensure a's acceptability, e.g. by adding an attack against c. In this paper, we focus on characterising explanations, not repairing AA frameworks.

The reminder of this paper is organised as follows. Section 2 reviews some background on AA and dispute trees. Section 3 introduces the two views of explanations. We will see that they do not in general coincide (although they do in Example 1). Section 4 gives the procedures of computing explanations with dispute trees. Section 5 discusses several issues with the difference between the two forms explanations and some other possible types of explanations. Section 6 reviews some related works. Section 7 concludes.

2   Background

Abstract Argumentation (AA) *frameworks* [9] are pairs $AF = \langle \mathcal{A}, \mathcal{R} \rangle$, consisting of a set of *arguments*, $\mathcal{A}$, and a binary *attack* relation, $\mathcal{R}$. For any attack $(a, b) \in \mathcal{R}$, a is the *attacking argument*.

Given an AA framework $AF = \langle \mathcal{A}, \mathcal{R} \rangle$, an *extension* $A \subseteq \mathcal{A}$ is *admissible* (in AF) if and only if $\forall a, b \in A$, there is no $(a, b) \in \mathcal{R}$ (A is *conflict-free*) and for any $a \in A$, if $(c, a) \in \mathcal{R}$, then there exists some $b \in A$ such that $(b, c) \in \mathcal{R}$.

Given an AA framework $AF = \langle \mathcal{A}, \mathcal{R} \rangle$, we say that an argument a is *in AF* if and only if $a \in \mathcal{A}$; we also say that an attack (a, b) is *in AF* or that a *attacks* b in AF if and only if $(a, b) \in \mathcal{R}$. Finally, we say that an argument a is *admissible* if and only if a is in some admissible extension.

Dispute Trees [10,11] are used to compute our explanations. Given an AA framework $AF = \langle \mathcal{A}, \mathcal{R} \rangle$, we will use the following version of dispute trees. A *dispute tree for* $a \in \mathcal{A}$ is a (possibly infinite) tree $\mathcal{T}$, such that:

1. every node of T is of the form $[L:x]$, labelled by an argument x (in AF) and assigned the status of either *proponent* (P) or *opponent* (O) (thus $L \in \{P, O\}$), but not both;
2. the root of T is $[P:a]$;
3. for every node n of the form $[P:b]$, for every argument c that attacks b in AF, there exists a child of n of the form $[O:c]$;
4. for every node n of the form $[O:b]$, there exists at most one child of n of the form $[P:c]$ such that c attacks b in AF;
5. there are no other nodes in T except those given by 1–4.

We say that a node of the form $[L:x]$ is a L node. The set of all arguments labelling P nodes in T is called the *defence set* of T, denoted by $\mathcal{D}(T)$. A dispute tree T is an *admissible dispute tree* if and only if:

1. every O node in T has a child, and
2. no argument in T labels both a P and an O node.

Theorem 3.2 in [12] states the following, given an AF and an argument a in AF:

1. If T is an admissible dispute tree for a, then $\mathcal{D}(T)$ is admissible (in AF).
2. If $a \in A$ where $A \subseteq \mathcal{A}$ is an admissible extension (in AF) then there exists an admissible dispute tree for a with $\mathcal{D}(T) = A'$ such that $A' \subseteq A$ and A' is admissible (in AF).

3   Two Different Notions of Explanation

We start with introducing the *pruning operator*, $\backslash$, as follows.

Definition 1. *Given an AA framework $AF = \langle \mathcal{A}, \mathcal{R} \rangle$ and a set of arguments $A \subseteq \mathcal{A}$, the* pruning operator, $\backslash$, *is defined as $AF \backslash A = \langle \mathcal{A}', \mathcal{R}' \rangle$, where*

- $\mathcal{A}' = \mathcal{A} \backslash A$,
- $\mathcal{R}' = \{(x, y) | (x, y) \in \mathcal{R} \text{ and } x \in \mathcal{A}', y \in \mathcal{A}'\}$.

Note that in this work we overload the operator $\backslash$ in several ways. Indeed, this operator is also used for the standard set difference operator and as defined later in Definitions 5 and 7. In all cases, it removes the second input from the first input.

We first introduce *arg-explanations*, giving explanations in the "argument-view".

Definition 2. *Given an AA framework $AF = \langle \mathcal{A}, \mathcal{R} \rangle$, let $a \in \mathcal{A}$ be such that a is not admissible in AF. Then, if there exists some $A \subseteq \mathcal{A}$, such that:*

1. *a is admissible in $AF \backslash A$, and*
2. *there is no $A' \subset A$ such that a is admissible in $AF \backslash A'$,*

then A is an arg-explanation *of a. Otherwise, $\{a\}$ is the* arg-explanation *of a.*

Given an arg-explanation A of some argument a, we say that a is the topic *argument for A.*

The intuition behind Definition 2 is that an arg-explanation of a non-admissible argument a is a minimal (with respect to set inclusion) set of arguments A such that if A is removed, then a becomes admissible. However, such A may not always exist. In such case, we take the view that the reason for a being not admissible is a itself. It is easy to see that this happens if and only if a attacks itself.

Proposition 1. *Given an AA framework $AF = \langle \mathcal{A}, \mathcal{R} \rangle$, let $a \in \mathcal{A}$. The arg-explanation of a is $\{a\}$ if and only if $(a, a) \in \mathcal{R}$.*

A non-admissible argument can have multiple arg-explanations, as illustrated in the following example.

Example 2. Given the AA framework in Fig. 1, there are two arg-explanations $\{b\}$ and $\{e\}$ for argument a. Indeed, removing either $\{b\}$ or $\{e\}$ from this AA framework makes the argument a admissible.

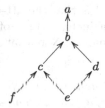

Fig. 1. AA framework for Example 2. Here the argument a has two arg-explanations ($\{b\}$ and $\{e\}$).

Proposition 2. *For any argument a in an AA framework $AF = \langle \mathcal{A}, \mathcal{R} \rangle$, if a is not admissible, then there is a non-empty arg-explanation of a.*

Proof (Sketch). By Proposition 1, if $(a, a) \in \mathcal{R}$, then the arg-explanation of a is $\{a\}$. Otherwise, since a is trivially admissible in the AA framework $AF' = \langle \{a\}, \{\} \rangle$, AF can always be reduced to AF' by removing arguments in $\mathcal{A}$.

We can see that arguments in an arg-explanation are always "related to" the argument being explained, formally given as follows.

Definition 3. *Given an AA framework $AF = \langle \mathcal{A}, \mathcal{R} \rangle$, let $x, y \in \mathcal{A}$. Then, x is related to y (in AF) if and only if:*

1. $x = y$; or
2. $(x, y) \in \mathcal{R}$; or
3. $\exists z \in \mathcal{A}$, such that $(x, z) \in \mathcal{R}$ and z is related to y.

Definition 3 is given recursively with (1) and (2) the base cases. Note that each argument is related to itself (by (1)). Note also that if there is no attack against an argument then the only argument related to it is the argument itself.

Proposition 3. *Let A be an arg-explanation for some non-admissible argument a in some AA framework $AF = \langle \mathcal{A}, \mathcal{R} \rangle$. For all $b \in A$, b is related to a (in AF).*

Proof (Sketch). This proposition holds by the observation that for any (non-admissible) argument a, arguments not related to a do not affect its admissibility.

We now turn our attention to *att-explanations*, which give explanations in the "attack-view".

Definition 4. *Given an AA framework $AF = \langle \mathcal{A}, \mathcal{R} \rangle$ let $a \in \mathcal{A}$ be such that a is not admissible in AF. Then an att-explanation of a is a set of attacks $R \subseteq \mathcal{R}$, such that*

1. *a is admissible in $\langle \mathcal{A}, \mathcal{R} \setminus R \rangle$;*
2. *there is no $R' \subset R$ such that a is admissible in $\langle \mathcal{A}, \mathcal{R} \setminus R' \rangle$.*

Given an att-explanation R of a, we say that a is the topic *argument for R.*

The intuition behind Definition 4 is that the att-explanation of an argument a is a minimal (with respect to set inclusion) set of attacks such that a becomes admissible if these attacks are removed. Note that such R always exists, as shown by the following proposition.

Proposition 4. *For any argument a in an AA framework, if a is not admissible, then there is an att-explanation of a and every att-explanation of a is non-empty.*

Proof (Sketch). Trivially, as if a is not attacked, then a is admissible. Thus, we can always construct an att-explanation of a by including attacks of the form $(\_, a)$.[1]

Similarly to Proposition 3, the following holds.

Proposition 5. *Let R be an att-explanation for a and $(x, y) \in R$. Then both x and y are related to a.*

Proof. (Sketch) This proposition holds as (1) if y is not related to a, then removing (x, y) does not affect the admissibility of a; and (2) if y is related to a, then x is.

One may hypothesise that arg-explanations and att-explanations of any argument a always coincide in the sense that the set formed by the attacking arguments in an att-explanation is an arg-explanation for a. The following example illustrates that this is not the case in general.

Example 3. We illustrate the difference between arg-explanations and attacking arguments in att-explanations. Consider the following AA framework AF:

---

[1] Here and after, _ denotes an anonymous variable as in Prolog.

Here, a is not admissible as it is attacked by both b and c. To make a admissible, we can either remove **both** b and c (as removing only one of them is insufficient) hence the arg-explanation for a is $\{b, c\}$; or we can remove **either** the attack (b, a) **or** the attack (c, a). Thus, the attacking arguments in att-explanations are either b or c.

One interpretation of this example is that both b and c are at odds with a; and b and c are in mutual conflict. To make a admissible, we can either eliminate both b and c (arg-explanation); or we can ally a with either b or c (att-explanation).

One may also hypothesise that for any argument a, its att-explanations are always "more compact" than its arg-explanations in the sense that *the set of arguments formed by attacking arguments in an att-explanation is no bigger than any arg-explanations*, as in the case of Example 3. This is not true in general, as illustrated below.

Example 4. Consider the following AA framework AF:

Here, a is not admissible and $\{(b, a), (f, e)\}$ is an att-explanation for a. We can see that removing any of these two attacks alone from AF is insufficient to render a admissible. The attacking arguments in this att-explanation are b and f. However, it is easy to see that the set formed by f alone is an arg-explanation. Thus, removing f alone from AF renders a admissible.

The following proposition gives a formal link between arg-explanation and att-explanation.

Proposition 6. *Let A be an arg-explanation for some argument a in an AA framework $\langle A, R \rangle$ and $S = \{(x, y) \in R \mid x \in A\}$. Then, there exists some att-explanation R for a such that $R \subseteq S$.*

Proof (Sketch). Trivially, as since A is an arg-explanation, removing A gives the same effect, as far as a is concerned, as removing all attacks from A.

4 Obtaining Explanations from Dispute Trees

Both arg-explanations and att-explanations can be obtained from dispute trees. Since admissible arguments correspond to admissible dispute trees (see Sect. 2), given a non-admissible argument a, no dispute tree with root argument a is admissible. We pose the question:

> *How do we turn a non-admissible dispute tree into an admissible dispute tree by removing (some of) its nodes?*

Answering this question effectively gives us arg-explanations for a. We provide an answer with *pruned trees*.

In this section we assume as given a general AA framework $AF = \langle \mathcal{A}, \mathcal{R} \rangle$.

Definition 5. *Given a dispute tree $\mathcal{T}$, the* pruned tree $\mathcal{T}'$ *(of $\mathcal{T}$) with respect to a set of arguments $A \subseteq \mathcal{A}$ (denoted with $\mathcal{T}' = \mathcal{T} \setminus A$) is a dispute tree such that a node $n = [\text{L}:x]$ is in $\mathcal{T}'$ if and only if the following three conditions hold:*

1. n is in $\mathcal{T}$; and
2. $x \notin A$; and
3. let $E = \{y | [\_:y]$ is an ancestor of n in $\mathcal{T}\}$; then $E \cap A = \{\}$.

The intuition behind Definition 5 is that given a dispute tree $\mathcal{T}$ and a set of arguments A, pruning $\mathcal{T}$ with respect to A yields another tree $\mathcal{T}'$ such that $\mathcal{T}'$ does not contain any node labelled by arguments in A or nodes that "hung below" nodes labelled by arguments in A.

Later we will refer to some pruned tree $\mathcal{T}' = \mathcal{T} \setminus A$ as (non-)admissible without specifying in which AA framework. Implicitly, we will assume that this framework is $AF \setminus A$.

Example 5 (Example 3 continued). An input dispute tree $\mathcal{T}$ for argument a is shown in Fig. 2 (left). Two pruned trees $\mathcal{T}' = \mathcal{T} \setminus \{c\}$ and $\mathcal{T}'' = \mathcal{T} \setminus \{b, c\}$ are shown in the same figure (in the middle and on the right, respectively). We can see that neither $\mathcal{T}$ nor $\mathcal{T}'$ are admissible dispute trees (in AF and in $AF \setminus \{c\}$, respectively). However, $\mathcal{T}''$ is an admissible dispute tree (in $AF \setminus \{b, c\}$).

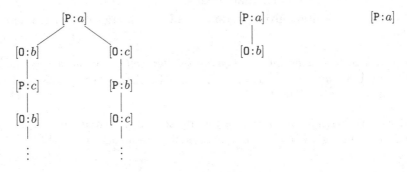

Fig. 2. Dispute tree $\mathcal{T}$ for argument a in Example 5 (left); a pruned tree $\mathcal{T}' = \mathcal{T} \setminus \{c\}$ (middle); a pruned tree $\mathcal{T}'' = \mathcal{T} \setminus \{b, c\}$ (right).

Trivially, the following proposition holds, stating that pruning a dispute tree with an empty set returns the same dispute tree.

Proposition 7. *Let $\mathcal{T}$ be a dispute tree. Then $\mathcal{T} \setminus \{\} = \mathcal{T}$.*

With pruned tree defined, we can identify arguments making a given dispute tree non-admissible, as follows.

Definition 6. *Given some argument a in AF, let T be a dispute tree for a. A tree-arg-explanation (with respect to T) is a set of arguments A such that*

1. $T \setminus A$ *is an admissible dispute tree (in $AF \setminus A$); and*
2. *there is no $A' \subset A$ such that $T \setminus A'$ is an admissible dispute tree (in $AF \setminus A'$).*

Intuitively, given a dispute tree T, a tree-arg-explanation is a minimal set of arguments such that the pruned tree $T \setminus A$ is admissible. For the dispute tree T in Example 5, $\{b, c\}$ is the only tree-arg-explanation for T.

Note that, since we require arg-explanations to be minimal (see Definition 2, condition 2), in general, tree-arg-explanations are not arg-explanations, as illustrated in the following example.

Example 6. Given the AA framework shown in Fig. 1, consider the two dispute trees, T_1 and T_2, for the argument a, shown respectively in the left and the right in Fig. 3. Although $T_1 \setminus \{e, f\}$ and $T_1 \setminus \{b\}$ are admissible, $T_1 \setminus \{c\}$ is not. Indeed, both $\{e, f\}$ and $\{b\}$ are tree-arg-explanations with respect to T_1.

Also, both $T_2 \setminus \{e\}$ and $T_2 \setminus \{b\}$ are admissible. Thus, both $\{e\}$ and $\{b\}$ are tree-arg-explanations with respect to T_2.

By Definition 2, $\{e\}$ and $\{b\}$ are arg-explanations for a and $\{e, f\}$ is not an arg-explanation, although it is a tree-arg-explanation with respect to T_1.

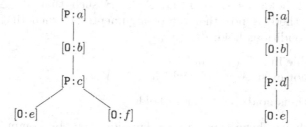

Fig. 3. Two dispute trees T_1 (left) and T_2 (right) for a in the AA framework in Fig. 1.

Proposition 8. *Given an argument $a \in \mathcal{A}$, for any $A \subseteq \mathcal{A}$, if a is admissible in $AF \setminus A$, then there is a dispute tree T for a in AF such that $T' = T \setminus A$ is an admissible dispute tree for a in $AF \setminus A$.*

Proof. If a is admissible in AF, then we let $A = \{\}$, by Proposition 7 and Theorem 3.2 in [12], this proposition holds.

If a is not admissible in AF, we need to show that T can be constructed from T'. We let T be the limit of the sequence $T_1, T_2, \dots, T_n$ constructed as follows:

1. $T_1 = T'$;
2. T_{i+1} is T_i with a new node [L:x] as the child of some node [_:y] such that
   (a) $x \in A$;
   (b) (x, y) is in AF;
   (c) T_{i+1} is a dispute tree.

With this construction, we know that $\mathcal{T}_n$ is a dispute tree for a as $\mathcal{T}_1$ is a dispute tree for a. We can see that $\mathcal{T}_n \setminus A = \mathcal{T}'$ as the specified construction "reverses" the pruning. Hence the proposition holds.

Proposition 8 sanctions that dispute trees give a "complete" approach for computing arg-explanations. In other words, if a set of arguments is an arg-explanation for some argument a (in some AA framework AF), then it will not be missed by looking at dispute trees for a (in AF).

With Proposition 8, we are ready to show the main result for computing arg-explanations with dispute trees, as follows.

Theorem 1. *Given an argument a in AF, let $TT = \{\mathcal{T}_1, \ldots, \mathcal{T}_n, \ldots\}$ be the set of all dispute trees for a and $S = \{A | A$ is a tree-arg-explanation with respect to $\mathcal{T}_i$, for any $\mathcal{T}_i \in TT\}$. For all $A \in S$, if there is no $A' \in S$ such that $A' \subset A$, then A is an arg-explanation for a.*

Proof. To show that A is an arg-explanation for a is to show

1. a is admissible in $AF \setminus A$; and
2. A is a minimal set (with respect to $\subseteq$) satisfying 1.

Condition 1 holds as, since $A \in S$, A is a tree-arg-explanation. Thus, there is some dispute tree $\mathcal{T}_i \in TT$ for a such that $\mathcal{T}_i \setminus A$ is an admissible dispute tree. By Theorem 3.2 in [12], a is admissible in $AF \setminus A$.

Condition 2 holds as there is no $A' \in S$ such that $A' \subset A$; and by Proposition 8, there is no other set of arguments A^* such that both of the following two conditions hold:

1. a is admissible in $AF \setminus A^*$; and
2. there does not exist $A_i \in S$ for which $A_i \subseteq A^*$.

As both conditions hold, the theorem holds.

Thus far, we have shown how arg-explanations can be computed with dispute trees (namely dispute trees are a "sound" mechanism for obtaining arg-explanations). In the rest of this section, we study obtaining att-explanations from dispute trees. We start with defining pruned trees with respect to attacks, as follows.

Definition 7. *Given a dispute tree $\mathcal{T}$, the pruned tree $\mathcal{T}'$ (of $\mathcal{T}$) with respect to a set of attacks R is a dispute tree (denoted with $\mathcal{T}' = \mathcal{T} \setminus R$) such that a node $n = [\text{L}:x]$ ($\text{L} \in \{\text{P}, \text{O}\}$) is in $\mathcal{T}'$ if and only if the following three conditions hold:*

1. *n is in $\mathcal{T}$; and*
2. *if n is a child of $n' = [\_:y]$ in $\mathcal{T}$, then $(x, y) \notin R$; and*
3. *let $S = \{n' | n'$ is an ancestor of n in $\mathcal{T}\}$; then for all $n_1 = [\_ : w] \in S$, $n_2 = [\_:z] \in S$ such that n_1 is a child of n_2, we have $(w, z) \notin R$.*

The intuition behind Definition 7 is that given a dispute tree $\mathcal{T}$ and a set of attacks R, pruning $\mathcal{T}$ with respect to R yields another tree $\mathcal{T}'$ such that $\mathcal{T}'$ does not contain any branch rooted at x with y the parent of x, where $(x, y) \in R$.

Example 7 (Example 5 continued). Given the dispute tree $\mathcal{T}$ for argument a shown in Fig. 2 (left), the pruned tree $\mathcal{T}^* = \mathcal{T} \setminus \{(c,a)\}$ is shown in Fig. 4. $\mathcal{T}^*$ is an admissible dispute tree.

Fig. 4. A pruned tree $\mathcal{T}^* = \mathcal{T} \setminus \{(c,a)\}$ for Example 7.

Following the same idea behind Definition 6, we define *tree-att-explanation* as follows.

Definition 8. *Given a dispute tree $\mathcal{T}$ for some argument a, a* tree-att-explanation *(with respect to $\mathcal{T}$) is a set of attacks $R \subseteq \mathcal{R}$ such that*

1. *$\mathcal{T} \setminus R$ is an admissible dispute tree; and*
2. *there is no set of attacks $R' \subset R$ such that $\mathcal{T} \setminus R'$ is admissible.*

In the same way that tree-arg-explanations are not always arg-explanations, tree-att-explanations are not always att-explanations, as illustrated in the following example.

Example 8. Given the AA framework shown in Fig. 5 (left), there are two dispute trees, $\mathcal{T}_1$ and $\mathcal{T}_2$, for argument a (shown respectively in the middle and the right in Fig. 5).

From $\mathcal{T}_1$, we see that $\{(h,c),(g,f)\}$ is a tree-att-explanation. Yet, from $\mathcal{T}_2$ we see that $\{(g,f)\}$ alone is also a tree-att-explanation. Thus, the former tree-att-explanation is not an att-explanation and the latter is.

Similarly to Proposition 8, the following proposition for att-explanations holds, sanctioning a form of "completeness" for obtaining att-explanations.

Proposition 9. *Given an argument a in AF, for any set of attacks R in AF, if a is admissible in $AF \setminus R$, then there is a dispute tree $\mathcal{T}$ for a in AF such that $\mathcal{T} \setminus R$ is an admissible dispute tree.*

Finally, we are ready to show the main result for obtaining att-explanations with dispute trees, as follows.

Theorem 2. *Given an argument a in AF, let $TT = \{\mathcal{T}_1, \ldots, \mathcal{T}_n, \ldots\}$ be the set of all dispute trees for a and $S = \{A | A$ is a tree-att-explanation with respect to $\mathcal{T}_i$, for any $\mathcal{T}_i \in TT\}$. For all $R \in S$, if there is no $R' \in S$ such that $R' \subset R$, then R is an att-explanation for a.*

The proof of Theorem 2 is similar to the one of Theorem 1.

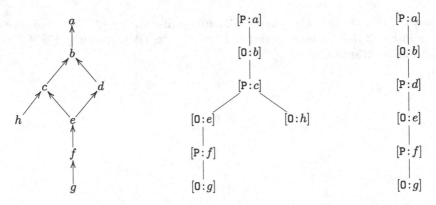

Fig. 5. AA framework in Example 8 (left); a dispute tree $\mathcal{T}_1$ for argument a (middle); another dispute tree $\mathcal{T}_2$ for a (right).

5 Discussion

In this paper, we have given two different notions of explanations, the "argument-view" and the "attack-view". Comparing the two, the following observations can be made.

Firstly, arg-explanations are more suitable for identifying "fixes" for arguments not being admissible. For instance, given an arg-explanation, to make the topic argument admissible, one can just add new attacks to all arguments in the arg-explanation. Thus, for dialectical applications such as *persuasion* in multi-agent systems (e.g. see [19,26]), identifying arg-explanations helps agents know effective attacking points, i.e. arguments to attack to render the topic admissible. It is easy to see that att-explanations do not grant this ability, as inserting new arguments attacking the attacking arguments in an att-explanation does not necessarily change the admissibility of the topic. For instance, inserting a new argument d attacking c in Example 3 does not make a admissible, though $\{(c,a)\}$ is an att-explanation and c is the attacking argument in (c,a).

Secondly, we have enforced minimality while defining both arg-explanations and att-explanations in Definitions 2 and 4, respectively. As a consequence, as illustrated in Examples 6 and 8, computing both arg-explanations and att-explanations requires the construction of all dispute trees for the topic argument. Constructing all dispute trees for an argument might be deemed to be too expensive computationally for certain applications. For both arg-explanations and att-explanations, in addition to tree-arg/att-explanations, we can consider *rel-arg/att-explanations* as alternatives, briefly discussed below.

The second conditions in Definitions 2 and 4, where minimality is required, can be relaxed to *relatedness*, i.e. for arg-explanations, informally:

A *rel-arg-explanation* for some non-admissible topic argument a is a set of arguments A such that: (1) if A is removed, then a becomes admissible; and (2) every argument in A is related to a as in Definition 3.

By Proposition 3, arg-explanations are rel-arg-explanations. Moreover, it is easy to see that tree-arg-explanations are also rel-arg-explanations. We observe that rel-arg-explanations are easy to obtain, e.g. the set of arguments labelling opponent nodes in a dispute tree gives a rel-arg-explanation. However, it can be viewed that such oversimplification renders rel-arg-explanation less useful for the purpose of recognising the "true source" that triggers the non-admissibility of the topic. Similar reasoning can be applied for att-explanations.

With rel-arg/att-explanations and arg/att-explanations at two extremes, one may think that tree-arg/att-explanations give a good compromise between the usefulness of such explanations and their computation complexity, i.e. obtaining a tree-arg-explanation requires computing a dispute tree with a minimal set of opponent arguments within the tree. Thus, for applications where computing arg/att-explanations is too expensive to be affordable, computing tree-arg/att-explanations could be a suitable alternative for understanding why the topic argument is not admissible.

Thirdly, in this work, we made no distinction between different arg/att-explanations. As illustrated in Example 2, in general, there are multiple arg-explanations for a single topic argument. In Example 2, one may argue that $\{e\}$ is a more reasonable explanation for a as it is the "root of the cause" whereas b is less suitable as it already has two "immediate responses", arguments c and d. However, such reasoning itself is unconvincing as it could be equally well argued that *"if the problem at b is addressed, then there is no need to worry about anything else"*. Similar reasoning can be applied to att-explanations as well. Thus, we take the view that making further distinction between arg/att-explanations is difficult and possibly application-dependent.

6 Related Work

[14,15] have introduced the *related admissibility* argumentation semantics to capture explanations for admissible arguments in both AA and Assumption-based Argumentation. Given an admissible argument as the topic, they model its explanations as a set of arguments defending the topic. They also use dispute trees to compute explanations. Roughly speaking, arguments in proponent nodes from an admissible dispute tree are an explanation for the argument in the root of the tree. They have not studied explanations for non-admissible arguments or explanations in the "attack-view".

[3] have studied revising AA frameworks by adding new arguments which may interact with existing arguments. They have studied the behaviour of the extensions of the augmented argumentation frameworks, taking also into account possible changes of the underlying semantics. Our work is orthogonal to theirs. We are interested in finding explanations for non-admissible arguments and the forms of explanations we study in this paper are concerned with removing arguments or attacks.

[22] have introduced dynamic argumentation frameworks and allowed various revision operators being applied. Their work is performed at a "meta-level" in the

sense that both the underlying logic for arguments and argumentative semantics are left unspecified. Their work is focused on understanding dynamic changes represented in argumentation frameworks and defining operators modelling these changes. Our work differs from theirs as we focus on abstract argumentation and generating explanations.

[16] have studied the minimal changes needed to make some arguments acceptable in an argumentation framework. They have considered two types of changes: adding or removing attacks. Their work is motivated by agents in persuasion. However, in their setting, the set of arguments in the argumentation framework is fixed and only certain attacks can be added or removed. Our study of att-explanations is closely related to their work. However, we have relied on different approaches (with dispute trees) for finding att-explanations whereas they have used a set of rewriting rules.

[6] have studied the impact of adding a new argument to an AA framework, particularly on the set of its extensions. The authors have studied several properties for this type of changes under the grounded and preferred semantics. They are not concerned with giving explanations to the (non-) acceptability of arguments. Comparing with their work, ours is not about revising AA frameworks, but identifying arguments and attacks that affect the non-acceptability of arguments.

[4] have studied the impact of removing a single argument from an AA framework on the set of extensions. Their work is situated in a legal context. Our work is different as we are not concerned with changes to all extensions when a particular argument is removed. Rather, half of our paper concerns which arguments are responsible for the non-admissibility of arguments.

[2] have studied different types of *expansions*, that is, different ways to modify an existing AA framework. In their work, they allow the addition of new arguments, as well as the addition/removal of attacks. The problem studied there is: given an argumentation system and a "goal set" E, find a minimal expansion such that E belongs to at least one extension of the modified system. Though related, they are clearly solving a different problem as we are not concerned with adding arguments or attacks.

[5] use the notion of *explanation dialogues* to represent dialogical proof procedures for abductive argumentation framework. Their notion of explanations is closer to the ones introduced in [14,15], i.e. focus on explanations for sentences (arguments) that are in certain extensions (acceptable), instead of non-acceptable arguments.

[23] also study explanations of arguments as two sets of arguments, a "removal set" and an "addition set". Roughly speaking, an argument can be made acceptable by removing arguments from the removal set and inserting arguments from the addition set. Though their notion of explanation is similar to our arg-explanations, their computation is not based on debate trees or forests. They have not considered att-explanations.

[1] present a work on explanation for failure query in inconsistent knowledge base with argumentation. Their work focuses on using argumentation dialogue

to explain a single type of query whereas ours aims at introducing a general theory of explanation for unacceptable arguments.

The literature on human-computer interaction includes a considerable amount of work on explanation in various contexts, e.g. for recommender systems [24], and on evaluating empirically various explanatory tools according to various criteria such as effectiveness and transparency [24]. We have focused on defining various notions of explanation for abstract argumentation, and in particular for non-membership of arguments in admissible extensions. It would be interesting in the future to evaluate empirically our techniques, and in particular the relative merits of the various notions of explanation we have defined according to criteria identified in the HCI literature.

We have defined tree-att-explanations (see Definition 8) in terms of a pruning operator over dispute trees. Other forms of pruning have been defined in the literature, e.g. in [8], but for different tasks and frameworks, e.g., in the case of [8], for improving query answering in Possibilistic Defeasible Logic Programming. It would be nonetheless interesting to study whether other forms of pruning could provide other notions of explanation for abstract argumentation, and whether our form of pruning could serve the purpose of defining explanatory methods in other frameworks.

7   Conclusion

Argumentation has its unique advantage in explaining the process and results of its computation. To fully exploit this advantage, [14, 15] study explanations for admissible arguments. In short, that work considers explanations for an admissible argument as arguments defending it. In this work, we shift our focus to explanations for arguments that are not admissible. We aim to be able to explain *why some argument is not admissible*. We take the view that an argument a is not admissible because of the presence of some arguments A or attacks R, such that if A or R are removed, then a becomes admissible. Thus, an explanation in the "argument-view" (arg-explanation) of a is A and an explanation in the "attack-view" (att-explanation) of a is R.

We have shown that, although exhibiting similarities, arg-explanations and att-explanations for the same argument do not always coincide. We have used dispute trees for obtaining both forms of explanations.

Explanations studied in this work are based on the admissibility semantics in abstract argumentation. In the future, we would like to explore explanations with other semantics and other argumentation formalisms. Note that in this paper we have already implicitly addressed explanations for arguments not belonging to any preferred extension [9], since preferred extensions are maximally admissible and every admissible extension is contained in some preferred extension; therefore, if an argument does not belong to any preferred extension then it does not belong to any admissible extension either. In addition, we plan to study other types of explanations, e.g. based on relatedness rather than minimality. The computation approach introduced in this work is based on dispute trees. It will be interesting to see if other approaches, e.g. labelling-based, can be developed. Moreover, explanations are studied in this work from a theoretical viewpoint. It would be very useful if experiments of our notions of explanations could be conducted with real users from a human-computer interaction perspective, e.g. along the lines of [7,21,24]. Finally, it would be interesting to study the various notions of explanation we have defined from a computational complexity perspective, to determine their computational viability.

Acknowledgements. This research was supported by the EPSRC TRaDAr project *Transparent Rational Decisions by Argumentation*: EP/J020915/1.

References

1. Arioua, A., Tamani, N., Croitoru, M., Buche, P.: Query failure explanation in inconsistent knowledge bases using argumentation. In: Proceedings of the COMMA, pp. 101–108 (2014)
2. Baumann, R.: What does it take to enforce an argument? minimal change in abstract argumentation. In: Proceedings of the ECAI, pp. 127–132 (2012)
3. Baumann, R., Brewka, G.: Expanding argumentation frameworks: Enforcing and monotonicity results. In: Computational Models of Argument: Proceedings of COMMA 2010, Desenzano del Garda, Italy, 8–10 September 2010, pp. 75–86 (2010)
4. Bisquert, P., Cayrol, C., de Saint-Cyr, F.D., Lagasquie-Scheix, M.-C.: Change in Argumentation Systems: Exploring the Interest of Removing an Argument. In: Benferhat, S., Grant, J. (eds.) SUM 2011. LNCS, vol. 6929, pp. 275–288. Springer, Heidelberg (2011)
5. Booth, R., Gabbay, D.M., Kaci, S., Rienstra, T., Torre, L.V.D.: Abduction and dialogical proof in argumentation and logic programming. In: Proceedings of the ECAI, pp. 117–122 (2014)
6. Cayrol, C., Saint-Cyr, F.D., Lagasquie-Schiex, M.: Change in abstract argumentation frameworks: Adding an argument. JAIR **38**, 49–84 (2010)
7. Cerutti, F., Tintarev, N., Oren, N.: Formal arguments, preferences, and natural language interfaces to humans: an empirical evaluation. In: ECAI 2014–21st European Conference on Artificial Intelligence, 18–22 August 2014, Prague, Czech Republic - Including Prestigious Applications of Intelligent Systems (PAIS 2014), pp. 207–212 (2014)
8. Chesñevar, C.I., Simari, G.R., Godo, L.: Computing dialectical trees efficiently in possibilistic defeasible logic programming. In: Baral, C., Greco, G., Leone, N., Terracina, G. (eds.) LPNMR 2005. LNCS (LNAI), vol. 3662, pp. 158–171. Springer, Heidelberg (2005)
9. Dung, P.M.: On the acceptability of arguments and its fundamental role in non-monotonic reasoning, logic programming and n-person games. AIJ **77**(2), 321–357 (1995)
10. Dung, P.M., Kowalski, R.A., Toni, F.: Dialectic proof procedures for assumption-based, admissible argumentation. AIJ **170**, 114–159 (2006)
11. Dung, P.M., Kowalski, R.A., Toni, F.: Assumption-based argumentation. In: Simari, G., Rahwan, I. (eds.) Argumentation in Artificial Intelligence, pp. 199–218. Springer, Heidelberg (2009)

12. Dung, P.M., Mancarella, P., Toni, F.: Computing ideal sceptical argumentation. AIJ **171**(10–15), 642–674 (2007)
13. Fan, X., Toni, F.: Decision Making with Assumption-Based Argumentation. In: Black, E., Modgil, S., Oren, N. (eds.) TAFA 2013. LNCS, vol. 8306, pp. 127–142. Springer, Heidelberg (2014)
14. Fan, X., Toni, F.: On computing explanation in abstract argumentation. In: Proceedings of the ECAI (2014)
15. Fan, X., Toni, F.: On computing explanations in argumentation. In: Proceedings of the AAAI (2015)
16. Kontarinis, D., Bonzon, E., Maudet, N., Perotti, A., van der Torre, L., Villata, S.: Rewriting Rules for the Computation of Goal-Oriented Changes in an Argumentation System. In: Leite, J., Son, T.C., Torroni, P., van der Torre, L., Woltran, S. (eds.) CLIMA XIV 2013. LNCS, vol. 8143, pp. 51–68. Springer, Heidelberg (2013)
17. Modgil, S., Prakken, H.: The ASPIC$^+$ framework for structured argumentation: a tutorial. Argum. Comput. **5**(1), 31–62 (2014)
18. Modgil, S., et al.: The added value of argumentation. In: Ossowski, S. (ed.) Agreement Technologies, vol. 8, pp. 357–403. Springer, Heidelberg (2013)
19. Prakken, H.: Formal systems for persuasion dialogue. Knowl. Eng. Rev. **21**(2), 163–188 (2006)
20. Rahwan, I., Simari, G.R.: Argumentation in Artificial Intelligence. Springer, Heidelberg (2009)
21. Rahwan, I., Madakkatel, M.I., Bonnefon, J.-F., Awan, R.N., Abdallah, S.: Behavioral experiments for assessing the abstract argumentation semantics of reinstatement. Cogn. Sci. **34**(8), 1483–1502 (2010)
22. Rotstein, N.D., Moguillansky, M.O., Falappa, M.A., García, A.J., Simari, G.R.: Argument theory change: Revision upon warrant. In: Computational Models of Argument: Proceedings of COMMA 2008, Toulouse, France, 28–30 May 2008, pp. 336–347 (2008)
23. Sakama, C.: Abduction in argumentation frameworks and its use in debate games. In: Nakano, Y., Satoh, K., Bekki, D. (eds.) JSAI-isAI 2013. LNCS, vol. 8417, pp. 285–303. Springer, Heidelberg (2014)
24. Tintarev, N., Masthoff, J.: Evaluating the effectiveness of explanations for recommender systems - methodological issues and empirical studies on the impact of personalization. User Model. User-Adapt. Interact. **22**(4–5), 399–439 (2012)
25. Toni, F.: A tutorial on assumption-based argumentation. Argument & Computation, Special Issue: Tutorials on Structured Argumentation **5**(1), 89–117 (2014)
26. Walton, D., Krabbe, E.: Commitment in Dialogue: Basic concept of interpersonal reasoning. State University of New York Press, Albany (1995)

Building Support-Based Opponent Models
in Persuasion Dialogues

Christos Hadjinikolis[(✉)], Sanjay Modgil, and Elizabeth Black

King's College London, London, UK
{christos.hadjinikolis,sanjay.modgil,elizabeth.black}@kcl.ac.uk

Abstract. This paper deals with an approach to opponent-modelling in argumentation-based persuasion dialogues. It assumes that dialogue participants (agents) have models of their opponents' knowledge, which can be augmented based on previous dialogues. Specifically, previous dialogues indicate relationships of support, which refer both to arguments as abstract entities and to their logical constituents. The augmentation of an opponent model relies on these relationships. An argument external to an opponent model can augment that model with its logical constituents, if that argument shares support relationships with other arguments that can be constructed from that model. The likelihood that the constituents of supporting arguments will in fact be known to an opponent, varies according to support types. We therefore provide corresponding quantifications for each support type.

1 Introduction

Strategy development in agent dialogues is an area that has received ample research interest in the last years [2,3,8,10,15,20–22]. Specifically, strategising in a dialogue concerns the selection of a particular locution among all available locutions, which by some measure is deemed optimal [7]. In competitive contexts, "optimal" is understood in terms of increasing a participant's self-interested utility. Since in such contexts the employed knowledge is usually distributed amongst the participants, agents are unaware of the locutions available to their opponents. Thus, they often assume models of their opponents' possible knowledge for simulating how a dialogue may evolve, and develop strategies accordingly.

Building and updating an opponent model (OM) is a challenging task. As Black and Hunter explain in [4], one needs to investigate how such models can be maintained and under what circumstances they can be useful, and go on to identify situations in which the use of particular model-update mechanisms may be disadvantageous. Generally, a common assumption is that OMs can be constructed on the basis of a participant's accumulated dialogue experience [10,15,21]. Specifically in the context of argumentation-based persuasion dialogues, some researchers propose that these models are augmented with external content (arguments), assuming relationships between the latter and information already in the model [10]. These relationships can be based on the notion of *support*.

E. Black et al. (Eds.): TAFA 2015, LNAI 9524, pp. 128–145, 2015.
DOI: 10.1007/978-3-319-28460-6_8

In [10], Hadjinikolis *et al.* rely on the $ASPIC^+$ framework for structured argumentation to define a dialogue system for persuasion. In this system agents are assumed to have models of their opponents' knowledge. This knowledge can be augmented based on a modeller's dialogue history using the notion of *reinstatement* support. For example, assume that two agents, Ag_1 (modeller) and Ag_2 (opponent) engage in a dialogue. Let A be an argument introduced by Ag_2 in a dialogue, countered by Ag_1 with argument B. If B is then countered by Ag_2 with a third argument C, we then assume a support relationship between A (the supported) and C (the supporter), in the sense that C reinstates A. Ag_1 can model such relationships as directed, weighted arcs, linking nodes that represent the associated arguments (e.g. $A \rightarrow C$), in what is referred to as a relationship graph (RG). An arc weight represents the frequency with which a certain argument is followed by a supporter in dialogues in which the modeller has participated, e.g. how often does C follow after A. Relying on this graph Ag_1 can augment an existing OM of another agent (e.g. Ag_3), to include the logical constituents of supporters, assuming that the latter are related to arguments that can be instantiated from the current state of that OM. For example, including in an OM the constituents of argument C, given that A can already be instantiated by that OM. Arc weights can then be used for the calculation of a probability value assigned to these constituents, which represents the modeller's confidence that an opponent is indeed aware of them.

In addition to reinstatement, other kinds of relationships can be used to identify support between arguments. For example, let an argument A be attacked by two arguments B_1 and B_2. One may argue that B_1 and B_2 support each other since they share the same attack target. Furthermore, more expressive kinds of support can be identified between arguments if one inspects their structure. For example, one may assume that an argument X supports an argument Y if they share the same conclusion/claim. This could also be assumed if X's claim appears as a premise in Y or in the antecedent of a rule in Y.

The purpose of this paper is to extend the work in [10] in the following ways. Firstly, it extends the notion of a RG by including a new kind of support relationship, concerned with arguments which attack the same target, allowing for another modelling alternative. Secondly, by inspecting the structure of related arguments, a refined categorisation of different support types is proposed, according to which support relationships are distinguished between low-level logical relationships and high-level abstract relationships. The first are special instances of the latter. It is then argued that in addition to abstract relationships, logical ones suggest a stronger connection between related arguments, which can be interpreted as an increased likelihood of them being mutually known to a certain opponent. Finally, a more fine grained quantification of these likelihoods is proposed, which reflects the properties of the support relationships they concern.

The paper is organised as follows. Sections 2.1 and 2.2 respectively present the $ASPIC^+$ framework for structured argumentation [13], and the $ASPIC^+$-based dialogue framework for persuasion presented in [9]. Using a framework for structured argumentation is necessary for investigating both abstract as well as logical support relationships between arguments. $ASPIC^+$ is chosen as a general and expressive framework, which accommodates many existing logical approaches to argumentation [13], allowing us to claim an analogous generality for our research. Section 3 elaborates on the categorisation of different support relationships between arguments, and on how they are modelled as weighted directed arcs between nodes of arguments in a $\mathcal{RG}$. Section 4 shows how these weights are quantified in a way that reflects the relationships they concern. Finally, Sect. 5 discusses our work in relation to how the notion of support is generally used in the literature, while Sect. 6 summarises our contributions and presents future work.

2   Background

2.1 $ASPIC^+$

$ASPIC^+$ [13] instantiates Dung's [6] abstract approach by assuming an unspecified logical language $\mathcal{L}$, and by defining arguments as inference trees formed by applying strict or defeasible inference rules of the form $\varphi_1, \ldots, \varphi_n \rightarrow \varphi$ and $\varphi_1, \ldots, \varphi_n \Rightarrow \varphi$, interpreted as 'if the *antecedents* $\varphi_1, \ldots, \varphi_n$ hold, then *without exception*, respectively *presumably*, the *consequent* φ holds'.

To define attacks, minimal assumptions on $\mathcal{L}$ are made; namely that certain wff (well formed formulæ) are a contrary or contradictory of certain other wff. Apart from this the framework is still abstract: it applies to any set of strict and defeasible inference rules, and to any logical language with a defined contrary relation. The basic notion of $ASPIC^+$ is an argumentation system.

Definition 1. *Let* $AS = (\mathcal{L}, ^-, \mathcal{R}, \leq)$ *be an* **argumentation system** *where:*

- *$\mathcal{L}$ is a logical language.*
- *$^-$ is a contrariness function from $\mathcal{L}$ to $2^{\mathcal{L}}$, such that:*
  - *φ is a contrary of ψ if $\varphi \in \overline{\psi}$ and $\psi \notin \overline{\varphi}$;*
  - *φ is a contradictory of ψ (denoted by '$\varphi = -\psi$'), if $\varphi \in \overline{\psi}$ and $\psi \in \overline{\varphi}$.*
- *$\mathcal{R} = \mathcal{R}_s \cup \mathcal{R}_d$ is a set of strict ($\mathcal{R}_s$) and defeasible ($\mathcal{R}_d$) inference rules such that $\mathcal{R}_s \cap \mathcal{R}_d = \emptyset$.*
- *$\leq$ is a pre-ordering on $\mathcal{R}_d$.*

Arguments are then constructed with respect to a knowledge base that is assumed to contain two kinds of formulæ.

Definition 2. *A* **knowledge base (KB)** *in an AS is a pair $(\mathcal{K}, \leq')$ where $\mathcal{K} \subseteq \mathcal{L}$ and $\mathcal{K} = \mathcal{K}_n \cup \mathcal{K}_p$ where these subsets of $\mathcal{K}$ are disjoint: $\mathcal{K}_n$ is the (necessary) axioms (which cannot be attacked); and $\mathcal{K}_p$ is the ordinary premises (on which attacks succeed contingent upon preferences), and where $\leq'$ is a pre-ordering on the ordinary premises $\mathcal{K}_p$.*

Arguments are now defined, where for any argument A, `Prem` returns all the formulas of $\mathcal{K}$ (*premises*) used to build A; `Conc` returns A's conclusion; `Sub` returns all of A's sub-arguments; and `Rules` returns all rules in A.

Definition 3. *An* **argument** *A on the basis of a knowledge base $(\mathcal{K}, \leq')$ in an argumentation system $(\mathcal{L}, ^-, \mathcal{R}, \leq)$ is:*

1. *φ if $\varphi \in \mathcal{K}$ with:* $\mathtt{Prem}(A) = \{\varphi\}$*;* $\mathtt{Conc}(A) = \varphi$*;* $\mathtt{Sub}(A) = \{\varphi\}$*;* $\mathtt{Rules}(A) = \emptyset$*.*
2. *$A_1, \ldots A_n \to/\Rightarrow \psi$ if $A_1, \ldots, A_n$ are arguments such that there exists a strict/defeasible rule* $\mathtt{Conc}(A_1), \ldots, \mathtt{Conc}(A_n) \to/\Rightarrow \psi$ *in $\mathcal{R}_s/\mathcal{R}_d$.*
   $\mathtt{Prem}(A) = \mathtt{Prem}(A_1) \cup \ldots \cup \mathtt{Prem}(A_n)$*;* $\mathtt{Conc}(A) = \psi$*;*
   $\mathtt{Sub}(A) = \mathtt{Sub}(A_1) \cup \ldots \cup \mathtt{Sub}(A_n) \cup \{A\}$*;*
   $\mathtt{Rules}(A) = \mathtt{Rules}(A_1) \cup \ldots \cup \mathtt{Rules}(A_n) \cup$
   $\{\mathtt{Conc}(A_1), \ldots, \mathtt{Conc}(A_n) \to/\Rightarrow \psi\}$

Three kinds of *attack* are defined for $ASPIC^+$ arguments. B can attack A by attacking a premise or conclusion of A, or an inference step in A. For the latter *undercutting* attacks, it is assumed that applications of inference rules can be expressed in the object language; the precise nature of this naming convention will be left implicit.

Definition 4. *A* **attacks** *B iff A undercuts, rebuts or undermines B, where:*

- *A* **undercuts** *argument B (on B') iff $\mathtt{Conc}(A) \in \overline{B'}$ for some $B' \in \mathtt{Sub}(B)$ of the form $B_1'', \ldots, B_n'' \Rightarrow \psi$.*
- *A* **rebuts** *argument B (on B') iff $\mathtt{Conc}(A) \in \overline{\varphi}$ for some $B' \in \mathtt{Sub}(B)$ of the form $B_1'', \ldots, B_n'' \Rightarrow \varphi$. In such a case A contrary-rebuts B iff $\mathtt{Conc}(A)$ is a contrary of φ.*
- *A* **undermines** *B (on B') iff $\mathtt{Conc}(A) \in \overline{\varphi}$ for some $B' = \varphi$, $\varphi \in \mathtt{Prem}(B) \setminus \mathcal{K}_n$. In such a case A contrary-undermines B iff $\mathtt{Conc}(A)$ is a contrary of φ.*

An undercut, contrary-rebut, or contrary-undermine attack is said to be preference-independent, otherwise an attack is preference-dependent.
Then, A **defeats** *B (denoted $A \to B$) iff A attacks B (denoted $A \rightharpoonup B$) on B', and either: $A \rightharpoonup B$ is preference-independent, or; $A \rightharpoonup B$ is preference-dependent and $A \not\prec B'$.*

Some kinds of attack succeed as *defeats* independently of preferences over arguments, whereas others succeed only if the attacked argument is not stronger than the attacking argument. The orderings on defeasible rules and non-axiom premises are assumed to be used in defining an ordering $\preceq$ on the constructed arguments. Unlike [13] a function p is explicitly defined in [9], that takes as input a KB in an *AS* (and so the defined arguments and orderings on rules and premises) and returns $\preceq$ (see [13] for ways in which such a function would define $\preceq$). Finally, $\prec$ is assumed to be the strict counerpart of $\preceq$. The combination of an argumentation system, a knowledge base and a function p, is called an *argumentation theory*.

Definition 5. *An* **argumentation theory** *is a triple $AT = (AS, KB, p)$ where AS is an argumentation system, KB is a knowledge base in AS and:*

$$p : AS \times KB \longrightarrow \preceq$$

such that $\preceq$ is an ordering on the set of all arguments that can be constructed from KB in AS.

2.2 The Dialogue Framework

In [9], Hadjinikolis *et al.* assume an environment of multiple agents $Ag_1, \ldots, Ag_\nu$, where each Ag_i can engage in persuasion dialogues in which its strategic selection of locutions may be based on what Ag_i believes its interlocutor (in the set $Ag_{j\neq i}$) believes. Each Ag_i maintains a model of its possible opponent agents that represents the logical information possible opponents may use to construct arguments and preferences, rather than just abstract arguments and their relations. All agents share the same contrary relation $^-$, the same language $\mathcal{L}$, and the same way of defining preferences over arguments based on the pre-orderings over non-axiom premises and defeasible rules (i.e., the same function p).

Definition 6. *Let $\{Ag_1, \ldots, Ag_\nu\}$ be a set of agents. For $i = 1 \ldots \nu$, the **agent theory** of Ag_i is a tuple:*

$$AgT_i = < S_{(i,1)}, \ldots, S_{(i,\nu)} >$$

where for $j = 1 \ldots \nu$, each sub-theory $S_{(i,j)}$ is what Ag_i believes is the argumentation theory $(AS_{(i,j)}, KB_{(i,j)}, p_{(i,j)})$ of Ag_j, and:

- *if $j = i$, $S_{(i,j)}$ is Ag_i's own argumentation theory.*
- *for any $i, j, k, m \in \{1 \ldots \nu\}$, it holds that:*

$$S_{(i,j)} = (AS_{(i,j)}, KB_{(i,j)}, p_{(i,j)}) \quad and \quad S_{(k,m)} = (AS_{(k,m)}, KB_{(k,m)}, p_{(k,m)})$$

be any two distinct sub-theories, then:

$$p_{(i,j)} = p_{(k,m)}, \quad \mathcal{L}_{(i,j)} = \mathcal{L}_{(k,m)} \quad and \quad {}^-(i,j) = {}^-(k,m).$$

Table 1. The discrete sets of logical elements found in each sub-theory of Ag_i's agent theory (AgT_i).

		1 $\mathcal{K}$	2 $\leq'$	3 $\mathcal{R}$	4 $\leq$
1	$S_{(i,1)}$	$\mathcal{K}_{(i,1)}$	$\leq'_{(i,1)}$	$\mathcal{R}_{(i,1)}$	$\leq_{(i,1)}$
2	$S_{(i,2)}$	$\mathcal{K}_{(i,2)}$	$\leq'_{(i,2)}$	$\mathcal{R}_{(i,2)}$	$\leq_{(i,2)}$
.	...	...	...	...	...
i	$S_{(i,i)}$	$\mathcal{K}_{(i,i)}$	$\leq'_{(i,i)}$	$\mathcal{R}_{(i,i)}$	$\leq_{(i,i)}$
.	...	...	...	...	...
ν	$S_{(i,\nu)}$	$\mathcal{K}_{(i,\nu)}$	$\leq'_{(i,\nu)}$	$\mathcal{R}_{(i,\nu)}$	$\leq_{(i,\nu)}$

A simplified version of an agent's AgT appears in Table 1. Essentially, the notion of an OM is captured by a sub-theory. For convenience, a simplified version of a sub-theory is assumed, of the form:

$$S_{(i,j)} = \{\mathcal{K}_{(i,j)}, \leq'_{(i,j)}, \mathcal{R}_{(i,j)}, \leq_{(i,j)}\}$$

which contains the discrete sets of logical elements assumed by the modeller (in this case Ag_i) to be known by each of its opponents ($Ag_{j\neq i}$), including the modeller's own sub-theory ($S_{(i,i)}$). Henceforth, we may omit subscripts identifying pre-orderings and rules specific to a given agent.

Dialogue participants are assumed to introduce arguments constructed in a common language $\mathcal{L}$, which attack those of their opponent, sharing an understanding of when one argument attacks another, based on the language dependent notion of conflict. Preferences may also be submitted in the dialogue against arguments, as a means of invalidating the success of an attack as defeat. *Commitment stores* are employed, to store the preferences and the logical constituents of the arguments introduced by each agent in a dialogue. These commitment stores are then used by the dialogue participants for directly updating the sub-theories (OMs) of their respective opponents, e.g. Ag_i can use the commitment store of its opponent Ag_j in a dialogue to *update* the contents of its sub-theory $S_{(i,j)}$.

Participants assume the roles of *proponent* (Pr) and *opponent* (Op), where the former submits an initial argument X, whose claim is the topic of the dialogue. The set of arguments $\mathcal{A}$ instantiated by the logical constituents submitted by both parties during the course of a dialogue, are assumed to be organised into a Dung framework, $AF = (\mathcal{A}, \mathcal{D})$, where $\mathcal{D}$ is the binary defeat relation on $\mathcal{A}$, i.e. $\mathcal{D} \subseteq \mathcal{A} \times \mathcal{A}$, defined on the basis of the attack relationships between the arguments, and the preferences introduced into the dialogue by both participants. Two sets of protocol rules are described: one for the grounded and one for the preferred semantics. These rules regulate turn-taking and the legal moves available to the participants in a dialogue, in a way that reflects their respective semantics. Conflicting preferences are resolved in favour of Op in the grounded case, and of Pr in the preferred[1].

Since the modelling of an opponent's preferences is not in the scope of this work, we only assume dialogue moves whose content is just arguments and leave the modelling of preferences to future work. Furthermore, since our interest is just to model opponent arguments in terms of how they appear in dialogues, rather than distinguishing between different dialogues with respect to different semantics (e.g. grounded, preferred), we define a general dialogue with minimal restrictions on the moves available to each participant at each point.

We define a dialogue $\mathcal{D}$ as a sequence of dialogue moves $< \mathcal{DM}_0, \ldots, \mathcal{DM}_n >$ of the form $\mathcal{DM} =< I, A >$, where $I \in \{Pr, Op\}$, $\overline{I} = Pr$ if $I = Op$ and vice-versa, and A is an argument in the set $\mathcal{A}_I$ instantiated from I's sub-theory ($S_{(I,I)}$) as well as from the commitment store of a participant's opponent. The content of $\mathcal{DM}_0$ is the initial argument for the topic of the dialogue. The legality of a dialogue move is regulated by explicit rules that, among others, account for the dialogical objective and a participant's role. For the purpose of this paper these are defined as follows:

Definition 7. $\mathcal{D} =< \mathcal{DM}_0, \ldots, \mathcal{DM}_n >$ *is a* **legal** *persuasion dialogue if:*

---

[1] Note that if agents play logically perfectly they can be shown to win iff the argument they move is justified under the grounded respectively preferred semantics in the framework constructed during the dialogue [9].

1. $\mathcal{DM}_0 =< Pr, X >$ *(the dialogue begins with Pr's move);*
2. *for $i = 0 \ldots n - 1$, if $\mathcal{DM}_i =< I, A \in \mathcal{A}_I >$ then $\mathcal{DM}_{i+1} =< \bar{I}, B \in \mathcal{A}_{\bar{I}} >$ (Pr and Op take turns);*
3. *for $i = 1 \ldots n$, each $\mathcal{DM}_i$ is a reply to some $\mathcal{DM}_j$, $j < i$ (alternative replies are allowed), where $\mathcal{DM}_j =< I, A >$, $\mathcal{DM}_i =< \bar{I}, B >$ and B attacks A.*

Since we assume multi-reply protocols which allow participants to *backtrack* and reply to previous opponent moves, dialogues can be represented as trees rather than sequences of moves. An example is shown in Fig. 1a, where Ag_1's moves $\mathcal{DM}_5$ & $\mathcal{DM}_7$ are used as alternative replies against Ag_2's move $\mathcal{DM}_1$.:

Definition 8. *Let $\mathscr{D} =< \mathcal{DM}_0, \ldots, \mathcal{DM}_n >$ be a dialogue and $\mathcal{M} = \{\mathcal{DM}_0, \ldots, \mathcal{DM}_n\}$ the set of moves in $\mathscr{D}$. Then $\mathcal{T} = \{\mathcal{M}, \mathcal{E}\}$ is a **dialogue tree** with root node $\mathcal{DM}_0$, and arcs $\mathcal{E} \subseteq \mathcal{M} \times \mathcal{M}$, such that for every two moves $\mathcal{DM}_i$ & $\mathcal{DM}_j$, $(\mathcal{DM}_i, \mathcal{DM}_j) \in \mathcal{E}$ means that $\mathcal{DM}_j$ is $\mathcal{DM}_i$'s target ($\mathcal{DM}_i$ replies to $\mathcal{DM}_j$).*

Every move in $\mathcal{M}$ that is not the target of another move is a *leaf-node*, while each distinct path from $\mathcal{DM}_0$ to a leaf node is a *dispute*. For a $\mathcal{T}$ with m leaf-nodes, $\Delta = \{d_1, \ldots, d_m\}$ is the set of all disputes in $\mathcal{T}$. Each new dispute results from a backtracking move by either of the participants. Note that for convenience we may represent a dialogue tree as $\mathcal{T} = \{d_1, \ldots, d_m\}$.

Provided a modeller's history of dialogues, Hadjinikolis *et al.* [10] model support relationships between arguments in these dialogues, in the form of a relationship graph ($\mathcal{RG}$). A $\mathcal{RG}$ is assumed to be incrementally constructed through a series of dialogues. It is composed of nodes which represent the set of all encountered opponent arguments (OAs) in a modeller's dialogue history, linked with directed, weighted arcs that represent support relationships between them.

Definition 9. *Let $\mathcal{H} = \{\mathscr{D}^1, \ldots, \mathscr{D}^k\}$ be an agent's **history** of dialogues and $\mathcal{A}^{\mathcal{H}}$ represent the set of arguments introduced by that agent's opponents in $\mathcal{H}$. Then a **relationship graph** ($\mathcal{RG}$) is a directed graph $\mathcal{RG} = \{\mathcal{A}^{\mathcal{H}}, R\}$, where $R \subseteq \mathcal{A}^{\mathcal{H}} \times \mathcal{A}^{\mathcal{H}}$ is a set of weighted arcs representing support relationships. For two arguments $A, B \in \mathcal{A}^{\mathcal{H}}$, we write r_{AB} to denote the arc $(A, B) \in R$, and denote the arc's weight as w_{AB} where $0 \leq w_{AB} \leq 1$.*

Note that arc weights are actually probability values. Thus, henceforth we may write $Pr(r_{AB})$ referring to r_{AB}'s weight w_{AB}, i.e. $Pr(r_{AB}) = w_{AB}$.

Finally, the augmentation process proposed in [10] consists of three steps. Let Ag_1 and Ag_2 be two agents about to engage in a dialogue. Let Ag_1 have a model of Ag_2's possible knowledge $S_{(1,2)}$ and let $\mathcal{RG}_1$ be Ag_1's relationship graph. First, instantiate a set $\mathcal{A}$ with all arguments that can be constructed from $S_{(1,2)}$. Second, identify a set $N_{\mathcal{A}}$ with arguments adjacent to $\mathcal{A}$ in $\mathcal{RG}_1$, where every $X \in N_{\mathcal{A}}$ is a supporter of some $Y \in \mathcal{A}$. Third, based on the arc weights on the support relationships between $\mathcal{A}$ and $N_{\mathcal{A}}$ compute and assign confidence values to the constituents of the arguments in $N_{\mathcal{A}}$, and augment $S_{(1,2)}$ with them.

3   Modelling Support Relationships

The modelling approach proposed in [10] assumes that if two arguments share a support relationship in a $\mathcal{RG}$, then if the supported in the relationship is assumed to be already known to a certain opponent, it is *likely* that the supporter is also known to that opponent. In contrast to [10] we assume more than just one type of support between arguments. This section presents four types of support, distinguishing them according to whether they are abstract or logical.

3.1   Abstract Support Relationships

Abstract support relationships are concerned with how *opponent arguments* appear in a dialogue structure. The first kind of support relationship we discuss is that of *reinstatement support (RS)*. Though not explicitly referred as such, this is the relationship on which the work in [10] relies on. The RS of an argument A (supported) by an argument B (supporter) is represented if B defends A as defined in [6]. An example of a RS identified in the dialogue tree of Fig. 1a is the one between arguments A and C in the sense that C reinstates A by attacking A's attacker B. Other such relationships are those between A and G, A and I, and C and E, for which corresponding arcs are instantiated to construct the RS-$\mathcal{RG}$ of Fig. 1b (where we assume Ag_2 is the modeller). The identification of these relationships as well as their representation in an $\mathcal{RG}$, is defined as follows.

Definition 10. *Let $\mathcal{RG} = \{\mathcal{A}^{\mathcal{H}}, R\}$ be a relationship graph and $RS \subseteq R$ be a subset of R representing all of the* **RS** *relationships. Let A and B be any two arguments respectively serving as the content of two opponent dialogue moves $\mathcal{DM}_i \in d_k$ and $\mathcal{DM}_j \in d_l$ in a dialogue tree $T = \{d_1, \ldots, d_m\}$. Let* level() *be a function applied on a $\mathcal{DM}$ that returns the level of the move in T. Then $\exists r_{AB} \in RS$ if:*

1. *$k = l$ (the two moves are in the same dispute);*
2. *$i < j$ ($\mathcal{DM}_i$ precedes $\mathcal{DM}_j$ in the dialogue);*
3. *level($\mathcal{DM}_j$) − level($\mathcal{DM}_i$) = 2.*

In this paper we now introduce the additional notion of a *common attack target support (CATS)* relationship. Intuitively, arguments which attack the same target support each other in the sense that they serve the same objective; to invalidate that target. An example of a CATS identified in the dialogue tree of Fig. 1a is the one between arguments C and G, in the sense that they both attack the same target (argument B). Notice that in contrast to RS relationships, each argument in a CATS relationship supports the other. Hence, arcs between these arguments are reciprocal.

Referring to Fig. 1a, CATS relationships exist between G and I, and C and I; hence the corresponding arcs in the CATS-$\mathcal{RG}$ of Fig. 1c. In general, arguments are linked in a $\mathcal{RG}$ if they appear in distinct disputes in the same dialogue, in reply to the same modeller argument, i.e. attacking the same target in a dialogue. We formally express this as follows.

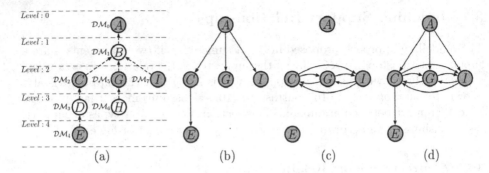

Fig. 1. (a) A T between Ag_1(grey) & Ag_2, (b) a RS-$\mathcal{RG}$, (c) a CATS-$\mathcal{RG}$, (d) the joint $\mathcal{RG}$.

Definition 11. *Let* $\mathcal{RG} = \{\mathcal{A}^\mathcal{H}, R\}$ *be a relationships graph. Let* d' *be a sub-dispute of a dispute* $d \in T$ *such that* $d' = < \mathcal{DM}_0, \ldots, \mathcal{DM}_k >$, *and A and B be two arguments respectively serving as the content of two opponent dialogue moves* $\mathcal{DM}_i$ *and* $\mathcal{DM}_j$ *in a dialogue tree* T. *Then* $\exists r_{AB}, r_{BA} \in CATS \subseteq R$, *if both* $\mathcal{DM}_i$ *and* $\mathcal{DM}_j$ *extend* d' *in* T, *and:*

- $\exists d_1' = < \mathcal{DM}_0, \ldots, \mathcal{DM}_k, \mathcal{DM}_i >$, *where* d_1' *is a sub-dispute of a* $d_1 \in T$, *and;*
- $\exists d_2' = < \mathcal{DM}_0, \ldots, \mathcal{DM}_k, \mathcal{DM}_j >$, *where* d_2' *is a sub-dispute of a* $d_2 \in T$.

Note that the reader might well assume the transitive closure of arcs in an $\mathcal{RG}$, so that, for example, the existence of arcs r_{CI} and r_{IC} might be inferred given the existence of arcs r_{CG} & r_{GI} (which infer r_{CI}) and r_{IG} & r_{GC} (which infer r_{IC}) (see Fig. 1). This can assist in reducing the explicit representation of arcs between *all* nodes that attack the same argument. However, as Definition 11 states, it is imperative that arguments are linked with $CATS$ relationships only if they appear *in the same dialogue tree*, attacking the same argument. Take for instance a case where, arguments C and G appear in the same dialogue attacking the same argument, B, while G and I appear in another dialogue attacking B again. In this case, simply relying on transitivity to assume a support link between C and I seems unreasonable, since the two attackers have never *jointly* appeared in the same dialogue attacking the same argument.

This is not to say that assuming a transitivity property is wrong or even counter-intuitive. It does make sense to assume that arguments which distinctly attack the same target may appear together in a future dialogue (or that, equivalently, may be mutually known to a certain opponent). However, the modelling perspective that this paper adopts requires that all linked arguments in a $\mathcal{RG}$ jointly appear in dialogues, as this bears on the likelihood that a certain argument will follow after a certain other.

3.2   Logical Support Relationships

We now turn to logical support relationships. As will be shown, they are in fact special instances of abstract support relationships and will therefore only affect the quantification of the weights assigned to the arcs they concern, i.e. no new arcs will be defined by identified logical supports. Note that we will motivate the need of using logical support relationships in Sect. 4, where we discuss the expectations implied by these relationships and how they positively affect the weighting of the arcs they concern.

In order to investigate logical relationships between arguments we turn to their structure. We exemplify by reference to an argumentation system $AS = (\mathcal{L}, ^-, \mathcal{R}, \leq)$, where:

- $\mathcal{L}$ is a language of propositional literals, composed from a set of propositional atoms $\{a, b, c, \dots\}$ and the symbols $\neg$ and $\sim$ respectively denoting strong and weak negation (i.e., negation as failure);
- α is a strong literal if α is a propositional atom or of the form $\neg\beta$ where β is a propositional atom;
- α is a wff of $\mathcal{L}$ if α is a strong literal or of the form $\sim \beta$ where β is a strong literal, and;
- for a wff α, α and $\neg\alpha$ are contradictories and α is a contrary of $\sim \alpha$.

Assume then a dialogue between two agents (Ag_1 and Ag_2) with structured arguments, as it appears in Fig. 2a.

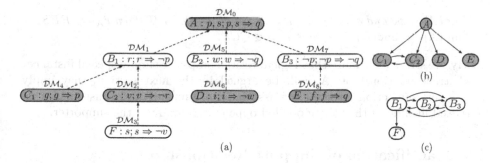

Fig. 2. (a) A dialogue between Ag_1(grey) and Ag_2, (b) the $\mathcal{RG}_s$ constructed by Ag_1 for Ag_2's arguments, and (c) the $\mathcal{RG}_s$ constructed by Ag_2 for Ag_1's arguments.

The first logical relationship we identify is *backbone support (BBS)*. The BBS concerns relationships where the supporter's claim is a formula in the antecedent of a rule in another (supported) argument, in response to a challenge (attack) on that formula (as described in [12]). For instance, take the RS relationship r_{AC_1} (Fig. 2b). Notice in Fig. 2a that C_1's claim p is in the antecedent of rule $p, s \Rightarrow q$ in A, which means that C_1 serves as a BBS for A, in response to the B_1's attack on p. Note that strictly speaking, B_1 attacks the *premise* p in A_1, and in principle BBS support can of course respond to an attack on the conclusion of a defeasible rule (rather than a premise) that supplies the formula in the antecedent of the rule in the supported argument. However, we focus on the formula in the antecedent, to accommodate extensions of our dialogue framework that allow the use of enthymemes as modelled in $ASPIC^+$ [11]; e.g., when A_1 is simply moved as the rule $p, s \Rightarrow q$, and the supporting argument effectively backward extends A_1 [18] in response to the challenge. Finally, notice that though r_{AC_2} is a RS relationship, it cannot be characterised as BBS.

The second kind of logical relationship is that of *common conclusion support (CCS)*. CCS bears on a participant's ability to support a certain claim in multiple ways. An example of a CCS can be identified in Fig. 2a between arguments B_2 and B_3 since they share the same claim $\neg q$. Notice again that while $r_{B_1 B_2}$, $r_{B_2 B_1}$, $r_{B_1 B_3}$, $r_{B_3 B_1}$, and $r_{B_2 B_3}$, $r_{B_3 B_2}$ concern CATS relationships, only the last two additionally concern CCS relationships.

At this point we must clarify that it is not the case that just CATS can also be CCS relationships or that just RS relationships can be BBS relationships. Take for example the CATS relationship $r_{B_1 B_3}$ (Fig. 2c). Notice that B_1 serves as a BBS for argument B_3 (Fig. 2a). Further notice that r_{AE} (Fig. 2b) is a RS which is also a CCS (Fig. 2a). These relationships are formally defined as follows.

Definition 12. *Let* $\mathcal{R}G = \{A^{\mathcal{H}}, R\}$ *be a relationship graph where* $R = RS \cup CATS$. *Let A and B be two arguments in* $A^{\mathcal{H}}$ *and* $r_{AB} \in R$. *Then* $BBS \subseteq R$ *is a subset of R representing all* **backbone support** *relationships, and* $CCS \subseteq R$ *is a subset of R representing all* **common conclusion support** *relationships, where if:*

- *$\mathrm{Conc}(A) = \phi$, and ϕ is in the antecedent of a rule in B, then $r_{AB} \in BBS$;*
- *$\mathrm{Conc}(A) = \mathrm{Conc}(B) = \phi$, then $r_{AB} \in CCS$.*

Lastly, we stress once more that logical relationships are simply special instances of abstract relationships. As will be argued in the next section, they imply a stronger connection between the associated arguments, and consequently an increased likelihood that the modelled opponent is aware of the supporter.

4   Quantification of Support Relationships

All arcs in a $\mathcal{R}G$ assume assignment of numerical weight values. These values express likelihoods, in the form of probability values, that a supporter argument can be constructed by the modelled opponent, contingent on the latter being aware of the supported argument. Weight assignation depends on the abstract as well as on the logical support type of a relationship. Thus, we assume that arc weights (w) are produced from two distinct sub-weights; one abstract w^α, and one logical w^λ. We propose that logical weights should have a positive impact on the overall weight of an arc, given that we interpret abstract and logical weights as probability values concerned with the *same* random event; that of the supporter in a relationship being known to an opponent, contingent on knowledge of the supported. We therefore define the weight of an arc to be equal to the joint probability value of its two sub-weights. All weight values are independent and identically distributed (i.i.d.).

Definition 13. *Let $\mathcal{H}$ be a modeller's history of dialogues, A and B two arguments of a $\mathcal{RG} = \{\mathcal{A}^{\mathcal{H}}, R\}$ induced from $\mathcal{H}$, and $r_{AB} \in R$ with a weight w_{AB}, where w^{α}_{AB} and w^{λ}_{AB} are respectively the* **abstract and logical sub-weights** *of w_{AB}. Then:*

$$w_{AB} = w^{\alpha}_{AB} + w^{\lambda}_{AB} - w^{\alpha}_{AB} \cdot w^{\lambda}_{AB}.$$

Different support types are quantified differently, and encode expectations regarding the awareness of the supporting arguments. For example, RS relationships imply that supporter opponent arguments are likely to follow after supported arguments in dialogues, as responses to challenges. The extent of that likelihood is defined by the frequency that this is shown to happen between two arguments, in a modeller's history of dialogues.

Assume, for example, that a modeller, Ag_1, monitors an opponent argument A, introduced by various opponents in a series of dialogues. Let A appear a total of 10 times in these dialogues, and is attacked by arguments introduced by Ag_1. Assume then that A is reinstated against those arguments by opponent arguments B, C and D, respectively 3, 4 and 1 times, while in two dialogues A is not reinstated by any argument. Then the abstract weights w^{α}_{AB}, w^{α}_{AC} and w^{α}_{AD} for the respective RS relationships r_{AB}, r_{AC} and r_{AD} will be $\frac{3}{10}$, $\frac{4}{10}$ and $\frac{1}{10}$. These weights represent how likely the supporting argument (e.g. B in r_{AB}) will be submitted by any given opponent, so as to reinstate the supported argument (e.g. A). This is the approach proposed in [10].

We produce an analogous ratio for the case of CATS, which represents how likely a modeller's argument will be attacked by a given pair of opponent arguments. As with RS relationships, CATS implies that supporting opponent arguments are likely to follow after supported arguments, as alternative attacks (replies). Again, this likelihood is defined by the frequency that this is shown to happen in a modeller's history of dialogues.

For example, suppose a modeller's argument A introduced in three dialogues with different agents, where Ag_1 monitors attacks on A. Assume that in the first dialogue A is attacked by opponent arguments B, C and D, in the second by B and C and in the third by B and D. One may then assume the following relationships: r_{BC}, r_{BD}, r_{CB}, r_{CD}, r_{DC} and r_{DB}. The weight for each of these relationships will be the number of times the arguments in each relationship appear jointly, divided by the number of times that the supported argument in the relationship appeared in distinct disputes attacking the common target. For example, C follows B two out of the three times that B attacks A, thus $w_{BC} = \frac{2}{3}$, while B follows C every time that C attacks A, $w_{CB} = \frac{2}{2}$. Hence, $w_{BD} = \frac{1}{3}$, $r_{CD} = \frac{1}{2}$, $w_{DC} = \frac{1}{2}$ and $w_{DB} = \frac{2}{2}$. Definition 14 formally describes these quantifications.

Definition 14. *Let $\mathcal{H}$ be a modeller's history of dialogues and $\mathcal{RG} = \{\mathcal{A}^{\mathcal{H}}, R\}$ the relationship graph induced from $\mathcal{H}$, where $R = RS \cup CATS$ are respectively the sets of reinstatement and common attack target support. Let $r_{AB} \in R$ with* *a weight* w_{AB}, *where* w_{AB}^{α} *is the* **abstract sub-weight** *of* w_{AB}. *Also let:*

$$(a) \text{ occurrences}_{RS}(\mathcal{H}, A, B) = C_{AB},$$
$$(b) \text{ instances}_{RS}(\mathcal{H}, A) = I_A,$$
$$(c) \text{ occurrences}_{CATS}(\mathcal{H}, A, B, C) = J_{AB},$$
$$(d) \text{ instances}_{CATS}(\mathcal{H}, A, C) = I_{AC},$$

be respectively:

(a) *a function that returns the number of times B follows after A in distinct disputes in* $\mathcal{H}$,
(b) *a function that returns the number of times A appeared in distinct disputes in* $\mathcal{H}$ *though not as a leaf,*
(c) *a function that returns the number of joint appearances of A and B against an argument C in the same dialogues in* $\mathcal{H}$,
(d) *a function that returns the number of appearances of A against an argument C in all dialogue of* $\mathcal{H}$.

Then:

$$w_{AB}^{\alpha} = \begin{cases} \frac{C_{AB}}{I_A} & \text{if } r_{AB} \in RS, \\ \frac{J_{AB}}{I_{AC}} & \text{if } r_{AB} \in CATS. \end{cases}$$

Let us turn now to the quantification of logical relationships. As stated earlier, we assume that logical relationships imply a stronger connection between arguments that already share abstract relationships. Our intuitive expectation of this strengthening rests on two assumptions. The first is that generally, if one perceives argumentation as a way of characterising the reasoning one uses to arrive at certain beliefs about the world, it is then reasonable to expect that rational agents would ideally have explored all possible lines of reasoning with respect to a claim. Hence, if an agent makes use of a (sub)argument claiming p, then there is some likelihood that the agent will be aware of other arguments concluding p. Secondly, in real-world dialogues agents move incomplete arguments (enthymemes) in a dialogue (recall our discussion in Sect. 3.2), so that challenges on a formula in the antecedent of a rule, motivates submission of a supporting argument claiming that formula (and so effectively backward extending the incomplete argument).

Based on these two assumptions we *expect* that participants are likely to be aware of multiple ways of arguing for a claim, having been faced with responding to challenges on the claim, as well as having had to respond to challenges on a formula in order to argue why that formula is believed. These expectations are justified by the existence of logical support relationships between some arguments. Take for instance the case of the BBS relationship r_{AC_1} (Fig. 2b). Here the introduction of $C_1 : g; g \Rightarrow p$ is caused by a challenge on $A : p; s; p, s \Rightarrow q$ that forces Ag_1 to reveal an alternative line of reasoning justifying p (in A p is already present as a premise), and hence an alternative line of reasoning justifying q (i.e. $g; g \Rightarrow p; s; p, s \Rightarrow q$). On the other hand, if the incomplete argument

$A' : s; p, s \Rightarrow q$ had been allowed, then the supporting C_1 would have backward extended A' to yield $g; g \Rightarrow p; s; p, s \Rightarrow q$. Similarly, the CCS relationship $r_{B2,B3}$ (Fig. 2c) suggests that Ag_2 has explored other alternatives for $\neg q$, which were revealed in the course of the dialogue, only when it became necessary.

Finally, there are many ways for quantifying the logical weights of an arc r_{AB}. One could focus on the supported argument in the relationship and using all the OM_s available to a modeller, produce a ratio by counting the number of opponents that are aware of (can construct) logical supporters of A. Then, divide that number with the number of opponents that are aware of *any* supporters of A. This quantification approach focusses on the distinction between logical and abstract relationships.

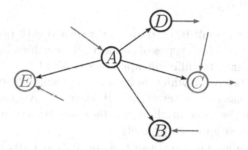

Fig. 3. An instance of a $\mathcal{RG}$ that focuses on the support relationships on argument A.

Take for instance argument A in Fig. 3 which appears to be supported by four arguments, B, C, D and E. Let us assume that out of these four supporters only B and D are logical supporters of A. Suppose that the modeller is operating in a multi-agent environment with a total of 20 agents (excluding the modeller). Let us further assume that out of those 20 agents, 10 can support A with at least one of the supporters, and that of those 10 only 4 are aware of either B either D or of both. This would yield a logical weight value both for r_{AB} and for r_{AD} equal to $\frac{4}{10}$, i.e.:

$$w^\lambda_{AB} = w^\lambda_{AD} = \frac{4}{10}.$$

Though in this case it may seem unreasonable that all logical relationships where A is the supported argument will have the same logical weight, this approach captures the intuition that if an argument A is logically supported by an opponent, then it is *likely* that that opponent will be aware of more logical supporters of A. That *likelihood* is depended on the number of logical supporters an argument has, and therefore the logical weight of an arc is quantified with respect to those supporters.

Other quantification perspectives with different objectives could focus on other aspects of these relationships, e.g. to further distinguish between BBS and CCS relationships. We therefore assume no absolute stance as to the exact way of quantifying logical support relationships and define a general logical weighting function as follows.

Definition 15. *Let AgT be an agent's agent theory containing all the sub-theories of its opponents, and $RG = \{\mathcal{A}^{\mathcal{H}}, R\}$ a relationship graph where BBS, $CCS \subseteq R$ are respectively the sets of backbone and common conclusion support arcs in R. Let $r_{AB} \in \{CCS, BBS\}$ with a weight w_{AB}. Then:*

$$\mathtt{weightL}(RG, r_{AB}, AgT) \rightarrow w_{AB}^{\lambda}$$

is a function that returns w_{AB}'s **logical sub-weight** w_{AB}^{λ}, *where $0 \leq w_{AB}^{\lambda} \leq 1$.*

5   Related Work

The notion of support is multifaceted and is concerned with positive interactions between arguments [17]. Many types of support relationships have been identified in the literature so far with different applications [5, 14, 16]. The most common type is that of reinstatement which is implicit in Dung's framework [6], and is understood in the sense of counter-attack. However, as Amgoud *et al.* argue [1], support does not use the same method as attack and thus counter-attack cannot capture the notion of support completely.

In this respect, different perceptions of the notion have been formalised in the literature, giving rise to a class of acceptability semantics defined within *bipolar argumentation framework (BAF)*, in which interactions between arguments concern both attack as well as support relationships. For example, Boella *et al.* [5] distinguish between what they refer to as *deductive support*, according to which an argument A supports an argument B if the acceptance of A implies the acceptance of B, and *defeasible support* where the previous implication holds only by default and it can be attacked. Similarly, Nouioua [14] assumes a perception of support referred to as *necessary support*, according to which if an argument A necessarily supports B, then acceptance of A is required for the acceptance of B. Also, Oren and Norman [16] introduce the idea of *evidential support*, distinguishing "special" arguments which serve as prima-facie or indisputable sources of truth, and "standard" arguments whose claims are not sufficiently justified, and need to be supported by the former so as to be considered acceptable. Finally, accrual of arguments for the same claim [19] can also be interpreted as support, where the accruing arguments mutually support each other.

Many of the above notions of support are motivated by logical relationships between the constituents of support-related arguments, such as those introduced in this paper. For example, in a similar sense to evidential support, BBS concerns relationships where the supporter is called to justify the antecedent of another argument (the supported), when the latter (which can be considered a standard argument) is challenged. In our case though, the supporter is not required to be a "special" argument. A case of deductive support can also be exemplified through BBS. Assume an argument $B : p; p \rightarrow q$ where p is an ordinary premise and $p \rightarrow q$ a strict rule which cannot be attacked. Assume then an argument $A : s; s \Rightarrow p$ which backbone-supports B. Since $p \rightarrow q$ cannot be attacked, acceptance of A should imply the acceptance of B. This is because any attack on B's premise p must also be by definition an attack on A's claim. Similarly, in the case of necessary support, one could say that A necessarily supports B. Also, CCS effectively models the accrual of mutually supporting arguments for the same claim.

Finally, we have considered extensions to our dialogical framework which allow for use of enthymemes, e.g., $A' : s; p, s \Rightarrow q$ supported by $C_1 : g; g \Rightarrow p;$. As argued by Modgil [12], logical instantiations of frameworks by given sets of formulae do not (for the purposes of argumentation-based inference where the claims of justified arguments identify the inferences from the instantiating formulae) warrant abstract representations of support relations in frameworks. Rather, support relations are useful in other settings, including dialogues. For example when incomplete arguments are moved (e.g., A'), and the missing elements are subsequently supported (e.g., with C_1). If one were to *start* with a set of formulae $\{g; g \Rightarrow p; s; p, s \Rightarrow q\}$, it would suffice to simply construct the argument $g; g \Rightarrow p; s; p, s \Rightarrow q$. In a dialogue, the latter is implicitly, and incrementally, constructed through moving A' and (in response to the challenge) the supporting $C1$. In these contexts, the use of such supporting relationships as well as relationships such as CATS, provide further value for opponent modelling purposes and for OM augmentation.

6   Conclusions and Future Work

This paper extended the work of Hadjinikolis *et al.* [10] in the following ways. Firstly, it extended the notion of a $\mathcal{RG}$ by introducing $CATS_s$ relationships between arguments, which is to the best of our knowledge a novel notion of support presented here, allowing for more modelling alternatives. Secondly, it proposed a distinction between abstract support relationships concerned with how arguments appear in the structure of dialogues, and logical relationships, concerned with relationships between the constituents of arguments already abstractly related. It then argued that (as in [12]) these relationships are redundant when considering logical instantiations for argumentation-based inference, but are needed in dialogical contexts, providing further value for opponent modelling purposes. Lastly, corresponding quantifications of the likelihoods implied by the presented support relationships were proposed.

We should clarify that the proposed modelling mechanism is not to be used for building an OM through its sole use, but rather to be jointly used with other mechanisms to augment an existing OM. Such mechanisms may concern: *direct collection* [10], where the constituents of arguments asserted in a dialogue by an opponent are directly added to its OM; the use of *virtual arguments* [20], based on which meta-levels of an OM are assumed, which contain arguments possibly known to an opponent that the modeller itself is not aware of, and; the employment of mechanisms concerned with removing data from an OM that are inconsistent with an opponent's behaviour [3]. Combined use of these mechanisms, rather than just the use of the one proposed in this paper, limits the possibility that a constructed OM will concern a system of supportive arguments of one's opponent, rather than a general representation of that opponent's knowledge—since OM_s will be built and updated based on more than just support relationships. Support is only used as a reasonable basis for inferring likelihoods that certain arguments, currently not members of an OM, could be known to a modelled opponent and should thus be included in its OM.

Future research will focus on the development of a methodology towards evaluating our modelling approach and validating our assumptions on the increased likelihoods implied by logical support relationships between arguments. Finally, we also intend to extend our work by including "why" locutions, which are expected to make logical relationships more evident.

References

1. Amgoud, L., Cayrol, C., Lagasquie-Schiex, M.C., Livet, P.: On bipolarity in argumentation frameworks. Int. J. Intell. Syst. **23**(10), 1062–1093 (2008)
2. Black, E., Atkinson, K.: Choosing persuasive arguments for action. In: Proceedings of the Tenth International Conference on Autonomous Agents and Multi-Agent Systems, AAMAS 2011, pp. 905–912 (2011)
3. Black, E., Coles, A., Bernardini, S.: Automated planning of simple persuasion dialogues. In: Bulling, N., van der Torre, L., Villata, S., Jamroga, W., Vasconcelos, W. (eds.) CLIMA 2014. LNCS, vol. 8624, pp. 87–104. Springer, Heidelberg (2014)
4. Black, E., Hunter, A.: Reasons and options for updating an opponent model in persuasion dialogues. In: Proceedings of the International Workshop on Theory and Applications of Formal Argumentation, TAFA 2015 (2015)
5. Boella, G., Gabbay, D.M., van der Torre, L.W.N., Villata, S.: Support in abstract argumentation. In: Proceedings of Computational Models of Argument, COMMA 2010, pp. 111–122 (2010)
6. Dung, P.M.: On the acceptability of arguments and its fundamental role in non-monotonic reasoning, logic programming and n-person games. Artif. Intell. **77**(2), 321–357 (1995)
7. Dunne, P.E., McBurney, P.: Concepts of optimal utterance in dialogue: selection and complexity. In: Dignum, F.P.M. (ed.) ACL 2003. LNCS (LNAI), vol. 2922, pp. 310–328. Springer, Heidelberg (2004)
8. Emele, C.D., Norman, T.J., Parsons, S.: Argumentation strategies for plan resourcing. In: Proceedings of the Tenth International Conference on Autonomous Agents and Multi-Agent Systems, AAMAS 2011, pp. 913–920 (2011)
9. Hadjinikolis, C., Modgil, S., Black, E., McBurney, P., Luck, M.: Investigating strategic considerations in persuasion dialogue games. In: Proceedings of the Starting AI Researchers' Symposium, STAIRS 2012, pp. 137–148. IOS Press (2012)
10. Hadjinikolis, C., Siantons, Y., Modgil, S., Black, E., McBurney, P.: Opponent modelling in persuasion dialogues. In: Proceedings of the International Joint Conference on Artificial Intelligence, IJCAI 2013, pp. 164–170. AAAI Press (2013)
11. Hosseini, S.A., Modgil, S., Rodrigues, O.: Enthymeme construction in dialogues using shared knowledge. In: Proceedings of Computational Models of Argument, COMMA 2014, pp. 325–332 (2014)

12. Modgil, S.: Revisiting abstract argumentation frameworks. In: Black, E., Modgil, S., Oren, N. (eds.) TAFA 2013. LNCS, vol. 8306, pp. 1–15. Springer, Heidelberg (2014)
13. Modgil, S., Prakken, H.: A general account of argumentation with preferences. Artif. Intell. **195**, 361–397 (2013)
14. Nouioua, F.: AFs with necessities: further semantics and labelling characterization. In: Liu, W., Subrahmanian, V.S., Wijsen, J. (eds.) SUM 2013. LNCS, vol. 8078, pp. 120–133. Springer, Heidelberg (2013)
15. Oren, N., Norman, T.J.: Arguing using opponent models. In: McBurney, P., Rahwan, I., Parsons, S., Maudet, N. (eds.) ArgMAS 2009. LNCS, vol. 6057, pp. 160–174. Springer, Heidelberg (2010)
16. Oren, N., Norman, T.J.: Semantics for evidence-based argumentation. In: Proceedings of Computational Models of Argument, COMMA 2008, pp. 276–284 (2008)
17. Polberg, S., Oren, N.: Revisiting support in abstract argumentation systems. In: Proceedings of Computational Models of Argument, COMMA 2014, pp. 369–376 (2014)
18. Prakken, H.: Coherence and flexibility in dialogue games for argumentation. Log. Comput. **15**(6), 1009–1040 (2005)
19. Prakken, H.: A study of accrual of arguments, with applications to evidential reasoning. In: Proceedings of the International Conference on Artificial Intelligence and Law, ICAIL 2005, pp. 85–94 (2005)
20. Rienstra, T., Thimm, M., Oren, N.: Opponent models with uncertainty for strategic argumentation. In: Proceedings of the Twenty-Third International Joint Conference on Artificial Intelligence, IJCAI 2013, pp. 332–338. AAAI Press (2013)
21. Riveret, R., Rotolo, A., Sartor, G., Prakken, H., Roth, B.: Success chances in argument games: a probabilistic approach to legal disputes. In: Proceedings of the Twentieth annual Conference on Legal Knowledge and Information Systems: JURIX, pp. 99–108 (2007)
22. Kovatsos, M., Rahwan, I., Fischer, F., Weiss, G.: Practical strategic reasoning and adaptation in rational argument-based negotiation. In: Parsons, S., Maudet, N., Moraitis, P., Rahwan, I. (eds.) ArgMAS 2005. LNCS (LNAI), vol. 4049, pp. 122–137. Springer, Heidelberg (2006)

The Hidden Power of Abstract Argumentation Semantics

Thomas Linsbichler[1]([✉]), Christof Spanring[1,2], and Stefan Woltran[1]

[1] TU Wien, Vienna, Austria
linsbich@dbai.tuwien.ac.at
[2] University of Liverpool, Liverpool, UK

Abstract. Abstract argumentation plays an important role in many advanced AI formalisms. It is thus vital to understand the strengths and limits of the different semantics available. In this work, we contribute to this line of research and investigate two recently proposed properties: rejected arguments and implicit conflicts. Given an argumentation framework F, the former refers to arguments in F which do not occur in any extension of F; the latter refers to pairs of arguments which do not occur together in any extension of F despite not being linked in F's attack relation. We consider four prominent semantics, viz. stable, preferred, semi-stable and stage and show that their expressive power relies on both properties. Among our results, we refute a recent conjecture by Baumann et al. on implicit conflicts.

1 Introduction

In recent years argumentation has emerged to become one of the major fields of research in Artificial Intelligence [6,16]. In particular, Dung's well-studied abstract argumentation frameworks (AFs) [11] are a simple, yet powerful formalism for modeling and deciding argumentation problems that are integral to many advanced argumentation systems, see e.g. [7]. The evaluation of AFs in terms of finding reasonable positions with respect to a given framework is defined via so-called argumentation semantics (cf. [1] for a recent overview). Given an AF F, an argumentation semantics σ returns acceptable sets of arguments $\sigma(F)$, the extensions of F. Several semantics have been introduced over the years [2,8,11,18] with motivations ranging from the desired treatment of specific examples to fulfilling certain abstract principles. One important line of research in abstract argumentation is thus the systematic comparison of the different semantics available. Hereby, the behaviour of extensions with respect to certain properties [3] has been analyzed and the expressive power of semantics [12,14,15,17] has been studied by identifying the set of extension-sets achievable under certain semantics. In this work we extend this analysis by investigating two fundamental properties which we describe next: implicit conflicts and rejected arguments.

An attack between arguments represents an explicit conflict. By the nature of most argumentation semantics, conflicts can also be implicit in the sense

© Springer International Publishing Switzerland 2015
E. Black et al. (Eds.): TAFA 2015, LNAI 9524, pp. 146–162, 2015.
DOI: 10.1007/978-3-319-28460-6_9

that some arguments do not occur together in any extension, although there is no attack between them. Given an AF, a natural question is, whether it can be transformed to an equivalent (under a semantics at hand) AF where every conflict is explicit (we will call these AFs analytic). In case the answer is no for a particular semantics σ, we can ascribe additional ("hidden") power to σ, since σ-extensions can deliver sets of conflicts which cannot be represented solely by attacks. A similar role can be played by rejected arguments, i.e. arguments that do not occur in any σ-extension. Hereby, it is of interest to understand in which ways rejected arguments contribute to the "strength" of a particular semantics. In other words, assume an AF delivers a set of σ-extensions $\mathbb{S}$, but some arguments are not member of any extension of $\mathbb{S}$. In case $\mathbb{S}$ cannot be expressed by an AF which is given only over arguments from $\mathbb{S}$, the rejected arguments (i.e. those in the AF which do no appear in $\mathbb{S}$) clearly contribute to the power of the semantics.

Not all semantics show the sort of "hidden power" we have outlined above. Let us consider the naive semantics which is defined as maximal conflict-free sets. Here, an argument is rejected if and only if it is self-attacking. In terms of expressiveness, this means that the same outcome can be achieved by just deleting the rejected arguments. Concerning implicit conflicts, two arguments occur together in a naive extension if and only if there is no attack between them and they are not self-attacking. Moreover, conflicts with self-attacking arguments can easily be made explicit, therefore a translation to an AF (given over the same arguments) with explicit conflicts only is always possible. In [5], the authors conjectured that such a translation also exists in the case of stable semantics.

In the present paper, we refute this conjecture and show that for all σ among stable, preferred, semi-stable and stage semantics, there exist AFs such that there is no AF equivalent under σ that contains solely explicit conflicts. This shows that under these semantics implicit conflicts allow to model scenarios that cannot be achieved by explicit conflicts alone. In addition, we give conditions guaranteeing translations to analytic AFs.

As a second main contribution, we study the role of rejected arguments by comparing the expressiveness of stable, preferred, semi-stable and stage semantics in the setting of compact AFs (i.e. AFs not containing rejected arguments). We show that the range of extension-sets one can get under stage and semi-stable semantics in this setting is strictly larger than under stable semantics, but all other combinations of semantics have incomparable expressiveness, hereby complementing recent results from [5].

2   Background

We assume a countably infinite domain $\mathfrak{A}$ of arguments. An argumentation framework (AF) is a pair $F = (A, R)$, where $A \subseteq \mathfrak{A}$ is non-empty and finite, and $R \subseteq A \times A$ represents the attack relation. The collection of all AFs is given as $AF_{\mathfrak{A}}$. Given an AF $F = (A, R)$, we write $a \rightarrowtail_F b$ for $(a, b) \in R$, and $S \rightarrowtail_F a$

(resp. $a \rightarrowtail_F S$) if $\exists s \in S$ such that $s \rightarrowtail_F a$ (resp. $a \rightarrowtail_F s$). Symmetric attacks $\{(a,b),(b,a)\} \subseteq R$ are denoted by $\langle a, b \rangle \in R$. For $S \subseteq A$, the *range* of S (wrt. F), denoted S_F^+, is the set $S \cup \{b \mid S \rightarrowtail_F b\}$. We drop the subscript F in $\rightarrowtail_F$ or S_F^+ if there is no ambiguity. For an AF $F = (B, Q)$ we use A_F and R_F to refer to B and Q, respectively. The composition of AFs F, G is defined as $F \cup G = (A_F \cup A_G, R_F \cup R_G)$.

Given $F = (A, R)$, an argument $a \in A$ is *defended* (in F) by a set $S \subseteq A$ if for each $b \in A$, such that $b \rightarrowtail_F a$, also $S \rightarrowtail_F b$. A set T of arguments is defended (in F) by S if each $a \in T$ is defended by S (in F). A set $S \subseteq A$ is *conflict-free* (in F), if there are no $a, b \in S$, such that $(a, b) \in R$. We denote the set of all conflict-free sets in F as $cf(F)$. A set $S \in cf(F)$ is called *admissible* (in F) if S defends itself. We denote the set of admissible sets in F as $adm(F)$.

The semantics we focus on in this work are the naive, stable, preferred, stage, and semi-stable extensions. Given $F = (A, R)$ they are defined as:

- $S \in naive(F)$, if $S \in cf(F)$ and $\nexists T \in cf(F)$ s.t. $T \supset S$;
- $S \in stb(F)$, if $S \in cf(F)$ and $S_F^+ = A$;
- $S \in prf(F)$, if $S \in adm(F)$ and $\nexists T \in adm(F)$ s.t. $T \supset S$;
- $S \in stage(F)$, if $S \in cf(F)$ and $\nexists T \in cf(F)$ s.t. $T_F^+ \supset S_F^+$;
- $S \in sem(F)$, if $S \in adm(F)$ and $\nexists T \in adm(F)$ s.t. $T_F^+ \supset S_F^+$.

3   Implicit Conflicts

The first property we investigate are implicit conflicts in an AF for a given semantics. We differentiate between the concept of an attack (as a syntactical element) and the concept of a conflict (with respect to the evaluation under a given semantics). In the following definition we recall the notion of explicit conflicts from [5] and then we define, based on this notion, three classes of AFs.

Definition 1. *Given some AF F, a semantics σ and arguments $a, b \in A_F$. If for any $S \in \sigma(F)$, $a \in S$ implies $b \notin S$, we say that a and b are in* conflict *in F for σ. If $(a, b) \in R_F$ or $(b, a) \in R_F$ we say that the conflict between a and b is* explicit *(in F), otherwise the conflict is called* implicit *(in F). An AF F is called* analytic *for σ (or σ-analytic) if all conflicts of $\sigma(F)$ are explicit in F. F is called* quasi-analytic *for σ if there is an AF G such that $A_F = A_G$, $\sigma(F) = \sigma(G)$ and G is analytic for σ. Finally F is called* non-analytic *for σ if it is not quasi-analytic.*

For $\mathbb{S} \subseteq 2^{\mathfrak{A}}$ and some semantics σ we say that $\mathbb{S}$ is an analytic extension-set *for σ if there is some σ-analytic AF F with $\sigma(F) = \mathbb{S}$. If there is some AF F with $\sigma(F) = \mathbb{S}$ but any such AF is non-analytic for σ, then $\mathbb{S}$ is called a* non-analytic *extension-set for σ.*

Example 1. Let us now consider a set of natural language arguments that might or might not be fictional. We have two researchers, one (A) specialising in applied theory of social networking, the other (B) in uncountable graph theory. After quite a few beers we have A claiming A_1: *"every single theory that is relevant today was invented less than ten years ago"*, somewhat unrelated to that B throws in his inner truth B_1: *"my research can be justified by its purely theoretical beauty alone"*. Now A however objects with A_2: *"research must always be motivated by practical applications"*, to which B replies B_2: *"many nowadays widely applied theories were considered useless in practice for decades or even centuries"*.

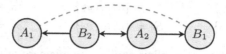

Fig. 1. Quasi-analytic AF for $\{stb, prf, sem, stage\}$, cf. Example 1.

Here naturally A_2 attacks B_1 and is in a mutual attack relationship with B_2, which additionally attacks A_1. The resulting AF F is also depicted in Fig. 1. For $\sigma \in \{stb, prf, sem, stage\}$ we have $\sigma(F) = \{\{A_1, A_2\}, \{B_1, B_2\}\}$, and thus there is an implicit conflict between A_1 and B_1, which means that F is not analytic. Now, adding e.g. (B_1, A_1) we obtain an equivalent (under σ) AF F', where all conflicts are explicit. Thus on a theoretical level F is quasi-analytic for σ and $\{\{A_1, A_2\}, \{B_1, B_2\}\}$ is an analytic extension-set.

However, observe that an interpretation of our set of arguments with an explicit conflict between A_1 and B_1 might not be practically justified, as these arguments seem rather unrelated with respect to their actual meaning.

Intuitively, an AF F is quasi-analytic if it can be translated to an AF G which has the same arguments as F and where all conflicts are explicit. It was conjectured in [5] that every AF containing implicit conflicts for stable semantics is quasi-analytic, in the sense that all implicit conflicts can be made explicit without adding further arguments. In line with the following definition, [5] claimed that ECC holds for stable semantics.

Definition 2. *We say that the* Explicit Conflict Conjecture (ECC) *holds for semantics σ if every AF is quasi-analytic for σ.*

While ECC holds for naive semantics as previously discussed, we will refute ECC for all semantics in $\{stb, prf, sem, stage\}$ by providing non-analytic AFs.

Example 2. Take into account the AF $F = (A, R)$ depicted in Fig. 2 which features an implicit conflict for stable semantics between a and b:

$$A = \{a, b, c\} \cup \{u_i, v_i, x_i, y_i \mid i \in \{1, 2\}\}$$
$$R = \{\langle a, c \rangle, \langle b, c \rangle\} \cup \{\langle \alpha_i, \beta_i \rangle \mid i \in \{1, 2\}, \alpha \in \{x, y\}, \beta \in \{u, v\}\}$$
$$\cup \{(u_i, a), (a, x_i), (v_i, b), (b, y_i), \langle u_i, v_i \rangle \mid i \in \{1, 2\}\}$$

In the following we refer to $M_{i1} = \{v_i\}, M_{i2} = \{u_i\}, M_{i3} = \{x_i, y_i\}$. The stable extensions of F can be separated into extensions containing c and others. For $i, j \in \{1, 2, 3\}$ the former are given as:

$$S_{ij} = \{c\} \cup M_{1i} \cup M_{2j}$$

If on the other hand $c \notin S$ one of a, b will be a member of S and thus:

$$S_1 = \{a, v_1, v_2\} \qquad S_3 = \{a, v_1, y_2\} \qquad S_5 = \{b, u_1, x_2\}$$
$$S_2 = \{b, u_1, u_2\} \qquad S_4 = \{a, y_1, v_2\} \qquad S_6 = \{b, x_1, u_2\}$$

Now clearly a and b share an implicit conflict, as one cannot be defended without the other being attacked. However observe that all the other conflicts implicitly defined by the extension-set $\mathbb{S} = \{S_1, S_2 \ldots S_6\} \cup \{S_{ij} \mid i, j \in \{1, 2, 3\}\}$ are already given explicitly in F. Furthermore the remaining (implicit or explicit) maximal conflict-free sets $S_a = \{a, y_1, y_2\}$ and $S_b = \{b, x_1, x_2\}$ neither attack b nor a respectively and thus are not stable extensions of F.

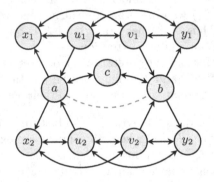

Fig. 2. Illustration of the AF from Example 2.

We now proceed by showing that Example 2 serves as a counter-example for ECC for stable semantics.

Theorem 1. *There are non-analytic AFs for stable semantics.*

Proof. Consider the stable extension-set $\mathbb{S}$ from Example 2. We will show that there is no AF $F = (A, R)$ with $A = \bigcup \mathbb{S}$, $stb(F) = \mathbb{S}$ and $(a, b) \in R$. (Observe that due to symmetry reasons we need not consider $(b, a) \in R$ and $(a, b) \notin R$.) For a contradiction take such an AF as given.

The extensions containing c ensure that there is no conflict between arguments c and α_i for $\alpha \in \{x, u, v, y\}$ and $i \in \{1, 2\}$. By definition any stable extension $S \in \mathbb{S}$ attacks all outside arguments, $S \rightarrowtail \alpha$ for $\alpha \in A \setminus S$. Hence from $S_3 = \{a, v_1, y_2\}$ being a stable extension we conclude $a \rightarrowtail c$ and $\{a, y_2\} \rightarrowtail \alpha_2$ for $\alpha \in \{x, u, v\}$. Similarly due to $S_4 = \{a, y_1, v_2\}$ we conclude that $\{a, y_1\} \rightarrowtail \alpha_1$

for $\alpha \in \{x, u, v\}$. But now by assumption $a \rightarrowtail b$ and thus for $S_a = \{a, y_1, y_2\}$ we acquire full range, $S_a \rightarrowtail \alpha$ for any $\alpha \in A \setminus S_a$, i.e. S_a becomes an unwanted stable extension. Therefore F is non-analytic.   □

We observe that in this counter-example for ECC for stable semantics the stable extensions coincide with semi-stable, preferred and stage extensions. With the following lemma this leads to some straight-forward generalizations.

Lemma 1. *Take some AF $F = (A, R)$ with $prf(F) = stb(F)$ (resp. $sem(F) = stb(F)$) as given. If F is quasi-analytic for preferred (resp. semi-stable) semantics, then it is also quasi-analytic for stable semantics.*

Proof. By assumption for $\sigma \in \{prf, sem\}$ there is a σ-analytic AF $G = (A, R_G)$ such that $\sigma(F) = \sigma(G)$. We want to show that $stb(G) = \sigma(G)$. Using the general relation $stb \subseteq \sigma$, it remains to show that $\sigma(G) \subseteq stb(G)$. To this end observe that any attack of F still represents an explicit conflict in G. Now for $S \in stb(F)$ we know that for all $a \in A \setminus S$ we have $S \rightarrowtail_F a$. Since by assumption also $S \in \sigma(F)$ this immediately implies an explicit conflict between S and a in G. Due to admissibility of σ-extensions we now have $S \rightarrowtail_G a$ for all $a \in A \setminus S$. Considering $\sigma \subseteq cf$ hence $S \in stb(G)$, resulting in $\sigma(G) = stb(G)$ and thus G being stb-analytic and also F being stb-quasi-analytic.   □

Using the AF F from Example 2 and the contraposition of Lemma 1 yields the following result, refuting ECC for preferred and semi-stable semantics.

Corollary 1. *There are non-analytic AFs for preferred and semi-stable semantics, respectively.*

The next example shows that some AFs proof to be non-analytic for preferred semantics while being quasi-analytic for the other semantics under consideration.

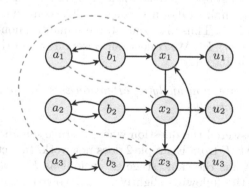

Fig. 3. A non-analytic AF for *prf* as used in Example 3.

Example 3. Take into account the AF F as depicted in Fig. 3. In the following we show that F is non-analytic for preferred semantics. For a contradiction we assume that there exists an analytic AF G with $A_F = A_G$ and $prf(F) = prf(G)$. We now investigate this hypothetical AF G. Observe that due to $S_b = \{b_1, b_2, b_3, u_1, u_2, u_3\} \in prf(F)$ there is no conflict between u_i and b_j for $i, j \in \{1, 2, 3\}$. Due to $A_1 = \{a_2, a_3, b_1, x_2, u_1, u_3\} \in prf(F)$ and symmetric versions thereof there is no conflict between u_i and a_j for $i, j \in \{1, 2, 3\}$, and for $i \neq j$ there is no conflict between x_i and u_j. In other words in G the u_i are in conflict only with the x_i for $i \in \{1, 2, 3\}$.

Furthermore we have an implicit conflict between a_1 and x_2, as accepting a_1 means rejecting b_1 and thus x_2 can be defended against x_1 only by x_3 which however is attacked by x_2. Due to $S_a = \{a_1, a_2, a_3\} \in prf(F)$ being admissible and G being analytic now $S_a \rightarrowtail_G x_2$. But then S_a defends u_2 and thus can not be a preferred extension in G. For symmetry reasons it follows that the implicit conflicts (a_i, x_j) of F cannot be made explicit for preferred semantics.

On the other hand for stable (or stage or semi-stable) semantics we observe that S_a is not an extension. Although the overall conflicts remain the same, this allows us to include conflicts (x_j, a_i) without any harm for the other extensions.

As there are no more implicit conflicts, thus for stable, semi-stable and stage semantics this AF is quasi-analytic.

Observe that for the AF F in Example 3 allowing additional self-attacking arguments would not alter the non-analytic nature of this example for preferred semantics, as in the hypothetical analytic AF G we have that S_a naturally is in conflict with any rejected argument and thus due to admissibility needs to attack all of these rejected arguments. Thus any AF realizing the extension-set $prf(F)$ is non-analytic for preferred semantics.

As shown in [12,14] the set of realizable extension-sets coincides for preferred and semi-stable semantics. We recall admissibility of semi-stable semantics and consider that any semi-stable extension is a preferred extension as well. As discussed above, we only make use of necessary explicit conflicts, admissibility and maximality of extensions. Thus also semi-stable semantics non-analytically realizes the extension-set $prf(F)$. We collect our observations in the following result which generalizes Corollary 1.

Theorem 2. *There are non-analytic extension-sets for preferred and semistable semantics, respectively.*

We still have not answered the question whether stage semantics possesses non-analytic AFs. The AF F from Example 2 does not work. In fact, the analytic AF G depicted in Fig. 4 has the same stage extensions as F, $stb(F) = stage(F) = stage(G)$. However, the following slightly more involved example yields a non-analytic AF for stage (and stable) semantics.

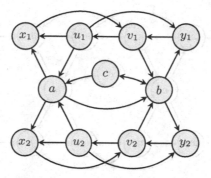

Fig. 4. Analytic AF for stage semantics, cf. Example 2.

Example 4. Take into account the AF $F = (A, R)$ depicted in Fig. 5 with:

$$A = \{a, b, c\} \cup \{u_i, v_i, x_i, y_i, r_i, s_i \mid i \in \{1, 2\}\}$$
$$R = \{\langle a, c \rangle, \langle b, c \rangle\} \cup \{\langle r_i, x_i \rangle, \langle s_i, y_i \rangle \mid i \in \{1, 2\}\}$$
$$\cup \{\langle \alpha_i, \beta_i \rangle \mid i \in \{1, 2\}, \alpha \in \{x, y\}, \beta \in \{u, v\}\}$$
$$\cup \{(u_i, a), (a, x_i), (v_i, b), (b, y_i), \{u_i, v_i\} \mid i \in \{1, 2\}\}$$

In the following we will refer to $M_{i1} = \{r_i, v_i, s_i\}, M_{i2} = \{r_i, u_i, s_i\}, M_{i3} = \{r_i, y_i\}, M_{i4} = \{x_i, s_i\}, M_{i5} = \{x_i, y_i\}$. The stable extensions of F can be separated into extensions containing c and others. For $i, j \in \{1 \ldots 5\}$ the former are given as:

$$S_{ij} = \{c\} \cup M_{1i} \cup M_{2j}$$

If, on the other hand, $c \notin S$, one of a, b will be a member of S:

$$S_1 = \{a, r_1, r_2, v_1, v_2, s_1, s_2\} \qquad S_4 = \{a, r_1, r_2, y_1, v_2, s_2\}$$
$$S_2 = \{b, r_1, r_2, u_1, u_2, s_1, s_2\} \qquad S_5 = \{b, r_1, u_1, x_2, s_1, s_2\}$$
$$S_3 = \{a, r_1, r_2, v_1, y_2, s_1\} \qquad S_6 = \{b, r_2, x_1, u_2, s_1, s_2\}$$

Similarly to Example 2 we have that a and b share an implicit conflict for stable and thus stage semantics, as $stb(F) = stage(F) = S = \{S_1 \ldots S_6\} \cup \{S_{ij} \mid i, j \in \{1 \ldots 5\}\}$. Again except for the implicit conflict between a and b all conflicts in F already are explicit, and the only other maximal conflict-free sets $S_a = \{a, r_1, r_2, y_1, y_2\}$ and $S_b = \{b, x_1, x_2, s_1, s_2\}$ are not stable extensions here.

Theorem 3. *There are non-analytic AFs for stage semantics.*

Proof. Consider the AF $F = (A, R)$ from Example 4. We first show that F is non-analytic for stable semantics by assuming a contradicting analytic AF of the same arguments and extensions. We will then use this observation to proceed similarly for stage semantics. For a hypothetical analytic AF $G = (A, R_G)$ with

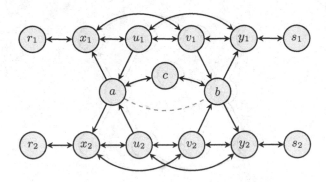

Fig. 5. Illustration of the AF from Example 4.

$stage(F) = stage(G)$ we show that $stb(G) \neq \emptyset$, implying $stb(G) = stage(G)$ and thus G being analytic also for stable semantics. For symmetry reasons, wlog. we assume $(a, b) \in R_G$. In what follows, we use the same naming schema for extensions as in Example 4.

For stable semantics we need $a \rightarrowtail c$, since e.g. S_1 has to be a stable extension. From $S_{33} \in stb(G)$, $a \rightarrowtail b$ by assumption and as observed $a \rightarrowtail c$ we conclude $S_a \in stb(G)$, as $c \in S_{33}$ is allowed to attack only a and b. Thus if G is analytic for stable semantics then $stb(F) \neq stb(G)$.

We now turn to stage semantics and have the following observations:

- Due to conflict-explicitness we need $s_1 \rightarrowtail y_1$, since otherwise $S_{55}^+ \subset S_{45}^+$; similarly we conclude $s_i \rightarrowtail y_i$ and $r_i \rightarrowtail x_i$;
- Furthermore necessarily $c \rightarrowtail a$, since otherwise $S_{11}^+ \subset S_a^+$;
- Now since u_i and v_i need to be in conflict we need $c \not\rightarrowtail b$, because otherwise at least one of S_{ij} for $i, j \in \{1, 2\}$ becomes a stable extension. By conflict-implicitness hence $b \rightarrowtail c$.
- From $c \rightarrowtail a$, $r_1 \rightarrowtail x_1$ and $s_1 \rightarrowtail y_1$ we conclude $u_1 \rightarrowtail v_1$ due to the danger of $S_{21}^+ \subset S_{11}^+$. Similarly $u_2 \rightarrowtail v_2$.
- Since $c \rightarrowtail a$ furthermore we need $x_i \rightarrowtail r_i$, $x_i \rightarrowtail u_i$ and $x_i \rightarrowtail v_i$, due to range comparison of M_{i4} and M_{i2}.
- By previous range observations we have to assume $b \not\rightarrowtail a$ and $u_i \not\rightarrowtail a$, since otherwise S_2 becomes a stable extension.
- But now $S_2^+ \subseteq S_b^+$, i.e. either we gain the unwanted extension S_b or we loose the desired extension S_2. □

Thus we have shown that for each semantics there exist non-analytic AFs. We now turn to positive results in the sense of making implicit conflicts explicit. Recall that for quasi-analytic AFs we require the set of arguments to remain unchanged in this context. This restriction indeed plays a vital role as shown next for the case of stable semantics.

Proposition 1. *For stable semantics and some AF F, if there is an implicit conflict between a and b then there is an AF G with $|A_G| = |A_F| + 1$, $R_G \supseteq R_F$, $(a, b) \in R_G$, $stb(G) = stb(F)$, and each implicit conflict for stb in G is implicit in F as well.*

Proof. Let F be an arbitrary AF with an implicit conflict between two arguments a and b. We define $R' = R_F \cup \{(a,b)\}$. Observe that $F' = (A, R')$ has the same and possibly more stable extensions as compared to F. By construction of F', any $S \in stb(F') \setminus stb(F)$ has $a \in S$ and $S \not\rightarrow_F b$. We collect the arguments of the unwanted extensions in $A_a = \bigcup(stb(F') \setminus stb(F))$ and observe that $A_a \not\rightarrow_F b$. Now define the AF G with $A_G = A_F \cup \{x\}$ and

$$R_G = R' \cup \{(x,x)\} \cup \{(x,v) \mid v \in A_a\} \cup \{(u,x) \mid u \in A_F \setminus A_a\}.$$

First note that obviously $|A_G| = |A_F| + 1$, $R_G \supseteq R_F$, and $(a,b) \in R_G$. Moreover, since the new argument x attacks or is attacked by every other argument, G does not introduce any further implicit conflicts compared to F. It remains to show that $stb(G) = stb(F)$. Let $S' \in stb(F)$ and assume that $b \in S'$. As by assumption b and a do not occur together in any stable extension of F, we know that $b \rightarrowtail_G x$ and thus $S' \in stb(G)$. On the other hand assume that $b \notin S'$. Then we have some $c \in S'$ with $c \rightarrowtail_F b$. If $S' \notin stb(G)$, then only because $S' \not\rightarrow_G x$, hence $S' \subseteq A_a$, a contradiction to $A_a \not\rightarrow_F b$. Therefore $S' \in stb(G)$. Now assume there is some $S \in stb(G)$ with $S \notin stb(F)$. By the construction of G this S must be among $stb(F') \setminus stb(F)$. However, we then have $S \not\rightarrow_G x$, a contradiction to $S \in stb(G)$, concluding the proof for $stb(F) = stb(G)$. $\qquad\square$

In contrast to preferred and semi-stable semantics (cf. Theorem 2) we observe the following interesting difference for stable and stage semantics when abstaining from a condition on the set of arguments.

Theorem 4. *All extension-sets for stable and stage semantics are analytic.*

Proof. Note that for any AF F there is an AF G such that $stb(G) = stage(F)$ [14] and the fact that $stb(F) \subseteq stage(F)$. Further as by definition any AF F is finite we can have at most finitely many implicit conflicts for semantics $\sigma \in \{stb, stage\}$, each of which can be removed by repeated application of Proposition 1. $\qquad\square$

To conclude this section we investigate the question of conditions such that ECC holds. We have mentioned in the introduction that every AF is quasi-analytic for naive semantics. This insight can be generalized as follows.

Proposition 2. *Let $\sigma \in \{stage, stb, sem, prf\}$. If for some AF F there exists an AF G such that $\sigma(F) = naive(G)$, then F is quasi-analytic for σ.*

Proof. Let F, G be AFs with $\sigma(F) = naive(G)$. We define the AF H with $A_H = A_F$ and $R_H = \{\langle a, b \rangle \mid (a, b) \in R_G, a, b \in \bigcup \sigma(F)\} \cup \{\langle a, x \rangle, (x, x) \mid a \in A_F, x \notin \bigcup \sigma(F)\}$. As this AF G provides the same conflicts as the AF F for naive semantics, we deduce that also the maximal conflict-free sets are the same, $naive(H) = naive(G)$. By definition of H, for any $S \in naive(H)$ and $a \in A_F \setminus S$ we have $S \rightarrowtail_H a$ and hence S is a stable extension of H. Finally observe that $stb(H) \subseteq \sigma(H) \subseteq naive(H)$ for any AF H, hence the result follows. $\qquad\square$

Another property which guarantees that ECC holds relies on the existence of what we call "identifying arguments". We say that an AF F is *determined* for semantics σ if for every $S \in \sigma(F)$ there exists an $a \in S$ such that for $S' \in \sigma(F)$ we have that $a \in S'$ implies $S' = S$. In other words, every σ-extension contains an identifying argument in the sense that it does not occur in any other σ-extension.

Proposition 3. *Let* $\sigma \in \{stb, prf, sem, stage\}$. *Then, any AF F determined for σ is quasi-analytic for σ.*

Proof. Consider an AF F determined for σ and for each $S \in \sigma(F)$ let a_S be some fixed identifying argument. Now take into account the sets $I = \{a_S \mid S \in \sigma(F)\}$ and $R_I = \{\langle a_S, a_{S'} \rangle \mid S, S' \in \sigma(F), S \neq S'\}$, clearly $\sigma((I, R_I)) = \{\{a_S\} \mid S \in \sigma(F)\}$. Furthermore let $O = A_F \setminus I$ be the remaining arguments of F and $R_O = \{\langle a, b \rangle \mid a, b \in O, a$ *and* b *are in conflict for* σ *in* $F\}$. We now define G as $A_G = A_F = O \cup I$ and $R_G = R_I \cup R_O \cup \{(a_S, b) \mid S \in \sigma(F), b \in (O \setminus S)\}$. Observe that I forms a clique within G, a clique that is not attacked by arguments in O. Since stable semantics is SCC-splittable [4], we can determine $stb(G)$ by first computing $stb((I, R_I)) = \{\{a_S\} \mid S \in \sigma(F)\}$ and then propagating, for each of these singleton extensions, the attacks to arguments in O. This leaves us, for each a_S with $S \in \sigma(F)$, with the AF $(S \setminus \{a_S\}, \emptyset)$ which clearly has $S \setminus \{a_S\}$ as only stable extension. Hence $stb(G) = stb(F)$. The result for preferred semantics, which is also SCC-splittable, follows in the same way. For $\theta \in \{stage, sem\}$ we get $stb(G) = \theta(F)$ in the same way as above and since $\theta(F) \neq \emptyset$ it follows that $\theta(G) = stb(G) = \theta(F)$.

Finally observe that all conflicts in G for σ (among I, among O or between I and O) are explicit by definition.   □

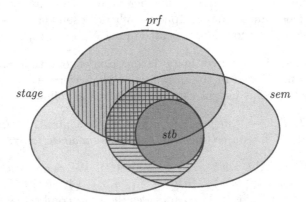

Fig. 6. A Venn-Diagram illustrating compact signatures of stable, semi-stable, stage and preferred semantics.

4 Rejected Arguments

In this section we analyze the impact of rejected arguments on the expressiveness of semantics. We do so by determining the limits of AFs without rejected arguments. We first recall some concepts introduced in [5].

Definition 3. *An AF F is called* compact *under semantics σ if $A_F = \bigcup \sigma(F)$. A set $\mathbb{S} \subseteq 2^{\mathfrak{A}}$ is called* compactly realizable *under σ if there is an AF F that is compact under σ and realizes $\mathbb{S}$, i.e. $A_F = \bigcup \sigma(F)$ and $\sigma(F) = \mathbb{S}$. The c-signature Σ_σ^c of σ is defined as set of all extension-sets compactly realizable under σ:*

$$\Sigma_\sigma^c = \{\sigma(F) \mid F \in AF_{\mathfrak{A}}, A_F = \bigcup \sigma(F)\}.$$

The following results put in relation the c-signatures of the semantics under consideration.

Theorem 5. *In accordance with Fig. 6, it holds that:*

- $\Sigma_{stb}^c \subseteq \Sigma_\sigma^c$ *for $\sigma \in \{stage, sem\}$;*
- $\Sigma_{prf}^c \setminus (\Sigma_{stb}^c \cup \Sigma_{sem}^c \cup \Sigma_{stage}^c) \neq \emptyset$;
- $\Sigma_{stage}^c \setminus (\Sigma_{stb}^c \cup \Sigma_{prf}^c \cup \Sigma_{sem}^c) \neq \emptyset$;
- $\Sigma_{stb}^c \setminus \Sigma_{prf}^c \neq \emptyset$;
- $(\Sigma_{prf}^c \cap \Sigma_{sem}^c) \setminus (\Sigma_{stb}^c \cup \Sigma_{sem}^c) \neq \emptyset$;
- $\Sigma_{sem}^c \setminus (\Sigma_{stb}^c \cup \Sigma_{prf}^c \cup \Sigma_{stage}^c) \neq \emptyset$.

Proof. The first two statements were shown in [5]. In the following we provide, as part of the proof, examples witnessing the remaining statements. The general procedure looks as follows: Let $\sigma_1, \ldots, \sigma_n$ and $\tau_1, \ldots, \tau_m$ be semantics. To show that $\left(\bigcap_{1 \leq i \leq n} \Sigma_{\sigma_i}^c\right) \setminus \left(\bigcup_{1 \leq j \leq m} \Sigma_{\tau_j}^c\right) \neq \emptyset$ holds, we fix some extension-set $\mathbb{S}$, provide an AF F with $\sigma_i(F) = \mathbb{S}$ for all $i \in \{1, \ldots, n\}$, and show that $\mathbb{S}$ is not compactly realizable under any of the semantics $\tau_1, \ldots, \tau_m$.

We begin by showing $\Sigma_{stage}^c \setminus (\Sigma_{stb}^c \cup \Sigma_{prf}^c \cup \Sigma_{sem}^c) \neq \emptyset$.

Example 5. Let $\oplus$ such that $a \oplus b = (a + b) \bmod 9$. Consider the AF $F = (\{a_0, \ldots, a_8\}, \{(a_i, a_j) \mid 0 \leq i < 9, j = i \oplus 1\})$, i.e. the directed cycle of nine arguments (Fig. 7). We get $stage(F) = \{\{a_i, a_{i\oplus2}, a_{i\oplus4}, a_{i\oplus6}\} \mid 0 \leq i < 9\}$. Now

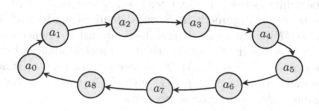

Fig. 7. A directed cycle of nine arguments.

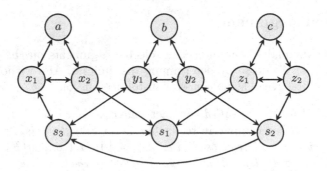

Fig. 8. AF showing $\Sigma_{stb}^c \setminus \Sigma_{prf}^c \neq \emptyset$.

assume this extension-set is compactly realizable under stable, preferred or semi-stable semantics, i.e. there is some G with $\sigma(G) = stage(F)$ ($\sigma \in \{stb, prf, sem\}$) and $A_G = A_F$. Since a_i and a_j occur together in some stage extension of F for all i, j with $i \oplus 1 \neq j$ and $i \neq j \oplus 1$, the only possible attacks in G are (a_i, a_j) with $i \oplus 1 = j$ or $i = j \oplus 1$. Now let $S_i = \{a_i, a_{i\oplus2}, a_{i\oplus4}, a_{i\oplus6}\}$. In order to have $S_i \in \sigma(G)$, a_i has to attack $a_{i\oplus8}$ and $a_{i\oplus6}$ has to attack $a_{i\oplus7}$, first for S_i to be maximal and second to be defended. Hence $R_G = \{\langle a_i, a_j \rangle \mid 0 \leq i < 9, j = i \oplus 1\}$ and $\sigma(G) = stage(F) \cup \{a_i, a_{i\oplus3}, a_{i\oplus6} \mid 0 \leq i < 3\}$, showing that there is no compact AF realizing $stage(F)$ under σ.

The following example witnesses that $\Sigma_{stb}^c \setminus \Sigma_{prf}^c \neq \emptyset$.

Example 6. Consider stable semantics for the AF F depicted in Fig. 8 and let $\mathbb{S} = stb(F)$ be its extension-set. Observe that neither $\{a, b, c\}$ nor any superset is a stable extension.

Assume there exists some AF G compactly realizing $\mathbb{S}$ under preferred semantics, i.e. $prf(G) = \mathbb{S}$ and $A_G = \bigcup \mathbb{S}$. One can check that F is analytic for stable semantics, i.e. for the AF G there can only be attacks between arguments being linked in Fig. 8.

Consider the extension $S = \{b, c, x_1, s_1\} \in stb(F)$. For $S \in prf(G)$ there are two possible reasons for $a \notin S$. Either a is in conflict with S or a is not defended by S. Assume a not to be defended by S. Then $x_2 \rightarrowtail a$ and $x_1 \not\rightarrowtail x_2$ and $s_1 \not\rightarrowtail x_2$. But then $x_2 \notin S$ defends itself, and in G either S is not a maximal admissible set or S is not an admissible set. It follows that a is in conflict with S, the only possibility being a conflict with x_1, hence $x_1 \rightarrowtail a$ ($a \rightarrowtail x_1$ is not sufficient since no other argument in S can defend x_1 against a). Considering $\{a, y_1, z_1, s_2\} \in stb(F)$, only a can defend itself against x_1, hence $a \rightarrowtail x_1$.

Similarly, one can justify the existence of symmetric attacks between a and x_2, b and y_i, and c and z_i ($i \in \{1, 2\}$). Therefore the set $\{a, b, c\}$ is admissible in G, hence there must be some $S' \in prf(G)$ with $S' \supseteq \{a, b, c\}$, a contradiction to $\mathbb{S}$ being realizable under the preferred semantics.

We proceed with an example showing that $(\Sigma_{prf}^c \cap \Sigma_{sem}^c) \setminus (\Sigma_{stb}^c \cup \Sigma_{stage}^c) \neq \emptyset$.

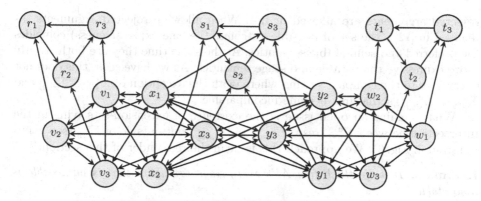

Fig. 9. AF showing $(\Sigma_{prf}^c \cap \Sigma_{sem}^c) \setminus (\Sigma_{stb}^c \cup \Sigma_{stage}^c) \neq \emptyset$.

Example 7. Consider the AF F from Fig. 9. We have $\mathbb{S} = sem(F) = prf(F) = \{\{v_i, y_j, r_i, s_j\} \mid 1 \leq i, j \leq 3\} \cup \{\{w_i, x_j, t_i, s_j\} \mid 1 \leq i, j \leq 3\} \cup \{\{v_i, w_j, r_i, t_j\} \mid 1 \leq i, j \leq 3\}$. For $\sigma = stage$ or $\sigma = stb$, assume there is an AF G with $\sigma(G) = \mathbb{S}$ and $A_G = \bigcup \mathbb{S}$. First note that for all $i, j \in \{1, 2, 3\}$ each pair $\{v_i, s_j\}, \{w_i, s_j\}, \{r_i, s_j\}, \{t_i, s_j\}$ is contained in some element of $\mathbb{S}$, hence there cannot be an attack between any of these pairs in G. Now let $S = \{v_i, w_j, r_i, t_j\}$ for some $i, j \in \{1, \ldots, 3\}$. We have $S_G^+ \subsetneq A_G \setminus \{s_1, s_2, s_3\}$, hence S cannot be a stable extension of G. Moreover, since G must be self-loop-free, $S \cup \{s_k\}$ with $1 \leq k \leq 3$ is conflict-free and obviously has a larger range than S. Therefore S cannot be a stage extension in G.

For the final result we will make use of the following lemma, which might be of interest on its own.

Lemma 2. *Let $\sigma, \tau \in \{stb, prf, sem, stage\}$ and F, G be τ-compact AFs such that $\tau(F) \notin \Sigma_\sigma^c$ and $A_F \cap A_G = \emptyset$. It holds that $\tau(F \cup G) \notin \Sigma_\sigma^c$.*

Proof. Assume there is some compact AF H such that $\sigma(H) = \tau(F \cup G)$. Since $A_F \cap A_G = \emptyset$, it follows that $\tau(F \cup G) = \tau(F) \times \tau(G)$. Due to compactness every argument $a \in A_F$ occurs together with every argument $b \in A_G$ in some τ-extension of $F \cup G$, meaning that H cannot contain any attack between a and b. Hence $\sigma(H) = \sigma(H_1) \times \sigma(H_2)$ with $A_{H_1} = A_F$ and $A_{H_2} = A_G$. Therefore it must hold that $\sigma(H_1) = \tau(F)$, a contradiction to the assumption that $\tau(F) \notin \Sigma_\sigma^c$. $\square$

Now we get $\Sigma_{sem}^c \setminus (\Sigma_{stb}^c \cup \Sigma_{prf}^c \cup \Sigma_{stage}^c) \neq \emptyset$ as follows: Let $F = F_1 \cup F_2$ where F_1 is the AF in Fig. 8 and F_2 is the AF in Fig. 9 (observe that for $A_{F_1} \cap A_{F_2} = \emptyset$ some renaming is necessary). From $sem(F_1) \notin \Sigma_{prf}^c$ (see Example 6) we get $sem(F) = (sem(F_1) \times sem(F_2)) \notin \Sigma_{prf}^c$ by Lemma 2. In the same way $sem(F) \notin \Sigma_{stb}^c \cup \Sigma_{stage}^c$ follows from $sem(F_2) \notin \Sigma_{stb}^c \cup \Sigma_{stage}^c$ (see Example 7).

This concludes the proof of Theorem 5. $\square$

Comparing the insights obtained from Theorem 5 with the results on expressiveness of semantics in [12] we observe notable differences depending on whether rejected arguments are allowed or not. When allowing rejected arguments (as utilised in [12]), the set of possible outcomes (i.e. the expressiveness) coincides for preferred and semi-stable semantics. At the same time they are both strictly more expressive than stable and stage semantics. As we have seen, this does not carry over to the compact setting where, with the exception of $\Sigma_{stb}^c \subset \Sigma_{sem}^c$ and $\Sigma_{stb}^c \subset \Sigma_{stage}^c$, signatures become incomparable.

What remains an open issue is the existence of extension-sets lying in the intersection between Σ_{prf}^c (resp. Σ_{sem}^c) and Σ_{stage}^c but outside of Σ_{stb}^c (see Venn-diagram in Fig. 6). We approach this issue in the remainder of this section.

Lemma 3. *In self-attack free AFs every stage extension that is admissible is also stable.*

Proof. Take some AF F and some admissible stage extension S, $S \in stage(F)$, $S \in adm(F)$ as given. Suppose there is some argument that is not in the range of S, i.e. $a \in A_F \setminus S_F^+$. Then by admissibility a cannot attack S, by assumption S does not attack a. Thus for $a \notin S$ we in fact would need $(a, a) \in R_F$. It follows that there is no such argument a and thus $S_F^+ = A_F$. Hence $S \in stb(F)$. $\square$

Proposition 4. *Let $\sigma \in \{sem, prf\}$ and F, G be compact AFs with $stage(F) = \sigma(G)$. If $stage(F) \notin \Sigma_{stb}^c$ then it holds that $F \neq G$ and G is non-analytic.*

Proof. Assume that $F = G$. Then $stage(F) = \sigma(F)$. But then by Lemma 3 also $\sigma(F) = stb(F)$, contrary to the assumption that $stage(F) \notin \Sigma_{stb}^c$. Therefore $F \neq G$. For a contradiction, wlog. assume G to be analytic (for any quasi-analytic H there is some corresponding analytic G). Observe that for stage extensions $S \in stage(F)$ and any argument $a \in A \setminus S$ it holds that either there is an explicit conflict between S and a in F, or a is self-attacking in F, since S_F^+ would not be maximal otherwise. With $stage(F) = \sigma(G)$ and G being analytic for the admissibility based semantics σ this means that $S \rightarrowtail_G a$, i.e. $S_G^+ = A$. With all σ-extensions becoming stb-extensions and $stb \subseteq \sigma$ we derive a contradiction to the initial statement: $stb(G) = stage(F)$. $\square$

Assume that for $\sigma \in \{prf, stage\}$ there exists an extension-set $\mathbb{S} \in (\Sigma_\sigma^c \cap \Sigma_{stage}^c) \setminus \Sigma_{stb}^c$, Proposition 4 says that $\mathbb{S}$ is compactly realized by different AFs under σ and $stage$, i.e. $stage(F) = \mathbb{S}$ and $\sigma(G) = \mathbb{S}$ with $F \neq G$. Moreover, G is non-analytic. Recent investigations encourage us to conjecture the following:

Conjecture 1. It holds that $(\Sigma_{prf}^c \cap \Sigma_{stage}^c) \setminus \Sigma_{stb}^c = (\Sigma_{sem}^c \cap \Sigma_{stage}^c) \setminus \Sigma_{stb}^c = \emptyset$.

5   Discussion

In this paper, we have analyzed the roles the concepts of implicit conflicts and rejected arguments play when it comes to comparing the expressiveness of prominent argumentation semantics like preferred, stable, semi-stable and stage semantics. Our first family of results show that implicit conflicts do play a role for the power of the semantics under consideration, thus rejecting a recent conjecture brought up in [5]. In the second part we have complemented results on compact signatures. Our findings show that it is the rejected arguments which, for instance, make semi-stable and preferred semantics equally powerful (as shown in [12]). Disallowing rejected arguments has in turn different effects for these semantics.

The study of implicit conflicts and rejected arguments not only contributes to the theoretical understanding of argumentation semantics. It can also give valuable insights for systems implementing reasoning tasks of abstract argumentation (e.g. [10,13]). Knowledge about the existence of certain implicit conflicts can be used by solvers to reduce the search-space of their algorithms.

The obvious open questions include the above conjecture as well as research on the exact relations between AFs, semantics, rejected arguments and implicit conflicts. For future work, we want to extend our investigations to further extension-based semantics as well as to labelling-based semantics [9]. The latter setting provides a richer and more fine-grained hierarchy of the concepts we have used here. For instance, an argument might be rejected since it is always out, always undecided, or never in. Moreover, quantitative aspects of implicit conflicts as well as rejected arguments, e.g. how their ratio differs from one semantics to another, may be considered. Finally, we want to study how our findings contribute to the analysis of semantics in the context of instantiation [7].

Acknowledgements. This research has been supported by the Austrian Science Fund (FWF) through projects I1102 and P25521.

References

1. Baroni, P., Caminada, M., Giacomin, M.: An introduction to argumentation semantics. Knowl. Eng. Rev. **26**(4), 365–410 (2011)
2. Baroni, P., Dunne, P.E., Giacomin, M.: On the resolution-based family of abstract argumentation semantics and its grounded instance. Artif. Intell. **175**(3–4), 791–813 (2011)
3. Baroni, P., Giacomin, M.: On principle-based evaluation of extension-based argumentation semantics. Artif. Intell. **171**(10–15), 675–700 (2007)
4. Baumann, R.: Splitting an argumentation framework. In: Delgrande, J.P., Faber, W. (eds.) LPNMR 2011. LNCS, vol. 6645, pp. 40–53. Springer, Heidelberg (2011)
5. Baumann, R., Dvořák, W., Linsbichler, T., Strass, H., Woltran, S.: Compact argumentation frameworks. In: Schaub, T., Friedrich, G., O'Sullivan, B. (eds.) Proceedings of the 21st European Conference on Artificial Intelligence (ECAI 2014). Frontiers in Artificial Intelligence and Applications, vol. 263, pp. 69–74. IOS Press (2014)
6. Bench-Capon, T.J.M., Dunne, P.E.: Argumentation in artificial intelligence. Artif. Intell. **171**(10–15), 619–641 (2007)
7. Caminada, M., Amgoud, L.: On the evaluation of argumentation formalisms. Artif. Intell. **171**(5–6), 286–310 (2007)
8. Caminada, M., Carnielli, W.A., Dunne, P.E.: Semi-stable semantics. J. Log. Comput. **22**(5), 1207–1254 (2012)

9. Caminada, M., Gabbay, D.M.: A logical account of formal argumentation. Studia Logica **93**(2), 109–145 (2009)
10. Cerutti, F., Dunne, P.E., Giacomin, M., Vallati, M.: Computing preferred extensions in abstract argumentation: a SAT-based approach. In: Black, E., Modgil, S., Oren, N. (eds.) TAFA 2013. LNCS, vol. 8306, pp. 176–193. Springer, Heidelberg (2014)
11. Dung, P.M.: On the acceptability of arguments and its fundamental role in nonmonotonic reasoning, logic programming and n-person games. Artif. Intell. **77**(2), 321–357 (1995)
12. Dunne, P.E., Dvořák, W., Linsbichler, T., Woltran, S.: Characteristics of multiple viewpoints in abstract argumentation. Artif. Intell. **228**, 153–178 (2015)
13. Dvořák, W., Järvisalo, M., Wallner, J.P., Woltran, S.: Complexity-sensitive decision procedures for abstract argumentation. Artif. Intell. **206**, 53–78 (2014)
14. Dvořák, W., Spanring, C.: Comparing the expressiveness of argumentation semantics. In: Verheij, B., Szeider, S., Woltran, S. (eds.) Proceedings of the 4th Conference on Computational Models of Argument (COMMA 2012). Frontiers in Artificial Intelligence and Applications, vol. 245, pp. 261–272. IOS Press (2012)
15. Dyrkolbotn, S.K.: How to argue for anything: Enforcing arbitrary sets of labellings using AFs. In: Baral, C., De Giacomo, G., Eiter, T. (eds.) Proceedings of the 14th International Conference on Principles of Knowledge Representation and Reasoning (KR 2014), pp. 626–629. AAAI Press (2014)
16. Rahwan, I., Simari, G.R. (eds.): Argumentation in Artificial Intelligence. Springer, Heidelberg (2009)
17. Strass, H.: The relative expressiveness of abstract argumentation and logic programming. In: Proceedings of the 29th AAAI Conference on Artificial Intelligence (AAAI 2015), pp. 1625–1631 (2015)
18. Verheij, B.: Two approaches to dialectical argumentation: admissible sets and argumentation stages. In: Meyer, J.J.C., van der Gaag, L.C. (eds.) Proceedings of the 8th Dutch Conference on Artificial Intelligence (NAIC 1996), pp. 357–368 (1996)

Argument Mining: A Machine Learning Perspective

Marco Lippi[(✉)] and Paolo Torroni

DISI, Università Degli Studi di Bologna, Bologna, Italy
{marco.lippi3,p.torroni}@unibo.it

Abstract. Argument mining has recently become a hot topic, attracting the interests of several and diverse research communities, ranging from artificial intelligence, to computational linguistics, natural language processing, social and philosophical sciences. In this paper, we attempt to describe the problems and challenges of argument mining from a machine learning angle. In particular, we advocate that machine learning techniques so far have been under-exploited, and that a more proper standardization of the problem, also with regards to the underlying argument model, could provide a crucial element to develop better systems.

1 Introduction

Argumentation is a multi-disciplinary research field which studies debate and reasoning processes, and spans across and ties together diverse areas such as logic and philosophy, language, rhetoric and law, psychology and computer science. Over the last decades, *computational* argumentation has come to be increasingly central as a core study within artificial intelligence [3], while some cognitive science theories indicate that the function of human reasoning itself is argumentative [27]. Argumentation started to become known even in the computational social sciences, where agent-based simulation models have been proposed, whose micro-foundation explicitly refers to argumentation theories [15,26]. This, together with the current hype of big data and tremendous advances in computational linguistics, created fertile ground for the rise of a new area of research called *argumentation* (or *argument*) *mining* (henceforth AM).

The growing excitement in this area is tangible. The initial studies started to appear only a few years ago in specific domains such as legal texts, online reviews and debate [7,28,39]. In 2014 alone there have been no less than three international events on argumentation mining.[1] While research on this topic

---

[1] The First ACL Workshop on Argumentation Mining, http://www.uncg.edu/cmp/ArgMining2014, SICSA Workshop on Argument Mining: Perspectives from Information Extraction, Information Retrieval and Computational Linguistics http://www.arg-tech.org/index.php/sicsa-workshop-on-argument-mining-2014, and the BiCi Workshop on Frontiers and Connections between Argumentation Theory and Natural Language Processing, http://www-sop.inria.fr/members/Serena.Villata/BiCi2014/frontiersARG-NLP.html.

© Springer International Publishing Switzerland 2015
E. Black et al. (Eds.): TAFA 2015, LNAI 9524, pp. 163–176, 2015.
DOI: 10.1007/978-3-319-28460-6_10

is gaining momentum, major commercial players have also joined in, as IBM recently funded a multi-million cognitive computing project whose core technology is AM.[2] But what is AM and what makes it so popular?

The main goal of AM is to automatically extract arguments from generic textual corpora, in order to provide structured data for computational models of arguments and reasoning engines.

The self-evident application potential of AM is one reason for its growing popularity. From an application perspective, AM could be considered in some respects as an evolution of sentiment analysis. Habernal et al. [20] state that, while the goal of opinion mining is to understand *what people think about something*, the aim of argumentation mining is to understand *why*, thus unveiling reasoning processes, rather than just detecting opinions and sentiment. Besides, more or less abstract computational argumentation models and theories now seem closer than ever to the "real world" and the community seems eager to contribute to the creation of significant domains where very expressive models and efficient algorithms developed in recent years can be tested and applied. Another reason of its rapid expansion is that AM poses a scientifically engaging challenge, especially from a machine learning (ML) perspective. Indeed, AM is a difficult NLP task that merges together many different components, such as information extraction, knowledge representation, and discourse analysis. This is also creating new opportunities in the computational argumentation community. Advanced statistical and subsymbolic reasoning methods have never been so tightly conjugated with a discipline, whose roots are in symbolic artificial intelligence.

Most notably, we see AM as a source of new opportunities for the formal argumentation community, drawing a bridge between formal models and theories and argumentative reasoning as it emerges from everyday life.

Due to the novelty of this research domain, at the present stage AM is not a well-defined problem with clear boundaries. On the contrary, AM is rather a broad umbrella for a new set of challenges where many different understandings coexist and contribute towards a common, if under-specified, objective. However, there are already many interesting results, and we feel that time is ripe for attempting an initial road map.

The aim of this article is thus to discuss achievements and challenges in AM from a ML angle. Our ambition is to help making this new domain accessible to scholars that do not necessarily have a computational argumentation background. For this reason, we will start by introducing models which, although well-known in computational argumentation, are crucial design choices that greatly influence the ML problem formulation. We will then proceed to review relevant ML techniques and discuss challenges that AM poses to ML research.

---

[2] More about IBM Debating Technologies at http://researcher.watson.ibm.com/researcher/view_group.php?id=5443.

2   Problem Formulation

The discipline of argumentation has ancient roots in dialectics and philosophy, as that branch of knowledge dedicated to the study and analysis of how statements and assertions are proposed and debated, and conflicts between diverging opinions are resolved [3]. Starting from the pioneering works by Pollock [33], Simari and Loui [40], and Dung [12], among others, models of argumentation have also spread in the area of AI, especially in connection with knowledge representation, non-monotonic reasoning, and multi-agent systems research, giving rise to a new field named "computational argumentation."

The two main approaches in computational argumentation are called *abstract* argumentation, and *structured* argumentation. The former is rooted in Dung's work, and it considers each argument as an atomic entity without internal structure. It thus provides a very powerful framework to model and analyze "attack" relations between arguments, or sets of them, which may or may not be *justified* according to some semantics. The latter proposes an internal structure for each argument, described in terms of some knowledge representation formalism. Structured argumentation models are those typically employed in AM, as defining the structure of an argument becomes crucial, when the goal is to extract portions of arguments from natural language.

Because there are many significant proposals for structured argumentation [4], it is impossible to give a single formal, universally accepted definition of structured argument. A rather comprehensive account of argumentation models under an argument analysis perspective is given by Peldszus and Stede [32]. A simple and intuitive characterization is given by Walton, who describes an argument as a set of statements consisting in three parts: a conclusion, a set of premises, and an inference from the premises to the conclusion [45]. In the literature, conclusions are sometimes referred to as *claims*, premises are often called *evidence* or *reasons*, and the link between the two, i.e., the inference, is sometimes called the *argument* itself. Besides this basic *claim/premise* argument model, other noteworthy models are due to Tuolmin [44] and Freeman [14].

Here is an example of a sentence containing a claim:[3]

> *Health risks can be produced by long-term use or excessive doses of anabolic steroids.*

The following sentence instead contains a premise, supporting the previous claim:

> *A recent study has also shown that long term AAS users were more likely to have symptoms of muscle dysmorphia.*

The term *argumentation* has historically referred to the process of constructing arguments and, since the advent of computational argumentation, to the process of determining the set of justified conclusions of a set of arguments. However, *argumentation mining* and *argument mining* are often used interchangeably and in a broad sense, as the field yet retains a strong element of conceptual exploration.

---

[3] All examples in this paper are taken from the IBM corpus, described in Sect. 4.

The task of detecting the premises and conclusion of an argument, as found in a text of discourse, is typically referred to as *detection* or *identification* [45]. More specific sub-tasks are *claim detection* [24] and *evidence detection* [36].

Being this a young research domain, not only its definitions but also its approaches and targets vary widely. Some research aims at extracting the arguments from generic unstructured documents, which is a fundamental step in practical applications [24], whereas other starts from a given set of arguments and focuses on aspects such as the identification of attack/support [10] or entailment [8] relations between them, or on the classification of argument schemes [13] in the sense of Walton et al. [46].

In the next section we will review ML methods for the task of automatically extracting arguments from text.

3   Methods

Argument mining is a complex, multi-faceted problem, which embraces many different concepts from various disciplines. For this reason, addressing AM usually requires dealing with a variety of intertwined sub-tasks. This intrinsic heterogeneity makes AM an extremely engaging application for machine learning, by involving aspects of natural language processing and understanding, information extraction, feature discovery and discourse analysis. All the argument mining frameworks proposed so far can be described as multi-stage pipeline systems, whose input is natural, free text document, and whose output is a mark-up document, where arguments (or parts of arguments) are annotated. Each stage addresses a sub-task of the whole AM problem, by employing one or more machine learning and natural language processing methodologies and techniques.

3.1   Argumentative Sentence Detection

A first stage usually consists of detecting which sentences in the input document are argumentative, which means that they contain an argument, or part thereof. This task is typically implemented by a machine learning classifier. A common implementation consists of training a binary classifier, with the goal of simply discarding propositions that are not argumentative, while a second classifier at a later stage in the pipeline will subsequently be trained to distinguish among various argument components (e.g., claims from premises). Alternatively, a single multi-class predictor could be employed to discriminate between all the possible categories of argument components.

In both cases, two crucial issues within this step involve (1) the choice of the classifier, and (2) the features to be used to describe the sentences. As for the adopted machine learning classifiers, many works in the literature so far have made attempts to compare several approaches, including Naïve Bayes classifiers [28,30], Support Vector Machines (SVM) [28,30], Maximum Entropy classifiers [28], Logistic Regression [24], Decision Trees and Random Forests [42].

The obtained results are in some cases conflicting, as for example in [28] the SVM model performs worse than Naïve Bayes, while in [42] the opposite happens. As a matter of fact, the vast majority of the aforementioned approaches have been based on classic, off-the-shelf classifiers, while all the effort has been focused on the creation of a set of highly engineered features, sometimes also obtained as the outcome of other external predictors [24]. It is therefore not surprising that the key element for achieving good performance has been shown to be the choice of the features, rather than the machine learning algorithm. Indeed, in several cases, different classifiers trained with the same feature sets lead to very similar performance.

Many works employ classical features for text representation, including bag-of-words representations of sentences, word bigrams and trigrams, part-of-speech information obtained with some statistical parser, information on punctuation, verb tenses and the use of some pre-determined list of key phrases [28,42]. An example fed to the machine learning classifier is therefore a sentence, typically represented as a vector x of k features $x = \{x_1, \ldots, x_k\}$, where x_j indicates the value of the j-th feature. In the formalism of bag-of-words, also extended to bigrams and trigrams, the j-th feature can indicate, for example, the presence, within the sentence, of the j-th word (or bigram, or trigram) of the dictionary. Yet, this classic and still widely used approach has a limitation: it does not capture the semantic similarity between different words, but only counts common terms in order to measure the similarity between two sentences. In this sense, for example, two terms such as *argue* and *believe* are orthogonal, and therefore they are as different as *argue* and *eat*. More advanced features try to incorporate linguistic and semantic information on the most informative words (typically verbs and nouns) in order to capture such similarities, by employing onthologies such as WordNet [24]. Some additional features are also used to mark the presence of certain syntactical descriptors, with the aim to detect recurrent structural patterns, but these methods are prone to overfitting, as they are typically well-suited for the corpus they have been constructed on. Even more sophisticated features include sentiment analysis indicators, subjectivity scores of sentences, dictionaries of keywords or keyphrases that may be highly informative of the presence of an argument [24]. Also in this case, the risk of obtaining methods that cannot generalize to different corpora is certainly not negligible, and, as a matter of fact, we are not aware of any method so far that has been extensively tested on a variety of different corpora.

Another key problem within this context is whether it is convenient to build systems that need to employ contextual information to detect argumentative sentences. The approach developed at IBM Research in Haifa, as a part of The Debater™ project, makes a strong use of the topic information (given in advance) when attempting to extract arguments [24]. Also in other specific applicative scenarios, as in the case of legal documents [28], features are very often highly dependent on the domain. While the use of contextual information can no doubt significantly boost the performance of the system in a given context, we remark that this is another element that could greatly limit the general applicability of the system across different contexts.

In a recent work [25] we propose to overcome these issues by employing an SVM based on structured kernels built upon constituency parse trees to identify sentences containing claims. Basically, the similarity between the structure of the parse trees is used in order to measure the similarity between sentences. In this way, the rhetorical structure of sentences is automatically captured by the implicit feature space, without the need of manually specifying the feature set, and without resorting to explicit contextual information.

Previous work by Rooney et al. [37] also considers kernel methods for an AM task. However, it only uses the sequence of parts-of-speech tags without exploiting the powerful representation of parse trees. The authors use their own tagging of the AraucariaDB (see Sect. 4).

3.2   Argument Boundaries Detection

Once the non-argumentative sentences have been discarded by the first stage of the pipeline, it is necessary to determine the exact boundaries of argument components, or "argumentative discourse units" [32]. Clearly, this phase greatly depends on the underlying argument model, since the AM system must be able to discriminate between all the possible components defined by the model of choice: claims and premises, for example, if we adopt the claim/premise model, or warrants, backings, qualifiers and rebuttals if we adopt the Toulmin model. Existing AM systems usually adopt the claim/premise model, because of its simplicity and generality. Yet, a recent work by Harbenal et al. [20] argues that different argumentation models could be better suitable for different application domains. For this reason, they employ the Toulmin model for the annotation of a corpus of web documents collected from blogs, forums, and news.

Regardless of the considered argument model, in addition to discriminating between all the possible argument components, this stage of the AM pipeline also needs to address a so-called *segmentation problem*, since a whole sentence does not necessarily correspond exactly to an argument component. In fact, we can distinguish between three different cases:

1. only a portion of the sentence coincides with an argument component;
2. two or more argument components can be present within the same sentence;
3. an argument component can span across multiple sentences.

For example, in the case of claims, the following sentence falls into the first category:

> A significant number of republicans assert that hereditary <u>monarchy is unfair and elitist.</u>

where the annotated claim is underlined. An example of a premise spanning more than a single sentence is the one below:

> When New Hampshire authorized a state lottery in 1963, it represented a major shift in social policy. No state governments had previously directly

run gambling operations to raise money. Other states followed suit, and now the majority of the states run some type of lottery to raise funds for state operations.

Most of the existing methods assume only one of the above possibilities, and they address the segmentation problem as a separate stage from the extraction of argumentative sentences [24, 28].

However, different solutions could in principle be exploited, for example resorting to structured output classifiers or to statistical relational learning models, which are capable of performing *collective classification* on a set of examples, rather than considering each of them independently. This framework allows to consider relationships and dependencies between examples and has shown to be a crucial element in many machine learning tasks on structured data [16]. A first step in this direction is observed in [18,31], where conditional random fields are used to perform the segmentation task for argument components.

Multi-class classification systems similar to the ones described in the previous section are typically employed to discriminate amongst different argument components, but sometimes they do not properly address the segmentation task [42]. In other cases, clauses (sub-sentences) resulting from the parsing of a sentence are considered as boundaries [28], or maximum likelihood systems are employed to identify the most probable boundaries of the argument components [24].

3.3   Argument Structure Prediction

Following the detection of argument components, a further stage in the pipeline has the aim to predict links between arguments or their components. As customary in machine learning, we speak in this case of *prediction* rather than *detection*, because the target of the classification is not a specific portion of the input document, but rather a connection (or link) between them. If the desired output consists in only relations between argument components, then the system will produce a sort of map of the arguments retrieved from the input text. Another possibility is to infer the connections between arguments, in which case support and attack relations have to be distinguished. This second point is a very important step, as the output of the AM system could be used as an input to a formal argumentation framework, so that different semantics could be applied to identify sets of arguments with desired characteristics.

As in the previous steps of the AM pipeline, even for structure prediction the implementation choices strongly depend on the underlying argument model. When considering a claim/premise model, for example, the task of inferring connections between claims and premises can be seen as a link prediction problem within a bipartite graph. With a more complex model, such as the Toulmin model, the link categories that can be predicted clearly grow, and more fine-grained predictors have to been designed, in order to correctly predict the connections between all the components. It is also worth noticing that some argument components can also be *implicit* within the original textual document: this is the case, for example, of *enthymemes*, or even of implicit warrants in the Toulmin model, corresponding to unsaid assumptions. Therefore, the argument structure prediction phase should, in principle, be able also to detect such implicit components and add them to the model: from a machine learning point of view, this is a highly challenging task, and currently no attempt has been made in this direction. A possible reference model for constructing enthymemes was proposed in [5].

In some cases, further simplifications can be modeled: in the work developed at the IBM Haifa Research Group, for example, premises (which they call *evidence*) are labeled given a certain claim [1]. In this way, the information regarding the claim can be used when detecting the evidence, and therefore there is no need to further predict the structure links, which are obtained (by definition) when predicting the evidence. In [42], a claim/premise model based on work by Freeman [14] is adopted, and thus attack/support links between argument components are predicted using a plain SVM binary classifier. In the context of legal documents, [28] adopt a manually-constructed context-free grammar to predict relations between argument components: this is a strongly domain-specific approach, based on the common structures of legal texts, which could hardly be applied to different application scenarios. Another quite popular approach is based on Textual Entailment (TE) [6] and aims to understand whether there exists an entailment relation between two given argument components.

4   Corpora

It is a fact that the whole AM process, based on ML and AI techniques, requires a collection of annotated documents, to be used as a training set for any kind of predictor. Constructing annotated corpora is, in general, a complex and time-consuming task, which requires to commit costly resources such as teams of experts, so that homogeneous and consistent annotations can be obtained. This is particularly true for AM, as the identification of argument components, their exact boundaries, and how they relate to each other can be quite complicated (and controversial!) even for humans. Moreover, very often the existing data sets have been built with slightly different goals or for some specific aim, and therefore they cannot always be used within all machine learning approaches.

As an example, several annotated corpora have been constructed with the goal of analyzing arguments and their relations. Among them, we mention the collections maintained by the University of Dundee,[4] which aggregate many datasets—including, notably, AraucariaDB—with annotated argument maps, in a variety of standardized formats. Another collection is the NoDE benchmark data base [9] which contains arguments obtained from a variety of sources, including Debatepedia[5] and ProCon[6]. Yet, due to the goal they were built for, these corpora do not put an emphasis on—and they often lack—the non-argumentative parts, which are necessary as negative examples for the training of some kind of discriminative machine learning classifier.

---

[4] http://corpora.aifdb.org.
[5] http://www.debatepedia.com.
[6] http://www.procon.org.

Furthermore, most of the AM systems proposed so far have been mainly used in pilot applications in specific domains only, where a few annotated corpora exist. Law has been the pioneering application domain for AM, and certainly among the most successful ones, with the work by Mochales Palau and Moens [28] on the European Court of Human Rights (ECHR) dataset for the extraction of claims and their supporting premises from a collection of structured legal documents. More recently, also the Vaccine/Injury Project (V/IP) [2] was carried out, with the goal of extracting arguments from a set of juridical cases involving vaccine regulations. Unfortunately, these corpora are not publicly available.

A new trend which is recently gaining attention is that of creating annotated data sets from biology and medicine texts [19,21]. This could be an extremely important step towards building ontologies and knowledge bases describing the links between either symptoms and diseases, or between genes and diseases, or even to assist personalized medicine prescriptions.

Rhetorical, philosophical and persuasive essays represent another interesting case study. The creation of a corpus from a collection of 19th century philosophical essays was proposed in [22]. A limited-scope but well-documented data set was proposed by Stab and Gurevych [41] as a collection of 90 persuasive essays. The topics covered are very heterogeneous. Due to the nature of the data, and to the annotation guidelines, only a few sentences in this corpus are non-argumentative. Being specifically designed for the analysis of persuasive essays, this corpus would likely not be the most appropriate choice for a training set, if the goal were to generalize to other kinds of data sources. In fact, these essays are annotated with claims, premises, and "major claims" (one per essay), these being highly domain-specific tags, often detected thanks to dedicated features, such as the position of the sentence within the essay.

A much larger data set is currently being developed at IBM Research,[7] starting from plain text in Wikipedia pages [1,36]. The purpose of this corpus is to collect context-dependent claims and evidence facts (i.e., premises), which are relevant to a given topic. At the time of writing, the data set covers 58 topics, for a total of 547 Wikipedia articles. The data set contains about 7,000 argumentative entities (claims or evidence), and is an extremely challenging benchmark. An approach to context-dependent claim detection on this corpus was proposed in [24], while a context-independent approach was applied in [25] for the same dataset.

Additional datasets were recently collected from online resources, including online reviews, blogs, and newspapers. Two of them have been developed by [38], for the task of extracting so-called *opinionated claims*: they consist in 285 LiveJournal blogposts and 51 Wikipedia discussion forums, respectively. Each dataset consists of 2,000 sentences. Another well-annotated corpus was developed by Habernal et al. [20], to model arguments following a variant of the Toulmin model. This dataset includes 990 instances, 524 of which are labeled as argumentative. A smaller corpus of 345 examples is annotated with finer tags. The authors report the annotation procedure in detail, together with a review

---

[7] https://www.research.ibm.com/haifa/dept/vst/mlta_data.shtml.

of the inter-agreement evaluation procedures of other existing corpora. Finally, data collected by web sources have been used also in [18], but unfortunately they are not publicly available.

5   Challenges

From the point of view ML, this blossoming research field poses new challenges and paves the way to unprecedented opportunities. We discuss them here.

Owing to the only recent development of the area, there is still a lack of general agreement regarding the models which should be adopted to build an AM system. Although one could argue that the intrinsic heterogeneous nature of data sources and application domains makes it difficult to propose a single and general model to be adopted in many contexts, yet we believe that some clarifications should be made in order to pose guidelines for the constructions of corpora. An attempt in this direction has certainly been made by several authors (e.g., see [20,24]). This process would bring a twofold benefit also on the ML side. First of all, it would allow more appropriate comparisons between different algorithms and techniques, as the same performance measurements could be applied to compare different approaches. Secondly, such a framework would also help the development of more general and context-independent methodologies, capable of performing AM on different kinds of data sources, since a novel system could be applied across different domains, exploiting what in ML is typically referred to as *transfer learning* [29].

From a more technical point of view, it is clear that, up to now, ML methodologies so far have been applied in AM pipelines only as off-the-shelf black boxes, while very often devolving the performance of the whole systems upon the sophistication of features employed. We believe that the time is ripe to move the ML contributions to AM a step forward, by trying more advanced algorithms, or even by developing specific approaches. Within this context, a crucial contribution will likely come from statistical relational learning, a recent area of ML dedicated to handling relational and structured data. The idea driving this research field is that relations between patterns often represent crucial information to build classifiers with high performance. When data is represented in a structured form, as it happens with the sequentiality of text, or with the graphical structure of argument maps, the potential of this kind of methodology is evident. Many of the approaches developed within this field also exploit logic formalisms to describe the domain of interest, thus allowing the embedding of background knowledge in the form of predicates and logic clauses. The success of statistical relational learning in relevant tasks somehow related to AM, such as link discovery in social and biological networks [17], information extraction and entity resolution in textual corpora [11,34], sequence tagging and sentence parsing [35] offers an additional very strong motivation. Another area of machine learning which may contribute to AM is active learning, where the learning systems actively ask for supervisions rather than being given in advance a fixed, static batch of supervised data. Active learning approaches have scored interesting results in several natural language processing applications [43] and thus they could be successfully applied also to some steps in the AM pipeline, being particularly useful when annotated data are hard to collect.

Last but not least, the AM community should certainly not ignore the huge impact that deep learning is bringing within artificial intelligence. Models based on deep architectures have obtained breakthrough results on a wide variety of applications, ranging from speech recognition and computer vision to natural language processing and understanding (e.g., see [23] and references therein). By dominating the ML scene in the last years, deep learning approaches are with no doubt among the novel methodologies which could bring decisive contributions to AM systems.

6 Conclusions

Argumentation mining represents a novel, exciting application domain for machine learning. Nevertheless, in spite of some promising initial results, there is still a lot of work to be done, in order to exploit all the potential of ML approaches within the AM community, and to build successful applications to be employed as an input to formal argumentation frameworks.

While other surveys have been dedicated to the modeling aspect of the AM tasks [32], this is the first step towards a more principled formulation of the problem from the ML point of view. In particular, this paper is a first attempt to highlight challenges and opportunities for ML systems in this area.

We argue that current approaches too often rely on methodologies that demand a great deal of effort in the development of powerful but highly domain-dependent features, and are thus difficult to generalize.

Moreover, we believe that a major obstacle to progress in AM is the lack of a standardized methodology for annotating relevant corpora. We find that most works define their own labeled corpora, hindering comparison between various approaches on the same dataset and between the performance of approaches across datasets.

We thus argue that a major effort should be put into the construction of annotated corpora that meet the needs of ML algorithms. In particular, if (as we believe) identifying relations between different arguments and between different argument components is a valuable output of prospective AM applications, then corpora should contain all the necessary annotations. As a matter of fact, argument structure prediction is the stage in the AM pipeline that has produced less results so far.

Finally, the methods we reviewed mostly target homogeneous and domain-specific data sources. An interesting direction could be developing AM techniques capable of handling heterogeneous data sources, as well as relational and structured data.

References

1. Aharoni, E., Polnarov, A., Lavee, T., Hershcovich, D., Levy, R., Rinott, R., Gutfreund, D., Slonim, N.: A benchmark dataset for automatic detection of claims and evidence in the context of controversial topics. In: Proceedings of the First Workshop on Argumentation Mining, pp. 64–68. Association for Computational Linguistics (2014)
2. Ashley, K.D., Walker, V.R.: Toward constructing evidence-based legal arguments using legal decision documents and machine learning. In: Francesconi, E., Verheij, B. (eds.) ICAIL 2013, Rome, Italy, pp. 176–180. ACM (2013)
3. Bench-Capon, T.J.M., Dunne, P.E.: Argumentation in artificial intelligence. Artif. Intell. 171(10–15), 619–641 (2007)
4. Besnard, P., García, A.J., Hunter, A., Modgil, S., Prakken, H., Simari, G.R., Toni, F.: Introduction to structured argumentation. Argum. Comput. 5(1), 1–4 (2014)
5. Black, E., Hunter, A.: A relevance-theoretic framework for constructing and deconstructing enthymemes. J. Log. Comput. 22(1), 55–78 (2012)
6. Cabrio, E., Villata, S.: Combining textual entailment and argumentation theory for supporting online debates interactions. In: Proceedings of the 50th Annual Meeting of the Association for Computational Linguistics (ACL 2012), pp. 208–212. Association for Computational Linguistics, Jeju, Korea (2012)
7. Cabrio, E., Villata, S.: Natural language arguments: A combined approach. In: Raedt, L.D., Bessière, C., Dubois, D., Doherty, P., Frasconi, P., Heintz, F., Lucas, P.J.F. (eds.) ECAI 2012–20th European Conference on Artificial Intelligence. Including Prestigious Applications of Artificial Intelligence (PAIS-2012) System Demonstrations Track, Montpellier, France, 27–31 August 2012, vol. 242, pp. 205–210. IOS Press (2012)
8. Cabrio, E., Villata, S.: A natural language bipolar argumentation approach to support users in online debate interactions. Argum. Comput. 4(3), 209–230 (2013)
9. Cabrio, E., Villata, S.: NoDE: A benchmark of natural language arguments. In: Parsons, S., Oren, N., Reed, C., Cerutti, F. (eds.) COMMA 2014. Frontiers in Artificial Intelligence and Applications, vol. 266, pp. 449–450. IOS Press (2014)
10. Chesñevar, C.I., McGinnis, J., Modgil, S., Rahwan, I., Reed, C., Simari, G.R., South, M., Vreeswijk, G., Willmott, S.: Towards an argument interchange format. Knowl. Eng. Rev. 21(4), 293–316 (2006)
11. Culotta, A., McCallum, A., Betz, J.: Integrating probabilistic extraction models and data mining to discover relations and patterns in text. In: Proceedings of the Main Conference on Human Language Technology Conference of the North American Chapter of the Association of Computational Linguistics, pp. 296–303. Association for Computational Linguistics (2006)
12. Dung, P.M.: On the acceptability of arguments and its fundamental role in nonmonotonic reasoning, logic programming and n-person games. Artif. Intell. 77(2), 321–358 (1995)
13. Feng, V.W., Hirst, G.: Classifying arguments by scheme. In: Lin, D., Matsumoto, Y., Mihalcea, R. (eds.) Proceedings of the Conference on 49th Annual Meeting of the Association for Computational Linguistics: Human Language Technologies, 19–24 June, 2011, Portland, Oregon, USA, pp. 987–996. ACL (2011)
14. Freeman, J.B.: Dialectics and the Macrostructure of Arguments: A Theory of Argument Structure, vol. 10. Walter de Gruyter, Berlin (1991)
15. Gabbriellini, S., Torroni, P.: A new framework for ABMs based on argumentative reasoning. In: Kamiński, B., Koloch, G. (eds.) Advances in Social Simulation. AISC, vol. 229, pp. 25–36. Springer, Heidelberg (2014)

16. Getoor, L.: Tutorial on statistical relational learning. In: Kramer, S., Pfahringer, B. (eds.) ILP 2005. LNCS (LNAI), vol. 3625, p. 415. Springer, Heidelberg (2005)
17. Getoor, L., Diehl, C.P.: Link mining: a survey. ACM SIGKDD Explor. Newsl. **7**(2), 3–12 (2005)
18. Goudas, T., Louizos, C., Petasis, G., Karkaletsis, V.: Argument extraction from news, blogs, and social media. In: Likas, A., Blekas, K., Kalles, D. (eds.) SETN 2014. LNCS, vol. 8445, pp. 287–299. Springer, Heidelberg (2014)
19. Green, N.: Towards creation of a corpus for argumentation mining the biomedical genetics research literature. In: Proceedings of the First Workshop on Argumentation Mining, pp. 11–18. Association for Computational Linguistics (2014)
20. Habernal, I., Eckle-Kohler, J., Gurevych, I.: Argumentation mining on the web from information seeking perspective. In: Cabrio, E., Villata, S., Wyner, A. (eds.) Proceedings of the Workshop on Frontiers and Connections between Argumentation Theory and Natural Language Processing, Forlì-Cesena, Italy, 21–25 July 2014. CEUR Workshop Proceedings, vol. 1341 (2014). CEUR-WS.org
21. Houngbo, H., Mercer, R.: An automated method to build a corpus of rhetorically-classified sentences in biomedical texts. In: Proceedings of the First Workshop on Argumentation Mining, pp. 19–23. Association for Computational Linguistics (2014)
22. Lawrence, J., Reed, C., Allen, C., McAlister, S., Ravenscroft, A.: Mining arguments from 19th century philosophical texts using topic based modelling. In: Proceedings of the First Workshop on Argumentation Mining, pp. 79–87. Association for Computational Linguistics (2014)
23. LeCun, Y., Bengio, Y., Hinton, G.: Deep learning. Nature **531**, 436–444 (2015)
24. Levy, R., Bilu, Y., Hershcovich, D., Aharoni, E., Slonim, N.: Context dependent claim detection. In: Hajic, J., Tsujii, J. (eds.) COLING 2014, Dublin, Ireland, pp. 1489–1500. ACL (2014)
25. Lippi, M., Torroni, P.: Context-independent claim detection for argumentation mining. In: Yang, Q., Wooldridge, M. (eds.) Proceedings of the Twenty-Fourth International Joint Conference on Artificial Intelligence, IJCAI 2015, Buenos Aires, Argentina, 25-31 July 2015, pp. 185–191. AAAI Press (2015)
26. Mäs, M., Flache, A.: Differentiation without distancing. explaining bi-polarization of opinions without negative influence. PLoS ONE **8**(11), e74516 (2013)
27. Mercier, H., Sperber, D.: Why do humans reason? argumento for an argumentative theory. Behav. Brain Sci. **34**, 57–74 (2011)
28. Mochales, R., Moens, M.F.: Argumentation mining. Artif. Intell. Law **19**(1), 1–22 (2011)
29. Pan, S.J., Yang, Q.: A survey on transfer learning. IEEE Trans. Knowl. Data Eng. **22**(10), 1345–1359 (2010)
30. Park, J., Cardie, C.: Identifying appropriate support for propositions in online user comments. In: Proceedings of the First Workshop on Argumentation Mining, pp. 29–38. Association for Computational Linguistics, Baltimore, Maryland, June 2014
31. Park, J., Katiyar, A., Yang, B.: Conditional random fields for identifying appropriate types of support for propositions in online user comments. In: Proceedings of the Second Workshop on Argumentation Mining. Association for Computational Linguistics (2015)
32. Peldszus, A., Stede, M.: From argument diagrams to argumentation mining in texts: A survey. Int. J. Cogn. Inf. Nat. Intell. (IJCINI) **7**(1), 1–31 (2013)
33. Pollock, J.L.: Defeasible reasoning. Cogn. Sci. **11**(4), 481–518 (1987)

34. Poon, H., Domingos, P.: Joint inference in information extraction. In: Proceedings of the Twenty-Second AAAI Conference on Artificial Intelligence, Vancouver, Canada, pp. 913–918. AAAI Press (2007)
35. Poon, H., Domingos, P.: Unsupervised semantic parsing. In: Proceedings of the 2009 Conference on Empirical Methods in Natural Language Processing, EMNLP 2009: Volume 1 - Volume 1, pp. 1–10. Association for Computational Linguistics, Stroudsburg (2009)
36. Rinott, R., Khapra, M., Alzate, C., Dankin, L., Aharoni, E., Slonim, N.: Show me your evidence - an automatic method for context dependent evidence detection. In: Proceedings of the 2015 Conference on Empirical Methods in NLP (EMNLP), Lisbon, Portugal, 17–21 September 2015, pp. 440–450. Association for Computational Linguistics (2015)
37. Rooney, N., Wang, H., Browne, F.: Applying kernel methods to argumentation mining. In: Youngblood, G.M., McCarthy, P.M. (eds.) Proceedings of the Twenty-Fifth International Florida Artificial Intelligence Research Society Conference, Marco Island, Florida, 23–25 May 2012. AAAI Press (2012)
38. Rosenthal, S., McKeown, K.: Detecting opinionated claims in online discussions. In: Sixth IEEE International Conference on Semantic Computing, ICSC 2012, Palermo, Italy, 19–21 September 2012, pp. 30–37. IEEE Computer Society (2012)
39. Saint-Dizier, P.: Processing natural language arguments with the <TextCoop> platform. Argum. Comput. 3(1), 49–82 (2012)
40. Simari, G.R., Loui, R.P.: A mathematical treatment of defeasible reasoning and its implementation. Artif. Intell. 53(23), 125–157 (1992)
41. Stab, C., Gurevych, I.: Annotating argument components and relations in persuasive essays. In: Hajic, J., Tsujii, J. (eds.) COLING 2014, Dublin, Ireland, pp. 1501–1510. ACL (2014)
42. Stab, C., Gurevych, I.: Identifying argumentative discourse structures in persuasive essays. In: Moschitti, A., Pang, B., Daelemans, W. (eds.) EMNLP 2014, Doha, Qatar, pp. 46–56. ACL (2014)
43. Thompson, C.A., Califf, M.E., Mooney, R.J.: Active learning for natural language parsing and information extraction. In: Bratko, I., Dzeroski, S. (eds.) Proceedings of the Sixteenth International Conference on Machine Learning (ICML 1999), Bled, Slovenia, 27–30 June 1999, pp. 406–414. Morgan Kaufmann (1999)
44. Toulmin, S.E.: The Uses of Argument. Cambridge University Press, Cambridge (1958)
45. Walton, D.: Argumentation theory: A very short introduction. In: Simari, G., Rahwan, I. (eds.) Argumentation in Artificial Intelligence, pp. 1–22. Springer, Heidelberg (2009)
46. Walton, D., Reed, C., Macagno, F.: Argumentation Schemes. Cambridge University Press, Cambridge (2008)

Arguing from Similar Positions:
An Empirical Analysis

Josh Murphy[(✉)], Elizabeth Black, and Michael Luck

Department of Informatics, King's College London, London, UK
{josh.murphy,elizabeth.black,michael.luck}@kcl.ac.uk

Abstract. Argument-based deliberation dialogues are an important mechanism in the study of agent coordination, allowing agents to exchange formal arguments to reach an agreement for action. Agents participating in a deliberation dialogue may begin the dialogue with very similar sets of arguments to one another, or they may start the dialogue with disjoint sets of arguments, or some middle ground. In this paper, we empirically investigate whether the similarity of agents' arguments affects the dialogue outcome. Our results show that agents that have similar sets of initially known arguments are less likely to reach an agreement through dialogue than those that have dissimilar sets of initially known arguments.

1 Introduction

Autonomous agents must often collaborate with others to achieve their goals, for example when it is impossible or inefficient to achieve them as individuals. One way for a group of agents to coordinate their actions is to participate in argument-based dialogues, which are structured interactions between participants, involving the exchange of formal arguments (e.g., [1]). There are many classes of argument dialogues, one such class being the deliberation dialogue, in which participants attempt to agree on an action. Such dialogues are a rational approach for agents to come to an agreement on how to act, allowing the opportunity for an agent not only to express their action preferences, but also to express the reasons for them. Thus, deliberation dialogues are important as a possible collaboration and coordination mechanism. However, if practical real-world applications for argument-based deliberation dialogues are to be developed, we need to understand the situations in which agents perform successfully in them.

The complexities of agent-based argument dialogues mean that often only a limited number of properties can be studied formally without making overly restrictive simplifications to the problem domain [2]. This can cause formal analysis of agent performance in such dialogues to be difficult. A complementary approach is to use simulation and empirical analysis; for example, Black and Bentley's experiments on simulations with a deliberation dialogue system found that argument-based deliberation dialogues typically outperform a basic consensus forming algorithm [3]. However, while their experiments explore a large and sensitive parameter space, they do not consider the similarity of arguments

E. Black et al. (Eds.): TAFA 2015, LNAI 9524, pp. 177–193, 2015.
DOI: 10.1007/978-3-319-28460-6_11

(they assume that agents have disjoint sets of initial arguments) which could be a contributing factor to the outcome of the dialogue.

In this paper, we also study the behaviour of deliberation dialogues using empirical methods, and investigate the dialogue system studied by Black and Bentley [3], first presented by Black and Atkinson [4]. We extend Black and Bentley's analysis by considering whether the *similarity* of arguments at the start of the dialogue affects the likelihood of whether agents successfully reach an agreement. This similarity of agent arguments at the start of a dialogue is likely to vary in real-world applications, so it is especially pertinent to understand how this property affects the outcomes of dialogues.

Our results demonstrate that the similarity of the sets of arguments known to each agent has a statistically significant effect on the likelihood of dialogue success. We find that, in contrast to our intuition, the higher the similarity of initial arguments the lower the likelihood of success. We provide a justification for this relationship and analyse the extent of its effect across the parameter space, helping to identify cases where the use of argument-based deliberation dialogues is likely to be useful. The contribution of this paper is thus an analysis of how the similarity of arguments known to agents at the start of a deliberation dialogue affects the likelihood that agents will reach agreement.

The paper is structured as follows. In Sect. 2 we recapitulate the model of the dialogue system originally presented by Black and Atkinson [4]. In Sect. 3 we describe our implementation and method of experimentation, including how we varied the similarity of the sets of arguments that agents initially know about. In Sect. 4 we present the results of our experiments, including an analysis of observed trends and a detailed description of the relationships between variables. We discuss related work in Sect. 5. Finally, in Sect. 6, we discuss avenues of future work.

2   Deliberation Dialogues

In this section we describe the model that specifies the deliberation dialogues investigated in this paper. This model is the same as that described by Black and Bentley [3], first presented by Black and Atkinson [4], and is based on the popular argument scheme and critical questions approach [5]. First we give details of the argumentation model that agents use to generate and evaluate arguments for and against different actions. We then describe the dialogue system used by agents to exchange these arguments, including the dialogue protocol that defines the structure of a deliberation dialogue, and the strategy that agents use to determine which of their arguments they will exchange.

2.1   Argumentation Model

Our key concern is with the performance of the system specified in [4], in which agents have knowledge about the state of the world, about the preconditions and effects of actions they can perform, and about values that are either promoted or demoted by particular changes to the state of the world (these values represent qualitative social interests that an agent wishes to uphold; for example, fairness, health benefit, or personal privacy [6]). An agent can use its knowledge to construct arguments for or against actions by instantiating a *scheme for practical reasoning* [7]: in the current circumstances R, we should/should not perform action A, which will result in new circumstances S, which will achieve goal G, which will promote/demote value V. For example, an agent with the goal to be at the park may be able to construct the following arguments for and against actions to achieve its goal (note that we omit the current and new circumstances from these arguments, assuming the reader can envisage appropriate instantiations).

- **A1:** We should *cycle* (action) because it promotes *personal well-being* (value) in achieving *getting to the park* (goal).
- **A2:** We should not *drive* (action) because it demotes *environmental well-being* (value) in achieving *getting to the park* (goal).
- **A3:** We should *drive* (action) because it promotes *timeliness* (value) in achieving *getting to the park* (goal).

The scheme for practical reasoning is associated with a set of characteristic critical questions (CQs), which can be used to identify challenges to proposals for action that instantiate the scheme. These critical questions each relate to one of three reasoning stages: *problem formulation*, which considers the knowledge agents have about the problem domain (e.g., whether the preconditions and effects of actions are correct, whether state transitions promote or demote particular values); *epistemic reasoning*, where agents determine the current circumstances; and *action selection*, where agents construct and evaluate arguments for and against different action options. The deliberation dialogues we study here consider only action selection, assuming that the other stages have been dealt with previously with other types of dialogue; this action selection stage determines three CQs for consideration (we use the numbering of CQs used in [7]; see [4] for a more detailed justification of the appropriateness of these CQs).

- **CQ 6:** Are there alternate ways of realising the same goal?
- **CQ 9:** Does doing the action have a side effect that demotes some other value?
- **CQ 10:** Does doing the action have a side effect that promotes some other value?

From these CQs we can identify attacks between arguments for and against actions to achieve a particular goal: two arguments *for* different actions attack one another (CQ6); an argument *against* an action a attacks another argument *for* the same action a (CQ9); two arguments *for* the same action that each promote different values attack one another (CQ10). Considering the example arguments given above, A1 attacks A3, A3 attacks A1, and A2 attacks A3.

Each agent has a (total-order) ranking over the values, referred to as its *audience*, which represents the importance it assigns to them. An agent uses its audience to determine the relative strength of arguments according to the values they each promote/demote, and thus whether an attack succeeds as a defeat. In the example above, an agent who finds personal well-being to be a more important value than timeliness will find argument A1 to be stronger than A3 and so will determine that A1 defeats A3, while A3's attack on A1 does not succeed as a defeat.

Given a set of arguments, the attacks between those arguments (determined by the CQs above), and a particular agent's audience, we evaluate the acceptability of an argument with respect to that agent with a Value Based Argumentation Framework (VAF) (introduced in [6]), an extension of the argumentation frameworks (AF) of Dung [8]. In an AF an argument is admissible with respect to a set of arguments S if all of its attackers are attacked by some argument in S, and no argument in S attacks an argument in S. In a VAF an argument succeeds in defeating an argument it attacks if its value is ranked higher than (if the attack is symmetric) or at least as high as (if the attack is asymmetric) the value of the argument attacked (according to a particular agent's audience). Arguments in a VAF are admissible with respect to an audience A and a set of arguments S if they are admissible with respect to S in the AF that results from removing all the attacks that are unsuccessful given the audience A. An argument is said to be *acceptable* to the agent if it is part of a maximal admissible set (a *preferred extension*) of the VAF evaluated according to the agent's audience.

An agent considers an action to be *agreeable* if it finds some argument *for* that action to be acceptable. Considering the example arguments given above, if an agent prefers *environmental well-being* to *timeliness*, which it prefers to *personal well-being*, it will find arguments A2 and A1 to be acceptable and conclude that the only agreeable action is to cycle (since this is the only action for which it has an acceptable argument). If, however, the agent prefers *timeliness* to *personal well-being*, which it prefers to *environmental well-being*, it will find arguments A2 and A3 to be acceptable, and so will determine that driving is the only agreeable action to achieve its goal.

Observe that arguments against actions are always acceptable given the instantiation of attacks derived from CQs and these are not considered by the agent in determining which actions it finds agreeable. Intuitively, this is because the CQs are concerned with evaluating presumptive proposals *for* performing some action. It would be possible (and we believe would not affect the results of our experiments) to adapt the VAF generation and evaluation so as to produce the same results in terms of agreeability of actions while avoiding the (perhaps unintuitive) case where both an argument for and an argument against an action are found to be acceptable; we choose here not to adapt the model in order that our results are relatable to previous work [3, 4].

We can also see that (as in [4]) if an attack is symmetric, then an attack only succeeds in defeat if the attacked argument's value is more preferred than the value of the argument being attacked; however, if an attack is asymmetric, then an attack succeeds in defeat if the attacking argument's value is at least as preferred as the value of the argument being attacked. Asymmetric attacks occur only when an argument against an action attacks another argument for that action; in this case, if both arguments' values are equally preferred, then it is undesirable for the argument for the action to withstand the attack. If we have a symmetric attack where the values of the arguments attacking one another are equally preferred, then it must be the case that each argument is for a distinct action but promotes the same value; here, the attack does not succeed as a defeat, since it is reasonable to choose either action.

We have described the mechanism that an agent uses to determine attacks between arguments for and against actions; it can then use an ordering over the values that motivate such arguments (its audience) in order to determine the acceptability of the arguments and, from this, the agreeability of actions. Next, we describe the dialogue system that agents use to jointly reason about the agreeability of actions.

2.2   Dialogue System

Deliberation dialogues take place between two participating agents (each with an identifier taken from the set $\mathcal{I} = \{x, \overline{x}\}$) and we assume that the dialogue participants have already agreed to participate in a deliberation dialogue in order to agree on an action to perform in order to achieve some mutual goal (this goal is the *topic* of the dialogue). At the start of the dialogue, each agent has available to it a set of arguments for and against actions to achieve the goal, which are those arguments it can construct from its private knowledge about the state of the world, the different actions that can be performed, and the values promoted or demoted by those actions. Each agent also has an audience (their personal ranking over the values).

During the course of the dialogue, agents take it in turns to make a single *dialogue move*. There are four types of dialogue move that participants may make:

- **assert** a positive argument (an argument *for* an action);
- **assert** a negative argument (an argument *against* an action);
- **agree** to an action;
- indicate that they have no arguments that they wish to assert (with a **pass**).

A dialogue terminates under two conditions: once two consecutive **pass** moves appear (in which case the dialogue is a *failure*, and no agreement has been reached), or two consecutive **agree** moves appear (in which case the dialogue is a *success*).

In order to evaluate which actions it finds agreeable at a point in the dialogue, an agent considers all the arguments it is aware of at this point and evaluates them as described in the previous section; it thus constructs a VAF consisting of the arguments it is initially aware of at the start of the dialogue and those arguments that have been asserted previously in the dialogue by the other agent, and evaluates this according to its audience. An action is *agreeable* to the agent if there is some argument *for* that action that it finds acceptable given this evaluation. Note that the set of actions that are agreeable to an agent may change over the course of the dialogue, due to it becoming aware of new arguments as they are asserted by the other participant.

A dialogue protocol specifies which moves are permissible for an agent x during x's turn in a deliberation dialogue with topic p as follows:

- It is permissible to **assert** an argument A iff the argument is for or against an action to achieve the topic p of the dialogue and A has not been asserted previously during the dialogue.
- It is permissible to **agree** to an action a iff either:
  - the immediately preceding move was an **agree** to the action a, or
  - the other participant $\bar{x}$ has at some point previously in the dialogue asserted a positive argument A for the action a.
- It is always permissible to **pass**.

While the dialogue protocol defines a set of moves it is permissible to make, an agent uses a particular *strategy* to decide which of the permissible moves to select. The *strategy* that our agents use is as follows.

- If it is permissible to **agree** to an action that the agent finds *agreeable*, then make such an **agree** move; otherwise
- if it is permissible to **assert** a positive argument *for* an action that the agent finds *agreeable*, then assert some such argument; otherwise
- if it is permissible to **assert** a negative argument *against* an action and the agent finds that action *not agreeable* then assert some such argument; otherwise
- make a **pass** move.

3   Investigating Similarity

Previous work has considered whether there is a relationship between the number of unique values and actions being argued over, the number of arguments known by agents, and the likelihood of agents reaching agreement through use of the deliberation dialogue system [3]. However, in those experiments the sets of arguments agents know at the start of the dialogue are always disjoint. It is possible, perhaps even likely, that in real world examples of agent dialogues there will be some overlap in the agents' initial argument sets. Thus, we are interested here in the question of whether the similarity of agents' initial arguments sets has an effect on the resulting dialogue.

To investigate this we perform experiments where we vary not only the number of unique values and actions being argued over and the number of arguments known, but also sim (a measure of the similarity of the sets of arguments known by each agent at the start of the dialogue). We thus require four parameters as follows.

1. acts : The number of unique actions that can be argued about.
2. vals : The number of unique values that can be promoted or demoted by the actions.

3. args : The number of unique arguments in the union of both agents' initial arguments.
4. sim : A measure of the similarity of the agents' sets of initial arguments.

To run experiments across the parameter space, a random scenario generator is required; this initialises the arguments known to each agent at the start of the dialogue (referred to as their *initial arguments*) and their audiences. For each run of the simulation, the scenario generator is given acts actions, and vals values. It then generates all possible arguments that can be constructed from the set of actions and the set of values: for each action and value pair there are two arguments that can be produced; one argument that claims performing the action will promote the value; and the other argument that claims performing the action will demote the value. Therefore, the set of all possible arguments contains $2 \times$ acts $\times$ vals many arguments.

Then, random arguments are removed from the set of all possible arguments until it contains args arguments. Note that if args $= 2 \times$ acts $\times$ vals then no arguments need to be removed. Half of the arguments remaining in the set are randomly distributed to one agent, with the other half being distributed to the other agent. The arguments that are distributed to an agent simulate the set of initial arguments that it can generate using its knowledge. The set of initial arguments distributed to an agent x is denoted R^x.

It is clear to see that, at this point, R^{x_i} and R^{x_j} would be disjoint sets. However, this is not always the case in agent dialogues. Two arguing agents are likely to have some overlaps in their knowledge and hence may be able to generate and communicate the same arguments. We introduce the sim parameter to determine how similar the sets R^{x_i} and R^{x_j} should be — the higher the value of sim the more arguments that are shared between agents. So, once R^{x_i} and R^{x_j} have initially been determined, (args/2) $\times$ sim random arguments from each set are copied into the other set. It can be seen that after this sharing process, if $sim = 1$ then agents will have args many arguments each, and the arguments the agents each have will be identical. Similarly, if sim $= 0$ then the agents will have args/2 arguments each, and the arguments each agent has will remain disjoint (note, this is equivalent to the situation studied by Black and Bentley [3]). The *total number of arguments* in a dialogue scenario refers to the sum of the number arguments initially known to one agent plus the number of arguments initially known to the other agent, and is calculated from the experiment parameters according to the following formula $\lceil$args $+$ (args $\times$ sim)$\rfloor$.

Our experiments investigate whether the similarity of agents' initial arguments has an effect on the simulated deliberation dialogues, across the following different parameter combinations.

- sim $\in \{0, 0.1, \ldots, 0.9, 1.0\}$,
- vals $\in \{2, 4, 6, 8, 10\}$,
- acts $\in \{2, 4, 6, 8, 10\}$,
- args $\in \{2, 3, \ldots, ($vals $\times$ acts $\times 2)\}$.

The randomised nature of the scenario generator and resulting simulated dialogue means that generated dialogues are not only sensitive to the input parameters, but also an element of chance. As a result, many dialogues must be simulated for each parameter combination: it is not sufficient only to run a single instance of a dialogue because two dialogues generated with the same parameter combination can still differ on the distribution of arguments among the agents, and the randomised aspect of the agents' strategy (agents select a random dialogue move when more than one is determined by the strategy). Thus, for each parameter combination, we simulate 1,000 dialogues and, for each dialogue, we record whether it ended successfully (with both agents having agreed on an action) or unsuccessfully (with agents failing to reach an agreement).

The argumentation model, dialogue system, and scenario generator were implemented in Java (independently from any argumentation libraries), and all simulations and experiments were run on a standard workstation computer. The source code can be found online at github.com/joshlmurphy.

4   Results

Black and Bentley [3] also studied the likelihood of success across the parameter space considered here, but only for dialogues in which sim = 0. By limiting our parameter space to dialogues in which sim = 0 we obtain a very close reproduction of results: we again witness that successful dialogues are more likely with higher numbers of actions and values, and we can observe the relationship between the total number of arguments and the likelihood that the dialogue ends successfully (for low numbers of values and actions there is a decrease in the likelihood of dialogue success as the number of arguments increases, while for higher numbers the relationship is more complex, with likelihood initially decreasing as the total number of arguments increases up to a certain point, after which the likelihood of dialogue success begins to increase).

However, by considering the different values of sim, we are able to make a number of empirical observations from which novel conclusions can be drawn. In each of the following subsections, we describe a particular aspect of our results, provide an explanation for what has been observed, and discuss the significance of the result.

A representative subset of our results is shown in Figs. 1–4. Figures 1–3 each presents three graphs showing the percentage of dialogues that end in success (y-axis), at different numbers of total arguments (x-axis), for different values of sim (the darker the shade of the plot, the lower the value of sim). The figures show the results for dialogues where vals = 2 (Fig. 1), vals = 6 (Fig. 2), and vals = 10 (Fig. 3). The graphs in each figure show the results for dialogues where acts = 2 (leftmost), acts = 6 (centre), and acts = 10 (rightmost). Each point represents the average of 1,000 simulated dialogues with that parameter combination. Similar results were seen across all combinations of vals and acts; we present only a representative sample here.

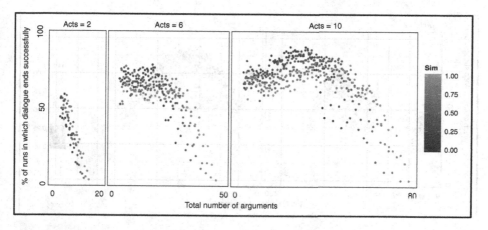

Fig. 1. Graphs to show relationship between total no. of arguments and % of dialogues that ended successfully, for different values of sim when vals = 2 (1000 runs for each parameter setting).

4.1 Dialogues Tend to Fail with Many Arguments

From the results in Figs. 1–3 we can see that dialogue success is very unlikely at high levels of total arguments (every graph tails into a 0 % rate of dialogue success as the number of total arguments tends towards its maximum value for the parameter combination). The reason for this is that if an agent believes every possible argument over a set of values and actions then it will find no action acceptable: all arguments for doing a particular action because that action promotes some value will be defeated by the negative argument that demotes that action for the same value, and hence the action will not be agreeable to the agent. In the case where agents start the dialogue with every possible argument over a set of values and actions, the agents begin the dialogue finding no actions agreeable and have no possibility of ever finding an action agreeable (since they know all arguments, no asserted argument during the dialogue will change the actions that are acceptable); this corresponds to the plot in the graphs where sim = 1, and the total number of arguments is 2 × acts × vals.

This observation cannot be made without considering dialogues in which sim ≠ 0 because, with low similarities, higher numbers of total arguments cannot be reached and so at low similarities, dialogues cannot have a large enough number of arguments to reveal this trend. This can be seen in Figs. 1–3 where no plots for sim = 0 exist beyond 50 % of the graphs' maximum of the number of total arguments.

Past a certain point, the more arguments an agent knows, the greater the chance that dialogue success is impossible, and this effect becomes severe at high levels of total number of arguments. Thus, it is not the case that the complete failure of dialogues for very high number of total arguments is the fault of the dialogue system but rather is down to the likely impossibility of an agent finding any action agreeable when knowing this many arguments. In real-world scenarios,

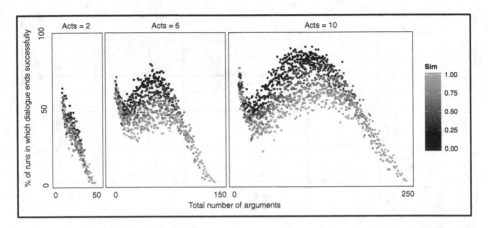

Fig. 2. Graphs to show relationship between total no. of arguments and % of dialogues that ended successfully, for different values of sim when vals = 6 (1000 runs for each parameter setting).

it is unlikely that an agent will have arguments both for an against an action motivated by the same value, since one would expect this to be resolved in the problem formulation stage of reasoning, and so we consider these types of dialogue to be unrealistic.

Thus, importantly, our results show that when using the deliberation dialogue, agents will not come to an agreement when it would not be rational for them to agree to do any of the possible actions. This result was proven theoretically by Black and Atkinson [4].

4.2   Dialogues are Less Successful as Sim increases

Given these initial results, we investigated whether the likelihood of success of a dialogue (measured by whether the dialogue ends in agreement or not) is affected by the similarity of the two agents' initial arguments (measured by the sim parameter). Looking at Figs. 1–3, we can see how the sim parameter affects the rate of dialogue success across different numbers of values, and actions, and total numbers of arguments. Perhaps surprisingly, the general trend is that agents that have similar sets of initial arguments are less likely to reach an agreement compared to agents that have dissimilar sets of initial arguments. The trend violates the intuition that agents with similar knowledge should be able to agree more easily. Indeed, this trend was present across the entire parameter space (except from when both acts = 2 and vals = 2, which we discuss in Sect. 4.3), so we present only a representative subset of the results. We observed very similar results for other combinations of vals and acts.

We assessed the relationship between the similarity of agents' initial arguments and the rate of success of the dialogue averaged over the total number of arguments in dialogues where the number of actions was 10 and the number of values was 10. This assessment was undertaken by calculating a Pearson

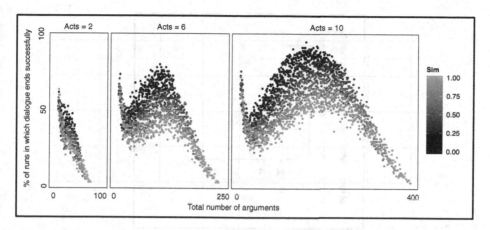

Fig. 3. Graphs to show relationship between total no. of arguments and % of dialogues that ended successfully, for different values of sim when vals = 10 (1000 runs for each parameter setting).

product-moment correlation coefficient, which showed that there is a very strong, negative relationship between the two variables (coefficient $r = -0.96$, statistical significance $p < 0.001$), indicating that the more similar the agents' initial arguments the less likely the dialogue will end in success. The scatterplot in Fig. 4 displays these results.

We explain this relationship as follows. When a dialogue is initialised with sim = 1 (i.e. agents' initial sets of beliefs are identical) any argument an agent asserts will already be known by the other agent. In these dialogues, the agents' sets of known arguments remain the same throughout the dialogue (since any asserted argument will already be known by both agents) so the actions an agent finds agreeable at the start of the dialogue remain the same at every subsequent turn. If agents do not have any agreeable actions in common at the start, then they never will, so the dialogue will fail. Conversely, when a dialogue is initialised with sim = 0 (i.e. agents' initial arguments are entirely disjoint), any argument an agent asserts throughout the dialogue will be novel for the other agent, potentially changing the actions it finds agreeable, and hence the actions that are agreeable to both agents. The more often an assert move changes the actions agreeable to both agents, the more likely it is that throughout the course of the dialogue there will be a point at which there is at least one action agreeable to both agents. In summary, the lower the similarity of the initial arguments, the greater the chance there will be at least one point in the dialogue at which agents mutually find at least one action agreeable, and hence the greater the chance of dialogue success.

Understanding the relationship between the similarity of agents' arguments at the start of a dialogue and the likelihood of dialogue success is important to understand situations in which deliberation dialogues are useful in trying to agree on an action; this can help identify real-world scenarios in which this technique can usefully be applied.

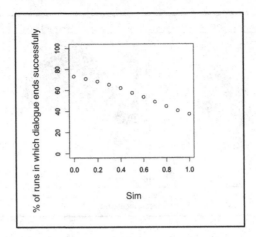

Fig. 4. A scatterplot to show the relationship between the similarity of initial belief sets and the rate of success of the dialogue averaged over the total number of arguments (1000 runs for each parameter setting), in dialogues where vals = 10 and acts = 10.

4.3   The Impact of Similarity Increases with the Number of Values

Varying sim for dialogues with a low number of values produces a relatively small effect on the likelihood of the success of the dialogue. For example, dialogues with 2 values are affected only slightly by changing sim; as can be seen in Fig. 1, the distances between plots for sim = 1 and sim = 0 are low, within 15 %. Looking at Fig. 2 where the dialogues have 6 values, the distances between plots for sim = 1 and sim = 0 are wider in general, and this is evidence of an increasing effect of sim at higher values. The distances are greater still for dialogues with 10 values, as seen in Fig. 3, where we observe a nearly 50 % difference in the likelihood of success of the dialogue between dialogues where sim = 1 and sim = 0.

Generalising these results, we can say that the impact of agents having similar sets of initial arguments on the likelihood of dialogue success increases as the number of values that agents argue over increases. This tells us that similarity has a large effect on the likelihood of dialogue success in such scenarios.

4.4   Success Most Likely at Around 50 % of Maximum Total
Arguments

For dialogues in which vals = 2 or acts = 2 we observe a general decrease in the likelihood of dialogue success as the total number of arguments increases. Furthermore, for dialogues in which acts = 2 we observe a *linear* decrease in the likelihood of dialogue success as the total number of arguments increases, regardless of the number values. This relationship can be seen in the relevant graphs in Figs. 1–3, and was also observed by Black and Bentley [3].

The relationship between the total number of arguments and the likelihood of success is more complex when we consider dialogues in which vals > 2 and acts > 2. The relationship can be described in three stages. First, in the lowest 10 % of a graph's maximum total number of arguments we observe a decrease in the likelihood of dialogue success similar to that in lower numbers of values and actions. However, in the second stage, after the 10 % point up to approximately 50 % of a graph's maximum total number of arguments, the trend reverses and we observe an increase in the likelihood of dialogue success as the total number of arguments increase. The trend reverses again in the third stage, after 50 % of a graph's maximum total number of arguments onward, where we observe a tail off towards a 0 % likelihood of dialogue success. This relationship can be seen in the relevant graphs in Figs. 1–2. This more complex relationship was not observed by Black and Bentley [3] because very high total numbers of arguments can only be reached by considering sim > 0. Dialogues with a low sim are less affected in the initial stage of the relationship and are more greatly affected in the second stage (the trough is shallower, and the peak is higher), whereas dialogues with a high sim are more affected in the initial stage of the relationship and are less affected in the second stage (the trough is deeper, and the peak is lower).

The shape of the relationship between the total number of arguments and the likelihood of dialogue success as described here would have been extremely difficult to prove using formal methods. However, by using the experimental approach we are able to investigate performance across the entire parameter space. The observation of the shape of the relationship is useful because it allows us to predict accurately the chance a dialogue will succeed for any given parameter combination.

5   Related Work

Our experiments are closely related to those of Black and Bentley [3], which are based on the same argumentation model and dialogue system [4] as the work presented in this paper. Their work was perhaps the first to use empirical methods to evaluate the benefit of using deliberation dialogues. In their experiments, they vary the number of values and actions being deliberated over, and the number of arguments available to agents at the start of the dialogue and show that the deliberation dialogue system typically outperforms consensus forming. Here, we expand the parameter space to also vary the similarity of the arguments that the agents have and show that this is an important factor in the success of a deliberation dialogue.

Kok *et al.* similarly take an empirical approach to the investigation of argument-based deliberation dialogues [9]. They focus on the expressive potential of argumentation by using a deliberation dialogue system that allows agents to communicate using elaborate arguments, assuming that agents that are able to express themselves better would be able to perform more efficiently and more effectively. They show that an arguing strategy offers increased effectiveness over a non-arguing strategy. In their work, agents' arguments are generated from their respective knowledge bases, but they do not consider how the performance of the dialogues depends on the similarity of these knowledge bases, or the similarity of arguments that are generated from them.

In considering groups, Toniolo *et al.* investigate how argument-based deliberation dialogues can be used by a team of agents that have their own potentially conflicting goals and norms [10]. Using an empirical evaluation of their model, they find that argument dialogues are a more effective means of agent coordination than collaborative plans (using the metric of the feasibility of the resulting plan). While their work does consider agents as heterogeneous with their own goals and norms, they do not consider how the similarity of their goals and norms (and hence their arguments) affects the quality of the plans produced.

Finally, Medellin-Gasque *et al.* present a dialogue protocol for deliberation and persuasion dialogues, in which agents argue over cooperative plans [11]. Interestingly, they investigate the impact of the agents' dialogue strategies on the result of the dialogue. Similar to our work, their dialogue system is based on the critical questions approach [5]. They implement 3 different agent strategies (a random strategy, and 2 strategies that place some priority over dialogue moves), which they test over a limited number of cases (20 initial states, generated from 4 different sets of information, and 5 different preference orders over values). Their results show that, for the cases and strategies tested, the quality of the outcome of the dialogue does not vary by altering the agents' strategies, but by using a priority strategy rather than a random strategy, the outcome can be reached more efficiently. Thus, agents' dialogue strategies can be an important consideration for dialogues, in at least some initial circumstances. In the results we present here, we have considered only a single dialogue strategy, however we have run some preliminary experiments that consider the performance of two other strategies. The first strategy we looked at selects a move to make at random from the entire set of moves permitted by the protocol. The other strategy is similar to that which is presented in this paper (in that it prefers agree moves, to moves that assert positive arguments, which it prefers to moves that assert negative arguments) but prioritises assert moves according to the agents preferences (i.e., will prefer to assert positive arguments for actions that promote more preferred values, and negative arguments against actions that demote less preferred values).

6   Discussion

Our results show how, in the argument-based deliberation dialogues investigated here, the similarity of agents' initial arguments affects the likelihood that a dialogue ends in success. We found dialogues with high similarities of initial arguments are less likely to end in agreement than dialogues with low similarities of initial arguments, because the higher the similarity of initial arguments the less potential for agents to reach a point in the dialogue at which there exists at least one action that is agreeable to both agents. Using an empirical approach, our investigation allowed a total analysis of the parameter space over a large sample size of dialogues. Our results identify scenarios in which using a deliberation dialogue is likely to lead to an agreement being reached.

In our investigation we explored the entire range of possible similarities of agents' initial arguments: from dialogues where agents started with entirely disjoint sets of initial arguments to dialogues where agents started with identical sets of initial arguments. Across this range we identified a statistically significant effect of similarity on the likelihood of dialogue success, but, it is unclear to what extent this range typically exists in real-world scenarios. The relationship between the sets of initial arguments we randomly generate to those seen in real-world applications is also not understood (for example, dialogues that were generated with a very high number of total arguments are probably not realistic). The lack of real-world data is an identified problem in research relating to applications of argumentation.

A potential solution for ensuring that our results relate to examples of argument dialogues in the real-world would be to use data from argument corpora for our experiments (e.g. [12]), rather than the randomly generated scenarios we used. An argument corpus is an organised collection of examples of real-world argument dialogues presented in a standardised format. However, there are three main limitations of current argument corpora. The first is that they are limited in the number of argument examples that they contain, and this would limit the viability of an experimental approach that uses this data. Basing conclusions on the small samples of data provided by argument corpora could be difficult to justify. In contrast, we were able to run 1,000 dialogues for each parameter combination (around 5.5 million dialogues), ensuring statistical significance of our observations. The second limitation is that the corpora typically focus on only a limited scope of topics: humans engage in deliberation dialogues on a wide range of topics, and only some of these are captured in current argument corpora (they tend to focus on legal or governmental dialogues). Focusing on only a subset of potential dialogue topics limits the conclusions that can be drawn from the data to that specific topic domain. The final limitation is the way in which arguments in the corpora are formatted. Transcription of natural language arguments to a standardised format is a complex process. Work is being done to allow this step to be done computationally (e.g. [13–15]), but, particularly as it is tied to the problem of natural language processing, it is likely to be a long time before this is an automatic and successful method. As a result, the transcribing and formatting of the arguments are often done by humans. This leads to a potential bias in the corpus, and could come from a number of sources: the human's aptitude for formal argumentation, personal opinions on the argument topic, and the knowledge the transcriber has of the argument topic.

There is a question as to whether measuring the quality of a deliberation dialogue simply on whether agents reach an agreement is the best or only measure. According to Walton and Krabbe [16], while there is a *public* goal to reach an agreement that is ascribed to by both agents in a deliberation dialogue, agents also have a *private* goal to influence the agreed upon action to one that is as favourable as possible to itself. Working out a suitable metric for the success of an agent's private goal is non-trivial as it is unclear how to accurately measure the influence an agent has had on the dialogue, and it is unclear how to measure which action is an agent's most favoured (should it be the agreeable action that promotes the highest value given local beliefs of the agent, or given global beliefs of the system). There are also other factors that could be used to measure the outcome of the dialogue: efficiency/speed of the dialogue (what resources were spent during the dialogue?), soundness of the agreed upon action (is the agreed upon action the best course of action from a global perspective?), and fairness (is the outcome representative of all of the agents' preferences?). For example, Black and Bentley assign scores to dialogue outcomes, depending on whether the agreed upon action is globally agreeable to both, one, or neither agent. However, there are many other possible ways to measure the quality of a deliberation dialogue.

Walton *et al.* [17] question whether models of deliberation dialogues are able to actually capture the richness and depth of human-like deliberation dialogues. Specifically, they consider dialogues in which information available to participants of the dialogue is dynamic. This is certainly a limitation of our investigations since the knowledge the agents have remains the same throughout the duration of the dialogue. If we extended the dialogue system to simulate changing knowledge of the environment during the course of the dialogue, an interesting investigation would be to see how the similarity of the information/arguments made available to both agents would affect the dialogue (i.e. what happens if the information made available to agents becomes gradually more different or if the information becomes gradually more similar?).

Though the investigations in this paper consider the similarity of agents' initial beliefs, they do not consider the similarity of agents' audiences (the ordering of their preferences over values). It may seem reasonable to predict that the more similar agents' preferences, the more likely they are to come to agreement. However, this hypothesis has not been tested, and we leave this for future work.

The dialogue system investigated in this paper allows for agents to argue about their beliefs, but not about their preferences. Giving agents the ability to argue about their preferences would allow for more sophisticated dialogues, and therefore may allow agents to reach agreement more often. However, in some settings it may be preferable that agents cannot argue about their preferences since agents may not wish to get into an overly sophisticated debate: in human-oriented domains one may want to discourage complex reasoning to ensure that the dialogue is easily understandable by a human, or in time-critical domains there may not be the computational resources available to facilitate more complex forms of dialogue.

References

1. McBurney, P., Parsons, S.: Dialogue games for agent argumentation. In: Simari, G., Rahwan, I. (eds.) Argumentation in Artificial Intelligence, pp. 261–280. Springer, New Year (2009)
2. Rahwan, I.: Argumentation in multi-agent systems. Auton. Agents Multi-Agent Syst. **11**, 115–125 (2005)
3. Black, E., Bentley, K.: An empirical study of a deliberation dialogue system. In: Modgil, S., Oren, N., Toni, F. (eds.) TAFA 2011. LNCS, vol. 7132, pp. 132–146. Springer, Heidelberg (2012)

4. Black, E., Atkinson, K.: Choosing persuasive arguments for action. In: Proceedings of the Tenth International Conference on Autonomous Agents and Multi-Agent Systems, pp. 905–912 (2011)
5. Walton, D.: Argumentation Schemes for Presumptive Reasoning. Lawrence Erlbaum Associates, Mahwah (1996)
6. Bench-Capon, T.: Agreeing to differ: modelling persuasive dialogue between parties without a consensus about values. Inf. Log. **22**(3), 231–245 (2002)
7. Atkinson, K., Bench-Capon, T.: Practical reasoning as presumptive argumentation using action based alternating transition systems. Artif. Intell. **171**(10–15), 855–874 (2007)
8. Dung, P.: On the acceptability of arguments and its fundamental role in non-monotonic reasoning, logic programming and n-person games. Artif. Intell. **77**, 321–357 (1995)
9. Kok, E., Meyer, J., Prakken, H., Vreeswijk, G.: Testing the benfits of structured argumentation in multi-agent deliberation dialogues. In: Proceedings of the Eleventh International Conference on Autonomous Agents and Multiagent Systems, pp. 1411–1412 (2012)
10. Toniolo, A., Norman, T., Sycara, K.: An empirical study of argumentation schemes for deliberative dialogue. In: Proceedings of the Twentieth European Conference on Artificial Intelligence, pp. 756–761 (2012)
11. Medellin-Gasque, R., Atkinson, K., Bench-Capon, T., McBurney, P.: Strategies for question selection in argumentative dialogues about plans. Argument Comput. **4**(2), 151–179 (2013)
12. Reed, C.: Argument corpora. Technical report, University of Dundee Technical report (2013). www.arg.dundee.ac.uk/corpora
13. Cardie, C., Green, N., Gurevych, I., Hirst, G., Litman, D., Muresan, S., Petasis, G., Stede, M., Walker, M., Wiebe, J.: (organising committee). In: Proceedings of the Second Workshop on Argumentation Mining, Workshop at the 2015 Conference of the North American Chapter of the Association for Computational Linguistics - Human Language Technologies (2015)
14. Lippi, M., Torroni, P.: Context-independent claim detection for argument mining. In: Proceedings of the Twenty-Fourth International Conference on Artificial Intelligence, pp. 185–191 (2015)
15. Cabrio, E., Villata, S.: A natural language bipolar argumentation approach to support users in online debate interactions. Argument Comput. **4**(3), 209–230 (2013)
16. Walton, D., Krabbe, E.: Commitment in Dialogue: Basic Concepts of Interpersonal Reasoning. SUNY Press, Albany (1995)
17. Walton, D., Toniolo, A., Norman, T.: Missing phases of deliberation dialogue for real applications. In: Proceedings of the Eleventh International Workshop on Argumentation in Multi-Agent Systems. Springer (2014)

ArgP2P: An Argumentative Approach for Intelligent Query Routing in P2P Networks

Ana L. Nicolini[✉], Ana G. Maguitman, and Carlos I. Chesñevar

Institute for Computer Science and Engineering (ICIC),
Consejo Nacional de Investigaciones Científicas y Técnicas (CONICET),
Universidad Nacional del Sur, Av. Alem 1253, (8000) Bahía Blanca, Argentina
{aln,agm,cic}@cs.uns.edu.ar

Abstract. The Internet is a cooperative and decentralized network built out of millions of participants that share large amounts of information. Peer-to-peer (P2P) systems go hand-in-hand with this huge decentralized network, where each individual node can serve content as well as request it. In this scenario, thematic search algorithms should lead to and benefit from the emergence of semantic communities that are the result of the interaction among participants. As a consequence, intelligent algorithms for neighbor selection should give rise to a logical network topology reflecting efficient communication patterns. When routing queries within a P2P network different conflicting issues may arise in individual nodes, such as deciding whether to propagate a query or to reject its processing. Such issues emerge in the context of incomplete and potentially inconsistent information in a distributed setting. To the best of our knowledge, current algorithmic approaches to P2P query processing are mostly based on a "reactive" approach, endowing the individual nodes with little or no intelligence. This paper presents a novel approach to use argumentation as part of the decision making machinery within individual nodes in a P2P network for thematic search. Our approach will rely on assumption-based argumentation (ABA). We provide a formalization for P2P networks for thematic search, on top of which intelligent algorithms based on ABA are specified. A case study is used to illustrate the proposed approach, providing insights into the performance of the new framework.

1   Introduction and Motivations

The Internet is a cooperative and decentralized network built out of millions of participants that share large amounts of information with other users. Peer-to-peer (P2P) systems go hand-in-hand with this huge decentralized network, where each individual node can serve content as well as request it. Thematic search is the process of seeking information related to a topic of interest. In the P2P scenario, thematic search algorithms should lead to and benefit from the emergence of semantic communities that are the result of the interaction among participants. As a result, intelligent algorithms for neighbor selection should give rise to a logical network topology reflecting efficient communication patterns [1].

© Springer International Publishing Switzerland 2015
E. Black et al. (Eds.): TAFA 2015, LNAI 9524, pp. 194–210, 2015.
DOI: 10.1007/978-3-319-28460-6_12

In this paper we propose a novel model for thematic search in P2P systems, where every node in the network has the ability to perform intelligent query routing by combining both *reactive* and *argumentative* behavior. Both nodes and queries are associated with topics. Therefore, each node needs to analyze the topic of an incoming query to determine if it is capable of answering the query or if the query needs to be forwarded to other nodes. Given a particular query Q, reactive behavior will correspond to hard-wired code used by an individual node in order to make decisions concerning Q. Such code follows a black-box model, and is typically based on specific features (e.g. whether the node is available for answering Q, whether the query Q is relevant to the node, etc.) without relying on knowledge representation and reasoning mechanisms. Argumentative behavior, on the other hand, is based on a dynamic knowledge base that captures the information acquired by the node during its lifetime, resulting from previous interactions with other nodes (e.g. whether there are reasons to believe that certain nodes are reliable to provide an answer for Q). The resulting knowledge base associated with each node will be usually incomplete and potentially inconsistent. Therefore, argumentative reasoning (formalized using assumption-based argumentation [10]) will provide every node with the ability for autonomous intelligent decision making, without interfering with the operation of the other peers. This will lead to a novel framework, called ArgP2P, that extends the traditional model for decision making in P2P thematic search, as each node will act as an autonomous agent with an inference engine which combines reactive and rational behaviors. A configuration parameter allows to set the frequency used by the node to behave reactively (just performing a black-box analysis for decision making) or rationally (i.e., applying argumentative inference to decide how to route a query). Since argumentation is a computationally expensive process, the use of this configuration parameter is crucial to ensure that the nodes' response time is reasonable in the context of a P2P search system, as will be described later.

ArgP2P applies argumentation to alleviate a common problem in P2P search frameworks, to which we refer as *Closed Communities Problem*. In this setting, as the interaction among peers increases the learning degree also increases leading to the formation of semantic communities. In this scenario one or more nodes can be disconnected from their community or can form another community with the same topic without being connected to each other. In Fig. 1 the logical network resulting from applying a thematic search algorithm is shown, in particular a logical network that presents a graphical visualization of the Closed Communities Problem. Each color represents a topic (similar colors represent similar topics) and a link joining two nodes represents that the nodes know each other. In this figure we can appreciate communities of nodes with related topics but we can also see related communities that are disconnected.

The goal of argumentation in the ArgP2P framework is to provide the nodes with the ability to decide, in an autonomous way, if it is the right time to explore the network beyond their specific communities. This action makes it possible to discover other potentially useful peers and helps connecting related communities that otherwise would remain disconnected.

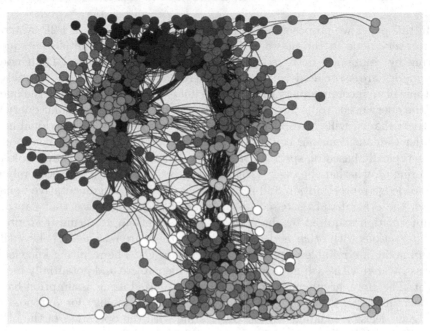

Fig. 1. Logical network resulting from applying a thematic search algorithm

The rest of this paper is structured as follows. Section 2 presents an overview of the main elements involved in P2P networks for thematic search, providing a suitable formalization and characterizing the main elements of the algorithm for an individual node. Section 3 summarizes the main elements of assumption-based argumentation (ABA). Section 4 presents a framework which integrates ABA within P2P thematic search. Section 5 presents a case study to illustrate how the proposed framework can be deployed in a P2P network. Section 6 discusses the main characteristics of our approach as well as some comparisons with related work. Finally, Sect. 7 summarizes the conclusions and discusses some future work.

2   P2P Networks for Thematic Search: Overview

A peer-to-peer [21] network is a distributed system in which every peer (host) communicates with other peers without the intervention of centralized hosts. Every peer in a P2P system has the potential to act as a client or as a server, sharing resources to work in conjunction. Robustness is an expected property of a P2P system, which accounts for maintaining the functionality and integrity of the system even if a peer fails. The absence of a central server distinguishes P2P networks from a client-server model. The most common applications of P2P networks are file sharing, distributed file storage, resource sharing and distributed computing. A good survey and discussion of P2P architectures and applications can be found in [3].

P2P network topologies are typically classified as *structured* [15] or *unstructured* [13], while some networks combine some properties of both [20]. A structured network is organized into a specific topology with a protocol aimed at ensuring a reasonable search performance. On the other hand, an unstructured network does not follow a specific pattern for the organization of its nodes and has a random topology. Because of this lack of structure, these networks have a relatively low search efficiency compared with the structured ones. As a consequence, the study of algorithms that improve search efficiency in unstructured P2P systems has been an active research area in the last years (e.g., [7,19,22,27]).

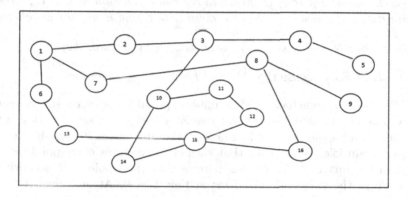

Fig. 2. Example of an unstructured P2P network

Figure 2 shows an example of an unstructured P2P network. In this network all participants (nodes) stand for devices such as personal computers, smartphones or large servers that exchange information. The typical way of routing queries in this kind of networks is by *flooding*. For example, node 1 generates a query message so that this query is sent through its adjacent nodes (nodes 2, 6 and 7). If these nodes do not provide an answer for the query, then they forward on their turn the query to their adjacent nodes, and so on, until an answer is found or the pre-established time to live (TTL) for the query message is reached.

The major limitations of flooding algorithms are the resulting network congestion and the possibility of not finding the answer to the query. Some results confirm that in order to solve this problem it is desirable that the participants send their queries to other participants that are specialized in the query topic. Thus, a query can be efficiently propagated in the network, suggesting that collaborative and distributed search can benefit from the user context and the existence of semantic communities [26].

Endowing the nodes with the ability to make decisions in an autonomous way gives them the possibility of routing queries to potentially relevant nodes based on some acquired knowledge about other peers' interests. Sometimes this knowledge is inconsistent and making the right decision is not a trivial issue. As we will see later, argumentative reasoning will provide a powerful complement for the traditional reactive behavior adopted by nodes to route queries.

2.1   Formalizing the Notion of P2P Network

A P2P network is a set of interconnected devices that exchange information. The static representation of a P2P network can be defined as a graph. However, in order to capture the flow of a query through the network, we will include a distinguished function to express time, characterizing a *dynamic* P2P network. Formally:

Definition 1. *A dynamic P2P network (or just P2P network) is a 3-uple $P = (\mathcal{N}, \mathcal{E}, S_t)$ where $\mathcal{N}$ is a (finite) set of nodes, $\mathcal{E}$ is a finite collection of edges (each edge is a pair of elements in $\mathcal{N}$) and a function S_t that captures the dynamic status of a node $n \in \mathcal{N}$ at a given time t, and is defined as follows:*

$$S_t : \mathcal{N} \longrightarrow Consult \cup Forward \cup \{reply, discard, idle\},$$

where $Consult =_{def} \{consult\} \times 2^{\mathcal{N}}$ and $Forward =_{def} \{forward\} \times 2^{\mathcal{N}}$.

In a P2P network a node has a finite number of possible states: consult by sending a query to a set of candidates nodes; forward a query to a set of nodes; reply a query, discard a message; and when none of the previous states apply, the node will just remain idle. We can see that each of these states corresponds with an element in the image of S_t. We will assume that the whole P2P network (i.e., every node in the network) initializes at time $t = 0$. At any given time t, a particular query will be associated with a set of nodes in the network (the ones which are processing the query at time t). We assume that the time counter will be incremented by 1 after a node processes the query. Next we show the formal characterization of the dynamic P2P network presented in Fig. 2, assuming that every node at time $t = 0$ is idle.

$P = (\mathcal{N}, \mathcal{E}, S_t)$
$\mathcal{N} = \{1, 2, ..., 16\}$
$\mathcal{E} = \{(1,2),(1,7),(1,6),(2,3),(2,1),(3,2),(3,10),(3,4),\ (4,3),\ (4,5),\ (5,4),\ (6,1),\ (6,13),$
$(7,1),\ (7,8),\ (8,7),\ (8,9),\ (9,8),\ (10,3),\ (10,14),\ (10,11),\ (11,10),\ (11,12),\ (12,11),$
$(12,15),\ (13,6),\ (13,15),\ (14,10),\ (14,15),\ (15,13),\ (15,16),\ (15,12),\ (15,\ 14),\ (16,8),$
$(16,15)\}$
$\forall n \in \mathcal{N}, S_0(n) = \text{idle}$

3   Assumption-Based Argumentation: Fundamentals

Argumentation has been identified as a way for understanding and reconciling differences and similarities of various existing formalisms for non-monotonic, default reasoning as studied in AI. This line of research has led to the development of different argumentation frameworks, notably abstract argumentation (AA) [8] and assumption-based argumentation (ABA) [5]. ABA is a general-purpose argumentation framework that can be instantiated to support various applications and specialised frameworks, including default reasoning frameworks [5,14,17], problems in legal reasoning [11], game-theory [9], practical reasoning and decision-theory [2,4,12,23]. However, whereas in AA arguments and attacks between arguments are abstract and primitive, in ABA arguments are deductions supported by assumptions. An attack by one argument against another is a deduction by the first argument of the contrary of an assumption supporting the second argument.

ABA is equipped with a computational machinery to determine the acceptability of claims by building and exploring a dialectical structure of a proponent's argument for a claim, an opponent's counter arguments attacking the argument, the proponent's arguments attacking all the opponent's counter arguments, and so on. This computation style, which has its roots in logic programming, has several advantages over other computational mechanisms for argumentation. The advantages are due mainly to the fine level of granularity afforded by interleaving the construction of arguments and determining their acceptability. For several reasons, included the previous one, ABA has turned out to be particularly applicable in the context of real-world problems (e.g. in grid computing [25]) and we will also use it as the underlying framework for our approach.

In what follows, we will provide the main definitions and concepts for ABA, in order to make this paper self-contained. For a complete description of assumption-based argumentation and its applications, the reader is referred to [24].

ABA Frameworks

An ABA framework is a tuple $\langle L, R, A, \rangle$ where

- $\langle L, R \rangle$ is a deductive system, with L the *language* and R a set of *rules*, that we assume of the form $\sigma_0 \leftarrow \sigma_1, ..., \sigma_m (m \geq 0)$ with $\sigma_i \in L (i = 0, ..., m)$; σ_0 is referred to as the head and $\sigma_1, ..., \sigma_m$ as the *body* of the rule $\sigma_0 \leftarrow \sigma_1, ..., \sigma_m$;
- $A \subseteq L$ is a (non-empty) set, referred to as *assumptions*;
- $^{-}$ is a total mapping from A into L; $\bar{a}$ is referred to as the *contrary* of a.

In ABA, *arguments* are deductions of claims using rules and supported by sets of assumptions, and *attacks* are directed at the assumptions in the support of arguments:

- *an argument for (the claim)* $\sigma \in L$ *supported by* $A \subseteq A$ ($A \vdash \sigma$ in short) is a deduction for σ supported by A (and some $R \subseteq R$)
- *an argument* $A_1 \vdash \sigma_1$ *attacks* an argument $A_2 \vdash \sigma_2$ iff σ_1 is the contrary of one of the assumptions in A_2.

Example. Let $\langle L, R, A \rangle$ be an ABA framework, where: $L=\{a,b,c,p,q,r,s,t\}$, $R=\{p \leftarrow q, a; q \leftarrow; r \leftarrow b, c\}$, $A=\{a,b,c\}$, and it holds that $\bar{a} = r; \bar{b} = s; \bar{c} = t$. Then the following arguments can be obtained:

$$\{\} \vdash q, \{a\} \vdash p, \{b,c\} \vdash r, \{a\} \vdash a, \{b\} \vdash b, \{c\} \vdash c$$

Arguments can be depicted as trees, as shown in Fig. 3 In this particular example, the following attack relationships hold: $\{b,c\} \vdash r$ attacks $\{a\} \vdash p$ as well as $\{a\} \vdash a$.

Fig. 3. Deductions for p (left), q (middle) and p (right) for the example presented in the "ABA frameworks" section.

Several *semantics* are available in ABA (e.g. grounded skeptical semantics, admissible semantics, etc.). In this paper we adopt the *grounded skeptical* semantics, which sanctions only one set of arguments as "winning". For space reasons the reader is referred to [24] for technical details.

4   The ArgP2P Framework

As discussed before, dynamic P2P networks take a black-box approach to deal with the query routing problem. Black-box approaches do not involve any form of inference, and simply rely on a basic analysis of certain local variables associated with an individual node to decide how to proceed. Such variables involve node features such as availability for answering an incoming query, relevance of the query to the nodes' interests, etc. These features are analyzed by each node by means of hard-wired code, resulting in reactive behavior and limited problem solving capabilities. Every query Q in thematic P2P search is always associated with a topic T (e.g. query = "prime numbers" and topic = "math") and each node of the network has a finite set of *topics* of interest (e.g. node 1 is interested in the set {math, physics}). A node interested in a specific topic is a potential node to reply queries about this topic, and every node in the network has knowledge about other nodes and their interest. This prompts the following definition:

Definition 2. *Let* $P = (\mathcal{N}, \mathcal{E}, S_t)$ *be a P2P network. For every node* $n \in \mathcal{N}$, *we define a* dynamic knowledge base KB_n *with the following form:*

$$KB_n = \langle (topic_1, \mathcal{N}_{topic_1}), (topic_2, \mathcal{N}_{topic_2}), ..., (topic_n, \mathcal{N}_{topic_n}) \rangle,$$

where $\mathcal{N}_{topic_i}$ *stands for a set of nodes associated with* $topic_i$.

The problem of this approach is that one or more nodes could be disconnected from other communities of nodes with the same topic or two communities[1] of nodes with the same topics could be disconnected from each other. Consequently some messages could never find an answer. The case study given in Sect. 5 will

---

[1] A community is a set of nodes with interest in related topics.

illustrate this problem. In order to solve it, we will extend the model by adding a decision-making component: the Argumentative Decision-Making System, that allows a node to decide whether it is necessary to explore the network, sending queries by flooding, which helps to discover other communities of nodes that share common interests.

In order to capture the relevant features associated with reactive and argumentative behavior, distinguished vectors of Boolean variables will be defined. Formally:

Definition 3. *Let* $P = (\mathcal{N}, \mathcal{E}, S_t)$ *be a P2P network. For every node* $n \in \mathcal{N}$, *an incoming query* Q *associated with a topic* T, *and a* KB_n *we define the following vectors of Boolean variables:*

$$RB_n(Q,T) = \langle availability(Q,T), relevance(Q,T), awareness(Q,T) \rangle,$$

where:

- *availability*(Q,T) *is true iff node* n *(interested in topic* T*) can answer an incoming query* Q *associated with topic* T;
- *relevance*(Q,T) *is true iff the topic* T *of the incoming query* Q *is relevant to node* n;
- *awareness*(Q,T) *is true iff node* n *knows other nodes interested in the topic* T *of the query* Q.

$$AB_n(KB_n) = \langle interest(KB_n), reliability(KB_n), congestion(KB_n), need\_to\_explore(KB_n) \rangle,$$

where

- *interest is true iff node* n *contains information in its knowledge base* KB_n *about other nodes and their interests;*
- *reliability is true iff the knowledge stored in* KB_n *provides reasons to believe that certain nodes are reliable;*
- *congestion is true iff the knowledge stored in* KB_n *provides reasons to believe that there exist paths to certain nodes that are congested;*
- *need_to_explore is true iff the knowledge stored in* KB_n *provides reasons to believe that it is necessary to explore the network.*

Definition 4. *Let* $P = (\mathcal{N}, \mathcal{E}, S_t)$ *be a P2P network. A Reactive Decision-Making System for a node* $n \in \mathcal{N}$, *denoted* $RDMS_n$, *is a hard-wired black box system that given a query* Q *associated with a topic* T, *takes* $RB_n(Q,T)$ *and* KB_n *and returns a decision* D *indicating how to route* Q *in* P. *Based on the query* Q, *its topic* T *and the knowledge base* KB_n *associated with the node* n, $RDMS_n$ *can choose one of the following courses of action:*

- Discard *the query* Q *if its TTL has expired;*
- Forward *the query* Q *to nodes interested in topic* T *when there is information in* KB_n *indicating to do so;*
- Forward *the query* Q *to adjacent nodes whenever the previous situation is not the case.*

Definition 5. *Let* $P = (\mathcal{N}, \mathcal{E}, S_t)$ *be a P2P network. An* Argumentative Decision-Making System *for a node* $n \in \mathcal{N}$, *a query* Q *and a topic* T *is denoted* $ADMS_n$ *and is an ABA program (based on* $KB_n, AB_n(KB_n), Q$ *and* T) *used to determine whether the decision* $need\_to\_explore(KB_n)$ *is warranted under grounded skeptical semantics.*[2] *If* $need\_to\_explore(KB_n)$ *is true, the system returns* true *and flooding is used as a strategy for routing the query, otherwise* false *is returned and the strategy for routing the query is the strategy obtaining from the* $RDMS_n$.

Definition 6. *Let* $P = (\mathcal{N}, \mathcal{E}, S_t)$ *be a P2P network. We define* **RDMS** *as the set of all the* $RDMS_n$ *systems for all* $n \in \mathcal{N}$. *Analogously, we define* **ADMS** *as the set of all the* $ADMS_n$ *systems for all* $n \in \mathcal{N}$.

Definition 7. *Let* $P = (\mathcal{N}, \mathcal{E}, S_t)$ *be a dynamic P2P network, an* ArgP2P framework *is a 3-uple* $(P, \textbf{RDMS}, \textbf{ADMS})$ *where:*

– P *is a P2P network,* $P = (\mathcal{N}, \mathcal{E}, S_t)$,
– **RDMS** *represents the Reactive Decision-Making component of* P, *and*
– **ADMS** *represents the Argumentative Decision-Making component of* P.

In Fig. 4 we present a graphical representation of the ArgP2P framework for a node n. This framework augments an already tested and implemented application [18] by adding an Argumentative Decision-Making component (indicated by the dotted square in the figure). In Algorithm 1 we present the high-level code of the RunNode algorithm for every node j in an ArgP2P framework. Algorithm 2 presents the high-level code of the Reactive Decision-Making System. Finally, the high-level code of the Argumentative Decision-Making System is presented in Algorithm 3. These algorithms model the most important features of the ArgP2P framework.

The main algorithm exhibits the interaction between the Reactive Decision-Making System ($RDMS_j$) and the Argumentative Decision-Making System ($ADMS_j$) in a node j. In order not to slow down the average response time of the node, note that $ADMS_j$ is invoked 1 out of every 15 executions of the code (this parameter is configurable, allowing to set the frequency for the operation of the Argumentative Decision-Making System in each node). The $RDMS_j$ checks the variables of the RB_j vector using the knowledge base KB_j and then makes a decision about how to route the query Q according to the knowledge acquired. The $ADMS_j$ builds an ABA program from vector AB_j and the knowledge base KB_j. Then it executes the program to reach a final decision about whether or not it is necessary to explore the network to increment its global knowledge.

---

[2] We are aware of different possible semantics for ABA. For illustrative purposes we have adopted the grounded skeptical semantics, even though other alternative semantics could be used. An in-depth analysis of these alternatives is outside the scope of this paper.

Algorithm 1. RunNode Code for every node j in a P2P framework.

Input: A query Q associated with a topic T.
Output: A decision D about what action to take after the arrival of the
query Q.
$count := count + 1$; \\ count is a global variable associated with every particular
node, initially set to 0, and incremented every time RunNode is executed.
LoadKnowledgeBase(KB_j); \\ Initializes the knowledge base with stored
information.
Decision $D :=$ ReactiveDecisionMaking(RB_j, Q, T, KB_j);
if *(count mod 15 = 0)* **then**
    If *(ArgumentativeDecisionMaking(AB$_j$, KB$_j$))* **then**
        $D = Forward\_to\_Adjacent\_Node$;
    end

end
return D.

Algorithm 2. ReactiveDecisionMaking for every node j ($RDMS_j$)

Input: A query Q associated with a topic T, a vector of variables RB_j and a
knowledge base KB_j.
Output: A decision D about what action to take after the arrival of the
query Q.
for *each $p_i \in RB_j$* **do**
    check(p_i, KB_j);
end
Decision $D :=$ makeDecision(Q, T,$RB_j(Q,T)$, KB_j);
return D.

Algorithm 3. ArgumentativeDecisionMaking for every node j ($ADMS_j$)

Input: A knowledge base KB_j and a vector of variables $AB_j(KB_j)$.
Output: Returns true iff $need\_to\_explore(KB_j)$ is warranted using grounded
skeptical semantics, otherwise it returns false.
boolean *result*;
constructABAprogram(KB_j,$AB_j(KB_j)$);
result$:=$ executeABAprogram($need\_to\_explore(KB_j)$);
return *result*.

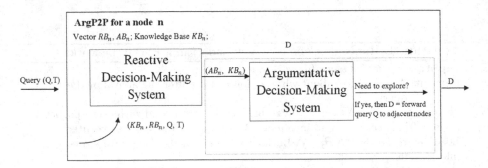

Fig. 4. High-level description of the components in every node n of an ArgP2P framework.

5   Case Study

Consider the P2P network in Fig. 2. Suppose that nodes 1, 2, 8 and 10 are interested in the topic *math* and have the knowledge shown in Table 1 about the rest of the network.

Table 1. Nodes' knowledge about the topic "math".

KB_n	Nodes associated with the topic "math"		
KB_1	5	8	10
KB_5	1	8	10
KB_8	1	5	10
KB_{10}	1	5	8

Suppose that node 1 generates a query message and sends it to the nodes that, according to its knowledge, are interested in the topic *math*. Figure 5(a) shows the initial paths followed by these messages, which are represented with dotted arrows. The formal representation of the network at time $(t = 1)$ is the following:

$$S_1(n) = \text{idle } \forall \ n \in \mathcal{N} - \{1\},$$
$$S_1(1) = (consult, \{5, 8, 10\}).$$

Then node 5 receives the forwarded message and it cannot answer the query so it forwards the message to the candidate nodes that it knows from KB_5 (except node 1 which is where the query was originated). Figure 5(b) illustrates this situation. Nodes 8 and 10 cannot answer the query either and forward the message by taking into account KB_8 and KB_{10} respectively. Figure 5(c) and (d) show this scenario. All these actions take place at time $t = 2$ and the formal representation is:

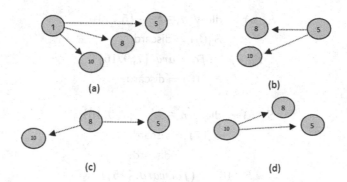

Fig. 5. Graphical representation of nodes sending messages at different time points when routing a query in a P2P network (case study).

$$S_2(n) = \text{idle} \ \forall \ n \in \mathcal{N} - \{5, 8, 10\},$$
$$S_2(5) = (forward, \{8, 10\}),$$
$$S_2(8) = (forward, \{5, 10\}),$$
$$S_2(10) = (forward, \{5, 8\}).$$

After forwarding the messages, node 5 receives a message from node 8 that was generated by node 1 and a message from node 10 that was also generated by node 1; finally node 10 receives a message from node 5 generated by node 1 and another from node 8 also originated in node 1. All these messages are discarded at time $t = 3$ because the receptor nodes already contain a message in their records with that identifier indicating that the node has already processed the message, and consequently node 1 will not be able to find the answer of the query. As a result, the actions at time $t = 3$ are the following:

$$S_3(n) = \text{idle} \ \forall \ n \in \mathcal{N} - \{5, 8, 10\},$$
$$S_3(5) = \text{discard},$$
$$S_3(8) = \text{discard},$$
$$S_3(10) = \text{discard}.$$

Assume that in order to solve this problem, node 8 decides to break the protocol and explore the network. Therefore, it will send messages to nodes 7, 9 and 16 at $t = 3$. Node 7 only has node 1 as an adjacent node, which is the same node that generated the query and therefore it is not considered. Node 9 has no potentially useful adjacent nodes to forward the message (the message arrived from node 8, so it is not considered). Node 16 will forward the message to node 15 (at time $t = 4$). Finally, at time $t = 5$, node 15 is able to answer the query originated by node 1.

$$S_3(n) = \text{idle } \forall \ n \in \mathcal{N} - \{5, 8, 10\},$$
$$S_3(5) = \text{discard},$$
$$S_3(8) = (forward, \{7, 9, 16\}),$$
$$S_3(10) = \text{discard}.$$

$$S_4(n) = \text{idle } \forall \ n \in \mathcal{N} - \{7, 9, 16\},$$
$$S_4(7) = \text{discard},$$
$$S_4(9) = \text{discard},$$
$$S_4(16) = (forward, \{15\}).$$

$$S_5(n) = \text{idle } \forall \ n \in \mathcal{N} - \{15\},$$
$$S_5(15) = \text{reply}.$$

When the $ADMS_8$ system is executed, an ABA program is built. The assumptions, rules and contraries that constitute the program can be automatically generated from knowledge that is readily available to the node from AB_8 and KB_8. This program allows node 8 to determine whether it is better or not to explore the network. In order to accomplish this, the node needs to deal with incomplete and potentially inconsistent information. As a consequence argumentative reasoning provides the appropriate mechanisms to reach a decision. If the node decides to explore, then it discards $RDMS_8$'s initial decision to forward the query message to potentially useful nodes. The following logic program corresponds to the ABA program generated by $ADMS_8$, as well as the associated derivation tree representing how the decision *"need to explore"* is reached. The resulting derivation tree is shown in Fig. 6. This example illustrates the fact that the ABA program will have to deal with inconsistent information. In particular the decision $need\_to\_explore$ is inconsistent with the decision $forward(1)$. Similarly, the assumption $notCongested(1)$ is inconsistent with the conclusion $congested(1)$.

$A = \{notCongested(1), notCongested(5), notCongested(10),$
$goodCandidate(1), goodCandidate(5), goodCandidate(10),$
$alwaysCongested(1), neverCongested(5), neverCongested(10),$
$longTimeToRespond(1), need\_to\_explore\}$

$R = \{math(1) \leftarrow; \ math(5) \leftarrow; math(10) \leftarrow; goodResponseRecord(1) \leftarrow;$
$goodResponseRecord(5) \leftarrow;$
$forward(1) \leftarrow math(1), notCongested(1), reliable(1);$
$forward(5) \leftarrow math(5), notCongested(5), reliable(5);$
$forward(10) \leftarrow math(10), notCongested(10), reliable(10);$
$congested(1) \leftarrow longTimeToRespond(1), alwaysCongested(1);$
$congested(5) \leftarrow longTimeToRespond(5), alwaysCongested(5);$
$congested(10) \leftarrow longTimeToRespond(10), alwaysCongested(10);$
$reliable(1) \leftarrow goodResponseRecord(1), goodCandidate(1);$

$reliable(5) \leftarrow goodResponseRecord(5), goodCandidate(5);$
$reliable(10) \leftarrow goodResponseRecord(10), goodCandidate(10);$
$notExplore \leftarrow forward(1);$
$notExplore \leftarrow forward(5);$
$notExplore \leftarrow forward(10)\}$

$\overline{notCongested(1)} = congested(1);$
$\overline{notCongested(5)} = congested(5);$
$\overline{notCongested(10)} = congested(10);$
$\overline{goodCandidate(1)} = badCandidate(1);$
$\overline{goodCandidate(5)} = badCandidate(5);$
$\overline{goodCandidate(10)} = badCandidate(10);$
$\overline{alwaysCongested(1)} = neverCongested(1);$
$\overline{neverCongested(5)} = alwaysCongested(5);$
$\overline{neverCongested(10)} = alwaysCongested(10);$
$\overline{longTimeToRespond(1)} = lowTimeToRespond(1);$
$\overline{need\_to\_explore} = forward(1);$
$\overline{need\_to\_explore} = forward(5);$
$\overline{need\_to\_explore} = forward(10);$
$\overline{need\_to\_explore} = notExplore;$

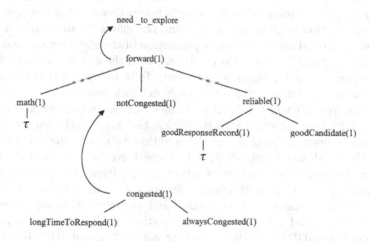

Fig. 6. Arguments and attacks involved in a derivation tree supporting the decision "*need_to_explore*". Pointing arrows denote attacks between arguments.

6   Discussion and Related Work

The concept of "knowledge sharing" is an emerging topic generally based upon cooperation between peers. This concept represents the trade-off between sharing knowledge to improve the global knowledge of the network and the cost of sending the messages with this information. The first step to sharing knowledge is to establish friendship relationships in a similar way as it is implemented in Self Learning Query Routing (SLPS) [6]. In the SLPS approach, the interests of the peers are learned based on their search result history, which allow to automatically construct friend relations based on the similarity of users' interests. In this routing model queries are routed to friend nodes following an unstructured pattern. If the searches in friend nodes fail, broadcast search will be executed. Each node ranks their friends from high to low according to the number of shared files and chooses the first top K nodes. As time goes on, a node can learn which are those friend nodes that share the same interests with it.

The identification of semantic communities can help predict the performance of a P2P search application. Akavipat et al. [1] evaluate algorithms for searching in P2P networks based on the concept of semantic similarity. Their experiments with different routing algorithms on their peer Web Search 6S (unstructured network) suggest that despite the use of an unstructured overlay network, peers' interactions lead to the formation of semantic communities.

All these approaches provide P2P whith some kind of intelligence in order to route queries to specific peers, but no one has the capability of determining whether or not the decision that was made is the best one to increment the global knowledge of the network. In an argumentative context a node with the ability to discern becomes an "agent". Kowalski [16] classified agents as *rational* or *reactive*. In general terms the difference between them is that a reactive agent receives a perception of the environment and translates it into a specific action; in contrast, a rational agent receives a perception of the environment and takes a certain time to "think" what action to take. Given these definitions, each of the nodes becomes a rational agent able to make fully independent decisions from which the node, its community or the whole network can benefit.

In the last years, there has been particular interest in deploying argumentation within P2P infrastructures. In particular, the ArguGRID project [25] aims at supporting service selection and composition in distributed environments, including the Grid and Service-oriented architectures, by means of argumentative agents, an agent environment, a service-composition environment, Peer-to-Peer technology and Grid middleware. Agents are argumentative in that they use argumentation-based decision-making and argumentation-supported negotiation of services and contracts. The integration of all technologies gives rise to the overall ArguGRID platform. In contrast with ArguGRID, our proposal introduces a framework where every node has an autonomous two-stage decision-making process with the only goal of routing queries efficiently in a P2P network, without negotiation between peers.

7   Conclusions and Future Work

In this paper we have outlined a novel model for thematic search in P2P networks, where every node in the network has the ability to combine both reactive and rational (argumentative) behavior. The argumentative inference engine is provided by an ABA program, which allows to enhance the decision-making capabilities in every node, based on knowledge acquired by the node during its lifetime. A configuration parameter allows to set the frequency by which argumentation is used during the decision making process (e.g. by setting the global variable *count* to 1, the node performs argumentative reasoning every time a query routing decision is to be made).

Part of our future work involves an empirical comparison between the ArgP2P framework and a purely reactive P2P framework. In addition, we plan to contrast the performance of different argumentative semantics and different *count values* for the nodes. Research in this direction is being pursued.

Acknowledgments. This research was funded by CONICET (PIP 112-201201-00487 and PIP 112-201101-01000),Universidad Nacional del Sur (PGI-UNS 24/N029) and ANPCyT(PICT 2014-0624).

References

1. Akavipat, R., Wu, L.-S., Menczer, F., Maguitman, A.G.: Emerging semantic communities in peer web search. In: Proceedings of the International Workshop on Information Retrieval in Peer-to-Peer Networks, P2PIR 2006, pp. 1–8. ACM, New York, NY, USA (2006)
2. Amaury Matt, P., Toni, F.: Argumentation-based agents for eprocurement
3. Androutsellis-Theotokis, S., Spinellis, D.: A survey of peer-to-peer content distribution technologies. ACM Comput. Surv. (CSUR) **36**(4), 335–371 (2004)
4. Besnard, P., et al.: Towards argumentation-based contract negotiation. Comput. Models Argument: Proc. COMMA **172**, 134 (2008)
5. Bondarenko, A., Toni, F., Kowalski, R.A.: An assumption-based framework for non-monotonic reasoning. LPNMR **93**, 171–189 (1993)
6. Chen, H., Gong, Z., Huang, Z.: Self-learning routing in unstructured p2p network. Int. J. Inf. Technol. **11**(12), 59–67 (2005)
7. Du, N., Wang, B., Wu, B.: Community detection in complex networks. J. Comput. Sci. Technol. **23**, 672–683 (2008)
8. Dung, P.M.: On the acceptability of arguments and its fundamental role in non-monotonic reasoning, logic programming and n-person games. Artif. Intell. **77**(2), 321–357 (1995a)
9. Dung, P.M.: On the acceptability of arguments and its fundamental role in non-monotonic reasoning, logic programming and n-person games. Artif. Intell. **77**, 321–357 (1995b)
10. Dung, P.M., Kowalski, R.A., Toni, F.: Assumption-based argumentation. Argumentation in Artificial Intelligence, pp. 199–218. Springer, Heidelberg (2009)
11. Dung, P.M., Thang, P.M.: Towards an argument-based model of legal doctrines in common law of contracts. In: Proceedings, CLIMA IX, vol. 7 (2008)
12. García, A.J., Simari, G.R.: Defeasible logic programming: An argumentative approach. Theor. Pract. Logic Program. **4**(1+2), 95–138 (2004)
13. Jin, X., Chan, S.-H.G.: Unstructured peer-to-peer network architectures. In Handbook of Peer-to-Peer Networking, pp. 117–142. Springer, Heidelberg (2010)
14. Kakas, K., Toni, F.: Computing argumentation in logic programming. J. Logic Comput. **9**(4), 515–562 (1999)

15. Korzun, D., Gurtov, A.: Structured peer-to-peer systems: fundamentals of hierarchical organization, routing, scaling, and security. Springer Science & Business Media (2012)
16. Kowalski, R.A.: Using meta-logic to reconcile reactive with rational agents. Metalogics and logic programming, pp. 227–242 (1995)
17. Kowalski, R.A., Toni, F.: Abstract argumentation. Artif. Intell. Law **4**(3–4), 275–296 (1996)
18. Nicolini, A.L., Lorenzetti, C.M., Maguitman, A.G., Chesñevar, C.I.: Intelligent algorithms for reducing query propagation in thematic p2p search. Anales del XIX Congreso Argentino de Ciencias de la Computación (CACIC), pp. 71–79. Mar del Plata, Buenos Aires, Argentina (2013)
19. Radicchi, F., Castellano, C., Cecconi, F., Loreto, V., Parisi, D.: Defining and identifying communities in networks. Proc. Natl. Acad. Sci. U.S. Am. **101**(9), 2658–2663 (2004)
20. Rosenfeld, A., Goldman, C.V., Kaminka, G.A., Kraus, S.: Phirst: A distributed architecture for P2P information retrieval. Inf. Syst. **34**(2), 290–303 (2009)
21. Schollmeier, R.: A definition of peer-to-peer networking for the classification of peer-to-peer architectures and applications. In: 2001 Proceedings of the First International Conference on Peer-to-Peer Computing, pp. 101–102 (2001)
22. Tang, C., Xu, Z., Dwarkadas, S.: Peer-to-Peer information retrieval using self-organizing semantic overlay networks. In: Proceedings of the 2003 Conference on Applications, Technologies, Architectures, and Protocols for Computer Communications, SIGCOMM 2003, pp. 175–186. ACM, New York, NY, USA (2003)
23. Toni, F.: Assumption-based argumentation for selection and composition of services. In: Sadri, F., Satoh, K. (eds.) CLIMA VIII 2007. LNCS (LNAI), vol. 5056, pp. 231–247. Springer, Heidelberg (2008)
24. Toni, F.: A tutorial on assumption-based argumentation. Argument Comput. **5**, 89–117 (2014)
25. Toni, F., et al.: The ArguGRID platform: An overview. In: Altmann, J., Neumann, D., Fahringer, T. (eds.) GECON 2008. LNCS, vol. 5206, pp. 217–225. Springer, Heidelberg (2008)
26. Voulgaris, S., Kermarrec, A., Massouli, L., van Oteen, M.: Exploiting semantic proximity in peer-to-peer content searching. In: Proceedings of the 10th IEEE International Workshop on Future Trends of Distributed Computing Systems, pp. 238–243. IEEE Computer Society, Washington, DC, USA (2004)
27. Wang, L.: Sofa: An expert-driven, self-organization peer-to-peer semantic communities for network resource management. Expert Syst. Appl. **38**, 94–105 (2011)

Persistence and Monotony Properties
of Argumentation Semantics

Tjitze Rienstra[1]([✉]), Chiaki Sakama[2], and Leendert van der Torre[3]

[1] Interdisciplinary Centre for Security, Reliability and Trust,
University of Luxembourg, Luxembourg City, Luxembourg
tjitze@gmail.com
[2] Wakayama University, Wakayama, Japan
sakama@sys.wakayama-u.ac.jp
[3] Computer Science and Communication, University of Luxembourg,
Luxembourg City, Luxembourg
leon.vandertorre@uni.lu

Abstract. We study a number of properties concerning the behaviour of semantics for Dung style abstract argumentation when the argumentation framework changes. The properties are concerned with how the evaluation of an argumentation framework changes if an attack between two arguments is added or removed. The results provide insight into the behaviour of these semantics in a dynamic context.

1 Introduction

Argumentation is a process that usually involves a series of steps taken to achieve a particular end. However, an argumentation framework (AF, for short) represents only a static snapshot of this process. To consider dynamics of argumentation, we need to consider AFs that change, for example due to the addition of new arguments and attacks. In this paper we focus on the behaviour of semantics for argumentation in a dynamic context, by studying properties related to how the evaluation of an AF changes if the AF changes.

Our work extends the growing literature on the general problem of change in Dung style argumentation theory. This includes studies of strong equivalence [12], enforcing [3] and revision in argumentation [6,10]. In particular, this paper extends the approach of Boella et al. [4,5], who studied *refinement* and *abstraction* principles, which are conditions under which the evaluation of an AF remains unchanged when an attack is added or removed. While they only focussed on semantics that yield a single extension or labelling, we extend their approach by considering three types of properties that also apply to semantics that yield multiple extensions or labellings:

- *XY* **Addition Persistence**: a σ labelling of an AF F in which x is labelled X and y is labelled Y is still a σ labelling of F after adding an attack from x to y.

E. Black et al. (Eds.): TAFA 2015, LNAI 9524, pp. 211–225, 2016.
DOI: 10.1007/978-3-319-28460-6_13

- *XY* **Removal Persistence**: a σ labelling of an AF F in which x is labelled X and y is labelled Y is still a σ labelling of F if removing the attack from x to y.
- *XY* **Skeptical Monotony**: if in all σ labellings of an AF F, x is labelled X and y is labelled Y, then adding an attack from x to y does not lead to new σ labellings.

We systematically check, for each combination of labels X and Y (relying on Caminada's three-valued labellings [7]) whether XY addition persistence, removal persistence and skeptical monotony are satisfied under the grounded, complete, preferred, stable and semi-stable semantics. Our results provide insight into the behaviour of these semantics in a dynamic context. For example, **OO** addition persistence reflects the principle that a point of view represented by a labelling L need not be revised due to the addition of an attack from x to y, if both x and y are labelled *out* in L. This is intuitive because the added attack does not introduce a conflict with respect to L in this case. We show that some combinations of X and Y yield counterintuitive properties that are, indeed, not satisfied under any of the semantics we consider. Other properties are intuitive, such as the above mentioned **OO** addition persistence, and are satisfied under some semantics but not under all.

The layout of this paper is as follows. In Sect. 2 we recall the necessary definitions concerning AFs, extension-based semantics and labelling-based semantics. In Sects. 3, 4 and 5 we introduce the addition persistence, removal persistence and skeptical monotony properties and we check whether they are satisfied or not. In Sect. 6 we discuss related work. In Sect. 7 we conclude and discuss a number of directions for future research.

2   Preliminaries

Formally, an AF is a directed graph represented by a set A of *arguments* and a binary relation $\rightsquigarrow$ over A called the *attack relation* [11]. To simplify our discussion we assume that A is a finite subset of a set $\mathcal{U}$ called the *universe of arguments*.

Definition 1. *Let $\mathcal{U}$ be a set whose elements are called* arguments. *An argumentation framework (AF, for short) is a pair $F = (A, \rightsquigarrow)$ where A is a finite subset of $\mathcal{U}$ and $\rightsquigarrow \subseteq A \times A$. We denote by $\mathcal{F}$ the set of all AFs.*

Given an AF $(A, \rightsquigarrow)$ we say that an argument $a \in A$ *attacks* an argument $b \in A$ if and only if $(a, b) \in \rightsquigarrow$. Given an AF F we denote by x^- (resp. B^-) the set of arguments attacking x (resp. some $x \in B$) and by x^+ (resp. B^+) the set of arguments attacked by x (resp. some $x \in B$).

2.1   Extension-Based Semantics

An extension-based semantics is defined by a condition that an extension (i.e., a set of arguments) must satisfy so that it represents a rationally acceptable set of arguments. Three basic conditions for an extension to be rationally acceptable are *conflict-freeness*, *admissibility* and *completeness*. An extension E is conflict-free if it is not self-attacking, admissible if it defends all its members, and complete if it furthermore includes all arguments that it defends. The notion of defence used here is defined as follows.

Definition 2 *[11]. Let $F = (A, \rightsquigarrow)$ be an AF. An extension $E \subseteq A$ defends an argument $y \in A$ if and only if for all $x \in A$ such that $x \rightsquigarrow y$, there is a $z \in E$ such that $z \rightsquigarrow x$. We define $\mathcal{D}_F(E)$ by $\mathcal{D}_F(E) = \{x \in A \mid E \text{ defends } x\}$.*

Definition 3 *[11]. Let $F = (A, \rightsquigarrow)$ be an AF. An extension $E \subseteq A$ is conflict-free iff for no $x, y \in E$ it holds that $x \rightsquigarrow y$; admissible iff E is conflict-free and $E \subseteq \mathcal{D}_F(E)$; and complete iff E is conflict-free and $E = \mathcal{D}_F(E)$.*

An extension-based semantics σ can be represented by a function $\mathcal{E}_\sigma : \mathcal{F} \rightarrow 2^{2^{\mathcal{U}}}$ satisfying $\mathcal{E}_\sigma((A, \rightsquigarrow)) \subseteq 2^A$. The following definition presents some of the most-used semantics, namely the complete (co), grounded (gr), preferred (pr), semi-stable (ss) and stable (st) semantics.

Definition 4. *Let $F = (A, \rightsquigarrow)$ be an AF.*

- $\mathcal{E}_{co}(F) = \{E \subseteq A \mid E \text{ is a complete extension of } F\}$
- $\mathcal{E}_{gr}(F) = \{E \in \mathcal{E}_{co}(F) \mid \nexists E' \in \mathcal{E}_{co}(F) \text{ s.t. } E' \subset E\}$
- $\mathcal{E}_{pr}(F) = \{E \in \mathcal{E}_{co}(F) \mid \nexists E' \in \mathcal{E}_{co}(F) \text{ s.t. } E \subset E'\}$
- $\mathcal{E}_{ss}(F) = \{E \in \mathcal{E}_{co}(F) \mid \nexists E' \in \mathcal{E}_{co}(F) \text{ s.t. } E \cup E^+ \subset E' \cup E'^+\}$
- $\mathcal{E}_{st}(F) = \{E \in \mathcal{E}_{co}(F) \mid E \cup E^+ = A\}$

The grounded extension can also be characterized by a fix point theory.

Proposition 1 *([11, Theorem 25]). Given an AF F, the grounded extension of F coincides with the least fixed point of $\mathcal{D}_F$.*

2.2 Labelling-Based Semantics

While an extension only captures the arguments that are accepted in a given position, a labelling assigns to each argument an *acceptance status*. This approach can be traced back to Pollock [13]. We follow Caminada [7], who defined the semantics considered here using three-valued labellings: **I** (accepted), **O** (rejected) and **U** (undecided). The benefit of labellings over extensions is that they permit us to distinguish not only arguments that are accepted and not accepted, but also those that are explicitly rejected and those that are undecided.

Definition 5. *A labelling of an AF $(A, \rightsquigarrow)$ is a function $L : A \rightarrow \{\mathbf{I}, \mathbf{O}, \mathbf{U}\}$. Given a label $l \in \{\mathbf{I}, \mathbf{O}, \mathbf{U}\}$ we define $L^{-1}(l)$ as $\{x \in A \mid L(x) = l\}$. Given an AF F, we let $\mathcal{L}(F)$ denote the set of all labellings of F.*

We also denote a labelling L by a set of pairs $\{(x_1, L(x_1)), \ldots, (x_n, L(x_n))\}$. Complete labellings are defined as follows.

Definition 6. *Let $F = (A, \rightsquigarrow)$ be an AF. A labelling $L \in \mathcal{L}(F)$ is complete if and only if for all $x \in A$, $L(x) = \mathbf{I}$ iff for all $y \in x^-$, $L(y) = \mathbf{O}$; and $L(x) = \mathbf{O}$ iff for some $y \in x^-$, $L(y) = \mathbf{I}$.*

The following definition introduces the labelling-based versions of the semantics presented in the previous section [8].

Definition 7. *Let $F = (A, \rightsquigarrow)$ be an AF.*

- $\mathcal{L}_{co}(F) = \{L \in \mathcal{L}(F) \mid L \text{ is a complete labelling of } F\}$
- $\mathcal{L}_{gr}(F) = \{L \in \mathcal{L}_{co}(F) \mid \nexists L' \in \mathcal{L}_{co}(F) \text{ s.t. } L'^{-1}(\mathbf{I}) \subset L^{-1}(\mathbf{I})\}$
- $\mathcal{L}_{pr}(F) = \{L \in \mathcal{L}_{co}(F) \mid \nexists L' \in \mathcal{L}_{co}(F) \text{ s.t. } L^{-1}(\mathbf{I}) \subset L'^{-1}(\mathbf{I})\}$
- $\mathcal{L}_{ss}(F) = \{L \in \mathcal{L}_{co}(F) \mid \nexists L' \in \mathcal{L}_{co}(F) \text{ s.t. } L^{-1}(\mathbf{U}) \subset L^{-1}(\mathbf{U})\}$
- $\mathcal{L}_{st}(F) = \{L \in \mathcal{L}_{co}(F) \mid L^{-1}(\mathbf{U}) = \emptyset\}$

The following proposition establishes a correspondence between extensions and labellings. It has been shown that this is a one-to-one mapping [8].

Proposition 2. *Let $F = (A, \rightsquigarrow)$ be an AF and let $\sigma \in \{co, gr, pr, ss, st\}$.*

- *If $L \in \mathcal{L}_\sigma(F)$ then $L^{-1}(\mathbf{I}) \in \mathcal{E}_\sigma(F)$.*
- *If $E \in \mathcal{E}_\sigma(F)$ then $L \in \mathcal{L}_\sigma(F)$, where L is defined by $L(x) = \mathbf{I}$, if $x \in E$, $L(x) = \mathbf{O}$, if $x \in E^+$ and $L(x) = \mathbf{U}$, otherwise.*

3   Addition Persistence Properties

We first consider *addition persistence*, defined with respect to two labels X and Y. We say that a semantics σ satisfies XY addition persistence whenever a σ labelling of an AF F in which x is labelled X and y is labelled Y is still a σ labelling of F after adding an attack from x to y. Formally:

Definition 8. *Let σ be a semantics and let $X, Y \in \{\mathbf{O}, \mathbf{I}, \mathbf{U}\}$. We say that σ satisfies XY addition persistence if and only if for all $(A, \rightsquigarrow) \in \mathcal{F}$ and $x, y \in A$, if $L \in \mathcal{L}_\sigma((A, \rightsquigarrow))$, $L(x) = X$ and $L(y) = Y$, then $L \in \mathcal{L}_\sigma((A, \rightsquigarrow \cup \{(x, y)\}))$.*

For some combinations of X and Y, the semantics we consider obviously do not satisfy XY addition persistence. These are **II**, **IU** and **UI** addition persistence. The reason is that no two arguments x and y such that x attacks y ever receive these combinations of labels in a complete labelling.

Proposition 3. *The grounded, complete, preferred and semi-stable semantics do not satisfy **II**, **IU** and **UI** addition persistence.*

Under the stable semantics, where arguments are never labelled **U**, all properties involving **U**-labelled arguments are trivially satisfied.

Proposition 4. *The stable semantics satisfies **UO**, **UU**, **UI**, **UO** and **UI** addition persistence but does not satisfy **II** addition persistence.*

For the remaining combinations of X and Y, XY addition persistence may be considered desirable. For example, **OO**, **OU** and **OI** addition persistence together reflect the principle that a point of view L need not be revised due to the addition of an attack from x to y, if x is labelled **O**. This is intuitive because the added attack does not in this case introduce a conflict with respect to L, as the argument from which the added attack originates is rejected. Consequently, the added attack does not invalidate the label assigned to y. Similar considerations apply to **UO**, **UU** and **IO** addition persistence, which also concern combinations where the added attack from x to y does not introduce conflict and does not invalidate the label assigned to y.

We now turn to the question whether the semantics we consider satisfy these remaining properties. Let us start with the grounded and complete semantics. While the grounded semantics satisfies **OO**, **OU**, **UO**, **UU** and **IO** addition persistence, it does not satisfy **OI** addition persistence.

Theorem 1. *The grounded semantics satisfies* **OO**, **OU**, **UO**, **UU** *and* **IO** *addition persistence but not* **OI** *addition persistence.*

Proof. Due to lack of space we only provide a proof sketch. Satisfaction can be proven by induction on the construction of the grounded extension of F as the fix point of $\mathcal{D}_F$. A counterexample for **OI** addition persistence is provided below.

The failure of **OI** addition persistence is due to the fact that the addition of an attack from an **O** to an **I** labelled argument may lead to a new complete labelling in which both arguments are **U**. This new labelling will become the new grounded labelling. This is demonstrated by the following example.

Example 1 (Failure of **OI** *addition persistence under the grounded semantics).* Consider an AF with two arguments a, b, where a attacks b. In the grounded labelling, a is labelled **I** and b is labelled **O**. If we add an attack from b to a the grounded labelling assigns **U** to a and b.

The complete semantics satisfies all properties satisfied by the grounded semantics but it also satisfies **OI** addition persistence.

Theorem 2. *The complete semantics satisfies* **OO**, **OU**, **OI**, **UO**, **UU** *and* **IO** *addition persistence.*

Proof. Follows easily from Definition 6. We omit this proof due to lack of space.

The preferred semantics satisfies all properties satisfied by the complete semantics, except for **UU** addition persistence.

Theorem 3. *The preferred semantics satisfies* **OO**, **OU**, **OI**, **IO** *and* **UO** *addition persistence but not* **UU** *addition persistence.*

Proof. Let $(A, \rightsquigarrow) \in \mathcal{F}$ and let $L \in \mathcal{L}_{pr}((A, \rightsquigarrow))$ be a labelling s.t. either $L(x) = \mathbf{O}$ or $L(y) = \mathbf{O}$. We prove that $L \in \mathcal{L}_{pr}((A, \rightsquigarrow \cup \{(x, y)\}))$. If $x \rightsquigarrow y$ we are done. For the case $x \not\rightsquigarrow y$, assume the contrary. We have $L \in \mathcal{L}_{co}((A, \rightsquigarrow \cup \{(x, y)\}))$ and thus there must be an $L' \in \mathcal{L}_{pr}((A, \rightsquigarrow \cup\{(x,y)\}))$ such that $L^{-1}(\mathbf{I}) \subset L'^{-1}(\mathbf{I})$. It then follows that either $L'(x) = \mathbf{O}$ or $L'(y) = \mathbf{O}$ and hence $L' \in \mathcal{L}_{co}((A, \rightsquigarrow))$. This contradicts $L \in \mathcal{L}_{pr}((A, \rightsquigarrow))$. Hence $L \in \mathcal{L}_{pr}((A, \rightsquigarrow \cup\{(x,y)\}))$. A counterexample for **UU** addition persistence is provided below.

Failure of **UU** addition persistence is due to the fact that an attack from a **U** to another **U** labelled argument may lead to a new complete labelling in which one of the two is labelled **I**. This new labelling will replace the old labelling as one of the preferred labellings. This is demonstrated by the following example.

Example 2 (Failure of **UU** *addition persistence under the preferred semantics).* Consider an AF with two arguments a, b, where a attacks b and a is self-attacking. The unique preferred labelling assigns **U** to a and b. If we add an attack from b to a the unique preferred labelling assigns **O** to a and **I** to b.

We already saw that addition persistence properties involving U-labelled arguments are trivially satisfied under the stable semantics. The remaining interesting properties are **OO**, **OI** and **IO** addition persistence. They are all satisfied.

Theorem 4. *Stable semantics satisfies* **OO**, **OI** *and* **IO** *addition persistence.*

Proof. This follows from the proof of Theorem 2 together with the fact that a labelling is stable if and only if it is complete and no argument is labelled **U**.

Under the semi-stable semantics, none of the remaining XY addition persistence properties are satisfied.

Theorem 5. *The semi-stable semantics does not satisfy* **IO**, **UO**, **OO**, **OU** *or* **OI** *addition persistence.*

We list here the counterexamples.

Example 3 (Failure of **IO**, **UO** *and* **OO** *addition persistence under semi-stable semantics).* The AF shown in Fig. 1 has a unique semi-stable labelling $L = \{(a, \mathbf{I}), (b, \mathbf{O}), (c, \mathbf{I}), (d, \mathbf{O}), (e, \mathbf{U}), (f, \mathbf{U})\}$. If we add an attack from a to b (labelled **I** and **O**); from f to b (labelled **U** and **O**); or from d to b (both labelled **O**), L is no longer a semi-stable labelling. Instead we get the unique semi-stable labelling $\{(a, \mathbf{I}), (b, \mathbf{O}), (c, \mathbf{O}), (d, \mathbf{I}), (e, \mathbf{O}), (f, \mathbf{I})\}$.

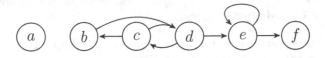

Fig. 1. Failure of **IO**, **UO** and **OO** addition persistence under semi-stable semantics.

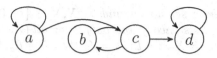

Fig. 2. Failure of **OU** addition persistence under semi-stable semantics.

*Example 4 (Failure of **OU** addition persistence under semi-stable semantics).*
The AF shown in Fig. 2 has a unique semi-stable labelling $L = \{(a, \mathbf{U}), (b, \mathbf{I}),$
$(c, \mathbf{O}), (d, \mathbf{U})\}$. If we add an attack from c to a (labelled **O** and **U**, respectively)
then L is no longer a semi-stable labelling. Instead we get the unique semi-stable
labelling $\{(a, \mathbf{O}), (b, \mathbf{O}), (c, \mathbf{I}), (d, \mathbf{O})\}$.

*Example 5 (Failure of **OI** addition persistence under semi-stable semantics).*
Consider an AF with three arguments a, b and c, where a attacks b, b attacks c
and c is self-attacking. The unique semi-stable labelling is $\{(a, \mathbf{I}), (b, \mathbf{O}), (c, \mathbf{U})\}$.
If we add an attack from b to a (labelled **O** and **I**, respectively) the unique
semi-stable labelling becomes $\{(a, \mathbf{O}), (b, \mathbf{I}), (c, \mathbf{O})\}$.

Let us summarize the results obtained in this section. At the start we established
that none of the semantics we consider satisfy **II**, **IU** and **UI** addition persistence, except the stable semantics, which does not satisfy **II** addition persistence
but trivially satisfies all properties involving **U**-labelled arguments. The complete
semantics can be considered the best behaved one, as it satisfies all remaining
properties, while the semi-stable semantics can be considered the worst behaved
one, as it satisfies none. Finally, the stable semantics is a degenerate case. It satisfies all properties, but all properties involving the label **U** are satisfied because
this label is never assigned to an argument in a stable labelling. Table 1 contains
an overview of the results.

Table 1. Overview of addition persistence properties.

Grounded:

X		
O	**U**	**I**
O ✓	✓	✓
Y **U** ✓	✓	-
I -	-	-

Complete:

X		
O	**U**	**I**
O ✓	✓	✓
Y **U** ✓	✓	-
I ✓	-	-

Preferred:

X		
O	**U**	**I**
O ✓	✓	✓
Y **U** ✓	-	-
I ✓	-	-

Stable:

X		
O	**U**	**I**
O ✓	✓	✓
Y **U** ✓	✓	✓
I ✓	✓	-

Semi-Stable:

X		
O	**U**	**I**
O -	-	-
Y **U** -	-	-
I -	-	-

4 Removal Persistence

We now consider the property of *removal persistence*. We say that a semantics
σ satisfies XY removal persistence whenever every σ labelling of an AF F in
which two arguments x and y are labelled X and Y, respectively, is still a σ
labelling of F after removing the attack from x to y. Formally:

Definition 9. *Let σ be a semantics and let $X, Y \in \{\mathbf{O}, \mathbf{I}, \mathbf{U}\}$. We say that σ satisfies XY removal persistence if and only if for all $(A, \rightsquigarrow) \in \mathcal{F}$ and $x, y \in A$, if $L \in \mathcal{L}_\sigma((A, \rightsquigarrow))$, $L(x) = X$ and $L(y) = Y$, then $L \in \mathcal{L}_\sigma((A, \rightsquigarrow \setminus \{(x,y)\}))$.*

Like in the previous section we now determine, for all semantics that we consider, and for all combinations of X and Y, whether XY removal persistence is satisfied or not. We first establish a number of obvious cases. First of all, **II**, **IU** and **UI** removal persistence are trivially satisfied under all semantics we consider, because these combinations of labels are never assigned by a complete labelling to any two arguments x and y where x attacks y. Similarly, all removal properties involving **U**-labelled arguments are trivially satisfied under the stable labellings, where argument are never labelled **U**. Furthermore **IO** removal persistence fails under all semantics we consider, because in a complete labelling, an argument is labelled **O** only if some attacker is labelled **I**. Thus, removing an attack from an argument labelled **I** in L to an argument labelled **O** in L may invalidate L. The same holds for **UU** removal persistence, which fails under all semantics we consider, except under the stable semantics, where it is trivially satisfied.

Proposition 5. *The grounded, complete, preferred and semi-stable semantics satisfy II, IU and UI removal persistence but do not satisfy IO and UU removal persistence.*

Proposition 6. *The stable semantics satisfies II, UO, UU, UI, OU and IU removal persistence but does not satisfy IO removal persistence.*

In the remainder of this section we focus on **OO**, **OU**, **OI** and **UO** removal persistence. All these properties may be considered desirable. For example, **OO** removal persistence reflects the principle that a point of view L need not be revised due to the removal of an attack from x to y, when both x and y are labelled **O** in L. This is an intuitive principle, because y is not in this case rejected due to being attacked by x, and removing it does not change whether or not the rejection of y is justified. Similar considerations apply to **OU**, **OI** and **UO** removal persistence, which all concern cases where the justification of the label assigned to the second argument does not rely on the label assigned to the first.

Let us start with the grounded, complete and preferred semantics.

Theorem 6. *The grounded, complete and preferred semantics satisfy OO, OU, OI and UO removal persistence.*

Proof. Grounded: Due to space constraints we only provide a sketch of the proof. The satisfied properties can be proven by induction on the construction of the grounded extension of an AF F as the fix point of $\mathcal{D}_F$. *Complete:* Follows easily from the definition of a complete labelling. *Preferred:* Let $(A, \rightsquigarrow) \in \mathcal{F}$ and let $L \in \mathcal{L}_{pr}((A, \rightsquigarrow))$ be a labelling s.t. $L(x) = \mathbf{O}$. We prove that $L \in \mathcal{L}_{pr}((A, \rightsquigarrow \setminus \{(x,y)\}))$. If $x \not\rightsquigarrow y$ we are done. For the case $x \rightsquigarrow y$, assume the contrary. We have $L \in \mathcal{L}_{co}((A, \rightsquigarrow \setminus \{(x,y)\}))$ and thus there must be an $L' \in \mathcal{L}_{pr}((A, \rightsquigarrow \setminus \{(x,y)\}))$ such that $L^{-1}(\mathbf{I}) \subset L'^{-1}(\mathbf{I})$. It then follows that $L'(x) = \mathbf{O}$ and hence

$L' \in \mathcal{L}_{co}((A, \rightsquigarrow))$. This contradicts $L \in \mathcal{L}_{pr}((A, \rightsquigarrow))$. Hence $L \in \mathcal{L}_{pr}((A, \rightsquigarrow \backslash \{(x, y)\}))$. This proves that the preferred semantics satisfies **OO**, **OU** and **OI** persistence. The proof for **UO** is similar.

Let us move on to the stable semantics. Proposition 6 already lists a number of properties that are trivially satisfied. The following theorem concerns the two remaining non-trivial properties.

Theorem 7. *The stable semantics satisfies **OO** and **OI** removal persistence.*

Proof. This follows from Theorem 6 together with the fact that a labelling is stable if and only if it is complete and no argument is labelled **U**.

Under the semi-stable semantics we see that all the remaining properties (**OO**, **OU**, **OI** and **UO** removal persistence) fail.

*Example 6 (Failure of **OO** and **OI** removal persistence under semi-stable semantics).* The AF shown in Fig. 3 has a unique semi-stable labelling $L = \{(a, \mathbf{O}), (b, \mathbf{I}), (c, \mathbf{O}), (d, \mathbf{I}), (e, \mathbf{O}), (f, \mathbf{U})\}$. If we remove the attack from a to e (both labelled **O**) then L is no longer a semi-stable labelling. Instead we get the unique semi-stable labelling $\{(a, \mathbf{I}), (b, \mathbf{O}), (c, \mathbf{I}), (d, \mathbf{O}), (e, \mathbf{I}), (f, \mathbf{O})\}$. Similarly, if we remove the attack from c to b (labelled **O** and **I**, respectively) then L is no longer semi-stable. Instead we get the unique semi-stable labelling $\{(a, \mathbf{O}), (b, \mathbf{I}), (c, \mathbf{I}), (d, \mathbf{O}), (e, \mathbf{I}), (f, \mathbf{O})\}$.

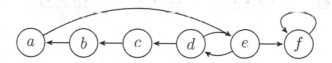

Fig. 3. Failure of **OO** and **OI** removal persistence under semi-stable semantics.

*Example 7 (Failure of **OU** removal persistence under semi-stable semantics).* The AF shown in Fig. 4 has a unique semi-stable labelling $L = \{(a, \mathbf{U}), (b, \mathbf{U}), (c, \mathbf{O}), (d, \mathbf{I}), (e, \mathbf{O}), (f, \mathbf{U})\}$. If we remove the attack from c to b (labelled **O** and **U**, respectively) then L is no longer a semi-stable labelling. Instead we get the unique semi-stable labelling $L = \{(a, \mathbf{O}), (b, \mathbf{I}), (c, \mathbf{I}), (d, \mathbf{O}), (e, \mathbf{I}), (f, \mathbf{O})\}$.

*Example 8 (Failure of **UO** removal persistence under semi-stable semantics).* The AF shown in Fig. 2 has a unique semi-stable labelling $L = \{(a, \mathbf{U}), (b, \mathbf{I}), (c, \mathbf{O}), (d, \mathbf{U})\}$. If we remove the attack from a to c (labelled **U** and **O**) then L is no longer a semi-stable labelling. Instead we get the unique semi-stable labelling $\{(a, \mathbf{U}), (b, \mathbf{O}), (c, \mathbf{I}), (d, \mathbf{O})\}$.

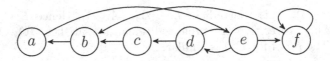

Fig. 4. Failure of **OU** removal persistence under semi-stable semantics.

Let us summarize the results obtained in this section. At the start we saw that under all semantics we consider, the **II**, **IU** and **UI** removal persistence are trivially satisfied. Furthermore, the **UU** and **IO** removal properties fail under all semantics, except for the stable semantics, which does not satisfy **IO** removal persistence but trivially satisfies all properties involving **U**-labelled arguments. As for the remaining properties, it holds that the grounded, complete and preferred semantics are all similar in that they all satisfy **OO**, **OU**, **OI** and **UO** removal persistence. However, the semi-stable semantics satisfies none of these properties. Table 2 contains an overview of these results.

Table 2. Overview of removal persistence properties.

Grounded:

	O	**U**	**I**
O	✓	✓	-
U	✓	-	✓
I	✓	✓	✓

(X across top, Y down left side)

Complete:

	O	**U**	**I**
O	✓	✓	-
U	✓	-	✓
I	✓	✓	✓

Preferred:

	O	**U**	**I**
O	✓	✓	-
U	✓	-	✓
I	✓	✓	✓

Stable:

	O	**U**	**I**
O	✓	✓	-
U	✓	✓	✓
I	✓	✓	✓

Semi-Stable:

	O	**U**	**I**
O	-	-	-
U	-	-	✓
I	-	✓	✓

5   Skeptical Monotony

Suppose that two arguments x and y are labelled X and Y in all σ labellings of F. The XY addition persistence property then implies that all σ labellings of F are also σ labellings of F after adding an attack from x to y. In other words, XY addition persistence implies that no σ labelling gets destroyed. But is it also the case that no new labellings are created? This is the property that we consider in this section. We call it *skeptical XY monotony*.

Definition 10. *Let σ be a semanitcs and let $X, Y \in \{\mathbf{O}, \mathbf{I}, \mathbf{U}\}$. We say that σ satisfies XY skeptical monotony if and only if for all $(A, \rightsquigarrow) \in \mathcal{F}$ and $x, y \in A$: If for all $L \in \mathcal{L}_\sigma((A, \rightsquigarrow))$, $L(x) = X$ and $L(y) = Y$, then $\mathcal{L}_\sigma((A, \rightsquigarrow \cup \{(x,y)\})) \subseteq \mathcal{L}_\sigma((A, \rightsquigarrow))$.*

Like before, it is obvious that for some combinations of X and Y, the semantics we consider do not satisfy skeptical XY monotony. If x and y are both labelled **I** then adding an attack creates a complete labelling which is not a complete labelling of the initial AF. Thus, skeptical **II** monotony fails, and skeptical **IU** and **UI** monotony fail for the same reason, except under the stable semantics, which does not satisfy **II** skeptical monotony but trivially satisfies all properties involving **U** labelled arguments.

Proposition 7. *The grounded, complete, preferred and semi-stable semantics do not satisfy* **II**, **IU** *or* **UI** *skeptical monotony.*

Proposition 8. *The stable semantics satisfies* **UO**, **UU**, **UI**, **UO** *and* **UI** *skeptical monotony but does not satisfy* **II** *skeptical monotony.*

In the rest of this section we focus on the remaining properties, namely **OO**, **OU**, **OI**, **UO**, **UU** and **IO** skeptical monotony. Again, all these properties may be considered desirable. For example, **OO** skeptical monotony reflects the principle that adding an attack between two arguments that are both labelled **O** in every labelling does not lead to the creation of new points of view on argument acceptance. This is intuitive because the added attack does not introduce a conflict with respect to any of the labellings of the initial AF. The other skeptical monotony properties may be considered desirable for the same reason. We now check whether the semantics we consider satisfy these properties.

Let us start with the grounded semantics. Because the grounded labelling is unique, there is no difference between XY skeptical monotony and XY addition persistence. Thus, the following result follows immediately from Theorem 1.

Theorem 8. *The grounded semantics satisfies* **OO**, **OU**, **UO**, **UU** *and* **IO** *skeptical monotony but not* **OI** *skeptical monotony.*

We move on to the complete semantics.

Theorem 9. *The complete semantics satisfies* **OO**, **OU**, **UO** *and* **IO** *skeptical monotony but not* **UU** *or* **OI** *skeptical monotony.*

Proof. Let $(A, \rightsquigarrow) \in \mathcal{F}$ and $x, y \in A$. If $x \rightsquigarrow y$ we are done. In the remainder we assume that $x \not\rightsquigarrow y$. The **OO**, **OU**, **UO** and **IO** cases can be reduced to the following two cases:

- For all $L \in \mathcal{L}_{co}((A, \rightsquigarrow))$, $L(y) = \mathbf{O}$. Then y is **O** in the grounded labelling of F. Hence there is a $z \in A$ s.t. $z \rightsquigarrow y$ and z is **I** in the grounded labelling of $(A, \rightsquigarrow)$. Furthermore since $x \not\rightsquigarrow y$ it holds that $x \neq z$. Theorem 1 implies that y is **O** and z is **I** in the grounded labelling of $(A, \rightsquigarrow \cup\{(x,y)\})$. Hence for all $L \in \mathcal{L}_{co}((A, \rightsquigarrow \cup\{(x,y)\}))$, $L(y) = \mathbf{O}$ and $L(z) = \mathbf{I}$. Definition 6 implies that $\mathcal{L}_{co}((A, \rightsquigarrow \cup\{(x,y)\})) \subseteq \mathcal{L}_{co}((A, \rightsquigarrow))$.
- For all $L \in \mathcal{L}_{co}((A, \rightsquigarrow))$, $L(x) = \mathbf{O}$ and $L(y) = \mathbf{U}$. Then x is **O** and y is **U** in the grounded labelling of F. Theorem 1 implies that x is **O** in the grounded labelling of $(A, \rightsquigarrow \cup\{(x,y)\})$. Hence for all $L \in \mathcal{L}_{co}((A, \rightsquigarrow \cup\{(x,y)\}))$, $L(x) = \mathbf{O}$. Theorem 6 implies that $\mathcal{L}_{co}((A, \rightsquigarrow \cup\{(x,y)\})) \subseteq \mathcal{L}_{co}((A, \rightsquigarrow))$.

Counterexamples for **OI** and **UU** skeptical monotony are provided below.

Example 9 (Failure of **OI** *and* **UU** *skeptical monotony under the complete semantics).* Consider an AF with two arguments a and b where a attacks b. This AF has a unique complete labelling $\{(a, \mathbf{I}), (b, \mathbf{O})\}$. Adding an attack from b to a leads to an additional complete labelling $\{(a, \mathbf{O}), (b, \mathbf{I})\}$. A counterexample for **UU** skeptical monotony can be constructed by making a self-attacking.

The preferred semantics satisfies none of the remaining properties.

Theorem 10. *The preferred semantics does not satisfy* **OO**, **OU**, **OI**, **UO**, **UU** *or* **IO** *skeptical monotony.*

Example 9 is also a counterexample for **OI** and **UU** skeptical monotony under the preferred semantics. Counterexamples for the other cases are provided below.

Example 10 (Failure of **IO** *and* **OO** *skeptical monotony under preferred semantics).* The AF shown in Fig. 3 has one preferred labelling $\{(a, \mathbf{O}), (b, \mathbf{I}), (c, \mathbf{O}),$ $(d, \mathbf{I}), (e, \mathbf{O}), (f, \mathbf{U})\}$. Adding an attack from e to c (both **O** in all preferred labellings) or from b to c (**I** and **O** in all preferred labellings) leads to a new preferred labelling that is not a preferred labelling of the initial AF: $\{(a, \mathbf{O}), (b, \mathbf{I}),$ $(c, \mathbf{O}), (d, \mathbf{O}), (e, \mathbf{I}), (f, \mathbf{O})\}$.

Example 11 (Failure of **OU** *skeptical monotony under the preferred semantics).* The AF shown in Fig. 2 has one preferred labelling $\{(a, \mathbf{U}), (b, \mathbf{I}), (c, \mathbf{O}), (d, \mathbf{U})\}$. Adding add an attack from c to a (labelled **O** and **U** in all preferred labellings) leads to a new preferred labelling that is not a preferred labelling of the initial AF: $\{(a, \mathbf{O}), (b, \mathbf{O}), (c, \mathbf{I}), (d, \mathbf{O})\}$.

Example 12 (Failure of **UO** *skeptical monotony under the preferred semantics).* The AF shown in Fig. 1 has one preferred labelling $\{(a, \mathbf{I}), (b, \mathbf{O}), (c, \mathbf{I}),$ $(d, \mathbf{O}), (e, \mathbf{U}), (f, \mathbf{U})\}$. Adding an attack from f to b (labelled **U** and **O** in all preferred labellings) leads to a new preferred labelling that is not a preferred labelling of the initial AF: $\{(a, \mathbf{I}), (b, \mathbf{O}), (c, \mathbf{O}), (d, \mathbf{I}), (e, \mathbf{O}), (f, \mathbf{I})\}$.

The stable semantics satisfies none of the XY skeptical monotony properties, except those that are trivially satisfied due to **U** labelled arguments, as established in Proposition 8.

Theorem 11. *Stable semantics does not satisfy* **OO**, **OI**, **IO** *skeptical monotony.*

For the **OO** and **IO** case, Example 10 can be turned into a counterexample by removing from the AF shown in Fig. 3 the argument f. For the **OI** case, Example 9 counts as a counterexample.

Like the preferred semantics, the semi-stable semantics satisfies none of the remaining XY skeptical monotony properties.

Theorem 12. *The semi-stable semantics does not satisfy* **OO**, **OU**, **OI**, **UO**, **UU** *or* **IO** *skeptical monotony.*

All counterexamples for the preferred case (Examples 9, 10, 11 and 12) also apply in the semi-stable case.

Let us summarize the results of this section. At the start we established that under all the semantics we consider, the **II**, **IU** and **UI** skeptical monotony properties fail. The exception is the stable semantics, which fails **II** skeptical monotony but trivially satisfies properties involving **U**-labelled arguments. Furthermore, the results for skeptical monotony under the grounded semantics coincide with the results of addition persistence. Finally, while the complete semantics still satisfies **OO**, **OU**, **UO** and **IO** skeptical monotony, the preferred and semi-stable semantics satisfy none of the skeptical monotony properties. Table 3 contains an overview of these results.

Table 3. Overview of skeptical monotony properties.

Grounded:

	X		
	O	U	I
O	✓	✓	✓
Y U	✓	✓	-
I	-	-	-

Complete:

	X		
	O	U	I
O	✓	✓	✓
Y U	✓	-	-
I	-	-	-

Preferred:

	X		
	O	U	I
O	-	-	-
Y U	-	-	-
I	-	-	-

Stable:

	X		
	O	U	I
O	-	✓	-
Y U	✓	✓	✓
I	-	✓	-

Semi-Stable:

	X		
	O	U	I
O	-	-	-
Y U	-	-	-
I	-	-	-

6 Related Work

As we mentioned, our work extends the approach of Boella et al. [4,5]. The refinement and abstraction principles that they studied are, in the single-extension case that they consider, equivalent to the addition and removal persistence properties. Indeed, the results we obtained for the grounded semantics coincide with theirs. As we discussed, our results extend theirs in a number of ways.

Our work is also related to earlier work we did on counterfactuals in argumentation. Sakama studied counterfactuals of the form $\alpha \Box\!\rightarrow \beta$ (meaning "if α were true then β would be true") where α and β are literals of the form $\mathbf{I}(x)$ or $\mathbf{O}(x)$ [15]. A counterfactual $\alpha \Box\!\rightarrow \beta$ is true w.r.t. an AF F and semantics σ if the change of F represented by α leads to the truth of β in all σ labellings of F. Here, the premise $\mathbf{O}(x)$ represents the addition of a new argument attacking x, while $\mathbf{I}(x)$ represents the removal of all attacks pointing to x. Rienstra's approach [14] is similar, and is based on a relation $\Vdash_\sigma^F$ determined by an AF F and semantics σ, between so called interventions and consequences. An intervention is a set of literals of the form $\mathbf{O}(x)$ or $\neg\mathbf{I}(x)$ that represent, respectively, addition of a new argument attacking x or of a new self-attacking argument attacking x. A formula ϕ is a consequence of an intervention Φ (written $\Phi \Vdash_\sigma^F \phi$) if the change represented by Φ leads to the truth of ϕ in all σ labellings of F. A number of properties that were studied using these models follow from the results that we have obtained. For example, failure of *Cautious Monotony* (if $\Phi \Vdash_\sigma^F \alpha$ and $\Phi \Vdash_\sigma^F \phi$ then $\Phi \cup \{\alpha\} \Vdash_\sigma^F \phi$) under the preferred semantics demonstrated by

Rienstra follows from the failure of **IO** skeptical monotony (Theorem 10). Similarly, the failure of *Cut* (if $\Phi \Vdash_\sigma^F \alpha$ and $\Phi \cup \{\alpha\} \Vdash_\sigma^F \phi$ then $\Phi \Vdash_\sigma^F \phi$) under the semi-stable semantics follows from the failure of **IO** addition persistence (Theorem 5).

Cayrol et al. [9] studied the impact on the evaluation of an argumentation framework when new arguments and attacks are added. They define a number of properties to characterize this impact. Examples are changes leading to a larger, unique, or smaller set of extensions, changes that are monotonic (every extension of the old AF is included in an extension of the changed AF) and monotony w.r.t. an argument (every argument included in an extension of the old AF is also included in an extension of the changed AF). Then they study the relation between these properties and determine some conditions under which the addition of an argument leads to a certain type of change.

The results we obtained can be contrasted with the characterization of the *strong equivalence* relation between AFs [12]. Two AFs are strongly equivalent with respect to a semantics if they generate equivalent sets of extensions, and this equivalence is robust with respect to the addition of new arguments and attacks to both AFs. The characterization of this relation shows that the presence and absence of an attack from an argument x to an argument y are indistinguishable if certain syntactical conditions are met. Examples of such conditions are that one or both of x and y are self attacking, or that y attacks x. Oikarinen and Woltran [12] have determined the exact condition for a number of different semantics. The results that we obtained also imply that in certain cases, the presence and absence of an attack between two arguments x and y are indistinguishable. In our case, however, the conditions are not syntactic but depend on the status of x and y.

7   Conclusion and Future Work

We studied a number of properties concerning the behaviour of semantics for abstract argumentation when the AF changes. The properties are concerned with how the evaluation of an AF changes if an attack between two arguments is added or removed. The results provide insight into the behaviour of these semantics in a dynamic context. In particular, we have shown that the complete semantics satisfies all the intuitive properties that we have considered, that the grounded, preferred and stable semantics fail some of them, and that the semi-stable semantics fail all of them.

We plan to extend the current line of research in a number of ways. First of all, we plan to study weaker versions of the properties considered in this paper, look at skeptical monotony with respect to removal and obtain results with respect to semantics that were not considered here. Furthermore, we plan to study connections between the properties considered here and in other work on the behaviour of semantics of argumentation, such as strong equivalence [12], input/output behaviour [1] and directionality [2]. Finally, we expect that the results we have obtained will be useful in the ongoing research into modelling dynamical aspects of abstract argumentation, such as counterfactuals, abduction and revision.

References

1. Baroni, P., Boella, G., Cerutti, F., Giacomin, M., van der Torre, L., Villata, S.: On the input/output behavior of argumentation frameworks. Artif. Intell. **217**, 144–197 (2014)
2. Baroni, P., Giacomin, M.: On principle-based evaluation of extension-based argumentation semantics. Artif. Intell. **171**(10–15), 675–700 (2007)
3. Baumann, R., Brewka, G.: Expanding argumentation frameworks: Enforcing and monotonicity results. In: COMMA 2010, Desenzano del Garda, Italy, 8–10 September 2010, volume 216 of Frontiers in Artificial Intelligence and Applications, pages 75–86. IOS Press, 2010
4. Boella, G., Kaci, S., van der Torre, L.: Dynamics in argumentation with single extensions: abstraction principles and the grounded extension. In: Sossai, C., Chemello, G. (eds.) ECSQARU 2009. LNCS, vol. 5590, pp. 107–118. Springer, Heidelberg (2009)
5. Boella, G., Kaci, S., van der Torre, L.: Dynamics in argumentation with single extensions: attack refinement and the grounded extension (extended version). In: McBurney, P., Rahwan, I., Parsons, S., Maudet, N. (eds.) ArgMAS 2009. LNCS, vol. 6057, pp. 150–159. Springer, Heidelberg (2010)
6. Booth, R., Kaci, S., Rienstra, T., van der Torre, L.: A logical theory about dynamics in abstract argumentation. In: Liu, W., Subrahmanian, V.S., Wijsen, J. (eds.) SUM 2013. LNCS, vol. 8078, pp. 148–161. Springer, Heidelberg (2013)
7. Caminada, M.: On the issue of reinstatement in argumentation. In: Fisher, M., van der Hoek, W., Konev, B., Lisitsa, A. (eds.) JELIA 2006. LNCS (LNAI), vol. 4160, pp. 111–123. Springer, Heidelberg (2006)
8. Caminada, M.W.A., Gabbay, D.M.: A logical account of formal argumentation. Stud. Logica **93**(2–3), 109–145 (2009)
9. Cayrol, C., de Saint-Cyr, F.D., Lagasquie-Schiex, M.-C.: Change in abstract argumentation frameworks: adding an argument. J. Artif. Intell. Res. **38**, 49–84 (2010)
10. Coste-Marquis, S., Konieczny, S., Mailly, J.-G., Marquis, P.: On the revision of argumentation systems: Minimal change of arguments statuses. In: 14th International Conference on Principles of Knowledge Representation and Reasoning, KR 2014, Vienna, Austria, 20–24 July 2014. AAAI Press (2014)
11. Dung, P.M.: On the acceptability of arguments and its fundamental role in nonmonotonic reasoning, logic programming and n-person games. Artif. Intell. **77**(2), 321–358 (1995)
12. Oikarinen, E., Woltran, S.: Characterizing strong equivalence for argumentation frameworks. Artif. Intell. **175**(14–15), 1985–2009 (2011)
13. Pollock, J.L.: Cognitive Carpentry: A Blueprint for How to Build a Person. MIT Press, Cambridge (1995)
14. Rienstra, T.: Argumentation in Flux - Modelling Change in the Theory of Argumentation. Ph.D. thesis, University of Luxembourg/University of Montpellier II (2014)
15. Sakama, C.: Counterfactual reasoning in argumentation frameworks. In: Proceedings of COMMA 2014, Frontiers in Artificial Intelligence and Applications, Atholl Palace Hotel, Scottish Highlands, UK, 9–12 September 2014, vol. 266, pp. 385–396. IOS Press (2014)

Argumentation-based Normative Practical Reasoning

Zohreh Shams[1]($\boxtimes$), Marina De Vos[1], Nir Oren[2],
Julian Padget[1], and Ken Satoh[3]

[1] Department of Computer Science, University of Bath, Bath, UK
{z.shams,m.d.vos,j.a.padget}@bath.ac.uk
[2] Department of Computer Science, University of Aberdeen, Aberdeen, UK
n.oren@abdn.ac.uk
[3] National Institute of Informatics, Tokyo, Japan
ksatoh@nii.ac.jp

Abstract. Reasoning about what is best for an agent to do in a particular situation is a challenging task. What makes it even more challenging in a dynamic environment is the existence of norms that aim to regulate a self-interested agent's behaviour. Practical reasoning is reasoning about what to do in a given situation, particularly in the presence of conflicts between the agent's practical attitude such as goals, plans and norms. In this paper we: (i) introduce a formal model for normative practical reasoning that allows an agent to plan for multiple and potentially conflicting goals and norms at the same time (ii) identify the best plan(s) for the agent to execute by means of argumentation schemes and critical questions (iii) justify the best plan(s) via an argumentation-based persuasion dialogue for grounded semantics.

1 Introduction

Autonomous agents operating in a dynamic environment must be able to reason and make decisions about actions in pursuit of their goals. In addition, in a normative environment an agent's actions are not only directed by the agent's goals, but also by the norms imposed on the agent. Norms are a well understood approach for declaratively specifying desirable behaviour by stating under which circumstances the performance of which actions or reaching which states are obliged or prohibited. When modelled as soft constraints, norms allow more flexible behaviour by defining a reward and punishment associated with compliance and violation. To avoid punishment, agents must comply with norms while pursuing their goals. However, if complying with a norm hinders a more important goal or norm, the agent should consider violating it. In order to decide what to do, an agent performing normative practical reasoning therefore needs to constantly weigh up the importance of goal achievement and norm compliance against the cost of goals being ignored and norms being violated, in different plans.

© Springer International Publishing Switzerland 2015
E. Black et al. (Eds.): TAFA 2015, LNAI 9524, pp. 226–242, 2015.
DOI: 10.1007/978-3-319-28460-6_14

Although practical reasoning frameworks that take norms into account exist (e.g. [8,11,16], there has been little attention paid to the explanation and justification of agents' decision making in such frameworks. The conflicts that arise between the practical attitudes of agents, such as goals, plans and norms, can make explaining the agent's decision making process very complicated. Argumentation has been shown to be a promising means for reasoning in the presence of inconsistent information [13]. In addition to assisting agents' reasoning, argumentation supports explaining agents' decision making via argumentation-based dialogues (e.g. [21]). Argumentation has previously been applied in practical reasoning and in the justification of the agent's decision making (e.g. [4,17,20]). However, the existing approaches suffer from at least one of the following problems: (i) the normative aspects of the agents operating in a dynamic environment are not taken into consideration [4,20]; (ii) the planning aspects of the practical reasoning problem is either abstracted away, or is not computationally implemented [4,17,20]; (iii) the conflicts identified between actions, goals, norms and plans are static and disregard the temporal essence of conflict [20].

In this paper we aim at presenting a model that integrates normative reasoning into practical reasoning. The model is implemented formally in a way that handles *durative* actions and time explicitly, hence enriching reasoning about conflicts. In order to develop a pattern of arguments to reason about conflicts in such a model, we use *argument schemes* and their associated *critical questions* [22]. Argument schemes are reasoning patterns expressed in natural language and critical questions are situations in which the scheme does not apply and are used to question the arguments constructed based on the schemes. These argument schemes employed in an argumentation framework (AF) enable the agent to identify and justify the best course of action. Although all of the existing approaches mentioned earlier use argumentation to identify the best course of actions for the agent to take, to the best of our knowledge our framework is the first one that uses the argumentation-based persuasion dialogue in [10] to engage in an internal dialogue to justify this choice.

The paper is organised as follows. After describing the formal model in the next section, we discuss arguments and their relations in Sect. 3. Section 4 demonstrates the dialogue used in this work, followed by an illustrative example in Sect. 5. Related work and conclusions are discussed in Sects. 6 and 7, respectively.

2   A Formal Model for Normative Practical Reasoning

This section offers a formal model and its semantics for normative practical reasoning. The foundation of this model is classical planning in which an agent is presented with a set of actions and a goal. Any sequence of actions that satisfies the goal is a solution for the planning problem. In Sect. 2.1 we extend the classical planning problem by substituting a single goal with a set of potentially inconsistent goals G and a corresponding set of norms N. A solution for such a problem is any sequence of actions that satisfies at least one goal. The agent has the choice of violating or complying with triggered norms, while satisfying its goals.

2.1   The Model

A normative temporal planning system is a tuple $P = (FL, \Delta, A, G, N)$ where FL is a set of fluents, Δ is the initial state, A is a set of durative STRIPS-like [14] actions, G denotes the set of agent goals and N denotes a set of norms imposed on the agent actions, that define what an agent is obliged or forbidden to do under certain conditions. We now describe each of these elements in more details.

Fluents. FL is a set of domain fluents that accounts for the description of the domain the agent operates in. A literal l is a fluent or its negation i.e. $l = fl$ or $l = \neg fl$ for some $fl \in FL$. For a set of literals L, we define $L^+ = \{fl | fl \in L\}$ and $L^- = \{fl | \neg fl \in L\}$ to denote the set of positive and negative fluents in L respectively. L is well-defined if there exists no fluent $fl \in FL$ such that $fl \in L$ and $\neg fl \in L$, i.e. if $L^+ \cap L^- = \emptyset$.

The semantics of the model are defined over a set of states S. A state $s \subseteq FL$ is determined by set of fluents that hold *true* at a given time, while other fluents (those not present) are considered false. A state $s \in S$ satisfies fluent $fl \in FL$ (i.e. $s \models fl$) if $fl \in s$ and it satisfies its negation $\neg fl$ if $fl \notin s$. This notation can be extended to a set of literals as follows: the set X is satisfied in state s, where $s \models x$, when $\forall x \in X \cdot s \models x$.

Initial State. The set of fluents that hold at the initial state is denoted by $\Delta \subseteq FL$.

Actions. A is a set of durative STRIPS-like actions, that is actions with preconditions and postconditions that take a non-zero duration of time to have their effects in terms of their postconditions. A durative action $a = \langle pr, ps, d \rangle$ is composed of well-defined sets of literals $pr(a), ps(a)$ to represents a's preconditions and postconditions and a positive number $d(a) \in \mathbb{N}$ for its duration. Postconditions are further divided into a set of add postconditions $ps(a)^+$ and a set of delete postconditions $ps(a)^-$. An action a can be executed in a state s if its preconditions hold in s (i.e. $s \models pr(a)$). The postconditions of a durative action are applied in the state s at which the action ends (i.e. $s \models ps(a)^+$ and $s \not\models ps(a)^-$).

The model allows concurrency unless there is a concurrency conflict between some actions, which prevents them from being executed in an overlapping period of time. Two actions a_1 and a_2 are in a concurrency conflict if the preconditions or postconditions of a_1 contradicts the preconditions or postconditions of a_2 [7].

Goals. G denotes a set of (possibly inconsistent) goals. Goals identify the state of affairs in the world that an agent wants to satisfy. Each goal $g \in G$ is defined as a well-defined set of literals, that should hold in order to satisfy the goal. Goal g is satisfied in the state s when $s \models g$. A set of goal $G_i \subseteq G$ is consistent iff $\not\exists g_1, g_2$ s.t. $g_1 \cup g_2$ is not well-defined.

Norms. N denotes a set of event-based norms to which the agent is subject. Each norm is a quadruple of the form $\langle d\_o, a_1, a_2, d \rangle$, where

- $d\_o \in \{o, f\}$ is the deontic operator determining the type of norm, which can be an obligation or prohibition.
- $a_1 \in A$ is the action that counts as the norm activation condition.
- $a_2 \in A$ is the action that is subject to obligation or prohibition.
- $d \in N$ is the norm deadline that is a time instant defined relative to the activation of the norm through the execution of a_1.

An obligation norm expresses that taking action a_1 obliges the agent to take action a_2 within d time units of norm activation. Such an obligation is complied with if the agent starts executing a_2 before the deadline and is violated otherwise. A prohibition norm expresses that taking action a_1 prohibits the agent from taking action a_2 within d time units of norm activation. Such a prohibition is complied with if the agent does not take a_2 before the deadline and is violated otherwise.

2.2   Semantics of the Model

Suppose that $P = (FL, \Delta, A, G, N)$ is a normative planning problem with the syntax given previously. A plan is represented by a sequence of actions taken at certain times, denoted as: $\pi = \langle (a_0, t_0), \cdots, (a_n, t_n) \rangle$, which means that action a_i is executed at time $t_i \in \mathbb{Z}^+$ s.t. $\forall i < j$ we have $t_i < t_j$. The total duration of a plan, $Makespan(\pi)$, is calculated by the relation: $Makespan(\pi) = max(t_i + d(a_i))$. The evolution of a sequence of actions for a given starting state $s_0 = \Delta$ is a sequence of states $\langle s_0, \cdots s_m \rangle$ for every discrete time interval from t_0 to m, where $m = Makespan(\pi)$. The transition relation between two states is defined by Eq. 1. If an action a_j ends at time t_i, state s_i results from removing all negative postconditions and adding all positive postconditions of action a_j to state s_{i-1}. If there is no action ending at s_i, s_i remains the same as s_{i-1}.

$$\forall i > 0 : s_i = \begin{cases} (s_{i-1} \setminus ps(a_j)^-) \cup ps(a_j)^+ & i = t_j + d(a_j) \\ s_{i-1} & \text{otherwise} \end{cases} \quad (1)$$

A sequence of actions π satisfies a goal, $s \models g$, if there is at least one state s_i in the sequence of states caused by the sequence of actions in π, such that $s_i \models g$. We therefore have $\pi \models G_j$ iff $\forall g \in G_j, \exists i \in [1, m]$ such that $s_i \models g$. An obligation $n_1 = \langle o, a_i, a_j, d \rangle$ is complied with in plan π (i.e. $\pi \models n_1$) if the action that is the norm activation condition has occurred $((a_i, t_i) \in \pi)$, and the action that is the subject of the obligation occurs $((a_j, t_j) \in \pi)$ between when the condition holds and when the deadline expires $(t_j \in (t_i, d + t_i))$. If a_i has occurred but a_j does not occur at all or occurs in a period other than the one specified, the obligation is violated (i.e. $\pi \not\models n_1$). In the case of prohibition $n_2 = \langle f, a_i, a_j, d \rangle$, compliance happens if the action that is the norm activation condition has occurred $((a_i, t_i) \in \pi)$ and the action that is the subject of the prohibition does not occur in the period between when the condition holds and when the deadline expires ($\nexists (a_j, t_j) \in \pi$ s.t. $t_j \in (t_i, d + t_i)$). If a_i has occurred and a_j occurs in the specified period, the prohibition norm is violated (i.e. $\pi \not\models n_2$).

Two obligation norms $n_1 = \langle o, a_1, a_2, d \rangle$ and $n_2 = \langle o, b_1, b_2, d' \rangle$ are in conflict in the context of plan π iff: (1) their activation conditions hold, (2) the obliged actions a_2 and b_2 have a concurrency conflict and (3) a_2 is in progress during the entire period over which the agent is obliged to take action b_2. On the other hand, a norm of type obligation $n_1 = \langle o, a_1, a_2, d \rangle$ and a norm of type prohibition $n_2 = \langle f, b_1, a_2, d' \rangle$ are in conflict in the context of plan π iff: (1) their activation conditions hold and (2) n_2 forbids the agent from taking action a_2 during the entire period over which n_1 obliges the agent to take a_2.

A norm of type obligation $n = \langle o, a_1, a_2, d \rangle$ and a goal g are in conflict, if taking action a_2 that is the subject of the obligation, brings about postconditions that are in conflict with the requirements of goal g. In addition, a norm of type prohibition $n = \langle f, a_1, a_2, d \rangle$ and a goal g are in conflict, if the postconditions of a_2 contribute to satisfying g, but taking action a_2 is prohibited by norm n. Sequence of actions $\pi = \langle (a_0, t_0), \cdots, (a_n, t_n) \rangle$ is a valid plan[1] and solution for P iff:

1. all the fluents in Δ hold at time t_0.
2. for each i, the preconditions of action a_i holds at time t_i, as well as through the execution of a_i.
3. a non-empty consistent subset of goals (i.e. $G_j \subseteq G$ and $G_j \neq \emptyset$) is satisfied in the path from initial state s_0 to the state holding at time t_m, where $m = Makespan(\pi)$.
4. there is no concurrency conflict between actions that are executed concurrently.
5. there is no conflict between any of the norms complied with.
6. there is no conflict between goals satisfied and norms complied with.

3   Argument Scheme and Critical Questions

The formal model explained in the previous section defines all possible plans Π that the agent can execute to satisfy at least one of its goals. Regarding norms, when the course of actions in a plan triggers a norm, the possible outcomes of violating or complying with that norm are generated separately. In order to identify the best plan(s) for the agent to execute, if any, we first augment the tuple $P = \langle FL, \Delta, A, G, N \rangle$ with a partial, irreflexive and transitive preference relation $Pref_{gn}$ that expresses agent's preferences over goals and norms: $Pref_{gn} \subseteq (G \cup N) \times (G \cup N)$. If the agent prefers satisfying goal α (or complying with norm α) over satisfying goal β (or complying with norm β), we have $(\alpha, \beta) \in Pref_{gn}$. The preference relation over plans, on the other hand, comes from the fact that the lesser number of violations is always preferred over more. Thus, plan π_1 is preferred over plan π_2, iff they satisfy the same set of goals, while π_1 has fewer violations. Assuming that the sets $satisfied_i$ and $violated_i$ define the set of satisfied goals and violated norms in plan π_i:

---

[1] We assume that plans are given by a sound planning system and make no further assumption about the implementation.

$satisfied_i = \{g_j | g_j \in G, \pi_i \models g_j\}$ and $violated_i = \{n_k | n_k \in N, \pi_i \not\models n_k\}$, we have: iff $satisfied_1 = satisfied_2, violated_1 \subsetneq violated_2$ then $(\pi_1, \pi_2) \in Pref_\pi$.

Having defined the preference relations $Pref_{gn}$ and $Pref_\pi$, we now use argument schemes and critical questions [22] to construct and evaluate a set of arguments involved in practical reasoning. The arguments and their relationships defined through arguments schemes and critical questions, respectively, plus arguments preferences that result from agent preferences discussed above, form a preference-based argumentation framework (PAF) [2]. The evaluation of such a PAF according to grounded semantics results in an unique extension containing a set of arguments that are justified in all senses. The choice of grounded semantics for sceptical reasoning has pragmatic and philosophical reasons that are discussed in details in [19]. By using a persuasion dialogue for the grounded semantics [10] in the next section, we justify how the plan argument(s) included in the grounded extension identify the best plan(s) for the agent to execute.

Definition 1. *A PAF is a triplet (Arg, Att, Pr) where Arg is a set of arguments, Att is a binary attack relation between arguments, $Att \subseteq Arg \times Arg$, and Pr is a (partial or complete) preordering on $Arg \times Arg$. Argument a is preferred over argument b iff $(a, b) \subset Pr$ and $(b, a) \notin Pr$. The defeat relation between two argument $Def \subseteq Arg \times Arg$ is therefore defined as: $\forall a, b \in Arg, a$ defeats b iff $(a, b) \in Att$ and $(b, a) \notin Pr$.*

The arguments, Arg, in the created PAF consists of three disjoint sets of arguments Arg_π, Arg_g, and Arg_n, obtained from three separate argument schemes defined in Sect. 3.1. The attack relation, Att, between arguments is instantiated through the application of six critical questions described in Sect. 3.2. The preference relations, Pr, between goal arguments and norm arguments results from the preference relations expressed by the agent over goals and norms: iff $(\alpha, \beta) \in Pref_{gn}$ then $(Arg_\alpha, Arg_\beta) \in Pr$. The same applies to plan arguments: iff $(\gamma, \lambda) \in Pref_\pi$ then $(Arg_\gamma, Arg_\lambda) \in Pr$.

3.1   Formal Model of Arguments

We now express three argumentation schemes in order to construct a set of arguments for normative practical reasoning: plan arguments, goal arguments and norm arguments. These arguments will be used to conduct the dialogue between a proponent that aims at convincing an opponent to accept why a particular plan should be executed. An opponent can question the proponent claim by asking why a certain goal was not satisfied in the proposed plan, or why a certain norm was violated.

AS1: This argument scheme results in constructing an argument for each plan (Arg_π) obtained from our formal model and is used by the agent to put forward a sequence of actions and as a proponent claims that the proposed sequence should be executed:

- In the initial state Δ
- The agent should perform sequence of actions $\pi = \langle (a_1, t_1), \cdots, (a_n, t_n) \rangle$
- which will realise set of goals G' ($\pi \models G'$) and complies with set of norms N' ($\pi \models N'$) and violates set of norms N'' ($\pi \not\models N''$)

AS2: This argument scheme results in constructing an argument for each goal that is *feasible*. A goal is feasible if it is satisfied in at least one plan. If a goal in not feasible, a rational agent should not adopt it or try to justify its adoption (for more details see [3]). A goal argument (Arg_g) is used by an opponent to explore why a goal is not satisfied in a plan, or to address the conflict between two goals or a goal and a norm:

- Goal g is a feasible goal of the agent
- Therefore, satisfying g is required.

AS3: This argument scheme results in constructing an argument for each norm (Arg_n) that is activated in at least one plan and is used by an opponent to explore why a norm is violated in a plan. It is also used to address the conflict between two norms or a goal and a norm. An activated norm is not necessarily activated in all plans. To allow reasoning about norms only in the context of the plans they are activated in, the norm (e.g. n_k) is augmented as (e.g. n_{ki}) where i is the index of the plan in which n_k is activated. Note that, this operation does not effect the preference relations discussed earlier. For instance, if the agent prefers satisfying g_2 to complying with norm n_1, $g_2 \succ n_1$, argument for this goal, Arg_{g_2}, is preferred to all the arguments for norm $Arg_{n_{1i}}$, where i is represents the plans in which norm n_1 was activated.

- Norm n_k is an activated norm imposed to the agent in plan π_i
- Therefore, complying with n_{ki} is required

3.2 Argument Interactions

The six critical questions in this section describe the ways arguments built in the previous section can attack each other. These CQs are associated to one or more AS, which are listed after each CQ.

CQ1 (AS2): Does a goal conflict with another goal? This CQ results in an attack between arguments for conflicting goals. Attacks caused by CQ1 are by definition symmetric and irreflexive. This can be formulated as:
Iff $g_1 \cup g_2$ is not well-defined then $(Arg_{g_1}, Arg_{g_2}), (Arg_{g_2}, Arg_{g_1}) \in Att$.

CQ2 (AS3): Does a norm conflict with another norm? Conflict between two norms is contextual based, the context being defined as the plan the norms are activated in. For instance, norms n_1 and n_2 might be in conflict in plan π_i (i.e., $Arg_{n_{1i}}$ and $Arg_{n_{2i}}$ attack each other) while they are conflict-free in plan π_j. Similar to CQ1, attacks caused by CQ2 are by definition symmetric and irreflexive. It is defined in Sect. 2.2 what it means for two norms to be conflicting. The definitions are formulated as follows.

Two obligation norms $n_1 = \langle o, a_1, a_2, d \rangle$ and $n_2 = \langle o, b_1, b_2, d' \rangle$ are in conflict in the context of plan π_i:

Iff $(a_1, t_{a_1}), (b_1, t_{b_1}), (a_2, t_{a_2}) \in \pi_i$, s.t. $t_{a_2} \in (t_{a_1}, t_{a_1} + d)$ and $(t_{b_1}, t_{b_1} + d') \subseteq (t_{a_2}, t_{a_2} + d(a_2))$ then $(Arg_{n_{1i}}, Arg_{n_{2i}}), (Arg_{n_{2i}}, Arg_{n_{1i}}) \in Att$.

A norm of type obligation $n_1 = \langle o, a_1, a_2, d \rangle$ and a norm of type prohibition $n_2 = \langle f, b_1, a_2, d' \rangle$ are in conflict in the context of plan π_i:

Iff $(a_1, t_{a_1}), (b_1, t_{b_1}) \in \pi_i$, s.t. $(t_{a_1}, t_{a_1} + d) \subseteq (t_{b_1}, t_{b_1} + d')$ then $(Arg_{n_{1i}}, Arg_{n_{2i}}), (Arg_{n_{2i}}, Arg_{n_{1i}}) \in Att$.

CQ3 (AS1): Is there any other preferred plan available? This CQ results in an attack from plan argument Arg_{π_1} to plan argument Arg_{π_2}, when plan π_1 is preferred over plan π_2. Attacks caused by CQ3 are by definition asymmetric and irreflexive:

Iff $(\pi_1, \pi_2) \in Pref_\pi$ then $(Arg_{\pi_1}, Arg_{\pi_2}) \in Att$.

CQ4 (AS1): Is there any conflict between a goal and a plan? This CQ results in an attack from a goal argument to a plan argument, when the goal is not satisfied in the plan. Attacks caused by CQ4 are by definition asymmetric and are formulated as:

Iff $\pi_i \not\models g_j$ then $(Arg_{g_j}, Arg_{\pi_i}) \in Att$.

CQ5 (AS2-AS3): Is there any conflict between a norm and a goal? The conflict between a norm and a goal is defined in Sect. 2.2 and is formulated below. Attacks caused by CQ5 are by definition symmetric.

A norm of type obligation $n_1 = \langle o, a_1, a_2, d \rangle$ and a goal g_j are in conflict:
iff $ps(a_2) \cup g_j$ is not well-defined then $\forall n_{1i}$, s.t. $\pi_i \in \Pi$: $(Arg_{n_{1i}}, Arg_{g_j})$, $(Arg_{g_j}, Arg_{n_{1i}}) \in Att$.

A norm of type prohibition $n_2 = \langle f, a_1, a_2, d \rangle$ and a goal g_j are in conflict:
iff $ps(a_2) \cap g_j \neq \emptyset$ then $\forall n_{2i}$, s.t. $\pi_i \in \Pi$: $(Arg_{n_{2i}}, Arg_{g_j}), (Arg_{g_j}, Arg_{n_{2i}}) \in Att$.

CQ6 (AS1): Is there any conflict between a norm and a plan? This CQ results in an attack from a norm argument to a plan argument, when the norm is violated in the plan. This asymmetric attack is formulated as: Iff $\pi_i \not\models n_j$ then $(Arg_{n_{ji}}, Arg_{\pi_i}) \in Att$.

3.3 Grounded Extension and Properties of Plan Arguments

We organise the instantiation of the arguments and their relations, as presented in the previous section, within a $PAF = (Arg, Att, Pr)$, which, based on Definition 1, can be mapped to a Dung $AF = (Arg, Def)$. The grounded extension of the AF, Gr, determines if a plan should be identified as a basis for the agent's action execution.

Property 1. For any plan π, $Arg_\pi \in Gr$ iff there is no plan better than π.

Property 2. Let ARG_π be the set of all plan arguments in the grounded extension: $ARG_\pi = \{Arg_\pi | Arg_\pi \in Gr\}$.

– if $ARG_\pi = \emptyset$, then a unique best plan does not exist.
– if $card(ARG_\pi) = 1$, then $Arg_\pi \in ARG_\pi$ is the best plan for the agent to execute.
– if $card(ARG_\pi) > 1$, then the preference information available is insufficient to identify a single best plan. Thus all $Arg_\pi \in ARG_\pi$ are the best plans and the agent can choose any of them as the basis of what to execute.

Property 3. If $card(ARG_\pi) = 1$ and Arg_π is the best plan then $\forall g_j \in G, n_k \in N$ s.t. $\pi \models g_j, \pi \models n_k$, we have: $Arg_{g_j}, Arg_{n_k} \in Gr$.

4   Persuasion Dialogue for Grounded Semantics

This section demonstrates a persuasion dialogue game for grounded semantics. The main motivation behind the development of argumentation-based dialogues is to bring the mathematical intuition behind the semantics closer to human way of interacting when trying to convince one another of their perspective. However, these dialogues have rarely been used in practice. The contribution of this paper is not in introducing a new dialogue, but instead is in applying an existing dialogue game to a practical reasoning problem, where the agent engages in this internal dialogue to justify why a plan(s) is the best plan(s) to execute. The purpose of the dialogue is to show that if a plan argument is in the grounded extension of an AF, the agent can dialectically point out the reason for why this particular course of action should be executed. The dialogue is based on Caminada's *complete and grounded labelling* that is stated in the following definition taken from [9].

Definition 2. *Let (Arg, Def) be a Dung argumentation framework, a (partial) argument labelling is a (partial) function $lab : Arg \rightarrow \{in, out, undec\}$. A non-partial argument labelling is called a complete labelling iff for each argument $a \in Arg$ it holds that a is labelled 'in' iff each attacker of a is labelled 'out' and a is labelled 'out' iff there exists an attacker of a that is labelled 'in'.*

A complete labelling is called the (unique) grounded labelling $\mathcal{L}_{gr}$ iff its set of in-labelled arguments is minimal (or equivalently, iff its set of out-labelled arguments is minimal, or iff its set of undec-labelled arguments is maximal among all complete labellings.

The persuasion dialogue for grounded semantics is defined such that for any argument $a \in Arg$ there exists a grounded discussion that is won by a proponent iff $\mathcal{L}_{gr}(a) = in$. A discussion move in this dialogue is a triple $\mathcal{M} = (\mathcal{P}, \mathcal{T}, \mathcal{L})$, where $\mathcal{P}$ is the player: $\mathcal{P} \in \{proponent, opponent\}$, $\mathcal{T}$ is one of the following moves: $\mathcal{T} \in \{claim, why, because, concede\}$ and $\mathcal{L}$ is a partial labelling. *claim* is always the first move in the dialogue put forward by proponent to claim that an argument is labelled *in*; *why* is a move available to the opponent to question the proponent about why an argument is labelled *in* or *out*; *because* is a move with which the proponent describes why a questioned argument is labelled in a particular way; and *concede* is the move uttered by the opponent to concede an argument being labelled *in* or *out* by the proponent earlier. The opponent is assumed to be maximally sceptical, conceding an argument is *in*, if it is already committed that all attackers are *out* and it concedes an argument is *out* if it is committed that at least one attacker is *in*.

The dialogue starts by the proponent (P) putting forward a claim that an argument is in *claim in(a)*. The proponent (P) and opponent (O) then take turns, while each turn for P contains a single *because* move, whereas in each turn O can play more than one *concede* and *why* move. However, O can question with *why* just one argument at a time. P gets committed to arguments used in *claim* and *because* moves, while O gets committed to *concede* moves. These moves can only be played if new commitment does not contradict a previous one. P uses the *because* move to provide reasons for *why* moves, put forward by O. The reason for an argument being labelled *in* can be provided only if all its attackers are labelled *out* and the reason for an argument being labelled *out* can be provided when at least one of its attackers is labelled *in*. When P or O cannot make any more moves the dialogue terminates. If on termination, O conceded the claim argument then P wins, otherwise O is the winner.

Using the dialogue described above, if there exists $Arg_\pi \in Arg$ s.t. $\mathcal{L}_{gr}(Arg_\pi) = in$, the proponent starting the discussion by move *claim in(Arg$_\pi$)* is guaranteed a winning strategy to justify plan π. The example in the following section shows the dialogue in action.

5   Illustrative Example

In this section, we provide a brief example that, for sake of space, just highlights the most important features of the proposed model. Let us consider an agent with the actions presented in Table 1. Apart from *attend_interview* that has duration two, the duration of all other actions is one. The agent has two goals namely, getting some qualification and going on strike. Getting the qualification requires the agent to pay the fee for the test, do an online theory test and attend an interview for oral examination: $g_1 = \{fee\_paid, test\_done, interview\_attended\}$. Going on strike on the other hand, requires the agent to be a member of union, not to go to work nor to attend any meeting on behalf of the company: $g_2 = \{union\_member, \neg office, \neg meeting\}$. Two of the agent's actions, *comp_funding* and *attend_interview*, have normative consequences captured in the two following norms:

$n_1 = \langle o, comp\_funding, attend\_meeting, 2 \rangle$: This norm expresses that if the agent uses company funds to pay the fee for the test she wants to take, she is obliged to attend a meeting on behalf of the company within 2 time units of execution of *comp_funding*.

$n_2 = \langle f, attend\_interview, attend\_meeting, 3 \rangle$: This norm expresses that attending the interview prohibits the agent from attending the meeting within 3 time units of taking action *attend_interview*.

Table 2 shows five plans for the agent, including the goal(s) satisfied and norms complied with or violated in each plan. The positive or negative signs next to each norm means the norm is being complied with or violated in the respective plan. The argumentation graph in Fig. 1 shows the arguments associated with plans, goals and norms in Table 2. Arguments $Arg_{\pi_1} - Arg_{\pi_5}$ are built based on $AS1$, Arg_{g_1} and Arg_{g_2} are based on $AS2$, and $Arg_{n_{11}} - Arg_{n_{25}}$ are based on $AS3$. The attack between arguments is labelled with the relevant critical question.

To show the role of agent preferences in reducing the two-way attacks to a one-way defeat, we assume two different set of preferences, Pr_1 and Pr_2 , for a PAF with set of Arg and Att in Fig. 1. Table 3 shows the agent preferences in the first column, while the second column translates the agent preferences to preferences between arguments. Finally, the grounded extension, Gr, of the argumentation graph based on each set of preferences is computed in the third column. In this specific example, each grounded extension includes a single plan, π_5 in Gr_1 and π_1 in Gr_2, that according to Property 2, is the best plan for the agent to execute.

Figures 2 and 3 show how by putting forward the argument for the best plan, that is Arg_{π_5} on the left hand side dialogue and Arg_{π_1} on the right hand side dialogue, the proponent can convince the opponent to accept this plan as the basis of what to do. Note that the dialogue is conducted after applying the preference information in Table 3 to the framework in Fig. 1. Moreover, these two dialogues are not the only possible dialogues. For example, in Fig. 3 instead of stating *because in*$(Arg_{n_{11}})$, the proponent could have put forward *because in*$(Arg_{n_{12}})$, or *because in*$(Arg_{n_{13}})$, or *because in*$(Arg_{n_{15}})$.

6   Related Work

Current work on argumentation-based practical reasoning can be broadly divided into two categories: logic-based (e.g. [1,3,15,20]) and scheme-based (e.g. [4,17]) approaches. In the former category (see details below) Dung's AF is used to generate a subset of consistent desires and plans to achieve them that are optimised in some sense. Whereas, in the approach proposed in this paper argumentation techniques, i.e. argument schemes and critical questions, are applied to a different step of the practical reasoning process, namely to identify and justify the best plan(s) out of a set of generated plans. Plans are generated by enabling the agent to plan for multiple goals together, which not only ensures the consistency of plans, it also gives a precise account of how the agent should execute the

Table 1. Agent actions

Preconditions	Actions	Postconditions
$\neg fee\_paid$	$comp\_funding$	fee_paid
$\neg test\_done, fee\_paid$	$take\_test$	$test\_done$
$\neg interview\_attended, fee\_paid$	$attend\_interview$	$interview\_attended$
$\neg meeting\_attended, office, fee\_paid$	$attend\_meeting$	$meeting\_attended$
$\neg union\_member$	$join\_union$	$union\_member$

Table 2. Agent plans

Plans	Goals	Norms
$\pi_1 = \langle (comp\_funding, 0), (attend\_meeting, 1),$ $(take\_test, 2), (attend\_interview, 3) \rangle$	g_1	$+n_{11}, +n_{21}$
$\pi_2 = \langle (comp\_funding, 0), (attend\_interview, 1),$ $(take\_test, 2) \rangle$	g_1	$-n_{12}, +n_{22}$
$\pi_3 = \langle (comp\_funding, 0), (attend\_interview, 1),$ $(attend\_meeting, 2), (take\_test, 3) \rangle$	g_1	$+n_{13}, -n_{23}$
$\pi_4 = \langle (join\_union, 0) \rangle$	g_2	N/A
$\pi_5 = \langle (join\_union, 0), (comp\_funding, 1),$ $(attend\_interview, 2), (take\_test, 3) \rangle$	g_1, g_2	$-n_{15}, +n_{25}$

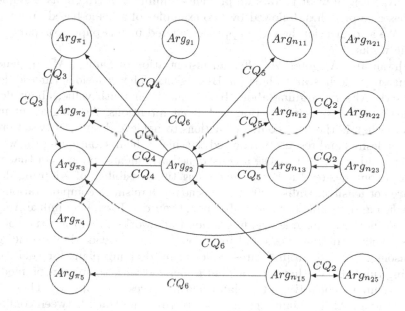

Fig. 1. Argumentation framework of the example

Table 3. Grounded extensions of graph 1

Agent preferences	Argument preferences	Grounded extension
$Pref_1 = \{(g_2, n_1),$ $(n_1, n_2)\}$	$Pr_1 = \{(Arg_{g_2}, Arg_{n_{11}}), (Arg_{g_2}, Arg_{n_{12}}),$ $(Arg_{g_2}, Arg_{n_{13}}), (Arg_{g_2}, Arg_{n_{15}}),$ $(Arg_{n_{11}}, Arg_{n_{21}}), (Arg_{n_{12}}, Arg_{n_{22}}),$ $(Arg_{n_{13}}, Arg_{n_{23}}), (Arg_{n_{15}}, Arg_{n_{25}})\}$	$Gr_1 = \{Arg_{g_1}, Arg_{g_2}, Arg_{n_{21}},$ $Arg_{n_{22}}, Arg_{n_{23}}, Arg_{n_{25}},$ $Arg_{\pi_5}\}$
$Pref_2 = \{(n_1, n_2),$ $(n_2, g_2)\}$	$Pr_2 = \{(Arg_{n_{11}}, Arg_{n_{21}}), (Arg_{n_{12}}, Arg_{n_{22}}),$ $(Arg_{n_{13}}, Arg_{n_{23}}), (Arg_{n_{15}}, Arg_{n_{25}}),$ $(Arg_{n_{21}}, Arg_{g_2}), (Arg_{n_{22}}, Arg_{g_2}),$ $(Arg_{n_{23}}, Arg_{g_2}), (Arg_{n_{25}}, Arg_{g_2})\}$	$Gr_2 = \{Arg_{g_1}, Arg_{n_{11}} Arg_{n_{21}},$ $Arg_{n_{12}}, Arg_{n_{13}}, Arg_{n_{15}},$ $Arg_{\pi_1}\}$

1. P: *claim in*(Arg_{π_5})
2. O: *why in*(Arg_{π_5})
3. P: *because out*($Arg_{n_{15}}$)
4. O: *why out*($Arg_{n_{15}}$)
5. P: *because in*(Arg_{g_2})
6. O: *concede in*(Arg_{g_2})
7. O: *concede out*($Arg_{n_{15}}$)
8. O: *concede in*(Arg_{π_5})

1. P: *claim in*(Arg_{π_1})
2. O: *why in*(Arg_{π_1})
3. P: *because out*(Arg_{g_2})
4. O: *why out*(Arg_{g_2})
5. P: *because in*($Arg_{n_{11}}$)
6. O: *concede in*($Arg_{n_{11}}$)
7. O: *concede out*(Arg_{g_2})
8. O: *concede in*(Arg_{π_1})

Fig. 2. Persuasion Dialogue for π_5 in Gr_1

Fig. 3. Persuasion dialogue for π_1 in Gr_2

actions in those plans (e.g. in which order, in what time, consequently or concurrently, etc.). In what follows we provide a summary of [15,20] as examples of logic-based approaches, followed by two examples of scheme-based approaches, [4,17]. We also mention how the approach offered in this paper compared with existing works.

Rahwan and Amgoud [20] offer an instantiation of Dung's AF for generating consistent desires and plans for BDI agents. They consider three different Dung style AFs for arguing about beliefs and their truth value, about desires and justification of their adoption and about intentions. Arguing about intention, i.e. what is the best course of actions to achieve desires, is based on the utility of desires and resources required to achieve them. Continuing the work of [20], Amgoud et al. [3] propose a constrained argumentation system that takes arguing about desires further by excluding the possibility of adopting desires that are not feasible. Unlike [20], there is no mechanism to compare various sets of justified and feasible desires. Hulstijn and van der Torre [15], unlike Amgoud [1,20], do not use multiple argumentation frameworks to capture the conflicts between beliefs, desires/goals and intentions/plans. Instead, they extract goals by reasoning forward from desires, followed by deriving plans for goals, using planning rules. Goals that have a plan associated with them, can be modelled as an argument consisting of a claim and its necessary support. These arguments form an AF for planning, in which there is an attack between conflicting plans. They then look for an extension of this AF that maximises the number of achieved desires as opposed to considering the quality or utility of these desires that is the base of comparison in [20].

The criticism about logic-based approaches is that the plan generation is not discussed and the main focus is on identifying a subset of consistent desires and their plans. However, it is not clear how, i.e. when and in which orders, the agent should execute those plans. More importantly and as it is discussed in [6], it is difficult to distinguish between states and actions, which results in the intrinsic worth of actions being neglected.

The most well-known scheme-based approach is the practical reasoning approach offered by Atkinson and Bench-Capon [4]. The approach uses Action-based Alternating Transition System (AATS) [23], which is instantiated based on the agent's knowledge of actions with pre- and post-conditions, and the values they promote. Using this AATS along with a set of arguments schemes and critical questions, arguments are generated for each available action. These arguments are then organised in a value-based argumentation framework (VAF) [5], where the preference between arguments is defined according to the values they promote and the goals they contribute to. Having said that there is no measurement of how much a value is promoted. The approach proposed by Oren [17] is also based on AATS and argumentation scheme and adopts several ideas from [4], however, unlike [4], it permits practical reasoning in the presence of norms. As a result preferences between arguments are defined based on considering all possible interactions between norms and goals instead of values and goals [4]. The work done in [21] also considers norms in collaborative planning, but unlike our work and [17], the norms are simply regimented, limiting the agent's normative reasoning capability to complying always with the imposed norms, without considering the possibility of violation. Permitting violation, allows the agent to weigh up outcomes of disregarding or adhering to a norm prior to committing to compliance or violation.

In order to avoid the shortcomings of logic-based approaches discussed in the third paragraph of this section, we have used scheme-based practical reasoning. Closest to our work is the approach in [17], however, instead of using AATS and evaluating all possible evolutions of the system, we approach this problem from a planning perspective, where only those evolutions that satisfy at least one goal are evaluated. The other difference is that [17] assumes that the conflict between different entities is inferred form paths, rather than being formulated in advance as it is in this work. Goal conflict for instance arises due to the fact that certain actions may achieve one but not another. Whereas, argument schemes and critical questions proposed here are based on the conflict formulated in the formal model level. Therefore, knowing that two goal conflict is used in the dialogue to explain why one was satisfied in a plan and the other one was not. In addition, in our approach, the justification of evaluation of plans to identify the best plan(s), is formulated using a persuasion dialogue game, in which the agent argues why a course of action should be taken.

7   Conclusion and Future Work

This paper proposes a formal framework for normative practical reasoning that is able to generate consistent plans for a set of conflicting goals and norms. The conflict between plans, goals and norms is managed by constructing arguments for these entities and instantiating an AF according to their relations. In order to bring transparency to the agent decision-making process when deciding which plan to execute, a persuasion dialogue is employed. Such a dialogue dialectically points out the reasons why (i) a goal/norm is or is not satisfied in a plan, (ii) a particular plan that pursues certain goals while violating and complying with some norms, should be the course of actions for the agent to execute. The main focus of future work is implementing the formal model.

Another area of future work is to extend the normative reasoning capability of the model by allowing state based norms. Such an extension would allow the expression of obligation and prohibitions to achieve or avoid some state before some deadline. A combination of event and state based norms (e.g. [12]) enriches the norm representation as well as normative reasoning. Furthermore, the normative reasoning can be extended by modelling permission norms as exceptions to obligation and prohibition norms (see [18] for more details).

Regarding the dialogue, at the moment, the preference-based AF constructed based on argument schemes and critical questions is converted to Dung's AF before being subjected to the persuasion dialogue. As a result the preference information is abstracted away in the dialogue. For instance, the reason for a goal not being satisfied in a plan could be because another goal that is in conflict with the former was satisfied in the plan. Knowing that the attack relation between two goals is symmetric, there must have been a preference relation that reduced the symmetric attack between the two goal arguments to an asymmetric one which is not explicit in the dialogue. We plan to make the dialogue game more informative by including information about preferences.

Traditionally, preferred semantics are used for practical reasoning because they preserve the agent's choices in case of unresolvable conflict between available courses of actions. By allowing multiple plans in the grounded extension, this choice is available to the agent. Having said that, as a part of future work, we are planning to apply preferred semantics to the problem presented in this paper and compare the result with grounded semantics.

References

1. Amgoud, L.: A formal framework for handling conflicting desires. In: Nielsen, T.D., Zhang, N.L. (eds.) ECSQARU 2003. LNCS (LNAI), vol. 2711, pp. 552–563. Springer, Heidelberg (2003)
2. Amgoud, L., Cayrol, C.: A reasoning model based on the production of acceptable arguments. Ann. Math. Artif. Intell. **34**, 1–3 (2002)
3. Amgoud, L., Devred, C., Lagasquie-Schiex, M.-C.: A constrained argumentation system for practical reasoning. In: Rahwan, I., Moraitis, P. (eds.) ArgMAS 2008. LNCS, vol. 5384, pp. 37–56. Springer, Heidelberg (2009)
4. Atkinson, K., Bench-Capon, T.J.M.: Practical reasoning as presumptive argumentation using action based alternating transition systems. Artif. Intell. **171**(10–15), 855–874 (2007)
5. Bench-Capon, T.J.M.: Value-based argumentation frameworks. In: Benferhat, S., Giunchiglia, E., (eds.) Non Monotonic Reasoning, pp. 443–454 (2002)
6. Bench-Capon, T.J.M., Atkinson, K.: Action-State Semantics for Practical Reasoning. In: The Uses of Computational Argumentation, Papers from the 2009 AAAI Fall Symposium, Arlington, Virginia, USA, 5–7 November 2009. vol. FS-09-06. AAAI Technical report. AAAI (2009)
7. Blum, A.L., Furst, M.L.: Fast planning through planning graph analysis. Artif. Intell. **90**(1), 281–300 (1997)
8. Broersen, J., Dastani, M., Hulstijn, J., Huang, Z., van der Torre, L.: The BOID architecture: conflicts between beliefs, obligations, intentions and desires. In: Proceedings of the Fifth International Conference on Autonomous Agents. AGENTS 2001. Montreal, Quebec, Canada, pp. 9–16. ACM (2001)

9. Caminada, M.: On the issue of reinstatement in argumentation. In: Fisher, M., van der Hoek, W., Konev, B., Lisitsa, A. (eds.) JELIA 2006. LNCS (LNAI), vol. 4160, pp. 111–123. Springer, Heidelberg (2006)

10. Caminada, M., Podlaszewski, M.: Grounded semantics as persuasion dialogue. In: Verheij, B., Szeider, S., Woltran, S., (eds.) Computational Models of Argument - Proceedings of COMMA 2012, Vienna, Austria, 10–12 September 2012, vol. 245. Frontiers in Artificial Intelligence and Applications. IOS Press, pp. 478–485 (2012)

11. Criado, N., Argente, E., Julián, V., Botti, V.: A BDI architecture for normative decision making. In: van der Hoek, W., Kaminka, G.A., Lespérance, Y., Luck, M., Sen, S., (eds.) 9th International Conference on Autonomous Agents and Multiagent Systems (AAMAS 2010), Toronto, Canada, 10–14 May 2010, vol. 1–3, pp. 1383–1384. IFAAMAS (2010)

12. De Vos, M., Balke, T., Satoh, K.: Combining event-and state-based norms. In: Gini, M.L., Shehory, O., Ito, T., Jonker, C.M., (eds.) International conference on Autonomous Agents and Multi-Agent Systems, AAMAS 2013, Saint Paul, MN, USA, 6–10 May 2013, pp. 1157–1158. IFAAMAS (2013)

13. Dung, P.M.: On the acceptability of arguments and its fundamental role in nonmonotonic reasoning, logic programming and n-person games. Artif. Intell. **77**(2), 321–358 (1995)

14. Fikes, R.E., Nilsson, N.J.: STRIPS: A new approach to the application of theorem proving to problem solving. In: Proceedings of the 2Nd International Joint Conference on Artificial Intelligence, IJCAI 1971, San Francisco, CA, USA, pp. 608–620. Morgan Kaufmann Publishers Inc., (1971)

15. Hulstijn, J., van der Torre, L.W.N.: Combining goal generation and planning in an argumentation framework. In: Delgrande, J.P., Schaub, T., (eds.) Non Monotonic Reasoning, pp. 212–218 (2004)

16. Kollingbaum, M.J., Norman, T.J.: NoA - A normative agent architecture. In: Gottlob, G., Walsh, T., (eds.) IJCAI-2003, Proceedings of the Eighteenth International Joint Conference on Artificial Intelligence, Acapulco, Mexico, 9–15 August 2003, pp. 1465–1466. Morgan Kaufmann (2003)

17. Oren, N.: Argument schemes for normative practical reasoning. In: Black, E., Modgil, S., Oren, N. (eds.) TAFA 2013. LNCS, vol. 8306, pp. 63–78. Springer, Heidelberg (2014)

18. Oren, N., Croitoru, M., Miles, S., Luck, M.: Understanding permissions through graphical norms. In: Omicini, A., Sardina, S., Vasconcelos, W. (eds.) DALT 2010. LNCS, vol. 6619, pp. 167–184. Springer, Heidelberg (2011)

19. Prakken, H.: Combining sceptical epistemic reasoning with credulous practical reasoning. In: Dunne, P.E., Bench-Capon, T.J.M, (eds.) Computational Models of Argument: Proceedings of COMMA 2006, 11–12 September 2006, Liverpool, UK, Frontiers in Artificial Intelligence and Applications. IOS Press, vol. 144, pp. 311–322 (2006)

20. Rahwan, I., Amgoud, L.: An argumentation-based approach for practical reasoning. In: Maudet, N., Parsons, S., Rahwan, I. (eds.) ArgMAS 2006. LNCS (LNAI), vol. 4766, pp. 74–90. Springer, Heidelberg (2007)

21. Toniolo, A., Norman, T.J., Sycara, K.P.: An empirical study of argumentation schemes for deliberative dialogue. In: De Raedt, L., Bessière, C., Dubois, D., Doherty, P., Frasconi, P., Heintz, F., Lucas, P.J.F., (eds.) ECAI 2012–20th European Conference on Artificial Intelligence. Including Prestigious Applications of Artificial Intelligence (PAIS-2012) System Demonstrations Track, Montpellier, France, 27–31 August 2012, vol. 242. Frontiers in Artificial Intelligence and Applications. IOS Press, pp. 756–761 (2012)
22. Douglas, D.N.: Argumentation Schemes for Presumptive Reasoning. Erlbaum Associates, Mahwah (1996)
23. Wooldridge, M., van der Hoek, W.: On obligations and normative ability: towards a logical analysis of the social contract. J. Appl. Log. 4(3–4), 396–420 (2006)

The Matrix Approach for Abstract Argumentation Frameworks

Yuming Xu[1] and Claudette Cayrol[2]([⊠])

[1] School of Mathematics, Shandong University, Jinan, China
xuyuming@sdu.edu.cn
[2] IRIT, University of Toulouse, Toulouse, France
ccayrol@irit.fr

Abstract. Matrices and the operation of dual interchange are introduced into the study of Dung's argumentation frameworks. It is showed that every argumentation framework can be represented by a matrix, and the basic extensions (such as admissible, stable, complete) can be determined by sub-blocks of its matrix. In particular, an efficient approach for determining the basic extensions has been developed using two types of standard matrix. Furthermore, we develop the topic of matrix reduction along two different lines. The first one enables to reduce the matrix into a less order matrix playing the same role for the determination of extensions. The second one enables to decompose an extension into several extensions of different sub-argumentation frameworks. It makes us not only solve the problem of determining grounded and preferred extensions, but also obtain results about dynamics of argumentation frameworks.

Keywords: Matrix · Argumentation · Extension · Reduction · Dynamics

1 Introduction

In recent years, the area of argumentation begins to become increasingly central as a core study within Artificial Intelligence. A number of papers investigated and compared the properties of different semantics which have been proposed for abstract argumentation frameworks [1–4, 7, 13, 14, 20, 22, 23].

Directed graphs have been widely used for modeling and analyzing argumentation frameworks (AFs for short) because of the feature of visualization [3, 10, 12, 14]. Furthermore, the labeling and game approach developed by Modgil and Caminada [7, 8, 18, 19] respectively are two excellent methods for the proof theories and algorithms of AFs. In this paper, we propose another novel idea, that is, the matrix representation of AFs.

Our aim is to introduce matrices and the operation of dual interchange into the study of AFs so as to propose new efficient approaches for determining basic extensions. First, we assign a matrix of order n for each AF with n arguments. This representation enables to establish links between extensions (under various

© Springer International Publishing Switzerland 2015
E. Black et al. (Eds.): TAFA 2015, LNAI 9524, pp. 243–259, 2015.
DOI: 10.1007/978-3-319-28460-6_15

semantics) of the AF and the internal structure of the matrix, namely sub-blocks of the matrix. Moreover, the matrix of an AF can be turned into a standard form, from which the determination of admissible and complete extensions can be easily achieved through checking some sub-blocks of this standard form. Furthermore, we propose the reduced matrix *wrt* conflict-free subsets, by which the determination of various extensions becomes more efficient. This approach has not been mentioned in the literature as we know. Finally, we present the reduced matrix *wrt* extensions and give the decomposition theory for extensions. It can be used to handle the semantics based on minimality and maximality criteria, for example, to determine the preferred extensions. It can also be related to the topic of directionality and enables us to obtain results about dynamics of AFs, which improve main results by Liao and Koons [17].

The paper is organized as follows. Section 2 recalls the basic definitions on abstract AFs. Section 3 introduces the matrix representation of AFs and the operation of dual interchange of matrices. Section 4 describes the characterization theorems for stable, admissible and complete extensions. Furthermore, we integrate these theorems and obtain two kinds of standard forms for matrices by dual interchanges. Section 5 presents the matrix reductions of AFs based on contraction and division of AFs, and some applications in AFs and dynamics of AFs. The proofs can be found in [11].

2   Background on Abstract AFs

In this section, we mainly recall the basic notions of abstract AFs [13,20].

Definition 1. *An abstract AF is a pair $AF = (A, R)$, where A is a finite set of arguments and $R \subseteq A \times A$ represents the attack relation. For any $S \subseteq A$, we say that S is conflict-free if there are no $a, b \in S$ such that $(a, b) \in R$; $a \in A$ is attacked by S if there is some $b \in S$ such that $(b, a) \in R$; $a \in A$ attacks S if there is some $b \in S$ such that $(a, b) \in R$; $a \in A$ is defended by (or acceptable wrt) S if for each $b \in A$ with $(b, a) \in R$, we have that b is attacked by S.*

We use the following notations inspired from graph theory. Let $AF = (A, R)$ be an AF and $S \subseteq A$. $R^+(S)$ denotes the set of arguments attacked by S. $R^-(S)$ denotes the set of arguments attacking S. I_{AF} denotes the set of arguments which are not attacked (also called initial arguments of AF).

An argumentation semantics is the formal definition of a method ruling the argument evaluation process. Two main styles of semantics can be identified in the literature: extension-based and labelling-based. Here, we only recall the common extension-based semantics of AF.

Definition 2. *Let $AF = (A, R)$ be an AF and $S \subseteq A$.*

- *S is a stable extension of AF if S is conflict-free and each $a \in A \backslash S$ is attacked by S.*

- S is admissible in AF if S is conflict-free and each $a \in S$ is defended by S. Let $a(AF)$ denote the set of admissible subsets in AF.
- S is a preferred extension of AF if $S \in a(AF)$ and S is a maximal element (wrt set-inclusion) of $a(AF)$.
- S is a complete extension of AF if $S \in a(AF)$ and for each $a \in A$ defended by S, we have $a \in S$.
- S is a grounded extension of AF if S is the least (wrt set-inclusion) complete extension of AF.

The common extension-based semantics can be characterized in terms of subsets of attacked/attacking arguments, due to the following results:

Proposition 1. *Let $AF = (A, R)$ be an AF and S a subset of A.*

- S is conflict-free if and only if (iff for short) $S \cap R^+(S) = \emptyset$ (or equivalently $R^+(S) \subseteq A \setminus S$)
- S is stable iff $R^+(S) = A \setminus S$
- S is admissible iff $R^-(S) \subseteq R^+(S) \subseteq A \setminus S$

Definition 3 [23]. *Let $AF = (A, R)$ be an AF, S a subset of A. The restriction of AF to S, denoted by $AF \mid_S$, is the sub-argumentation framework (sub-AF for short) $(S, R \cap (S \times S))$.*

Remark 1. For any nonempty subset S of A, the set A can be divided into three disjoint parts: S, $R^+(S)$ and $A \setminus (S \cup R^+(S))$. In our discussion on division of AF, the sub-AF $AF \mid_{A \setminus (S \cup R^+(S))}$ will play an important role. We call it the remaining sub-AF wrt S, or remaining sub-AF for short.

3 The Matrix Representation

Let $AF = (A, R)$ be an AF. It is convenient to put $A = \{1, 2, ..., n\}$ whenever the cardinality of A is large. Furthermore, we usually give the set A a permutation, for example $(i_1, i_2, ..., i_n)$, when dealing with the AF practically.

Definition 4. *Let $AF = (A, R)$ be an AF with $A = \{1, 2, ..., n\}$. The matrix of AF corresponding to the permutation $(i_1, i_2, ..., i_n)$ of A, denoted by $M(i_1, i_2, ..., i_n)^1$, is a boolean matrix of order n, its elements being determined by the following rules: (1) $a_{s,t} = 1$ iff $(i_s, i_t) \in R$ (2) $a_{s,t} = 0$ iff $(i_s, i_t) \notin R$. We usually denote the matrix $M(1, 2, ..., n)$ by $M(AF)$.*

Example 1. *Given $AF = (A, R)$ with $A = \{1, 2, 3\}$ and $R = \{(1, 2), (2, 1), (3, 2)\}$, represented by the following graph:*

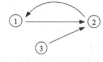

---

[1] strictly speaking, it should be denoted by $M_{AF}(i_1, i_2, ..., i_n)$.

According to Definition 4, the matrices of AF corresponding to the permutations
$(1,2,3)$ and $(1,3,2)$ are

$$\begin{pmatrix} 0 & 1 & 0 \\ 1 & 0 & 0 \\ 0 & 1 & 0 \end{pmatrix} \quad and \quad \begin{pmatrix} 0 & 0 & 1 \\ 0 & 0 & 1 \\ 1 & 0 & 0 \end{pmatrix}$$

Definition 5. *Let $AF = (A, R)$ be an AF with $A = \{1, 2, ..., n\}$. A dual inter-change on the matrix $M(i_1, ..., i_k, ..., i_l, ..., i_n)$ between k and l, denoted by $k \rightleftharpoons l$, consists of two interchanges: interchanging k-th row and l-th row; interchanging k-th column and l-th column.*

Lemma 1. *Let $AF = (A, R)$ be an AF with $A = \{1, 2, ..., n\}$, then $k \rightleftharpoons l$ turns the matrix $M(i_1, ..., i_k, ..., i_l, ..., i_n)$ into the matrix $M(i_1, ..., i_l, ..., i_k, ..., i_n)$.*

The dual interchange $k \rightleftharpoons l$ also turns the matrix $M(i_1, \cdots, i_l, \cdots, i_k, \cdots, i_n)$ into the matrix $M(i_1, ..., i_k, ..., i_l, ..., i_n)$. So, for any two matrices of an AF corre-sponding to different permutations of A we can turn one matrix into another by a sequence of dual interchanges. In this sense, we may call them to be equivalent matrix representations of the AF.

Example 1 (cont'd). By the dual interchange $1 \rightleftharpoons 2$, we can turn the matrix $M(1, 2, 3)$ into the matrix $M(2, 1, 3)$.

$$\begin{pmatrix} 0 & 1 & 0 \\ 1 & 0 & 0 \\ 0 & 1 & 0 \end{pmatrix} \underset{1 \rightleftharpoons 2}{} \begin{pmatrix} 0 & 1 & 0 \\ 1 & 0 & 0 \\ 1 & 0 & 0 \end{pmatrix}$$

4   Characterizing the Extensions of an AF

In this section, we mainly focus on the characterization of various extensions in the matrix $M(AF)$. The idea is to establish the relation between the extensions (viewed as subsets) of $AF = (A, R)$ and the sub-blocks of $M(AF)$.

4.1   Characterizing the Conflict-Free Subsets

The basic requirement for extensions is conflict-freeness. So, we will discuss the matrix condition which insures that a subset of an AF is conflict-free.

Definition 6. *Let $AF = (A, R)$ be an AF with $A = \{1, 2, ..., n\}$, and $S = \{i_1, i_2, ..., i_k\} \subseteq A$. The $k \times k$ sub-block*

$$M^{i_1, i_2, ..., i_k}_{i_1, i_2, ..., i_k} = \begin{pmatrix} a_{i_1, i_1} & a_{i_1, i_2} & \cdots & a_{i_1, i_k} \\ a_{i_2, i_1} & a_{i_2, i_2} & \cdots & a_{i_2, i_k} \\ . & . & \cdots & . \\ a_{i_k, i_1} & a_{i_k, i_2} & \cdots & a_{i_k, i_k} \end{pmatrix}$$

of $M(AF)$ is called the cf-sub-block of S, and denoted by $M^{cf}(S)$ for short.

Theorem 1. *Given $AF = (A, R)$ with $A = \{1, 2, ..., n\}$, $S = \{i_1, i_2, ..., i_k\} \subseteq A$ is conflict-free iff the cf-sub-block $M^{cf}(S)$ is zero.*

Example 1 (cont'd). $M^{cf}(\{1, 3\}) = \begin{pmatrix} 0 & 0 \\ 0 & 0 \end{pmatrix}$, $M^{cf}(\{1, 2\}) = \begin{pmatrix} 0 & 1 \\ 1 & 0 \end{pmatrix}$, and

$M^{cf}(\{2, 3\}) = \begin{pmatrix} 0 & 0 \\ 1 & 0 \end{pmatrix}$. By Theorem 1, $\{1, 3\}$ is conflict free, $\{1, 2\}$ and $\{2, 3\}$ are not.

4.2   Characterizing the Stable Extensions

As shown in Sect. 2, a subset S of A is stable iff $R^+(S) = A \setminus S$. So, except for the conflict-freeness of S, we only need to concentrate on whether the arguments in $A \setminus S$ are attacked by S. This suggests the following definition:

Definition 7. *Let $AF = (A, R)$ be an AF with $A = \{1, 2, ..., n\}$, $S = \{i_1, i_2, ..., i_k\} \subseteq A$ and $A \setminus S = \{j_1, j_2, ..., j_h\}$. The $k \times h$ sub-block*

$$M^{i_1, i_2, ..., i_k}_{j_1, j_2, ..., j_h} = \begin{pmatrix} a_{i_1, j_1} & a_{i_1, j_2} & \cdots & a_{i_1, j_h} \\ a_{i_2, j_1} & a_{i_2, j_2} & \cdots & a_{i_2, j_h} \\ \cdot & & \cdots & \cdot \\ a_{i_k, j_1} & a_{i_k, j_2} & \cdots & a_{i_k, j_h} \end{pmatrix}$$

of $M(AF)$ is called the s-sub-block of S and denoted by $M^s(S)$ for short.

In other words, we take the elements at the rows $i_1, i_2, ..., i_k$ and the columns $j_1, j_2, ..., j_h$ in the matrix $M(AF)$. For any matrix or its sub-block, the i-th row is called the i-th row vector and denoted by $M_{i,*}$, the j-th column is called j-th column vector and denoted by $M_{*,j}$.

Theorem 2. *Given $AF = (A, R)$ with $A = \{1, 2, ..., n\}$. A conflict-free subset $S = \{i_1, i_2, ..., i_k\} \subseteq A$ is a stable extension iff each column vector of the s-sub-block $M^s(S) = M^{i_1, i_2, ..., i_k}_{j_1, j_2, ..., j_h}$ of $M(AF)$ is non-zero, where $(j_1, j_2, ..., j_h)$ is a permutation of $A \setminus S$.*

Example 1 (cont'd). We consider the conflict-free subsets $\{1\}$ and $\{1, 3\}$. Since the second column vector of $M^s(\{1\}) = (1 \ 0)$ is zero and the only column vector of $M^s(\{1, 3\}) = \begin{pmatrix} 1 \\ 1 \end{pmatrix}$ is non-zero, we claim that $\{1, 3\}$ is a stable extension of AF but $\{1\}$ is not, according to Theorem 2.

4.3   Characterizing the Admissible Subsets

As shown in Sect. 2, a subset S of A is admissible if and only if $R^-(S) \subseteq R^+(S) \subseteq A \setminus S$. There may be arguments in $A \setminus S$ which are not attacked by S. Such arguments should not attack S. This suggests to explore the representation in $M(AF)$ of the relation between $R^-(S)$ and $R^+(S)$.

Definition 8. *Let* $AF = (A, R)$ *be an* AF *with* $A = \{1, 2, ..., n\}$, $S = \{i_1, i_2, ..., i_k\} \subseteq A$ *and* $A \setminus S = \{j_1, j_2, ..., j_h\}$. *The* $h \times k$ *sub-block*

$$M^{j_1, j_2, ..., j_h}_{i_1, i_2, ..., i_k} = \begin{pmatrix} a_{j_1, i_1} & a_{j_1, i_2} & \cdots & a_{j_1, i_k} \\ a_{j_2, i_1} & a_{j_2, i_2} & \cdots & a_{j_2, i_k} \\ \cdot & \cdot & \cdots & \cdot \\ a_{j_h, i_1} & a_{j_h, i_2} & \cdots & a_{j_h, i_k} \end{pmatrix}$$

of $M(AF)$ *is called the a-sub-block of* S *and denoted by* $M^a(S)$.

In other words, we take the elements at the rows $j_1, j_2, ..., j_h$ and the columns $i_1, i_2, ..., i_k$ in the matrix $M(AF)$.

Theorem 3. *Given* $AF = (A, R)$ *with* $A = \{1, 2, ..., n\}$. *A conflict-free subset* $S = \{i_1, i_2, ..., i_k\} \subseteq A$ *is admissible iff any column vector of the s-sub-block* $M^s(S)$ *corresponding to a non-zero row vector of the a-sub-block* $M^a(S)$ *is non-zero, where* $(j_1, j_2, ..., j_h)$ *is a permutation of* $A \setminus S$.

Example 1 (cont'd). We consider the conflict-free subsets $\{1\}$ and $\{2\}$. Since $M^s(\{1\}) = \begin{pmatrix} 1 & 0 \end{pmatrix}$ and $M^a(\{1\}) = \begin{pmatrix} 1 \\ 0 \end{pmatrix}$, the column vector $M^s_{*,1}$ of $M^s(\{1\})$ corresponding to the non-zero row vector $M^a_{1,*}$ of $M^a(\{1\})$ is non-zero, we claim that $\{1\}$ is admissible in AF by Theorem 3.

However, from $M^s(\{2\}) = \begin{pmatrix} 1 & 0 \end{pmatrix}$ and $M^a(\{2\}) = \begin{pmatrix} 1 \\ 1 \end{pmatrix}$ we know that the column vector $M^s_{*,2}$ of $M^s(\{2\})$ corresponding to the non-zero row vector $M^a_{2,*}$ of $M^a(\{2\})$ is zero. So, $\{2\}$ is not admissible in AF according to Theorem 3.

4.4   Characterizing the Complete Extensions

From the viewpoint of set theory, every complete extension S separates A into three disjoint parts: S, $R^+(S)$ and $A \setminus (S \cup R^+(S))$. Except for the conflict-freeness of S, we need not only to consider whether S is attacked by the arguments in $A \setminus (S \cup R^+(S))$, but also to see if every argument in $A \setminus (S \cup R^+(S))$ is attacked by some others in $A \setminus (S \cup R^+(S))$. This suggests the following definition.

Definition 9. *Let* $AF = (A, R)$ *be an* AF *with* $A = \{1, 2, ..., n\}$, $S = \{i_1, i_2, ..., i_k\} \subseteq A$ *and* $A \setminus S = \{j_1, j_2, ..., j_h\}$. *The* $h \times h$ *sub-block*

$$M^{j_1, j_2, ..., j_h}_{j_1, j_2, ..., j_h} = \begin{pmatrix} a_{j_1, j_1} & a_{j_1, j_2} & \cdots & a_{j_1, j_h} \\ a_{j_2, j_1} & a_{j_2, j_2} & \cdots & a_{j_2, j_h} \\ \cdot & \cdot & \cdots & \cdot \\ a_{j_h, j_1} & a_{j_h, j_2} & \cdots & a_{j_h, j_h} \end{pmatrix}$$

of $M(AF)$ *is called the c-sub-block of* S *and denoted by* $M^c(S)$ *for short.*

In other words, we take the elements at the rows $j_1, j_2, ..., j_h$ and the columns $j_1, j_2, ..., j_h$ in the matrix $M(AF)$.

Theorem 4. *Given $AF = (A, R)$ with $A = \{1, 2, ..., n\}$. An admissible extension $S = \{i_1, i_2, ..., i_k\} \subseteq A$ is complete iff*

(1) if some column vector $M^s_{*,p}$ of the s-sub-block $M^s(S)$ is zero, then its corresponding column vector $M^c_{*,p}$ of the c-sub-block $M^c(S)$ is non-zero and

(2) for each non-zero column vector $M^c_{*,p}$ of the c-sub-block $M^c(S)$ appearing in (1), there is at least one non-zero element a_{j_q,j_p} of $M^c_{*,p}$ such that the corresponding column vector $M^s_{*,q}$ of the s-sub-block $M^s(S)$ is zero, where $\{j_1, j_2, ..., j_h\} = A \setminus S$ and $1 \leq q, p \leq h$.

Example 2. *Let $AF = (A, R)$ with $A = \{1, 2, 3, 4, 5\}$ and $R = \{(2, 5), (3, 4), (4, 3), (5, 1), (5, 3)\}$. The matrix and graph of AF are as follows:*

$$M(AF) = \begin{pmatrix} 0 & 0 & 0 & 0 & 0 \\ 0 & 0 & 0 & 0 & 1 \\ 0 & 0 & 0 & 1 & 0 \\ 0 & 0 & 1 & 0 & 0 \\ 1 & 0 & 1 & 0 & 0 \end{pmatrix}$$

By Theorem 3, we have that $S = \{1, 2\}$ is admissible. Let $i_1 = 1, i_2 = 2, j_1 = 3, j_2 = 4, j_3 = 5$. Note that $M^s(\{1, 2\}) = \begin{pmatrix} 0 & 0 & 0 \\ 0 & 0 & 1 \end{pmatrix}$ has two zero column vectors $M^s_{*,1} = \begin{pmatrix} 0 \\ 0 \end{pmatrix}$ and $M^s_{*,2} = \begin{pmatrix} 0 \\ 0 \end{pmatrix}$. Their corresponding column vectors in $M^c(\{1, 2\}) = \begin{pmatrix} 0 & 1 & 0 \\ 1 & 0 & 0 \\ 1 & 0 & 0 \end{pmatrix}$ are $M^c_{*,1} = \begin{pmatrix} 0 \\ 1 \\ 1 \end{pmatrix}$ and $M^c_{*,2} = \begin{pmatrix} 1 \\ 0 \\ 0 \end{pmatrix}$ respectively, which
are all non-zero. For $a_{j_2 j_1} = a_{43} = 1$ in $M^c_{*,1}$, the corresponding column vector $M^s_{*,2}$ in $M^s(\{1, 2\})$ is zero. For $a_{j_1 j_2} = a_{34} = 1$ in $M^c_{*,2}$, the corresponding column vector $M^s_{*,1}$ in $M^s(\{1, 2\})$ is also zero. According to Theorem 4, we claim that $\{1, 2\}$ is a complete extension of AF.

By now, we can determine three basic extensions by checking the sub-blocks of the matrix $M(AF)$. Note that in each theorem the rules are obtained directly from the corresponding definition of extensions. So, there is no more advantage than judging by definitions. In the next subsection, we will improve the rules to achieve some standard form by which one can determine the extensions easily.

4.5   The Standard Forms of the Matrix $M(AF)$

In linear algebra, one can reduce the matrix of a system of linear equations into row echelon form by row transformations in order to find the solution easily. Similarly, we will use dual interchanges to reduce the matrix of AFs into standard forms, by which the extensions discussed above can be easily determined. In the sequel, two standard forms are introduced *wrt* different semantics.

Theorem 5. *Given $AF = (A, R)$ with $A = \{1, 2, ..., n\}$, $S = \{i_1, i_2, ..., i_k\} \subseteq A$ and $A \backslash S = \{j_1, ..., j_h\}$. By a sequence of dual interchanges $M(AF)$ can be turned into the matrix $M(i_1, i_2, ..., i_k, j_1, j_2, ..., j_h)$, which has the following form*

$$\begin{pmatrix} M^{cf}(S) & M^s(S) \\ M^a(S) & M^c(S) \end{pmatrix},$$

where $M^{cf}(S), M^s(S), M^a(S), M^c(S)$ are the cf- sub-block, s-sub-block, a-sub-block, c-sub-block of S respectively.

Corollary 1. *Given $AF = (A, R)$ with $A = \{1, 2, ..., n\}$, $S = \{i_1, i_2, ..., i_k\}$, $A \backslash S = \{j_1, ..., j_h\}$. Let $M(i_1, i_2, ..., i_k, j_1, ..., j_h)$ be the matrix of AF corresponding to the permutation $(i_1, i_2, ..., i_k, j_1, ..., j_h)$, as in Theorem 5.*

1. *S is conflict-free iff the cf-sub-block $M^{cf}(S) = 0$*
2. *S is stable iff the cf-sub-block $M^{cf}(S) = 0$ and every column vector of the s-sub-block $M^s(S)$ is non-zero.*

Example 1 (cont'd). $S = \{1, 3\}$ is a conflict-free subset of AF. By the dual interchange $2 \rightleftarrows 3$, $M(AF)$ can be turned into the following matrix:

$$M(1, 3, 2) = \begin{pmatrix} 0 & 0 & 1 \\ 0 & 0 & 1 \\ 1 & 0 & 0 \end{pmatrix}.$$

Since $M^s(S) = \begin{pmatrix} 1 \\ 1 \end{pmatrix}$, $\{1, 3\}$ is a stable extension of AF by Corollary 1.

We have obtained a partition matrix of order two, composed by four kinds of sub-blocks, from which we can determine the conflict-free status and stable status of S. However, there is no new information about the admissible and complete status of S. We can go further since, for any conflict-free subset S, A can be divided into three disjoint subsets: S, $R^+(S)$ and $A \backslash (S \cup R^+(S))$. So we obtain a new partition of order three.

Theorem 6. *Given $AF = (A, R)$ with $A = \{1, 2, ..., n\}$ and $S = \{i_1, i_2, ..., i_k\} \subseteq A$ a conflict-free subset. By a sequence of dual interchanges $M(AF)$ can be turned into the matrix $M(i_1, i_2, ..., i_k, j_{t_1}, ..., j_{t_q}, j_{s_1}, ..., j_{s_l})$*

$$= \begin{pmatrix} 0_{k,k} & 0_{k,q} & S_{k,l} \\ A_{q,k} & C_{q,q} & E_{q,l} \\ F_{l,k} & G_{l,q} & H_{l,l} \end{pmatrix} = \begin{pmatrix} 0_{k,k} & M^s(S) \\ M^a(S) & M^c(S) \end{pmatrix}$$

where $A \backslash S = \{j_{t_1}, ..., j_{t_q}, j_{s_1}, ..., j_{s_l}\}$, $k + q + l = k + h = n$, and each column vector of $S_{k,l}$ is non-zero.

Corollary 2. *Given $AF = (A, R)$ with $A = \{1, 2, ..., n\}$, $S = \{i_1, i_2, ..., i_k\}$, $A \backslash S = \{j_{t_1}, ..., j_{t_q}, j_{s_1}, ..., j_{s_l}\}$. Let $M(i_1, i_2, ..., i_k, j_{t_1}, ..., j_{t_q}, j_{s_1}, ..., j_{s_l})$ be the matrix of AF corresponding to the permutation $(i_1, i_2, ..., i_k, j_{t_1}, ..., j_{t_q}, j_{s_1}, ..., j_{s_l})$ as in Theorem 6.*

1. S is an admissible extension iff $A_{q,k} = 0$
2. S is complete iff $A_{q,k} = 0$ and each column vector of $C_{q,q}$ is not zero.

Example 1 (cont'd). $S = \{1\}$ is conflict-free. By the dual interchange $2 \rightleftarrows 3$, $M(AF)$ can be turned into the following matrix:

$$M(1, 3, 2) = \begin{pmatrix} 0\,0\,1 \\ 0\,0\,1 \\ 1\,0\,0 \end{pmatrix}.$$

Note that here $i_1 = 1, j_{t_1} = 3$ and $j_{s_1} = 2$ with $k = 1, q = 1, l = 1$. Since $S_{k,l} = S_{1,1} = (1)$, $A_{q,k} = A_{1,1} = (0)$, we claim that $\{1\}$ is an admissible extension of AF according to the first item of Corollary 2.

Example 2 (cont'd). $S = \{1, 2\}$ is conflict-free. Note that $M(AF)$ has already the standard form we need for S. Here, $i_1 = 1, i_2 = 2, j_{t_1} = 3, j_{t_2} = 4$ and $j_{s_1} = 5$ with $k = 2, q = 2, l = 1$. Because $S_{k,l} = S_{2,1} = \begin{pmatrix} 0 \\ 1 \end{pmatrix}$, $A_{q,k} = A_{2,2} = \begin{pmatrix} 0\,0 \\ 0\,0 \end{pmatrix}$, and $C_{q,q} = C_{2,2} = \begin{pmatrix} 0\,1 \\ 1\,0 \end{pmatrix}$, we conclude that $\{1, 2\}$ is a complete extension of AF according to the second item of Corollary 2.

5   Matrix Reduction

For some purposes or under some conditions, we can simplify the AFs and their matrices. In this section, we will mainly discuss the matrix reduction *wrt* conflict-free subsets and *wrt* some extensions. Related results can be applied to the computation of various extensions and to the dynamics of AFs.

5.1   Matrix Reduction Based on Contraction of AFs

In Sect. 4, we proposed to characterize the stable (admissible, complete) extensions of an AF by dividing A into two or three parts, and then considering the interaction between these different parts. This suggests to contract one part of an AF (namely a conflict-free subset) into a single argument by drawing up some rules. And thus, the matrix can be reduced into another matrix of less order which plays the same role for our purpose.

Definition 10. *Let $M(AF)$ be the matrix of an AF. The addition of two rows of the matrix $M(AF)$ consists in adding the elements in the same position of the rows, with the rules $0 + 0 = 0, 0 + 1 = 1, 1 + 1 = 1$. The addition of two columns of the matrix $M(AF)$ is similar as the addition of two rows.*

For a conflict-free subset $S = \{i_1, i_2, ..., i_k\}$, we try to contract the sub-block $M^{cf}(S)$ into a single entry in the matrix and make this entry share the same status as $M^{cf}(S)$ *wrt* extension-based semantics. The matrix $M(AF)$ can be reduced into another matrix $M_S^r(AF)$ of order $n - k + 1$ by the following rules: Let $1 \leq t \leq k$. For each s such that $1 \leq s \leq k$ and $s \neq t$,

1. adding row i_s to the row i_t,
2. adding column i_s to the column i_t, then
3. deleting row i_s and column i_s.

The matrix $M_S^r(AF)$ is called the reduced matrix *wrt* the conflict-free subset S, or the reduced matrix *wrt* S for short.

Correspondingly, the original AF can be reduced into a new one with $n - k + 1$ arguments by the following rules:
Let $A \setminus S = \{j_1, j_2, ..., j_h\}$ and $1 \leq t \leq k$. For each s such that $1 \leq s \leq k$ and $s \neq t$, and each q such that $1 \leq q \leq h$,

1. adding (i_t, j_q) to R if $(i_s, j_q) \in R$,
2. adding (j_q, i_t) to R if $(j_q, i_s) \in R$, then
3. deleting all (i_s, j_q) and (j_q, i_s) from R.

Let R_S^r denote the new relation and $A_S^r = \{i_t\} \cup (A \setminus S)$, then (A_S^r, R_S^r) is a new AF called the reduced AF *wrt* S. Obviously, the reduced matrix $M_S^r(AF)$ is exactly the matrix of (A_S^r, R_S^r).

Theorem 7. *Given $AF = (A, R)$ with $A = \{1, 2, ..., n\}$. Let $S = \{i_1, i_2, ..., i_k\} \subseteq A$ be conflict-free and $1 \leq t \leq k$. Then S is stable (resp. admissible, complete, preferred) in AF iff $\{i_t\}$ is stable (respectively admissible, complete, preferred) in the reduced AF (A_S^r, R_S^r).*

Example 1 (cont'd). Since $S = \{1, 3\}$ is conflict-free, $M(AF)$ can be turned into the following reduced matrix according to the above rules (S is contracted into $\{1\}$):

$$M_S^r(AF) = \begin{pmatrix} 0 & 1 \\ 1 & 0 \end{pmatrix}.$$

The corresponding reduced AF is (A_S^r, R_S^r) where $A_S^r = \{1, 2\}$ and $R_S^r = \{(1, 2), (2, 1)\}$. The graph of (A_S^r, R_S^r) is as follows:

Note that $\{1\}$ is stable in (A_S^r, R_S^r), and $S = \{1, 3\}$ is stable in AF.

Furthermore, we can extend the above idea to two disjoint conflict-free subsets and turn the matrix of AF into a reduced matrix of less order.

Let $S_1 = \{i_1, i_2, ..., i_k\}$ and $S_2 = \{j_1, j_2, ..., j_h\}$ be two conflict-free subsets of A such that $S_1 \cap S_2 = \emptyset$. We try to contract the sub-block $M^{cf}(S_1)$ and $M^{cf}(S_2)$ into two entries in the matrix and make them share the same status as $M^{cf}(S_1)$ and $M^{cf}(S_2)$ *wrt* extension-based semantics. The matrix $M(AF)$ can be reduced into another matrix $M_{S_1, S_2}^r(AF)$ of order $n - k - h + 2$ by the following rules:

Let $1 \leq t \leq k$ and $1 \leq s \leq h$. For each p such that $1 \leq p \leq k$ and $p \neq t$, and each q such that $1 \leq q \leq h$ and $q \neq s$,

1. for S_1, adding row i_p to the row i_t, adding column i_p to the column i_t,
2. for S_2, adding row j_q to the row j_s, adding column j_q to the column j_s, then
3. deleting row i_p and column i_p,
4. deleting row j_q and column j_q.

The matrix $M^r_{S_1,S_2}(AF)$ is called the reduced matrix wrt the disjoint conflict-free subsets S_1 and S_2, or the reduced matrix wrt (S_1, S_2) for short. Correspondingly, the original AF can be reduced into a new one with $n-k-h+2$ arguments by the following rules:
Let $1 \le t \le k$ and $1 \le s \le h$. For each p such that $1 \le p \le k$ and $p \ne t$, each q such that $1 \le q \le h$ and $q \ne s$, each $i \in A \setminus S_1$, and each $j \in A \setminus S_2$,

1. adding (i_t, i) to R if $(i_p, i) \in R$, adding (i, i_t) to R if $(i, i_p) \in R$,
2. adding (j_s, j) to R if $(j_q, j) \in R$, adding (j, j_s) to R if $(j, j_q) \in R$,
3. deleting all (i_p, i) and (i, i_p) from R,
4. deleting all (j_q, j) and (j, j_q) from R.

Let $R^r_{S_1,S_2}$ denote the new relation and $A^r_{S_1,S_2} = \{i_t, j_s\} \cup (A \setminus (S_1 \cup S_2))$, then $(A^r_{S_1,S_2}, R^r_{S_1,S_2})$ is a new AF called the reduced AF wrt (S_1, S_2). Obviously, $M^r_{S_1,S_2}(AF)$ is exactly the matrix of $(A^r_{S_1,S_2}, R^r_{S_1,S_2})$.

Theorem 8. *Given $AF = (A, R)$ with $A = \{1, 2, ..., n\}$. Let $S_1 = \{i_1, i_2, ..., i_k\}$ and $S_2 = \{j_1, j_2, ..., j_h\}$ be two conflict-free subsets of AF such that $S_1 \cap S_2 = \emptyset$. Let $1 \le t \le k$ and $1 \le s \le h$, then*

- *S_1 is stable (respectively admissible, complete, preferred) in AF if and only if $\{i_t\}$ is stable (respectively admissible, complete, preferred) in $(A^r_{S_1,S_2}, R^r_{S_1,S_2})$,*
- *S_2 is stable (respectively admissible, complete, preferred) in AF if and only if $\{j_s\}$ is stable (respectively admissible, complete, preferred) in $(A^r_{S_1,S_2}, R^r_{S_1,S_2})$.*

Example 3. *Let $AF = (A, R)$ with $A = \{1, 2, 3, 4\}$ and $R = \{(1, 2), (2, 3), (3, 4), (4, 1)\}$. The matrix and graph of AF are as follows.*

$$M(AF) = \begin{pmatrix} 0 & 1 & 0 & 0 \\ 0 & 0 & 1 & 0 \\ 0 & 0 & 0 & 1 \\ 1 & 0 & 0 & 0 \end{pmatrix}$$

Since $S_1 = \{1, 3\}$ and $S_2 = \{2, 4\}$ are two disjoint conflict-free subsets of AF, $M(AF)$ can be turned into the following reduced matrix according to the above rules(S_1 is contracted into $\{1\}$ and S_2 is contracted into $\{2\}$):

$$M^r_{S_1,S_2}(AF) = \begin{pmatrix} 0 & 1 \\ 1 & 0 \end{pmatrix}$$

Obviously, $\{1\}$ and $\{2\}$ are stable in $(A^r_{S_1,S_2}, R^r_{S_1,S_2})$. By Theorem 8, $S_1 = \{1, 3\}$ and $S_2 = \{2, 4\}$ are stable in AF.

Theorems 7 and 8 make it more efficient for us to determine whether a conflict-free subset is one of the basic extensions.

5.2   Matrix Reduction Based on Division of AFs

The division of AFs into sub-AFs has already been considered [17] for handling dynamics of AFs. Indeed many other issues in AFs can be dealt with by the division of AFs. For example, the grounded extension can be viewed as the union of two subsets I_{AF} and E: I_{AF} consists of the initial arguments of AF and E is the grounded extension of the remaining sub-AF $AF\mid_B$ *wrt* I_{AF} (where $B = A \setminus (I_{AF} \cup R^+(I_{AF})))$.

According to the maximality criterion, a preferred extension coincides with an admissible extension E from which the associated remaining sub-AF $AF\mid_C$ (where $C = A \setminus (E \cup R^+(E)))$ has no nonempty admissible extension.

Building Grounded and Preferred Extensions. Let S be an admissible extension of $AF = (A, R)$, and AF_1 be the remaining sub-AF *wrt* S. The basic extensions of AF_1 can be determined by applying the theorems obtained in Sect. 4. So, the matrix $M(AF_1)$ becomes the main object of our concentration. We call it the reduced matrix *wrt* the extension S.

For each extension T of AF_1, the matrix $M(AF)$ can be turned into a standard form *wrt* $S \cup T$ by a sequence of dual interchanges. Based on the results obtained in Sect. 4, we have the following theorem.

Theorem 9. *Let $AF = (A, R)$, $S \subseteq A$ be an admissible extension of AF, and $B = A\setminus(S \cup R^+(S))$. If $T \subseteq B$ is an admissible (resp. stable, complete, preferred) extension of the remaining sub-AF $AF\mid_B$ wrt S, then $S \cup T$ is an admissible (resp. stable, complete, preferred) extension of AF.*

Example 4. *Let $AF = (A, R)$ with $A = \{1, 2, 3, 4\}$ and $R = \{(1, 2), (2, 1), (2, 4), (3, 4)\}$. The matrix and graph of AF are as follows.*

$$M(AF) = \begin{pmatrix} 0 & 1 & 0 & 0 \\ 1 & 0 & 0 & 1 \\ 0 & 0 & 0 & 1 \\ 0 & 0 & 0 & 0 \end{pmatrix}$$

$S = \{3\}$ is an admissible extension of AF, $R^+(S) = \{4\}$ and $B = A \setminus (S \cup R^+(S)) = \{1, 2\}$. So, the matrix and graph of the remaining sub-AF wrt S are as follows:

$$M(AF\mid_B) = \begin{pmatrix} 0 & 1 \\ 1 & 0 \end{pmatrix}$$

Since $T = \{2\}$ is admissible in $AF\mid_B$, by Theorem 9, we conclude that $S \cup T = \{2, 3\}$ is admissible in AF.

These combination properties of extensions can also be used for computing related extensions.

A grounded extension can be built incrementally starting from an admissible extension. If AF has no initial argument, then the grounded extension S of AF is empty. Otherwise, let I_1 be the set of initial arguments of AF, then I_1 is an admissible extension of AF. Next, we consider the sub-AF $AF \mid_{B_1}$ where $B_1 = A \setminus (I_1 \cup R^+(I_1))$. If it has no initial argument, then the grounded extension $S = I_1$. Otherwise, let I_2 be the set of initial arguments of $AF \mid_{B_1}$ and $B_2 = B_1 \setminus (I_2 \cup R^+(I_2))$. By Theorem 9, $I_1 \cup I_2$ is an admissible extension of AF. This process can be done repeatedly, until some $AF \mid_{B_t}$ has no initial argument, where $1 \leq t \leq n$. It is easy to verify that $S = I_1 \cup ... \cup I_t$ is the grounded extension of AF.

A preferred extension is defined as a maximal (*wrt* set inclusion) admissible extension. So, it can be also built incrementally starting from some admissible extension. Let S_1 be any admissible extension of AF, and $B_1 = A \setminus (S_1 \cup R^+(S_1))$. If $B_1 = \emptyset$ or the sub-AF $AF \mid_{B_1}$ does not have nonempty admissible extension, then S_1 is a preferred extension of AF. Otherwise, let S_2 be an nonempty admissible extension. Then, $S_1 \cup S_2$ is an admissible extension of AF by Theorem 9. Let $B_2 = B_1 \setminus (S_2 \cup R^+(S_2))$, then it is a sub-AF of $AF \mid_{B_1}$. This process can be done repeatedly, until some sub-AF $AF \mid_{B_s}$ has no nonempty admissible extension where $1 \leq s \leq n$. It is easy to verify that $S = S_1 \cup ... \cup S_t$ is a preferred extension of AF.

Handling Dynamics of Argumentation Frameworks. In recent years, the research on dynamics of AFs has become more and more active [5,6,9,10,15,17, 21]. In [10] Cayrol et al. introduced change operations to describe the dynamics of AFs, and systematically studied the structural properties for change operations. Based on these notions, Liao et al. [17] concentrated their attention on the directionality of AFs and constructed a division-based method for dynamics of AFs. In the following, we introduce the reduction of a matrix *wrt* an extension in an unattacked subset of the AF and give the decomposition theorem of extensions for dynamics of AFs.

Directionality is a basic principle for extension-based semantics. According to [1,3], the following semantics have been proved to satisfy the directionality criterion: grounded semantics, complete semantics, preferred semantics and ideal semantics. Directionality is based on the unattacked subsets. So, we recall the definition of unattacked subset.

Definition 11. *Given $AF = (A, R)$, a non-empty set $U \in A$ is unattacked if and only if there is no $a \in A \setminus U$ such that a attacks U.*

Let U be an unattacked subset of $AF = (A, R)$. Let E_1 be an admissible extension in the sub-AF $AF \mid_U$, then we have a remaining sub-AF $AF \mid_T$ with $T = A \setminus (E_1 \cup R^+(E_1))$. In order to determine the extensions of $AF \mid_T$, we can apply the theorems obtained in Sect. 4. So, the matrix $M(AF \mid_T)$ becomes the main object of our concentration. We call it the reduced matrix *wrt* E_1.

For each conflict-free subset E_2, we can turn the matrix $M(AF)$ into one of the standard forms *wrt* $E_1 \cup E_2$ by a sequence of dual interchanges. Based on the results obtained in Sect. 4, we derive the following theorem.

Theorem 10. *Let $AF = (A, R)$ and U an unattacked subset of AF. $E \subseteq A$ is an admissible extension of AF iff $E_1 = E \cap U$ is admissible in the sub-AF $AF \mid_U$ and $E_2 = E \cap T$ is admissible in the remaining sub-AF $AF \mid_T$ wrt E_1 (where $T = A \setminus (E_1 \cup R^+(E_1)))$.*

Example 4 (cont'd). $U = \{1, 2\}$ is an unattacked subset of AF, and $E_1 = \{1\}$ is an admissible extension in the sub-AF $AF \mid_U$. Since $T = A \setminus (E_1 \cup R^+(E_1)) = \{3, 4\}$, the matrix and graph of the remaining sub-AF *wrt* E_1 are as follows:

$$M(AF \mid_T) = \begin{pmatrix} 0 & 1 \\ 0 & 0 \end{pmatrix} \qquad \text{③} \longrightarrow \text{④}$$

Obviously, $\{3\}$ is admissible in $AF \mid_T$. According to Theorem 10, $\{1, 3\}$ is admissible in AF.

Remark 4. Theorem 10 still holds for other extensions which satisfy the directionality principle. Namely, we can replace "admissible" by "complete, preferred, grounded or ideal".

Theorem 10 provides a general result for AFs. However it happens that this result plays an important role when applied to dynamics of AFs. In order to describe this application, we need to present basic notions related to dynamics of AFs. We focus on the work described in [17].

Let U_{arg} be the universe of arguments. Different kinds of change can be considered on $AF = (A, R)$. (1) adding (or deleting) a set of interactions between the arguments in A, we denote this set by $\mathcal{I}_A$. (2) adding a set $B \subseteq U_{arg} \setminus A$ of arguments, we can also add some interactions related to it, including a set of interactions between A and B and a set of interactions between the arguments in B. The union of these two sets of interactions is denoted by $\mathcal{I}_{A:B}$. (3) deleting a set $B \subseteq A$ of arguments, we will also delete all the interactions related to it, including the set of interactions between $A \setminus B$ and B and the set of interactions between the arguments in B. The union of these two sets of interactions is denoted by $\mathcal{I}_{A \setminus B:B}$. (4) after deleting the set $B \subseteq A$ of arguments, we can continue to delete some interactions between the arguments in $A \setminus B$. This set of interactions is denoted by $\mathcal{I}_{A \setminus B}$, similar as in (1).

An addition is represented by a tuple $(B, \mathcal{I}_{A:B} \cup \mathcal{I}_A)$ with $B \subseteq U_{arg} \setminus A$, and a deletion is represented by a tuple $(B, \mathcal{I}_{A \setminus B:B} \cup \mathcal{I}_{A \setminus B})$ with $B \subseteq A$.

Definition 12 [17]. *Given $AF = (A, R)$. Let $(B, \mathcal{I}_{A:B} \cup \mathcal{I}_A)$ be an addition and $(B, \mathcal{I}_{A \setminus B:B} \cup \mathcal{I}_{A \setminus B})$ be a deletion. The updated AF wrt $(B, \mathcal{I}_{A:B} \cup \mathcal{I}_A)$ and $(B, \mathcal{I}_{A \setminus B:B} \cup \mathcal{I}_{A \setminus B}))$ is defined as follows:*

$$AF^{\oplus} = (A, R) \oplus (B, \mathcal{I}_{A:B} \cup \mathcal{I}_A) = (A \cup B, R \cup \mathcal{I}_{A:B} \cup \mathcal{I}_A)$$
$$AF^{\ominus} = (A, R) \ominus (B, \mathcal{I}_{A \setminus B:B} \cup \mathcal{I}_{A \setminus B}) = (A \setminus B, R \setminus (\mathcal{I}_{A \setminus B:B} \cup \mathcal{I}_{A \setminus B}))$$

Now, let us apply Theorem 10 to the study of dynamics of AFs. The following two corollaries can be obtained directly.

Corollary 3. *Let $AF = (A, R)$, $AF^\oplus$ be the updated AF wrt an addition and U an unattacked subset in $AF^\oplus$. If E_1 is admissible in the sub-AF $AF^\oplus |_U$, and E_2 is admissible in the remaining sub-AF wrt E_1, then $E_1 \cup E_2$ is admissible in $AF^\oplus$. Conversely, for each admissible extension E of $AF^\oplus$, $E_1 = E \cap U$ is admissible in $AF^\oplus |_U$ and $E_2 = E \cap T$ is admissible in $AF^\oplus |_T$.*

Corollary 4. *Let $AF = (A, R)$, $AF^\ominus$ be the updated AF wrt a deletion and U an unattacked subset in $AF^\ominus$. If E_1 is admissible in the sub-AF $AF^\ominus |_U$, and E_2 is admissible in the remaining sub-AF $AF^\ominus |_T$ wrt E_1, then $E_1 \cup E_2$ is admissible in $AF^\ominus$; Conversely, for each admissible extension E of $AF^\ominus$, $E_1 - E \cap U$ is admissible in $AF^\ominus |_U$ and $E_2 = E \cap T$ is admissible in $AF^\ominus |_T$.*

Remark 5. The above two corollaries still hold if we replace "admissible" by "complete, preferred, grounded or ideal".

Since they are based on the division of AF and the directionality principle, the above two corollaries play a similar role as the main results in [17] when applied to dynamics of AFs. The basic idea in [17] is to divide an updated AF into three parts: an unaffected, an affected, and a conditioning part. The status of arguments in the unaffected sub-framework remains unchanged, while the status of the affected arguments is computed in a special argumentation framework (called a conditioned argumentation framework) that is composed of an affected part and a conditioning part. [17] has proved that under semantics that satisfy the directionality principle the extensions of the updated framework can be obtained by combining the extensions of an unaffected subframework and the extensions of the conditioning part.

However, in our approach, the remaining sub-AF $AF^\oplus |_T$ (or $AF^\ominus |_T$) has a simpler structure (and so is easier to compute) than the conditioning subframework of [17].

6 Concluding Remarks and Future Works

The matrix approach of AFs was constructed as a new method for computing basic extensions of AFs. For any conflict-free subset S, the matrix $M(AF)$ can be turned into one of the two standard forms by a series of dual interchanges. And thus, determining whether S is an extension can be achieved by checking some sub-blocks related to S. The underlying set A of arguments can be divided into three parts: the conflict-free set S, the attacked set $R^+(S)$ and the remaining set $A \setminus (S \cup R^+(S))$. Deciding whether S is admissible only requires to check whether the remaining set $A \setminus (S \cup R^+(S))$ attacks S. In this sense, the matrix approach is a structural (or integrated) method, which is different from checking the defended status of every argument of S.

The matrix approach of AFs can be applied to find new theories of AFs. For any conflict-free subset S of an AF, the matrix $M(AF)$ can be turned into a reduced matrix *wrt* S. The reduced matrix corresponds to a new AF with less arguments obtained by contracting the conflict-free subset S into one argument. This method has not appeared in the literature as we know. Moreover, for any admissible extension E of an AF, we can turn the matrix $M(AF)$ into a reduced matrix *wrt* E. The reduced matrix wrt extensions, when combining with the division of AFs, can be used to handle topics related to the maximality and directionality criteria. For example, we can compute the preferred extensions, and deal with the dynamics of AFs. It remains to evaluate the computational complexity of the operations. That is a first direction for further development of our work.

The matrix approach can be used for other applications. One direction for further research is to study the structural properties and status-based properties of dynamics of AFs as defined by [10]. Another topic is related to the matrix equation of AFs. We plan to find the equational representation of various extensions, by the solution of which we can obtain all the extensions *wrt* a fixed semantics. An interesting attempt has been made in this direction by [16].

References

1. Baroni, P., Giacomin, M.: On principle-based evaluation of extension-based argumentation semantics. Artif. Intell. **171**(10–15), 675–700 (2007)
2. Baroni, P., Giacomin, M.: Skepticism relations for comparing argumentation semantics. Int. J. Approximate Reasoning **50**(6), 854–866 (2009)
3. Baroni, P., Giacomin, M., Guida, G.: SCC-recursiveness: a general schema for argumentation semantics. Artif. Intell. **168**(1–2), 162–210 (2005)
4. Bench-Capon, T., Dunne, P.: Argumentation in artificial intelligence. Artif. Intell. **171**(10–15), 619–641 (2007)
5. Boella, G., Kaci, S., van der Torre, L.: Dynamics in argumentation with single extensions: abstraction principles and the grounded extension. In: Sossai, C., Chemello, G. (eds.) ECSQARU 2009. LNCS, vol. 5590, pp. 107–118. Springer, Heidelberg (2009)
6. Boella, G., Kaci, S., van der Torre, L.: Dynamics in argumentation with single extensions: attack refinement and the grounded extension. In: 8th International Joint Conference on Autonomous Agents and Multi- Agent Systems AAMAS 2009, pp. 1213–1214. Budapest May (2009)
7. Caminada, M.: Semi-stable semantics. In: Proceedings of the First International Conference on Computational Models of Argument COMMA 2006, pp. 121–130. IOS Press, Liverpool (2006)
8. Caminada, M.: An algorithm for computing semi-stable semantics. In: Mellouli, K. (ed.) ECSQARU 2007. LNCS (LNAI), vol. 4724, pp. 222–234. Springer, Heidelberg (2007)
9. Carbogim, D.: Dynamics on formal argumentation. Ph.D. thesis (2000)
10. Cayrol, C., de St-Cyr, F.D., Lagasquie-Schiex, M.: Change in abstract argumentation frameworks: adding an argument. J. Artif. Intell. Res. **38**(1), 49–84 (2010)
11. Cayrol, C., Xu, Y.: The matrix approach for abstract argumentation frameworks. Rapport de recherche RR-2015-01-FR, IRIT, University of Toulouse (February 2015). http://www.irit.fr/publis/ADRIA/PapersCayrol/Rapport-IRIT-CX-2015-02.pdf

12. Dimopoulos, Y., Torres, A.: Graph theoretical structures in logic programs and default theories. Theoret. Comput. Sci. **170**(1–2), 209–244 (1996)
13. Dung, P.: On the acceptability of arguments and its fundamental role in non-monotonic reasoning, logic programming and n-person games. Artif. Intell. **77**, 321–357 (1995)
14. Dunne, P.: Computational properties of argument systems satisfying graph-theoretic constrains. Artif. Intell. **171**, 701–729 (2007)
15. Falappa, M., Garcia, A., Simari, G.: Belief dynamics and defeasible argumentation in rational agents. In: Proceedings of the NMR 2004. pp. 164–170. Whistler, Canada (2004)
16. Gabbay, D.M.: Introducing equational semantics for argumentation networks. In: Liu, W. (ed.) ECSQARU 2011. LNCS, vol. 6717, pp. 19–35. Springer, Heidelberg (2011)
17. Liao, B., Li, J., Koons, R.: Dynamics of argumentation systems: a division-based method. Artif. Intell. **175**, 1790–1814 (2011)
18. Modgil, S.: Reasoning about preferences in argumentation frameworks. Artif. Intell. **173**, 901–934 (2009)
19. Modgil, S., Caminada, M.: Proof theories and algorithms for abstract argumentation frameworks. In: Simari, G., Rahwan, I. (eds.) Argumentation in Artificial Intelligence, pp. 105–129. Springer, Heidelberg (2009)
20. Rahwan, I., Simari, G.: Argumentation in Artificial Intelligence. Springer, Heidelberg (2009)
21. Rotstein, N., Moguillansky, M., Garcia, A., Simari, G.: An abstract argumentation framework for handling dynamics. In: Proceedings of the NMR 2008, pp. 131–139 (2008)
22. Verheij, B.: A labeling approach to the computation of credulous acceptance in argumentation. In: Proceedings of the IJCAI 2007, pp. 623–628. MIT Press (2007)
23. Vreeswijk, G.: Abstract argumentation system. Artif. Intell. **90**, 225–279 (1997)

Author Index

Printed in the United States
By Bookmasters